Writing and Publishing Your Thesis, Dissertation, and Research

A Guide for Students In the Helping Professions

P. Paul Heppner
University of Missouri - Columbia

Mary J. Heppner
University of Missouri - Columbia

BROOKS/COLE
CENGAGE Learning™

Australia • Brazil • Japan • Korea • Mexico • Singapore • Spain • United Kingdom • United States

BROOKS/COLE
CENGAGE Learning™

Writing and Publishing Your Thesis, Dissertation, and Research: A Guide for Students in the Helping Professions
P. Paul Heppner and Mary J. Heppner

Publisher: Lisa Gebo

Acquisitions Editor: Julie Martinez

Assistant Editor: Shelley Gesicki

Editorial Assistant: Amy Lam

Technology Project Manager: Barry Connolly

Marketing Manager: Caroline Concilla

Marketing Assistant: Mary Ho

Project Manager, Editorial Production: Katy German

Print/Media Buyer: Jessica Reed

Permissions Editor: Sarah Harkrader

Production Service: Shepherd, Inc.

Copy Editor: Jeanne Patterson

Cover Designer: Larry Didona

For product information and technology assistance, contact us at
Cengage Learning Customer & Sales Support, 1-800-354-9706

For permission to use material from this text or product, submit all requests online at
www.cengage.com/permissions
Further permissions questions can be emailed to
permissionrequest@cengage.com

Library of Congress Control Number: 2003102662

ISBN-13: 978-0-534-55974-8

ISBN-10: 0-534-55974-3

Brooks/Cole Cengage Learning
20 Davis Drive
Belmont, CA 94002-3098
USA

Cengage Learning is a leading provider of customized learning solutions with office locations around the globe, including Singapore, the United Kingdom, Australia, Mexico, Brazil, and Japan. Locate your local office at:
www.cengage.com/global

Cengage Learning products are represented in Canada by Nelson Education, Ltd.

To learn more about Brooks/Cole, visit
www.cengage.com/brookscole

Purchase any of our products at your local college store or at our preferred online store
www.cengagebrain.com

Printed in the United States of America
7 8 9 10 11   17 16 15 14 13

We dedicate this book to all of the students at the University of Missouri who we have worked with over the years who have stimulated us to understand and become better teachers and mentors to students writing their theses or dissertations. We hope the next generation of students can benefit from our experiences with you.

Brief Contents

Table of Contents

Chapter 3

Overview: Setting the Stage for the Thesis or Dissertation 38

Chapter 4

Searching and Reviewing the Relevant Literature: Finding What Has Come Before   52

Chapter 5

Research Hypotheses: The Motor That Drives the Study   67

Chapter 6

Writing Your Literature Review: Integration and Case Building   82

Chapter 9

Exclusion Is Easier, Inclusion Is Better: Diversifying Samples Co-authored with M. Meghan Davidson   *179*

Chapter 13

Qualitative Results: The Meaning-Making Process   305

Chapter 14

The Discussion: Making the Data Sing   327

Preface and Acknowledgments

We wrote this book for those learning how to actually write the major components of a thesis or dissertation. Both of us have taught courses focused on writing theses and dissertations. From our combined experience of over 20 years of teaching these courses, we have found that it is often helpful for students to have the key elements of each thesis/dissertation chapter clearly identified and to have corresponding examples of those elements or sections. We have noticed that students often experience affective reactions in many phases of writing their thesis or dissertation. However, rarely do texts explore the affective issues that can impede students' progress and provide suggestions in how to deal with these issues. Thus, we have designed this book to explicitly discuss the affective issues related to writing a thesis or dissertation and to provide many examples from actual theses and dissertations that illustrate typical ways to write many sections of each chapter.

In many ways this book represents a "how to" book; our goal is to provide more specific guidance for students to facilitate the writing of proposals and final drafts of their theses and dissertations. Thus, each chapter provides specific information about sections that are commonly found in theses and dissertations: how to write research hypotheses, how to write descriptions of inventories, how to write the results of data analyses using different statistical analyses. Our goal is to provide the basic rationale for common elements of each major chapter of the thesis/dissertation; then we provide numerous examples to illustrate exactly how previous students have written these sections. Although the content of readers' theses or dissertations most likely will differ from the examples in the book, the examples serve to concretely identify some of the key elements in the chapters.

Note that this book is not intended to teach students about how to design studies, how to conduct data collection, or how to conduct statistical procedures. These topics are beyond the focus of this book and have been covered previously in other books. Rather, this book focuses on how to write various sections of each thesis or dissertation chapter, such as the results chapter. We do, however, provide several recommendations where students can obtain relevant information pertaining to each chapter, such as conducting various statistical procedures or design issues. In many ways this book on writing the thesis and dissertation does dovetail nicely with *Research Design in Counseling* by Heppner, Kivlighan, and Wampold (1999). Whereas the Heppner et al. (1999) text focuses on research design issues for planning and conducting a study, this text extends that book by facilitating the subsequent writing of the thesis or dissertation. We expect that, together, these two books will provide students with more complete information about conducting and writing research.

We emphasize throughout the text that conducting a thesis or dissertation is not a linear process but, rather, one that typically intertwines activities such as the literature search, generation of hypotheses, and data analyses as the researcher progresses in developing and conducting the study and writing the results. Consequently, we do not encourage you to use this text in a linear way, but rather to refer to chapters as needed. In essence, this book focuses on writing the five major chapters of a thesis or dissertation and includes other important topics such as developing and writing hypotheses, working with your advisor, considering ethical issues, compiling citations and reference lists, diversifying samples, and publishing the study in a professional journal. We encourage you to examine the detailed Table of Contents and read (and re-read) relevant sections that are most helpful at any particular time.

It is critical to work closely with your advisor throughout the process of writing a thesis or dissertation. Although there are some general procedures that are typically used across colleges and universities, as well as advisors, a great deal of variability also exists. Thus, even though we may be teaching one particular style, or protocol, it is critical for you to be in close communication with your advisor (and department) about the most appropriate stylistic procedures. We do *not* want you to simply adopt the writing styles in this book and defend your stylistic choice by claiming that it is what Heppner and Heppner recommended! Rather, we suggest that you examine the writing examples to determine common elements used to write the major sections of each chapter, then modify them according to the writing styles/preferences employed at your institution. It is essential for you to understand that, in the end, it will be your advisor, your thesis/dissertation committee, and your graduate school who will approve the thesis or dissertation at your institution; thus, adhering to the local procedures and protocols is essential.

This book was written specifically for students who are writing theses or dissertations in Counseling Psychology, Counselor Education, and Clinical Psychology, although others in the behavioral and social sciences will find the book useful as well. Most of the examples are from these disciplines, which make them more relevant for readers in those specialties, although certainly other students will also find the book useful.

In writing the book, we have had assistance from four of our outstanding graduate students who have themselves written master's theses, are now in our doctoral program at the University of Missouri–Columbia, and are at various stages of completing their doctoral dissertations. We want to recognize the exceptional work these four students have provided. Yu-Wei Wang co-authored the two chapters on qualitative methods and qualitative results. M. Meghan Davidson co-authored the chapter on increasing the diversity of samples. Dong-Gwi Lee and Hyun-Joo Park co-authored the extensive chapter on writing quantitative results. We sincerely thank these authors for their expertise and care in contributing to this text.

We wish to thank a number of individuals at the University of Missouri–Columbia who read drafts of these chapters and gave us invaluable feedback. Lisa Spanierman utilized earlier drafts of some chapters in a class she taught on research design and provided very useful pedagogical feedback on those chapters. In addition, several students provided useful feedback on several chapters. We specifically thank the following individuals for helping us to learn how students were reacting to the chapters: Cari Bacon, Brande Baird, Beth Dietrich, Michelle Gibler, Dr. Mae-Hyang Hwang, Terrie Nagel, Scott Sandstead, Anne Berry Scott, Sara Summers, Lamara D. Warren, and David Wilson.

We also want to thank faculty and students in a research methods class we co-taught while we were Fulbright Fellows at National Taiwan Normal University (Taipei) in the winter of 2002 where we utilized earlier drafts of our chapters. Specifically, a special thanks to our host, Dr. Li-Fei Wang for her help in co-teaching the course and broadening our discussion of design issues, as well as in teaching how to write various sections of the thesis/dissertation in another culture. Yu-Wei Wang also deserves thanks for her assistance in co-teaching the course and working with the students. Thanks to all of the students in the class who endured our English; they provided excellent feedback on the chapters and helped us understand the many cross-cultural differences in conducting research in Taiwan and the United States: Jung Jen, Kai-Hsan Lin, Chia-Huei Lin, Pay-Yi Hsu, Yen-Ju Kang, Shiu-Chiao Tsai, Ai-Ju Wu, Tzu-Ying Ou, Ai-Hua Yang, and Ling Hsu Wei.

We also want to thank two very able research assistants, Min Huang and Zhaohui Sheng at the University of Missouri–Columbia, who were very helpful in numerous detail tasks in completing the book—from arranging references to identifying inconsistencies or missing passages to soliciting permissions for the larger passages we included in the book. We sincerely thank the authors of the theses and dissertations that we cite in the text. Our sincere thanks to Peggy Francomb of Shepherd Inc. and Jeanne Patterson for their excellent work with copyediting this book. Also to Anne Scott for her assistance in proofing the final manuscript.

Finally, our thanks to Julie Martinez of Wadsworth/Brooks Cole for her support and patience in helping us develop this book, Shelly Gesicki and anonymous reviewers who provided us with very useful feedback and revisions, and Caroline Concilla for marketing the book. We very much appreciate our long-standing relationship with Wadsworth/Brooks Cole.

SETTING YOURSELF UP FOR SUCCESS

Alleviating Barriers That May Impede Your Progress

STUDENT ONE: *I have set up a schedule for myself to work 2 hours every morning, Monday through Thursday. I set up a special workspace where I can really spread out my stuff and leave it spread out. I have talked to my partner about really giving me quiet space for those 2 hours, and she's been great about staying clear for that time. I set a goal of four to six pages each day. But when I actually sit down to write on a portion of my thesis, I seem to get into a cycle. I write for a period of time and then I run into a snag of some kind. Sometimes I don't like my writing and I pull it out of the printer and rip it up. Sometimes I start obsessing about something my advisor said, and I then end up questioning my whole idea. The snag can be any of a number of things. Soon the 2 hours are up and I am far from my goal of four pages. Then I feel bad about myself and start questioning if this is something I can really do. I find it almost impossible to come back to it the next day, and then a week goes by before I can get myself motivated to go back at it.*

STUDENT TWO: *I know I have to get this done, but I find it hard to get motivated. I am taking a lot of credits this semester and my research assistant position is really demanding. Seems like those deadlines always seem more pressing, and so I crank out that work first while the dissertation always gets put on the back burner. I also get to feeling that I am working all the time and I need a break, some balance of fun in my life. So even though I know I should be doing some work on it in the evenings, I find myself going out to the bars with my friends instead. I think I really need to put this off till summer when I have more time. But that is what I said last summer too, and I ended up not getting anything accomplished. My advisor was gone for the summer, so I just didn't have the structure I needed to get it done.*

You can hear the struggle in these students' voices as they talk about the barriers they are encountering as they try to develop their theses and dissertations. Some of these barriers are tangible, like finding the time and space to actually do the work. Most of them, however, are emotional or have an emotional basis. Emotion is a natural component of the thesis- or dissertation-creation process. Identifying the emotional components in an honest, shame-free manner is the first step in developing a work pace. The purpose of this chapter is to help you position yourself for success by identifying the barriers that may block your productivity and developing plans for eliminating them. Of all the chapters in this book, this may be the most important one. We urge you to refer back to it frequently! We have worked with hundreds of graduate students over the years, and we have not worked with a single student who could not do the work required of a thesis or dissertation. As students admitted into competitive graduate programs, you are bright enough to handle this task. Barriers are the product of various obstacles within your environment and within yourselves.

Some students complete their thesis or dissertation but only under extreme duress. Their masters or doctoral program may put them on probation due to lack of progress, or they may receive threatening letters indicating that if they do not complete by a certain date, they will be dismissed from the program. These students are often bitter because of this experience and graduate from the university with a very unsatisfied feeling. This is not the kind of outcome we want for any student. Students invest so much time, money, and energy into getting a masters or doctoral degree. They often do well in the program and have good connections with faculty, peers, and the institution; but the experiences around the thesis or dissertation cause those feelings to sour. These students end up feeling bad about themselves and the institution from which they are graduating. Graduating should feel like the culmination of a tremendous accomplishment and should be a time of honor and celebration, not shame, anger, and self-doubt.

Similarly, the institution invests a lot in the student. Some of that investment may be financial, but the faculty and staff that make up the training program typically devote a great amount of time to student selection and training. Faculties want students to succeed. When students drop out of the program or leave without completing their theses or dissertations, this does not reflect well on the training program. Once admitted, most training programs are committed to seeing that students leave the program successfully.

Thus, in this first chapter, we want you to develop the ability to identify and problem solve barriers that may prevent you from completing your thesis or dissertation. First, we identify the most common barriers perceived by students. Then we discuss specific ways of overcoming these barriers, though we understand that what works for one student may not work for another.

Factors That May Impede Your Success

Note that no matter how well prepared a student is, barriers occur that are a normal part of the process. The important thing is to be able to identify when they are happening and to develop ways to move through them. Over the years, students have identified eight prominent obstacles:

1. Lack of time
2. Lack of space
3. Nonsupport from partners, families, friends
4. Lack of organization
5. Emotional and psychological obstacles
6. "Shoulds" students tell themselves
7. A poor working relationship with your advisor
8. Lack of control with data collection and analyses

Lack of Time

You must realize that a thesis or dissertation is considerably different from most writing tasks you have previously done. Typically, in classes where a paper is assigned, students are able to put minimal time into the paper and "pull it out" in a few days (or a long night) before it is due. However, this is not possible for a thesis or a dissertation. A thesis or a dissertation is too big to accomplish by "pouring it on" for a 100-yard dash. We advise you to throw this notion about writing your thesis/dissertation out the window right now! Rather, we suggest you think of your thesis or dissertation as a marathon. Successfully writing your thesis/dissertation will take time and care to accomplish, even when separated into the manageable pieces that we discuss in this book.

To successfully complete your thesis/dissertation, you need to identify and protect time to work on this project and this project only. We have found that consistently having time to work is the key. Finding a consistent routine or schedule is critically important. "Today is Thursday, this is my writing day," or, "It is 7 A.M., I am writing now for a 2-hour block." Many people find that having smaller blocks of time (2 hours, 6 days a week) is more helpful than having one big block of time; but this is something you will need to decide based on the realities of your life and other tasks, as well as your own style and what has worked best for you in the past. Ask yourself: "In the past, when I have had a big project to do, what kind of time worked best for me?" Time of day is also a critical factor. When do you have the clearest mind and maximum energy for the writing? Some people work best the first thing in the morning, when their home or office is quiet and their mind is fresh. Others find themselves much more productive in the afternoon or evening. When you work does not matter; that you do work effectively does matter. Think about your own biorhythms. What would be the best time for you?

After you have identified an effective time to work, the next step is keeping that time sacred and protected. We all have many things pulling on our time. Family members need help. Company is coming and the house is a "disaster area." There is no food in the refrigerator. A paper is due in another class. Stephen Covey and his colleagues (1996), in his best selling book *First Things First,* (1994) used the analogy of big rocks and sand. If we fill up a jar with sand (or all the small details of making a life), finding the space to put in several big rocks (those things you prioritize as being really important to accomplish) is virtually impossible; in this case, your thesis or dissertation should be one of the big rocks in your life. If you put the big rocks in first, you will be amazed how much sand you can fill in around them. Think of your thesis or dissertation time as a big rock; give it top priority and block it out in your daily planner. Do not let people make you feel guilty about taking that time, and do not let other things encroach upon this time. If you are not accustomed to setting boundaries and if people in your social network are not used to respecting those boundaries, you may benefit from reading *Better Boundaries: Owning and Treasuring Your Life* (Black & Enns, 1997); these authors provide a range of helpful suggestions for setting appropriate boundaries in your personal and professional life. For example, perhaps your friend calls you every night and talks on the phone for hours about her relationship problems. Perhaps you have attempted to set a boundary and tell her that your evening hours are the only time you can work on your writing and that you would ask that she does not call until after 10 P.M. If she continues calling, she is clearly not respecting your boundary. You may need to take more drastic measures, for example, unplugging the telephone. Setting and maintaining important boundaries are really lifelong skills that you will benefit from long after the thesis or dissertation is completed.

Lack of Space

A problem for some students is that they lack the space to effectively do their work. For example, consider Gerardo. Gerardo would work sometimes at his kitchen table, sometimes in the library, other times at the local breakfast hangout, or still other times in his departmental cubicle. Each time he would transport his materials but never have all the resources he needed for the various tasks. He constantly misplaced resources and even pages he had written. Some days he wrote a lot, other days he wrote very little and spent more time talking to friends, especially when he went to the breakfast place and the departmental cubicle. In short, Gerardo's approach to this task was very unorganized and, in essence, in disarray.

Having a place to store all of your resources and materials to effectively work on your thesis or dissertation is essential for most students. Even if you are living in tight quarters, try to find a place where you can spread out your work and leave it for a long period of time. One of our students bought an old door at a flea market and put two old chests of drawers under both ends. It made a wonderful, large workspace without costing much. Try to organize your workspace with folders that are clearly marked; deadlines posted; and a sufficient amount of paper, pencils, and computer supplies ready for your use. An APA style manual is also very helpful to have nearby. Having a special place to work on your thesis or dissertation is another really important gift to give yourself. Perhaps a candle burning by your side provides a soothing feeling for you. Having live plants or soft piano music playing on the stereo can make the workplace more desirable for some students. Having whatever can make you want to enter this space and use it is the goal. If your space is a corner in a damp, chilly basement, the likelihood of wanting to go there is not very great.

We discuss positive self-talk under the section on emotional and psychological obstacles. However, for this section, one way of cueing yourself to stay focused and positive is by posting positive self-statements by your work area. "I am competent to do this." "I just need to stay focused and on track." "Perseverance is the key." "Just take it one step at a time." "This will make a good contribution to the literature." Whatever statements are most helpful to keep you motivated and on track are good ones to have at ready view. In addition, using the wall space above the desk as an idea board is helpful for some students. Other students have found that their timetable or progress chart posted on the wall can be a motivating visual.

Nonsupport from Partners, Families, and Friends

Because a thesis or dissertation is a large undertaking, it will impact your relationships in all kinds of ways. Friends and family will probably have less of your time. People in your life may have feelings that need to be addressed. Partners may feel jealous of the time that you are working on the thesis/dissertation. Friends may feel that you never have time for them anymore. Addressing these issues with significant people in your life is important, as is keeping them well informed about the process, how long it will take, and what you are trying to accomplish. Asking them for what you need is also important. For example, you may want to negotiate for tangible things: "I need to have 2 hours of time everyday to work on this project. Can you help me carve out that time and help me keep that time sacred?" or "Would you be able to cook dinner each night so that I am able to devote that time to my thesis?" In addition, you may need to negotiate psychological support: "This process is really scary for me; I find myself not believing that I can really do this. I really need you to support me in this and reassure me that I can get this done." "I have a tendency to get angry and resentful toward other people when I am not feeling very self-efficacious myself—if you hear me doing that, could you gently point it out? Blaming others is a way I keep myself from being productive, and I want to be aware of when I am doing it." If you have made attempts to express your needs and develop allies to help you in this process but still feel blocked, time with a trusted person or even a few sessions with a counselor may be invaluable to you.

Social support can be one of the most important elements to success in meeting your goals. Think about other creative ways of getting the support you need. Some of our students started a regular weekly lunch to problem solve and provide support and encouragement to each other. Creating a regular support group of this kind may be valuable to you in keeping on track with your thesis or dissertation. The people you pick for this are important. Although you may benefit from structured "debriefing" or "check-in" time to engage in catharsis about the process so that you can proceed with the task at hand, the last thing you need is someone who will bring you down or enable you to procrastinate. Getting in lengthy discussions about what your advisor is *not* doing to help you may not be a productive use of your time. You need people who are affirming and supportive and who can provide instrumental help if you run into a snag.

Lack of Organization

Getting and staying well organized are very important aspects of success with your thesis or dissertation. If you are already slightly compulsive, you are ahead of the game. If you are not, you will need to work hard to get organized. Because the thesis/dissertation is a very large task, you will have piles of articles you have copied, books, and notes from meetings with your advisor, lists of references that you will need at some future date, and so on. Even keeping track of exactly what your hypotheses are and how you are going to test them requires organization. If you have half your papers at your workspace, some in your car, and a few at the kitchen table, you will spend a lot of time trying to find what you need to start working. If you did not start making a reference list immediately, the likelihood that you will forget where you found that wonderful quote is high, and you will spend many hours going through piles of paper trying to find it. Thus, even if it goes against your nature, set up a system to organize the papers, articles, references, and other resources that work for you. A well-organized system will save you a great deal of time and countless heartaches and will help you feel much more in control of your work.

The computer is also a place where organization is important. Developing clearly marked folders on your computer is helpful. Label drafts of documents with the date so that you are sure you have the most current draft of a particular section. Back up everything so that losing your hard work if and when your computer crashes is not an issue.

Emotional and Psychological Obstacles

Once you get your time and space identified, significant people in your life on board, and an organizational scheme, it should be smooth sailing, right? For some people, the answer is yes. For most people, however, the answer is no. Most people who are doing a thesis or dissertation have a range of psychological and emotional barriers that can create large obstacles for their progress. Having emotional reactions is normal and natural; but, if the emotions are producing negative mindsets for you and are causing you to feel bad about yourself, these emotions need to be examined and altered.

Most students are not aware of their psychological dynamics when they are going through this process. Even very psychologically minded individuals do not cue in on such issues as: When am I feeling nervous, panicky? What is causing me to procrastinate on talking to my advisor about my idea? Why is it that whenever I think of the actual hypotheses and statistical analysis, I feel hopeless? Why am I feeling angry with my advisor? Why was it when Jane talked about her dissertation topic, I felt inadequate?

The first step in combating emotional and psychological barriers is being aware of your feelings. Identifying your cognitive and emotional reactions and patterns as you go through the process of doing a thesis or dissertation is critically important. Sometimes your body may be giving you signs that have not yet reached the level of conscious thought or feeling. For example, as your advisor starts talking about your proposal meeting and getting your committee together, you may notice your breathing going shallow. As your professor talks in class about an upcoming deadline for your Chapter 1, your hands may feel sweaty. These are important cues that something is going on. Reinforce yourself for being aware of these cues, as this is an important first step: simply telling yourself that you are proud of yourself for having enough self-awareness to recognize these emotional reactions. Also focus on when your body feels relaxed. What is being said or what are you experiencing in your environment that is bringing about a calmer, more in-control feeling?

Also attend closely to your thoughts throughout the day. What are you telling yourself? For example, when you hear someone else talk about his or her thesis or dissertation, are you saying to yourself, "That is really a good idea; mine is really pathetic compared to that"? When your advisor asks you what your hypotheses are and you respond, do you find yourself feeling inadequate? "She [or he] didn't seem too impressed. I think she thought it was a dumb idea. She tried to say it was a good idea, but I think she really thought it wouldn't make much of a contribution." Monitor these thoughts and feelings. They are very important and may tell you something about your fears and anxieties. Also consider talking to the person about your feelings. For example, it may be very helpful to check out your perceptions with your advisor and see how on target these perceptions really were.

The second step is trying to identify why you are feeling and thinking these things at this time. Analyzing what is underlying such self-talk and the physiological signs of anxiety and fear can be a complex process. For many people the underlying issue is one of self-esteem or, more specifically, one of lack of self-efficacy for the task at hand. *Self-esteem* is a broader term used to describe a global feeling about oneself; often we do not feel we are good enough. *Self-efficacy* is a more specific term used to describe a lack of self-confidence in one's ability to perform the specific tasks related to completing the thesis or dissertation. Self-efficacy has been demonstrated to affect the length of time spent on the task, perseverance when obstacles arise, and ultimate success with the project (Bandura, 1986).

Thus, you need to analyze what is creating your particular fear, anxiety, anger, and so on. One very good way of doing this is to keep a journal of your experience or incorporate this information into an existing journal. Each day, take some time to analyze what you are experiencing emotionally or cognitively in this process:

> Talked to Mike today about his thesis. He was talking about developing a spreadsheet to organize all of his data. When he was talking, I found myself feeling small and inadequate. I started hyping myself by saying stuff like, you have got to get going, and you are falling behind. But when I got home to work during my block of thesis time, I vegged out in front of the television instead. I think a couple things were going on. First, I felt competitive with Mike and inadequate because I don't know the first thing about spreadsheets. I feel like he is smarter than I am and that I don't quite measure up. It makes me wonder if I can complete this thing.

By taking the time to reflect on your feelings and thoughts about the process, you can then be better equipped to take action and overcome thoughts and feelings that may be serving as obstacles to your progress.

The third and final step in this process is developing strategies to overcome these thoughts and feelings. Some possible steps follow:

1. *Modify your self-talk.* When you find yourself thinking negative thoughts, cue yourself to change them. In the preceding case, you may say: "Mike is very competent in some ways. I have many competencies as well." "I don't think I need a spread sheet for my work; but, if I do, sounds like Mike may be a good resource for me."

2. *Recognize when psychological and emotional blocks are causing you to avoid thesis and dissertation tasks, and strategize ways to cope with them.* Problems, including theses and dissertations, are solved or completed by moving forward. The most self-defeating obstacle is to avoid the project, as avoidance halts your progress. Whatever you do, do not avoid the thesis or dissertation; it is too big to avoid. Try hard not to

become derailed in the process, although most people do from time to time. When you do, find ways to quickly get yourself back on track so that you keep moving forward, even if only in small steps. Recognizing when and how you get derailed and finding effective ways of getting out of this derailment sooner may be one of your most important self-learnings in this process.

3. *Recognize that the mechanisms that you have used in previous stressful situations are probably the same ones you will use here.* Some of those mechanisms may be effective for your coping. If so, use them. However, many times our mechanisms for handling stress are not productive. Think about other times you have been stressed in your life. For example, some people become very avoidant. They think of any number of reasons why they cannot do the task today, or this week, or this month. They clean their closets and all their drawers; they remodel their basement in order to have a good writing space. They get a puppy, or buy a house, or have a baby. Whatever they can do to avoid getting to work on the thesis or dissertation is their goal, consciously or unconsciously. Other people get rebellious or angry with others in their lives. For example, they get angry at: "This stupid requirement. Why do I want to get a Ph.D. anyway? I am not the egghead type." Or "If my advisor wasn't so busy with his own work, I could have had this done a year ago." Or "This dissertation class I am taking is not helping at all. I can't believe she's spending all this time talking about barriers rather than helping us get down to the meat of the matter." If you can become aware of the mechanisms you are using, you can also modify them.

4. *Find role models who are successful in their academic lives and who can model healthy self-care as well.* Many graduate programs even within psychology and education do not model healthy self-care. Often you see faculty who have little balance in their lives and who have not found appropriate ways to handle their own job stresses. Finding models who set appropriate boundaries, take the time and space they need for their own priorities, and have some reasonable balance in their work and personal lives can be invaluable to you as you attempt these same things in your own life.

5. *Take care of your body as well as your mind during this process.* If you are not getting adequate sleep, nutrition, or exercise, it is much more difficult to recognize the emotional and psychological issues you are experiencing. *The Wellness Workbook* by John Travis and Regina Sara Ryan (1988) may be a helpful resource to you in setting up your own "wellness plan" "self-care contract." Being a graduate student can be very stressful. Determining how you are currently handling stress and what more you could be doing to take care of yourself during this time is a vital element in the success of your project.

"Shoulds" Students Tell Themselves

One specific form of psychological obstacle that many students seem to have is giving themselves a long list of "shoulds" about their thesis or dissertation:

> I should have started this last summer when I had more time.
> I should have taken that additional statistics course when I had the chance.
> I should have switched advisors a long time ago.
> I should be able to think of a more creative topic than this one.

Shoulds are very dangerous cognitive messages because they tend to keep the student thinking about perceived shortcomings in the past rather than taking action in the present. They are also a powerful way students beat themselves up. Proposing and conducting a thesis or dissertation are stressful enough for most students, without adding to that stress a long list of shoulds. This is a time to be gentle with yourself and reinforce your strengths rather than kick yourself for past failures. As with other emotional and psychological barriers, the first step is becoming aware of your shoulds; what are you telling yourself that you should have done? Next, consciously try to substitute a positive affirmation to replace the should. Instead of *I should have started this last summer when I had more time,* try *Great! I am getting going at this thesis now.* Instead of *I should have taken that additional statistics course when I had the chance,* try *If I need additional help with the specific statistical analysis I am using in my study, I can consult with Marge or perhaps sit in on a couple weeks of the course this semester.*

Getting rid of shoulds is not negating the fact that everyone makes mistakes and that some of those mistakes may make writing the thesis or dissertation more difficult, but dwelling on these missed opportunities does not serve a purpose at the present time. The *If only* and *What if* thinking takes up precious time that is better spent on problem solving and moving ahead.

A Poor Working Relationship with Your Advisor

Hopefully, by the time you are working on your thesis or dissertation, you have developed a good working relationship with your advisor. Advisory relationships vary, however, in terms of the amount and kind of contact each student may have with his or her advisor. Initially, when you begin conceptualizing and working on your study, you will need to have regular contact with your advisor so that he or she is fully informed about your ideas, progress, and struggles along the way. Take the initiative now of scheduling regular meetings with your advisor, if you have not already done so. This time each week with your advisor to discuss your progress can provide motivation and structure for you to get things accomplished. E-mail can be another important tool for regularly staying in touch with your advisor.

Most advisors are interested in having students complete their thesis or dissertation in a timely manner and are almost always invested in helping students with this task. Having advisees who are "all but dissertation" (ABD), "all but thesis" (ABT), or continually struggling in the program is not a good reflection on advisors, so your progress is important to your advisor. Some advisees develop contracts with their advisors in which they let the advisors know what they need. For example, an advisee may say, "It is important for me to feel your support and feel like you are informed about my progress. I would like to check in once a week, if only for 15 minutes, to update you and tell you about any problems or concerns I am having." In other words, you have a right to ask for what you need and what you think will make the process go more smoothly for you.

Unfortunately, situations occur in which the advisor is not providing appropriate support to the student and, in fact, is serving as a barrier to the student's progress. Although how advisors define their role varies, certain basic assistance seems appropriate to expect. We discuss the relationship with your advisor and committee in more depth in Chapter 10; for now, note that switching to a different advisor may at times be an appropriate option. Other committee members or faculty may be interested in helping you if changing advisors is not advisable.

Lack of Control of Data Collection and Analyses

Many times students find it necessary and desirable to solicit help with their data collection and their data analysis. People who have grant and institutional support can provide unique opportunities for students to do research for their theses/dissertations that they would have been unable to do otherwise. These opportunities often allow students to work as part of a team with others who are interested in a similar topic. Particularly if this is an interdisciplinary team, diverse perspectives on your topic can be provided. There are some pitfalls, however, to keep in mind. Be extremely clear with the people with whom you are collaborating about what you need. For example, talk specifically about what freedom you have to include your own measures, how many participants you need, when you need them, what access you have to the data for your analyses, and what publication opportunities exist for you. If these issues are not clearly discussed, disappointments and sometimes significant problems can arise, such as the following student reports indicate:

- I had understood them to say that I could have access to 40 incest survivors who were clients in their agency; in the end they were only able to provide 17 incest survivors, which was not enough to do any of the types of analysis I needed for my research hypotheses.
- I had told them I wanted to study collective self-esteem, and I had given them a copy of the instrument I wanted to use. After my proposal

meeting, they determined that their test battery was too large and so they substituted a shorter self-esteem scale instead. This shorter scale did not measure the construct I was interested in and, thus, did not serve my purposes at all.

- I guess I hadn't made it clear enough that this research was for my dissertation and that I wanted sole authorship on the study I had carved out. They said that since they had provided all the subjects and even paid them to take the instruments that they expected joint authorship.

Data analysis is another area in which students often decide to seek consultation. With the growing complexity of statistical analysis techniques, many students need assistance. Nonetheless, *staying in control* of the data analysis process is what is important. Your committee will expect that you are knowledgeable about the statistical analysis you used in your research. They will ask you questions about why you made certain decisions. It is not a suitable response to say, "I don't know; that is what my statistical consultant told me to do." You need to have a firm grasp of what was done and, conceptually, why it was done in the manner it was. While there are no universal rules about how much help statistical consultants can provide, it is widely accepted that the student is responsible for understanding the analyses. In general, the more you are in control of both data collection and data analyses, the better.

CONCLUSIONS

In the big picture, very few students who reach the point of thesis on dissertation are unable to do the work necessary to complete the thesis on dissertation because of a lack of skills, knowledge, or expertise. So why are there so many ABDs and ABTs wandering around? The answer from our experience is really internal barriers: lack of self-efficacy or self-esteem, chronic procrastination, or a belief that the thesis/dissertation symbolizes something that the person fears. Becoming aware of what may be standing in your way is an important first step. Developing an active plan to overcome the barrier is the next critical step.

EXERCISE 1.1 STRENGTHS AND BARRIERS

Many students with whom we have worked have found it helpful to complete the following *strengths and barriers* exercise as they were getting started with their thesis or dissertation. The exercise provides a structured way of examining those areas where you may have particular strengths and, conversely, areas where there are obstacles in your path. We recommend that you take some time to reflect on the following questions.

Lack of Time

1. What time can I set aside to work regularly on my study?
2. What might get in the way of my being able to keep that time only for my thesis or dissertation?
3. What actions can I take now to ensure that this time will not be interrupted for other purposes?
4. Can I decrease time at my job?

Lack of Space

5. What physical space do I have in which to work on my study?
6. What do I need to do to make that space more functional and welcoming?
7. What may happen to cause this space to be unavailable to me?
8. What actions can I take now to ensure that this space will be available to me for the duration of my thesis/dissertation work?

Nonsupport from Partners, Families, Friends

9. What kinds of support will I need from partners, friends, and family during this process?
10. What barriers or obstacles might partners, friends, or family create to slow my progress?
11. What plan do I have for talking with partners, friends, or family about what I need from them during this process?

Lack of Organization

12. What do I need to do to get myself organized to start this process?
13. What are specific organizational schemes that I think will be helpful to me in this process?

Emotional and Psychological Obstacles

14. What are the primary emotional and psychological obstacles I see myself having that may slow my progress with my thesis or dissertation?
15. Do I fully understand the origins of these obstacles?
16. What can I do, specifically, to help keep these emotional and psychological barriers from derailing my thesis or dissertation work?

"Shoulds" Students Tell Themselves

17. What "shoulds" do I tell myself regarding this thesis or dissertation process?
18. What messages can I use to replace the "shoulds"?

A Poor Working Relationship with Your Advisor

19. How strong is my working relationship with my advisor?
20. What fears do I have about working with him/her on this process?
21. What steps can I take at this point to ensure that I get what I need from my advisor?

Lack of Control of Data Collection and Analysis

22. How much control will I have over my data-collection process?
23. What actions can I take to gain maximum control?
24. How much control will I have over my data analyses?
25. What actions can I take to gain maximum control?

Analysis of Strengths

26. What do I see as the primary strengths I bring to this process of writing a thesis or dissertation?

EXERCISE 1.2 MY THESIS OR DISSERTATION SELF-CARE PLAN/CONTRACT WITH MYSELF

From completing the *strengths and barriers* exercise, you have hopefully come away with a number of ideas for things you can do to actively approach obstacles and take care of yourself in the process. Please write a specific plan for self-care that you will use during your thesis or dissertation process.

Identifying Your Topic and Making It Researchable

The first step to conducting a thesis or dissertation is finding a topic that will sustain a student's effort through the long process ahead. For some students this is the easiest part; they have known what they want to study from the time they entered graduate school or even before.

> TAMARA: *I have known I wanted to study eating disorders in adolescent girls ever since I was in high school. I just saw some of my friends struggling with issues of body image; they seemed tormented by their bodies and forever wanting them to look different than they did. Other friends seemed so much more comfortable with their bodies, although their bodies were no more beautiful than the dissatisfied friends were. I want to know what made the difference. I think if we were clearer about the factors that lead to positive and negative body image we would be able to help parents and girls with this troubling phenomenon. I think this will be a really interesting thesis to conduct.*

But, unlike Tamara, for many, choosing a topic is one of the hardest parts of their graduate degree. The thought of developing a "completely original" idea for such a large project may seem overwhelming and beyond their capabilities.

> JOHN: *This has always seemed like the hardest part of the doctoral program to me. Even when I was applying, I remember thinking, "How am I ever going to come up with an idea that no one has ever thought of before?" I think I am a reasonably intelligent person, but research is not my thing. I keep avoiding thinking about this requirement for my doctorate, because it makes me very anxious.*

We have written this chapter for students like both John and Tamara. Clearly, John needs some information and support in making this decision. You may think that Tamara is well on her way to developing her thesis, but she has just completed step one of a multistep process. She has identified her passion. She still needs to turn that passion into a researchable topic.

In this chapter, we first discuss affective aspects of choosing a topic. As we discussed in Chapter 1, we believe that attending to your emotional reactions can facilitate the successful completion of your project. Next, we discuss eight distinct factors that are often involved in selecting a thesis or dissertation topic. These include issues related to whether the topic (a) is congruent with your research skill level, (b) is in your advisor's primary line of research, (c) helps you clear a needed hurdle en route to your "real life," (d) builds on previous research you have done, (e) helps you develop a particular skill, (f) helps you transition into a particular career field, (g) represents a deep and abiding passion, (h) brings understanding to a major societal issue, and (i) can be researched within an acceptable/practical amount of time.

Once we have clarified the potential factors involved in selecting your thesis or dissertation topic, we discuss specific ways of selecting a topic, that is, (a) reading the literature; (b) consulting with local, national, and international experts; (c) testing a psychological theory; and (d) finding topics through applied experience. We then address the issue of turning your topic into a researchable idea. This discussion includes (a) the size and scope of the investigation, (b) the level of complexity involved, and (c) how different research designs answer different questions within the same content area. Next, we discuss the critically important phase of writing your specific research questions. Finally, we suggest some Web sites to explore for possible ways of funding your thesis or dissertation.

Thus, in this chapter we seek to accomplish a great deal. Our goal is to clarify for you (a) the affective reactions often associated with starting to develop and refine a topic, (b) the factors involved in choosing a dissertation topic, (c) specific ways to find an appropriate topic, (d) how to turn that global topic into a researchable idea, and (e) how to write research questions that begin to frame the important issues and relationships the thesis or dissertation will address.

THE AFFECTIVE SIDE: FOCUSING ON YOUR FEELINGS

We want you to reflect on the thoughts and feelings associated with this process of clarifying a topic. We first discuss an affective continuum that ranges from excitement and joy to fear and anxiety. You may feel excited about the creative process and even, to some extent, thrilled to begin a process you have been thinking about for a long time. You may feel you are finally at a point where you can truly pursue something about which you are deeply passionate. Unlike other projects that may have been dictated by others, you now can follow your own interests, and you may find it gratifying to "test your wings."

At other times you may feel fear and anxiety. For example, some students have feared, even dreaded, the thesis or dissertation since entering graduate school and have worried about whether they, like John, can think of an "original idea." This notion of original thought has been seen as a defining element of the graduate research requirements (particularly the dissertation); moreover, this notion of originality has sometimes been interpreted as identifying a topic that not only has never been researched before but will also produce original, earth-shattering, and influential research on this topic! Sounds like a pretty formidable task, does it not? Heppner, Kivlighan, and Wampold (1999) warned against this interpretation of "original research":

> It is the rare trainee who believes at the outset that he or she can make a "real contribution" to the field; after all we are talking about *science!* Most often the inexperienced researcher interprets "original contribution" much too broadly and tries to develop a new topic area by creating a new assessment instrument to measure a new construct, a new research methodology to collect the data previously not collected, and new statistical procedures to handle old problems. In reality most experienced researchers would feel quite a sense of accomplishment if they did all these things in an entire career. (p. 32)

Thus, part of controlling anxiety or concern about the thesis or dissertation is developing realistic expectations and understanding that most research (even by accomplished researchers) simply builds on research that has already been done. Some of the most successful theses or dissertations simply extend a line of knowledge one step further in an area by examining one new variable within a well-established line of research, such as collecting data on a previously underrepresented sample, testing a new methodology, or trying a new statistical analysis. Thus, some of you may be giving yourself messages like John was in the earlier example: "I am not creative and don't have original ideas." We encourage you to alter those statements to ones like "Thousands of other students are going through this process of selecting a topic for their research; if they can do it; I can do it." "I am not alone in this process, I have good people to discuss my ideas with." We believe that students need to analyze what it is they are saying to themselves and devise appropriate alternative statements to use. At this stage, you need to develop the kind of statements that serve to control anxiety and allow you to approach the tasks at hand.

Another very common affective reaction at this point is fear of foreclosure on a topic. Throughout graduate school, students have had the luxury of thinking about ideas and possible research topics. "Maybe I will do my thesis on career counseling outcomes, or maybe I will examine the effects of post traumatic stress disorder (PTSD) on rape survivors." As the time for the thesis/dissertation draws nearer, the student must decide on a topic and persevere with that topic over the course of the next couple of years. For some people, this leads to feelings of anxiety. If you are experiencing these feelings, you may need to explore their origins. For some people, these feelings come from not wanting to commit to something and then later coming to the realization that they are really not that interested in the topic or that it basically is not a very good idea. For others, who are very divergent thinkers, having to narrow down a topic and commit to it has never been an easy task. For still others, making this commitment means grieving for the topics they are not going to pursue. Some see selection of the topic as the first step on a journey that is fraught with barriers and fears. They may feel they do not have the requisite skills, so starting this process, by explicitly choosing a topic, represents the first step to publicly exposing their weaknesses. Whatever the etiology of these feelings and beliefs, the outcome is often avoidance of some sort.

First of all, you should realize that these types of concerns and fears are very common in graduate students and developmentally normal. Almost every student has doubts, even students who have had considerable research experience. Nonetheless, take time to reflect on your own affective reactions at this point and develop ways (discussions with advisors, support groups with fellow students, therapy) to address such beliefs and fears so they do not halt progress on your thesis or dissertation. We encourage you to remain open to and monitor your feelings throughout this process, as they can be very informative about what is promoting and impeding the progress of the thesis or dissertation. In short, although such feelings of anxiety are normal, you must not let them become debilitating and block your progress.

FACTORS IN SELECTING A RESEARCH TOPIC

Selecting a research topic is a process that is often influenced by a number of goals or factors. Students approach the thesis or dissertation with very different levels of interest, skill, and commitment to the process. Some students may have allotted 2 years to complete their study, while others have one semester; the time factor often influences the type of research students can select. Students should consider a broad range of factors and goals for conducting a thesis or dissertation. Some students will be trying to make a transition into a slightly different career field, for example, from an emphasis on applied clinical work to forensic psychology. Their dissertation or thesis may help them make that transition. Other students may be thinking of developing some specific statistical skills that they have wanted to learn; still others will have a deep and abiding passion for an area of research and use the thesis or dissertation to help them answer some questions that are close to their soul. For most students, more than one factor goes into this decision. For example, in addition to researching a topic because it is one of interest, you may also acquire a new skill in the process. In this section, we review eight common goals or factors in selecting a research topic. We invite you to think about which of these factors are important to you and how you will integrate the factor into your topic selection process. Note that not all eight factors will be important for any one student. For some students, only one or two factors will be important. We provide this list so that you can think about your own unique situation and determine which factors are salient to you.

Assessing One's Level of Research Skill

A very important factor for you to consider is your level of previous research experience and the level and type of research skills you possess. This is a time for you to carefully evaluate your research strengths and to realistically assess how much guidance and assistance you will need in this process. Consider the following examples:

> Ming became involved in research as an undergraduate. She entered data, coded qualitative data, and attended research team discussions. When she went to graduate school, she joined other research teams and took on increasingly challenging roles. She contributed to conceptual and design issues, she started to understand the advantages and disadvantages of different types of designs, she became well acquainted with the things that can and often do go wrong in various aspects of the research process. Over time she became quite facile in conducting various statistical analyses. Ming also was active in writing sections of manuscripts; initially polishing first drafts; then writing first drafts of the methods, results, and later the introduction and discussion sections. In essence, she was being socialized over many years in the varied tasks of conducting research. She also published articles with her advisor and other faculty and for one study was the first author on a study she spearheaded. It is important to note not only that Ming had a lot of research skills but that these skills were acquired over hundreds of hours across many years.

Ming's experience is in sharp contrast to Joel's:

> Joel was not involved with research as an undergraduate. At that time he was planning a career in a practice setting and did not see the need to acquire research skills. He obtained a master's degree at an institution that gave the option of doing a manuscript rather than a thesis. The manuscript could be an integrative review of the literature rather than an empirical study. Joel chose the manuscript option and wrote a review of the literature on male gender role identity and its impact on men's mental health. Although Joel took all of the required statistics and research design courses and received passing grades in those classes, he did not apply that knowledge to an actual research project. In essence, the whole research enterprise seemed rather distant and unfamiliar to Joel.

Ming and Joel form two ends of a continuum in terms of their level of research skills. Ming seems well equipped to conduct her dissertation, whereas Joel will need to learn many aspects of the research process along the way. While both Ming and Joel can be successful in conducting their research, Joel may have to work harder to learn about all the steps necessary to conduct a research project.

Assessing your research skills is a critical activity, and we encourage you to discuss your self-assessment with your advisor. Although such discussions may be anxiety producing, especially for people like Joel, they not only provide a reality check but also provide the advisor with important information about your skills. Your skill level is one of the most important considerations in selecting a thesis or dissertation topic. For example, if you are a person with a great deal of skill, you may be able to work in an area that is less familiar to your advisor. You may have the skills to pursue a topic with less of a need for close, ongoing supervision. You have already had experience in most, if not all, of the aspects of the research process and, thus, will be able to anticipate and prevent many problems or questions that arise. Conversely, if your situation is more similar to that of Joel's, we strongly encourage you to consider working closely with your advisor on a topic in which your advisor has a fair amount of expertise. Learning the myriad of skills related to conducting your thesis or dissertation will require a great amount of work on both your part and on the part of your advisor. This process will be made easier if one of the two of you (namely, your advisor) is working in an area of comfort and expertise. In many ways, successfully completing the thesis or dissertation is directly related to the skills that the advisor and student bring as a team.

Assessing skills will also help you to define the scope of your project. If you have never had a qualitative course, designing a major qualitative thesis or dissertation is probably not wise. If you have never taken a course nor had experience in structural equation modeling (SEM), designing and testing a complex structural model are probably not good ideas either. This is particularly true if the student's advisor is not skilled in such topics (e.g., qualitative research or SEM techniques).

We have seen the occasional student who is following a passion and being a real "trail-blazing pioneer" in a particular research area but who does not have the skills or someone with specific expertise to help with the study. Students often feel that they are in a deep morass, unable to move forward, becoming more and more frustrated with each new obstacle, and unable to find people who can provide all the assistance needed to help them move forward. Because this is a very difficult spot to be in, we emphasize the importance of examining your own strengths and weaknesses with regard to the research process as an important step in selecting your research topic.

Following the Advisor's Areas of Expertise

Apart from your level of research skills, several other important factors should be considered when deciding whether to follow a primary advisor's line of research or develop your own research area. Each has clear advantages. Continuing in an advisor's line of research most often provides an enormous head start over selecting your own area of research. Typically, faculty have spent many years thinking, reading, writing, collecting data, developing and refining methodologies, and conceptualizing next steps in their research area. From the advisor's perspective, being a helpful advisor is usually much easier when the student has selected a topic in which the advisor has expertise. In these situations, the advisor can typically recommend seminal readings, discuss typical methodologies, identify obstacles, and recommend model articles on which to base future lines of inquiry. All of this can be a tremendous help. Many of the pitfalls, false starts, and methodological nightmares that can occur when you are first developing a study in an area can largely be avoided if you choose to work in an area in which your advisor has a lot of expertise.

Conversely, some students may not have the same research interests as their advisor (maybe they never did, or maybe their interests have changed over the course of their graduate training). In this case, their lack of passion or even interest for the area may result in a lackluster performance on this important project. We strongly encourage you to brainstorm ways that both your and your advisor's interests and areas of expertise can be accommodated and even maximized in the process. Sometimes, getting the best of both worlds is possible.

Clearing a Hurdle

> *I really don't want to do this thesis project. I have always wanted to be a practitioner and I don't understand how doing a thesis is going to help me be a better counselor. It just seems to me like this is one more hurdle that we have to jump in graduate school and I resent that it is such a time-consuming one at that.*

Although we would like all students to view their thesis or dissertation as a wonderful learning experience and one that will help them contribute to the larger society, learn new skills, and add to the knowledge base of the field, we realize that for some the thesis or dissertation is perceived to be a hurdle to get over on the way to pursuing their "real life." Although we personally find it sad that something as potentially growth producing as a thesis or dissertation primarily represents a barrier, we understand that sometimes events transpire throughout the process and this becomes the case. Again, you must honestly clarify what your goals are related to your thesis or dissertation. If you view it as a hurdle to be cleared on your way to something else, you may want to consider taking a very streamlined project in your advisor's primary line of research as we have already discussed. Even in these situations, we urge you to think about what you can learn from this process in order to make it a more worthwhile endeavor for you. Life is very short, and spending your time on activities that are not meaningful can be a waste of that precious time. In working with students, we have found that often we can identify something in the project that provides meaning. We encourage you to seek out aspects of your project that can be useful to you.

Continuing a Previous Line of Research

You might have conducted previous research in an area either as a part of a research team, as an assignment for a class, or perhaps for your honors thesis; now you may want to build on your previous research for your thesis or dissertation. Advantages to engaging in such programmatic research are that you know some of the research literature in this area, you are aware of the methodological issues involved, and you can easily identify several studies that would build on previous research. Continuing a line of work in which you have had previous experience is definitely easier. Moreover, such programmatic research adds in a more substantive way to the knowledge base in that particular area and often answers more specific questions within the area.

However, sometimes students continue with a research topic only because they thought it would be an easier route to complete the thesis or dissertation. In actuality, they lost their original interest, enthusiasm, and commitment for the area; it was simply a task to be done. If you feel that you have lost interest in a topic, we encourage you to seriously examine whether the time saved by continuing in an area is worth the personal cost. The thesis or dissertation takes a sustained commitment over a period of time. Conducting work on a topic in which you no longer have interest can make it a very arduous process. Thus, weigh the costs and benefits of continuing to conduct research in a previous area of interest and expertise.

Developing Specific Skills

Another factor to consider in selecting a research topic is the type of skills that you want to acquire or hone and how these skills will be useful in your career. For example, sometimes students want to expand their knowledge of a particular *methodology* like grounded theory. Alternatively, students may want to expand their knowledge of a particular *literature* like attachment theory. Sometimes students see *skill acquisition* as the primary motive for conducting a thesis or a dissertation in a particular area. For example, one of our students was very eager to apply the skills he had learned in his latent-variables classes. He saw these skills as being very important to future projects he might do. His faculty mentor had a large data set that would allow him to conduct a series of model-fitting studies. The topic itself was not one that held a great deal of interest for him, but the process of being able to use the data to hone his skills in Structural Equation Modeling (SEM) was highly salient to him. Another student was interested in learning more about feminist therapy. She designed a thesis examining the role of the client's feminist identity development on the process and outcome of counseling conducted using a feminist approach. Through this project, she learned a great deal about feminist therapy and some of the factors that lead to effective outcome. Thus, we encourage you to think not only about the content of your dissertation but also about the types of skills you may want to learn from the process of conducting this research. The time and energy devoted to this project is great; thus, considering carefully what can be learned through the process of the investigation seems relevant.

Promoting a Transition into a Chosen Career Field

Some students select a thesis or dissertation topic to acquire and demonstrate knowledge or expertise on a topic relevant to a particular career field. For example, you may want to work in a women's counseling center; thus, conducting a thesis or dissertation on some aspect of feminist therapy may provide you with specialized knowledge that may be very helpful in securing your ideal type of employment. You may want to use your psychology or education degree within a less-traditional setting, such as business or industry. Since your degree itself is not specifically geared toward this work setting, an impressive thesis or dissertation on a topic of relevance to business provides a number of potentially important pieces of information. For example, aside from the obvious content of the topic itself (e.g., measuring trust in corporate settings, dealing with resistance to change in organizations), the potential employer will also know that you were interested and motivated enough to design and conduct a lengthy project in this area. Moreover, your dissertation or thesis may reflect your ability to work effectively with business personnel, to gain their trust and access to business samples. In addition, it demonstrates how your training adds to the knowledge base of another discipline. Thus, we encourage you to consider your own career development as one factor in selecting a research topic. For example, where do you wish to become employed and how can the thesis or dissertation help you to acquire that type of employment?

Following a Personal Passion

Some students experience excitement about their thesis or dissertation because they have selected a topic where they feel a great deal of passion. Sometimes their passion arises out of an injustice they perceive or experienced; sometimes they have had a family problem that has caused them to feel a strong desire to find solutions to help other people with similar problems; sometimes they have had particularly meaningful and positive experiences working with a particular client group and want to understand more about that group. In essence, these students feel that their thesis or dissertation is an opportunity to make a professional contribution or some kind of difference on a particular topic about which they care deeply. Sometimes when students feel this kind of passion, they regard their thesis or dissertation as one part of their mission in life. This kind of feeling can provide powerful motivation for a student in completing his or her thesis or dissertation. Students often report, for example, that they cannot wait to find out the results of their data analysis. This kind of passion sustains students through the difficult tasks involved in the process.

The other side of this issue is whether the topic is *too* personally relevant and *too* emotionally charged for the student to be objective in his or her scientific inquiry. Although being passionate is great, too much intensity concerning a topic can result in consuming energy or losing the scientific objectivity necessary to conduct this level of scientific inquiry. We have occasionally seen students who were perhaps too emotionally involved in a topic; for example, investigating the psychological impact of the death of a child on parents when the student has just suffered the loss of his or her own child. We have seen students who felt so strongly about a topic that they had a personal agenda and desire to prove something about a topic or had an "ax to grind." So, prudence dictates examining your passions to determine if they are at a level that leads to continued and sustained interest and motivation or at a level that is prohibitive or reduces your ability to objectively examine the results.

Responding to a Significant Societal Need

Closely related to researching an area of passion is selecting a research topic because the student wants to make a contribution to alleviating a significant societal need. For example, some students want to help reduce school violence, racial tension, and prejudice or help patients cope with the challenges of living with chronic and debilitating diseases. Of course, one study will not solve such significant societal needs but some students gain satisfaction and meaning from being one small part of the work toward a solution. For some students, working toward alleviating a significant societal need is a personal passion or part of their life mission.

Applied professions such as counseling have a long history of responding to societal needs (see Heppner, Casas, Carter, & Stone, 2000). Many students who choose to enter the helping professions have deep and abiding values of helping others in some way. We strongly encourage you to consider selecting a research topic that may contribute to alleviating one small area of a significant societal need.

Acceptable/Practical Time Considerations

The time it takes for a project to be completed is clearly an important factor to consider when selecting a topic. Master's and doctoral students have a finite amount of time to be in a training program and to complete its requirements. When selecting a topic and defining the parameters of what will be investigated, students must assess a realistic time line for their project. The amount of time determined to be appropriate may vary from student to student. Some may view their thesis or dissertation research as a critical part of starting a line of research that they will pursue over the next years of their career. They may see it as appropriate to devote several years to the project. Other students may see it as practical to only devote a couple semesters to their project. Carefully consider the amount of time you have to pursue this project and select a topic that can be researched effectively within those time parameters.

Thus, you will consider many different factors when selecting a thesis or dissertation topic. Most students see their thesis or dissertation as serving more than one of these potential factors. Often students hope to investigate an area of passion that meets an important societal issue and helps them to develop skills that will be important to future research. We hope that by reading about these various factors, you will become clear about which factors are important to you in selecting a topic.

FINDING RESEARCH TOPICS

There are many ways to find research topics. Perhaps most important, you must keep an open and reflective mind in order to identify and develop topics. A critical first step is recognizing potential topics. To aid in identifying and—most importantly—remembering potential topics, some students carry a small notebook and jot notes about topics that seem particularly interesting to them. Ideas come from classes, other students, practice work, faculty, professional conferences, and reading the professional literature. One of our students found the idea for her study on Asian parental expectations after watching the movie *The Joy Luck Club*. Potential ideas are everywhere! In this section, we provide four major ways to find and refine research topic ideas: (a) reading the professional literature, (b) talking to experts, (c) applying or testing theory, and (d) examining applied experiences.

Reading the Professional Literature

Perhaps the most often recommended way to identify a possible research topic is by examining the professional literature. Reading widely both within and outside your field of interest is likely to spark a number of ideas. Sometimes students find it helpful to read the back issues of several of the premiere journals of their field as well as relevant handbooks. If you have narrowed the topic, sometimes it is helpful to read more focused resources. If you are interested in "something in the area of treating borderline personalities," then focusing on the last decade of literature in that area would be most helpful for starting to identify a topic. For example, a student of ours was interested in "something in the area of career interventions." We recommended that she examine the *Journal of Vocational Behavior*, which publishes yearly reviews of the literature on career development and vocational behavior. She also found several excellent chapters in the *Handbook of Counseling Psychology* (Brown & Lent, 2000) on career interventions. Through reading these sources, she was able to hone her idea to a much more specific and targeted one. Thus, we encourage you to read relevant as well as potentially related literature, paying particular attention to the limitations and suggestions for future research sections of the articles and chapters. This is a time-consuming process that may take many hours to accomplish, but there is no substitute for examining the existing literature in your interest areas to identify and refine a potential research topic.

Talking to Experts in the Field

In addition to reading the professional literature, you are encouraged to make appropriate use of professionals within your interest areas. Sometimes experts may be on your local campus or in the community. If your campus has a relevant expert, you will be expected to consult with that expert at some point in the process of developing your research idea. Students often need to go farther afield to national or international colleagues. Sometimes students are surprised by how interested and willing many experts are in discussing their areas of expertise. Most often researchers feel honored by students' interest in their work and are very willing to answer questions if they are posed in an appropriate manner. Following are two types of email messages from students.

> *Dr. Heppner. Currently I am working with Professor Albright at the University of Good Hope on what I hope will become my thesis for my master's degree. I have read with interest your 1999 article in* Journal of Counseling Psychology (JCP) *where you and your colleagues examined culture specific rape prevention programming for African American and White college students. I found it very interesting and inspiring. I would like to do my thesis in the area of rape prevention as well and wondered what you thought would be a good next step with that research? I was thinking that I might like to expand this idea to working with Asian American men at my college. I was also thinking that I would like to examine the attribute of personal entitlement that Fischer (1998) has discussed as being an important variable in predicting rape myth acceptance in White men. I would think this variable would be less prevalent in Asian men. I know you are very busy, but I would very much appreciate it if you had any thoughts about this idea. Thanks for your time and good luck with your work. I hope I have the opportunity to meet you sometime.*

In contrast, please read the following note:

> *Mary, You don't know me, but I want to do a study on career indecision. I remember reading an article awhile back that you did on*

this and was wondering if you had any ideas of related topics I could pursue. What key articles should I be looking at that were done in the last 10 years? Have you done any more work on this topic? I am wondering if you could write me back right away, because I am in a class where they made it a requirement that we talk to three professors about our topic, and turn in what they said. The assignment is due the day after tomorrow.

Researchers who are active in the field receive numerous requests from students and other faculty regarding our research. Queries like the first example are a great deal more rewarding to receive and respond to than the second. In the first example, the student had obviously read and studied Mary's most recent work. She had obviously thought deeply about the topic and developed some ideas about how she might proceed. Most important, the student asked questions that were tailored specifically to Mary's work, which was very appropriate. The student was also gracious, respectful of the Mary's time, and thankful for any feedback provided. Mary found herself wanting to respond and provide as much help as she could to this young scholar.

The second student clearly did little preparation before contacting Mary. He was unclear about the specific publication, leaving Mary confused about which article he was referencing. The student also did not do even the most rudimentary literature search in the area of career indecision and was asking general questions that, most likely, his local faculty could easily answer. The student seemed to be contacting Mary largely because it was a class assignment and came across as if this project were busy work rather than a functional consultation. He had not thought to consult in a timely fashion, as the assignment was due in another day. Mary's reaction to this email was mixed. She understood that this individual was young, just learning, and probably not being mentored or supervised by someone who would teach appropriate ways of contacting professionals. Because of this she responded to him as best she could but also emphasized that she could be more helpful if he would do more preparation, narrow his topical area, and have specific questions uniquely tailored to her expertise.

In sum, although we encourage consultation with professionals and experts in the field, we urge you to do so in a planful and respectful manner. You should definitely have conducted a literature search in your area of interest and have some specific questions tailored to the consultant's expertise. This type of email and subsequent phone contacts can cultivate a good professional relationship with the person; conversely, the professional can be left with a negative first impression if you are unprepared or disrespectful of the person's time and expertise.

Testing Theory

A considerable amount of research within education and psychology relates to testing theory. This is essential work and can be a tremendously important contribution to the field. Many theories have received only limited empirical evaluations. In addition, many theories have been tested using only majority populations. Due to an overreliance on using undergraduates to test some theories, examining the generalizability of such theories with other populations is needed (see Chapter 9 for more information on researching nonmajority populations). Thus, you may want to consider whether your research could be guided by a particular theory and how to develop empirical ways of testing certain aspects of the theory or the theory as a whole. Do not limit yourself to theories within your own discipline. Sometimes theories from other specialty areas or disciplines provide new ways of examining topics in another discipline. For example, social psychological theories such as Bandura's self-efficacy theory (1997) and Petty's and Cacioppo's elaboration likelihood model of attitude change (1986) have been tested in applied areas of psychology and have greatly expanded existing knowledge bases. Thus, as you are reading in other specialty areas for classes or projects, consider whether the theoretical models would be potentially useful to test in a different setting or with different populations.

Examining Applied Experiences

Be particularly vigilant of possible questions needing answers in practice settings. Often the best questions for research investigations derive from practice settings. Sometimes certain practices are maintained out of habit but not adequately tested empirically. In addition, sometimes practitioners have developed new intervention techniques or other new ideas that seem to be effective but now need empirical support. Remember that research can inform practice but the reverse is also true; practice can inform research. In short, identifying areas in practice that are in need of further investigation can lead to highly important contributions to the professional literature.

Reading the literature, talking to experts, applying and testing theories, and examining your experiences as a practitioner are all important routes to identifying and refining research topics. Remain vigilant for ideas and maintain a curious and inquisitive approach to finding and refining research topics.

DEVELOPING A TOPIC INTO A RESEARCHABLE STUDY

At this point, let us assume that you have identified a general topic on which to conduct your thesis or dissertation. For example, most students start with topics that are very broad, such as multicultural counseling training, attachment theory, incest survivors, or post traumatic stress disorders. The task now becomes refining the topic in ways that make it a researchable study. In some respects, determining the global topic of research is only the first step; the next and often more challenging step for most students is turning that global topic into a researchable study that is feasible, testable, and significant. In the following section, we examine five important areas to consider in taking a global topic and making it specific enough to be testable, that is, we discuss ways to narrow the focus of a thesis or dissertation. With this goal in mind, we discuss strategies related to (a) narrowing the scope of the study and identifying possible variables, (b) using theory to guide the selection of variables, and (c) using research questions to focus the study on certain hypothesized relationships among the variables. Remember that the goal at this point is simply to narrow the focus of the thesis or dissertation, not necessarily to finalize the specific hypotheses of the study. Narrowing the focus of the study allows the student to then examine the relevant literature in greater detail in order to make even more informed decisions about designing the thesis or dissertation.

Narrowing the Scope for a Study and Identifying Possible Variables

"Is this big enough?" is a frequently asked question of students who are at the early stages of developing a thesis or dissertation topic. Often the advisor's response is, "That is way too big, that is a career's worth of programmatic research." Sometimes the novice researcher has trouble gauging the magnitude of a project and determining what scope is appropriate. Our general criteria are that the thesis and dissertation should represent substantial amounts of work that will make a significant, publishable contribution to the literature of a field. Students often take more than a year to conduct and complete a thesis and 1 to 2 years for a dissertation. But the thesis or dissertation should not be a life's work. Thus, as a general rule, narrow your research topic for your thesis or dissertation such that the study can be conducted, analyzed, and written in roughly 1 year.

Finding the appropriate scope for a study is an important part of defining the parameters of the investigation. Let us place the thesis or dissertation into perspective using an analogy about the Grand Canyon. To portray the many facets of the Grand Canyon, one could use a video camera; the thesis or dissertation is the equivalent of one still photograph, perhaps of one small section of the trail or one beautiful overhanging rock. That photograph can provide some very important information that depicts the essence of some part of the canyon; yet, what it is able to portray about the whole canyon is very limited.

Sometimes, sketching a rudimentary diagram of many of the general research areas within a particular topic is useful to not only understand but also differentiate the major research areas. Within each major research area are literally hundreds of studies, and each study provides a snapshot of one aspect of the research in that major research area. Sometimes sketching such figures also helps students to clarify their research interests and subsequently narrow their literature search. As a general rule, we encourage students to limit their thesis or dissertation to just one major research area. Students may ask themselves what part of this topic is of most interest to them? What areas are they most committed to investigating? The decision to focus on one major area reduces what is often unwieldy complexity in research topics, as well as reducing the literature that needs to be reviewed to a smaller and more manageable number of studies.

Another consideration when deciding on the appropriate scope for a study is the number of variables under investigation. Rarely is a study based on one variable. In the past, studies commonly examined only two variables, such as the effect of one form of discipline on a child's self-esteem. As the knowledge base has progressed within applied psychology and education, so have the statistical tools that allow researchers to examine more complex relations that are most frequently the result of a host of potential factors. Thus, few studies in current literature explore only the relationship between two variables. We suggest that you identify several variables of potential importance to your investigation. One strategy for identifying possible variables is to again ask yourself more specific questions. What ideas or variables appear to hold most promise within the major research areas you have selected? What kind of information is missing on this research topic? (Thus, what variables are missing from the previous research?) Be sure to use the past literature, as well as your expertise and intuition, to generate a range of questions for your thesis or dissertation.

Using Theory to Guide the Initial Selection of Variables

As you develop and narrow your thesis or dissertation topic, you will often find that this process is best informed or guided by theory. By using theory, researchers are often able to identify and select variables and predicted relationships among variables based on previously described theoretical bases. Reading seminal theoretical articles in a particular research area provides direction by giving you a framework with which to understand a particular line of research or in which to integrate your thoughts on a topic.

A critical part of developing a topic into a study is developing a cogent rationale for the importance of or need for the study and the variables used in the study. Thus, readers (and especially committee members) will typically be asking questions such as: What guided the selection of these particular variables? Why did you select these particular questions? And, perhaps most important, what are the underlying mechanisms that may account for the predicted relationships you are hypothesizing in the investigation

(Tracey & Glidden-Tracy, 1999)? A theory often provides the answers to these types of questions. In essence, in these studies the investigator is testing the utility of a theory. Sometimes research topics, for whatever reason, are without useful guiding theories and, thus, discovery research strategies are most appropriate. Sometimes the knowledge base on a relatively new topic is such that a qualitative study without guiding theory is most appropriate. However, as a general rule, you should use theory to guide your research, particularly the identification of variables and hypothesized relationships among variables.

Sometimes these theories come from related specialty areas or disciplines. For example, much of the study of rape prevention has been theoretically grounded in a prominent social psychological theory of attitude change, the elaboration likelihood model of attitude change. The theory allows the researchers to predict relationships between the type of rape-prevention intervention and the likelihood of desired attitude change. Thus, the researchers have a framework for developing and testing the specific intervention and for discussing the results within a broader knowledge base. As you further develop your idea, utilize theories to help inform and shape your study. Moreover, do not limit yourself to theories within your specialty area; rather, examine theories of related disciplines that may help inform your specific area.

FURTHER REFINING A TOPIC BY IDENTIFYING INITIAL RESEARCH QUESTIONS

Oftentimes, the best way to refine a global topic into a researchable topic is to begin developing actual research questions to be tested. Research questions are another way of stating what you want to learn from your research. Research questions usually inquire about relationships among variables. For example: Is there a relationship between the sex of the counselor and the level of counselor self-disclosure in therapy? In this question, two variables are the focus of inquiry, sex of the counselor and counselor self-disclosure. Another example of research question is: What is the effect of counselor self-disclosure on the client's perceptions of the counselor? Or, on another topic: Does conflict resolution training reduce the incidence of school violence? Research questions not only serve to guide research to provide new knowledge about relationships among variables but also help solve societal problems as well as promote the development of theory (Tracey & Glidden-Tracey, 1999). In Chapter 6, we focus more specifically on appropriately writing research questions and hypotheses; but, at this early point in the process, we are simply encouraging you to begin developing possible research questions to further narrow your topics and, subsequently, to guide your literature review (see Chapter 4). Keep three criteria in mind as you begin to develop your research questions: testability, feasibility, and significance.

Testability

First, to what extent can the variables in the research questions be assessed or measured? If variables have been studied previously and strong psychometric instruments are available to measure these variables, the research question can be more easily tested from a quantitative perspective. Conversely, the study will present more challenges, perhaps even insurmountable challenges, if all or most of the variables are not easily assessed and have not been previously studied. As you proceed to conduct your literature review (see Chapter 4 and Chapter 7), examine to what extent previous investigators have used similar variables as you intend and how they assessed those constructs (see Heppner et al., 1999, for information about operationalizing variables).

Feasibility

Second, what is the feasibility of conducting a study on the research questions of interest? As you begin to conduct literature reviews and conceptualize the methods of the study, you need to assess how much time, energy, money, and other types of support the study will necessitate; is the study feasible to conduct given the time and resources you have available? Conducting this assessment of feasibility at this time and perhaps scaling back the study if it appears to require more resources than are currently available is much better than getting involved in the study and then determining it is not feasible.

Significance

Finally, evaluate your research question in terms of how useful this question is to the profession and to society. Does the research question address an important and significant societal need? Does the research question have the potential to result in a significant contribution to the professional literature? Similarly, does this study have the potential to be published in a professional journal in your specialty area? As we have already outlined, theses and dissertations can serve many functions; nonetheless, you need to assess whether this study has the potential to add to the professional literature or to the larger society.

In short, at this point, you should not only be developing research questions that are consistent with your goals for conducting the thesis or dissertation but also be evaluating the testability, feasibility, and significance of their questions.

GRANT SUPPORT FOR GRADUATE RESEARCH

Some topics and methodologies you choose require little financial support. Others may not be doable if you are not able to find grants or contracts to support your research. Many federal agencies and private foundations offer support for graduate students to pursue degrees, conduct research, participate in special projects, and write dissertations. We have provided a sampling of grant opportunities related to education, counseling, and psychology (see "Grant Opportunities" following Exercises 2.1). While some of these opportunities are general in focus, others are very specific. When considering grant applications, you should carefully read proposal guidelines to determine the appropriateness of the program to your specific research before beginning the application process.

CONCLUSIONS

Conceptualizing a meaningful and feasible topic for your thesis or dissertation is the first step in producing a successful product. The purpose of this chapter is to acquaint you with important factors to consider in choosing a topic. In highlighting a number of factors to consider in selecting a research topic, we are in essence suggesting that the thesis or dissertation can serve different functions for different students. We invite you to evaluate your situation and determine which of these functions are most important for you to consider.

Moreover, we emphasize the importance of reflecting on your topic and variables of interest; we strongly encourage you to begin to develop and write down potential research questions. Having these tentative research questions will help to focus the literature search and review. You may feel that developing research questions at this point is premature. Please understand that these questions are not "carved into stone" and do not necessarily represent your actual study. In fact, these questions are likely to change as you progress with your work. As you read more and begin to understand the literature of your area in a more complex way, you will probably refine your questions several times before actually conducting your investigation. However, beginning to even tentatively identify research questions often helps to begin to narrow the study into a manageable focus. After you have written a first draft of your research questions, we suggest that you begin to evaluate your research questions in terms of testability, feasibility, and significance. This is often a useful time to talk to your advisor to further consult about the direction of the thesis or dissertation project and potentially revise your tentative research questions.

EXERCISE 2.1 DEVELOPING A FOCUS TO YOUR RESEARCH TOPIC

1. List your top learning priorities for your research.
2. In what ways are these learning priorities related to your career goals and values?
3. What variables in your research topic interest you the most?
4. List possible research questions within your topic that interest you the most.

For each research question, evaluate the (a) feasibility (or how realistic it is) to conduct this study, (b) testability, and (c) significance of the study in addressing current societal needs and making meaningful contributions to the professional literature.

GRANT OPPORTUNITIES

Grants for Improving Doctoral Dissertation Research—Human Cognition and Perception
Agency: National Science Foundation
Deadline: Continuous
Amount: $8,000 (North America); $12,000 (Other areas)
Guidelines: http://www.nsf.gov/cgi-bin/getpub/nsf01113

The NSF's Division of Behavioral and Cognitive Sciences awards grants to doctoral students to improve the quality of dissertation research. The Human Cognition and Perception program supports basic research on human cognitive and perceptual functions and the development of these functions in children. Research supported by the program encompasses a broad range of theoretical perspectives and a variety of methods.

Grants for Improving Doctoral Dissertation Research—Sociology
Agency: National Science Foundation
Deadlines: Feb 15 and Oct 15
Amount: $7,500 maximum
Guidelines: http://www.nsf.gov/cgi-bin/getpub/nsf01113

The NSF's Division of Social and Economic Sciences awards grants to doctoral students to improve the quality of dissertation research. The Sociology program supports research on problems of human social organization, demography, and processes of individual and institutional change.

Dissertation Research Award
Agency: American Psychological Association, Science Directorate

Deadline: Sept 16
Amount: $1,000 (approximately 50 awards made annually)
Guidelines: http://www.apa.org/science/dissinfo.html

This program assists science-oriented doctoral students of psychology. The dissertation may be in any area of psychological research.

Clara Mayo Grants
Agency: Society for the Psychological Study of Social Issues (SPSSI)
Deadline: March 31
Amount: $1,000
Guidelines: http://www.spssi.org/mayo.html

Four awards are available to support master's theses or pre-dissertation research on aspects of sexism, racism, or prejudice. Studies of the application of theory or design of interventions or treatments to address these problems are welcome.

Grants-in-Aid Program
Agency: Society for the Psychological Study of Social Issues (SPSSI)
Deadlines: Nov 13 and April 1
Amount: $1,000
Guidelines: http://www.aapg.org/foundation/gia/about.html

Graduate student research is available for scientific research in social problem areas related to the basic interests and goals of SPSSI.

Dissertation Fellowship Program
Agency: Association for Institutional Research (AIR)
Deadlines: Jan 15
Amount: $15,000
Guidelines: http://www.airweb.org/page.asp/page=40

Fellowships are available for doctoral students beginning their dissertation work. Support assists students in the acquisition, analysis, and reporting of data from the National Center for Educational Statistics (NCES) and the National Science Foundation (NSF) data sets. The program supports research on postsecondary education that promises a significant contribution.

Dissertation Grants Program
Agency: American Educational Research Association
Deadlines: Sept 5, Jan 10, and March 20
Amount: $15,000
Guidelines: http://www.aera.net/programs/

The program's goals are to (a) stimulate research on U.S. education policy and practice-related issues, with a priority for those involving mathematics and science education using NSF and NCES data sets; (b) improve the U.S. educational research community's knowledge of data available at NSF and NCES and how to use them; and (c) increase the number of U.S. educational researchers using the data sets.

Dissertation Fellowship Program
Agency: Spencer Foundation
Deadlines: Oct 7
Amount: $20,000
Guidelines: http://www.spencer.org/programs/fellows/dissertation.htm

The Foundation seeks to encourage a new generation of scholars from a variety of fields to undertake research relevant to the improvement of education. Fellowships support individuals whose dissertations show potential for bringing fresh and constructive perspectives to the history, theory, or practice of formal or informal education anywhere in the world.

AERA/OERI Dissertation Grants Program
Agency: American Education Research Association and the U.S. Department of Education Office of Educational Research and Improvement
Deadlines: Oct 15, Apr 15
Amount: $15,000 for 1-year projects; $25,000 for 2-year projects (four awards per year)
Guidelines: http://www.aera.net/anews/announce/af01-002.htm

These grants are intended to provide doctoral students with time to write their dissertations. The program seeks to (a) stimulate research on fundamental educational issues, with a priority for the education of poor, urban, or minority students, as well as for mathematics and literacy education; (b) attract a cadre of talented scholars and enhance their research preparation; (c) build a network of scholars whose collaborations focus on high-priority educational issues; and (d) contribute to basic knowledge, the improvement of practice, and the informing of policy in educationally important contexts.

Dissertation Fellowships
Agency: American Association of University Women (AAUW)
Deadlines: Nov 1
Amount: $20,000 (51 awards)
Guidelines: http://www.aauw.org/3000/fdnfelgra/american.html

Dissertations are available to women in their final year of a doctoral degree program. Fellowships are open to applicants in all areas of study except engineering.

Graduate Student Program
Agency: U.S. Fulbright Program
Deadlines: varied
Amount: varied (1,000 awards granted annually)
Guidelines: http://www.iie.org

The U.S. Student Program is designed to give recent B.S./B.A. graduates, master's and doctoral candidates, and young professionals and artists opportunities for personal development and international experience. Most grantees plan their own programs. Projects may include university coursework, independent library or field research, classes in a music conservatory or art school, special projects in the social or life sciences, or a combination. It is the Board's policy that grants be awarded to the best-qualified students regardless of degree level. Preference, however, will be given to candidates who have recently received the baccalaureate degree. These candidates are not restricted as to field of study, nor will they be required to have formulated long-term specific educational or career goals beyond those necessary for a successful experience abroad. Master's degree candidates, young professionals and Ph.D. candidates are expected to have fully developed program of study/research that can be completed during the grant period.

National Research Service Awards for Individual Predoctoral Fellows
Agency: National Institute of Mental Health
Deadlines: April 5, August 5, and December 5
Amount: The annual stipend for predoctoral individuals is $16,500. An allowance of up to $2,500 per predoctoral fellow per 12-month period will be provided to the sponsoring institution to help defray such expenses as research supplies, equipment, travel to scientific meetings, and related items for the individual fellow, and to offset appropriate administrative costs of graduate research training. NIH will reimburse 100% of the cost of tuition up to $3,000 and 60% of tuition costs above $3,000 for the predoctoral fellow. Guidelines: http://grants.nih.gov/grants/guide/pa-files/PA-00-125.html

The NIMH and other institutes of the National Institutes of Health (NIH) provide National Research Service Awards (NRSAs) to individuals for doctoral-level training. These institutes award NRSA individual predoctoral fellowships to promising applicants with the potential to become productive, independent investigators in the scientific mission areas of these institutes. This program will provide predoctoral training support for doctoral candidates that have successfully completed their comprehensive examinations or the equivalent by the time of award and will be performing dissertation research and training.

OVERVIEW

Setting the Stage for the Thesis or Dissertation

Chapter 1 of the dissertation or thesis is analogous to the introduction of a journal article. You may even think of it as the first part of the article you will eventually submit when your dissertation or thesis is complete. In a journal article, however, the overview is usually two to three pages; in a thesis or dissertation, it is generally eight to ten pages. The purpose, however, is virtually identical. Overviews should serve the following key functions:

1. Engage the reader in the topic.
2. Build a rationale for why this study is important to do.
3. Include potential implications for the study.
4. Concisely state the purpose of the study.
5. List the hypotheses and the research questions.
6. Provide needed definitions, parameters, limitations, and assumptions.

Although the overview chapter comes first in the thesis or dissertation, we recommend writing it after you have written Chapter 2 (Review of the Literature) and Chapter 3 (Methods). As we stress throughout this book, writing a thesis or dissertation is not a linear process. Most students find themselves going back and forth as they proceed through the process of developing and conducting their thesis or dissertation. They read and study the literature and then realize they need to add a different hypothesis. They read an article that has a brilliant methodological suggestion and then modify part of their methods chapter. This nonlinearity is a good thing! That is, if you find yourself involved in this nonlinearity, then you are doing the kind of thinking you should be doing! You are uncovering the complexity of the topic area and allowing your thinking to be informed and improved by new information as you uncover it. This nonlinearity may frustrate you if you are a novice researcher. You may think research actually happens in the neat and methodical way it is described in professional journals. You may blame yourself for not getting it "right the first time." Rather, you should be saying to yourself, "This is exactly the kind of critical thinking I should be doing about my project."

Thus, when it comes to the task of constructing the overview or introductory chapter of the thesis or dissertation, most students have difficulty clearly articulating the purpose, rationale, and hypotheses before they have carefully and critically reviewed the literature in the area and before they have thought through all the methodological issues involved in their study. In fact, we have found that some students have such a difficult time with this particular chapter that, if they try to write it first, it serves as an obstacle to their progress.

This chapter requires a great deal of preparation before it can be done well. You may want to initially treat this chapter as a short, two-page concept paper that you will expand into a full chapter after you have written Chapter 2 and Chapter 3. A brief concept paper simply provides the "bare bones" of how you are conceptualizing your study. Concept papers can often provide you with a focus to proceed with your literature review and the development of your methods. After you have had a chance to study and integrate the literature in Chapter 2 and analyze the methodological issues inherent to this line of research, you are in a much better position to write the overview chapter. The concept paper is also a good way to communicate your initial thinking to your advisor or potential committee members. The important thing is not to allow the difficulty of writing the full overview chapter to serve as an obstacle to progress. We have found that once students get involved in their literature reviews—reading and analyzing the studies that have come before—they feel much more confident to come back to the writing of the overview chapter.

THE FUNNEL: AN ESSENTIAL WRITING TOOL

A particular structural writing tool—the funnel—is critical in helping chapters flow. A funnel, a tool with a wide portion at the top and an extremely narrow portion at the bottom, provides a good analogy for the shape of the overview and the literature-review chapters. The idea is to start out broadly and then to quickly narrow the writing to the specific study being proposed. Thus, you may be engaging the reader with startling national statistics about the extent of a major social problem but quickly narrowing to issues that are of particular relevance to your study. A common problem of novice writers is the habit of providing too much general information on a topic (e.g., race relations in the United States) and not enough on the specific area that their thesis or dissertation will cover (e.g., the impact of white racial identity status on mentors in a big brother program). Another common writing problem is that novice writers often switch from the global to the specific and back to the global again. As you are writing, think funnel. Look at the shape of your overview chapter and your literature-review chapter. Are you seeing the shape of a funnel? Do you start out with the most broad issues you want to include and then consistently move toward a more and more narrow perspective until you are providing the exact research questions and hypotheses you will be using for your thesis or dissertation? As you begin a new topic, again start broad and move to the specifics. You will have mini funnels inside the big funnel.

Graphically drawing a funnel of your research project such as the one depicted in Figure 3.1 may be helpful to you. In this figure, the student is doing her research on rape-prevention interventions with a high-school population. She is using social norming theory as her theoretical framework. She starts out with some brief national prevalence statistics that are general, then quickly moves to the prevalence rates in high schools, her target sample. She is conducting an intervention study aimed at preventing sexual assault, so she next critiques the existing prevention literature, followed by a more focused method-

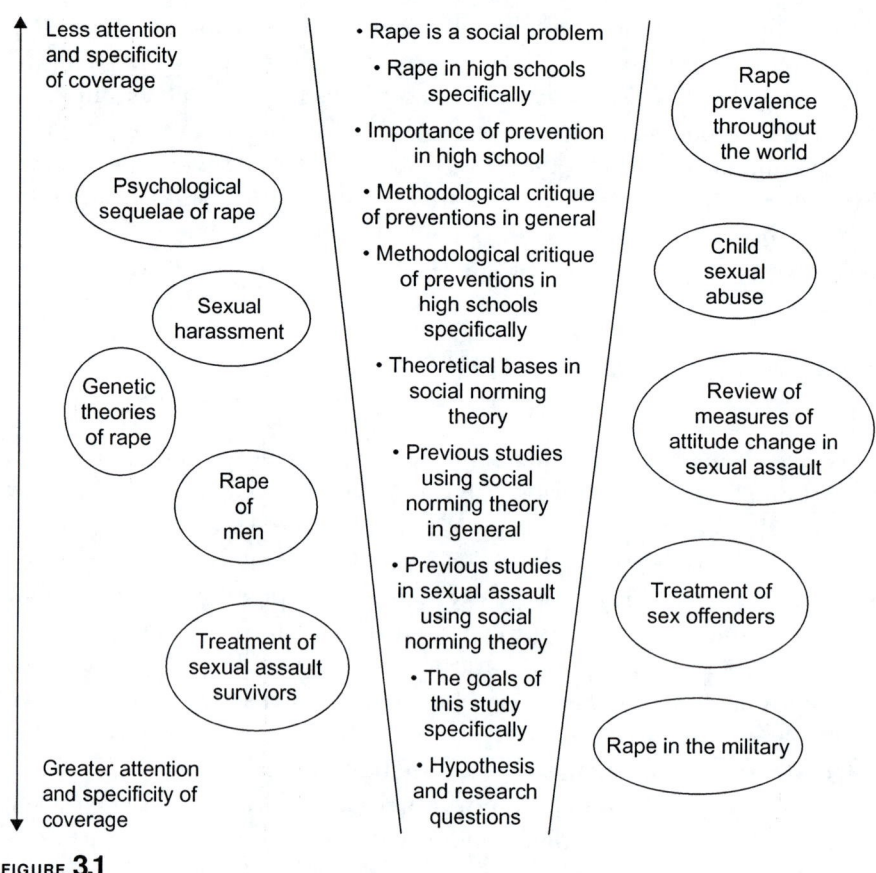

FIGURE 3.1

The Funnel.

ological critique of the prevention efforts at the high-school level. Since her theoretical framework is social norming theory, she describes the basic tenets of the theory, then provides a brief review of how it has been used to guide intervention studies in general (which in this case have largely been alcohol abuse prevention studies), then reviews the very limited literature on the use of social norming theory to guide sexual assault prevention studies. This leads the reader directly to the research questions and hypotheses that are being investigated in the present study. The arrow on the side of the diagram indicates that the amount of coverage of each of these topics grows more in depth as the chapter proceeds; that is, the author probably just has a paragraph on general prevalence statistics but may provide several pages describing in great detail the key research investigations that have been conducted using social norming theory as a theoretical framework for the design of sexual assault prevention interventions. Also note that numerous other topics related to sexual assault are outside the funnel and thus do not appear in the overview or the literature review at all. These topics are not central to building a case for this particular study and are thus excluded from these chapters. Think more about this funnel shape as we discuss the key elements that make up an effective overview chapter.

KEY ELEMENTS OF THE OVERVIEW CHAPTER

Engage the Reader in the Topic

The thesis or dissertation is a long and highly detailed piece of work. A certain amount of commitment is required for anyone to plunge into a thesis or dissertation and read it. Thus, the introduction must engage readers and let them know this is worthy of their time and energy. This topic is important. It is interesting. Readers need to know about this research because it has personal relevance for their lives. Putting thought and time into engaging the reader at this point will prepare you well to abbreviate this section for the eventual journal article that summarizes findings from the dissertation or thesis. Engagement can be achieved in a variety of ways. Compelling statistics regarding the extent of the problem are often used to engage the reader. A brief scenario of a typical presenting problem of a client may also be used. Dramatic statements or scenarios that relate to the issue or philosophical pondering of the topic can also be effective in engaging readers and causing them to care about the topic and the findings. Some specific methods of engaging the reader are illustrated in the examples that follow.

USING STATISTICS

In recent years, it has become increasingly clear that sexual harassment is a serious problem in both workplace and educational settings. The largest-scale studies of the incidence of sexual harassment in the workplace have all found that staggeringly large numbers of women have been subjected to this problem. The U.S. Merit Systems Protection Board (USMSPB) surveyed 23,964 federal workers in the early 1980s and found that 42% of the women had experienced sexual harassment (USMSPB, 1981); their follow-up study 6 years later yielded similar results (USMSPB, 1987). Gutek (1985) surveyed 1,232 women representative of the workforce in Los Angeles and found that 53% had experienced sexual harassment. Most recently, the National Victim Center asked about sexual harassment experiences in its latest sexual assault survey of 3,020 women, of whom 2,720 had been employed at some point. Preliminary results (cited in Koss et al., 1994) found a lower incidence of sexual harassment (17.5%), but this study included only more severe instances of harassment by supervisors that the respondents themselves labeled as sexual harassment. Most surveys of women university students have found that about 30% have reported at least one incident of sexual harassment. However, the most extensive survey of college women to date (Fitzgerald, Schullman, et al., 1988) found that approximately half of the women had experienced some form of harassment from their professors and instructors. Many researchers agree that these estimates are low, because the full range of sexual harassment was not assessed. (Cohen, 1995, p. 1)

Note in the preceding example how Cohen built the case for the importance of her study on the prevention of sexual harassment in higher education by presenting statistics that highlight the extent of the problem. Note also that she presents these statistics in an order that goes from statistics that are broad and related to U.S. workers in general to narrow and related to university students suffering from harassment by a professor. Through this method, Cohen is demonstrating the funnel principle and helping readers see that this is a generalizable problem in the United States as a whole and also that the problem of harassment is an important issue on college campuses, where she is conducting her research.

USE OF PHILOSOPHICAL PONDERING ABOUT HUMAN DEVELOPMENT

In childhood, we long for adulthood and the privileges that come with age. In adulthood, we often look back at youth and wish that we could start over. The question of what it means to be grownup continues to elude us, yet to preoccupy us, sometimes in our own private attempts to achieve this elusive state and, more often, in our attempts to prepare our children for the responsibilities that come with its conference. In modern times, we have come to realize the importance for development of the years that begin with puberty and end with emancipation: adolescence. This prolonged period between childhood and adulthood has been acknowledged as vital in a successful transition to adulthood (Harter, 1990; Patterson, Sochting, & Marcia, 1992). (Llorens, 1998, pp. 1–2)

Note in this example how Llorens engages readers by pondering the developmental issues of adolescents. Through this method, she helps readers reflect back on that period of time and the difficulties of transitioning to the adult world. Llorens' investigation examined the issue of psychological loss that occurs in adolescent girls as they pass from childhood to adulthood. Through engaging readers in remembering their own adolescence, she helps them to see how important her topic really is.

USE OF DRAMATIC STORIES FROM FAMILIAR EVENTS

As the world watched the evening news (American Broadcasting Company, 1991), a man in Los Angeles, California, was beaten by a gang of armed men. Some took an active role in the beating, others stood by actively encouraging those doing the beating. Still others stood mute as they watched. On another night, in Kansas City, Missouri, the world again watched as several armed men beat another man senseless. This victim's hands were bound behind his back. He offered no offensive action and was unable to defend himself effectively (ABC, 1991). Later, the world again watched as yet another man was beaten in Houston, Texas, by a group of armed men. This man was also bound and unable to defend himself (ABC, 1991). The scenes were captured on tape by citizens with video cameras. They witnessed and provided for the world to witness the aggressive and at times brutal acts committed by police officers. We as a nation are experiencing an apparent increase in the number of incidents in which police officers are caught "on camera" venting their frustrations on citizens. (Patterson, 1994, p. 1)

With these powerful and dramatic examples taken from the headlines, Patterson captures his audience. Readers find themselves asking, "Why is this happening?" "What causes the police to become so enraged and violent?" "What can be done?" These are exactly the kinds of questions Patterson wants readers to ask because his research will be conducted to answer these kinds of questions. Thus, the reader feels compelled to read on, to find out why these acts of violence occur and what can be done about them. These student authors have already begun to build a rationale for their studies through these engaging leads. In each case, the reader begins to understand that this is an important issue. Now the students need to convince readers that the rationale for the specific studies they are proposing seems appropriate to answer the questions raised by their engaging leads.

Build a Convincing Rationale for Why This Study Is Important to Do

Once you have the reader engaged and the reader understands that the problem is of some magnitude or importance, you then need to offer facts and evidence to convince the reader that the particular study is also appropriate and important enough to be done. Do not assume that just because readers think the global area of the study is important (childhood depression) that they will necessarily know that this particular study needs to be done. You need to convince readers that this topic has not been examined in the way you plan to examine it. Perhaps you are using variables that hold particular promise that have never been examined; or the instrument that you are constructing and validating is better in some key ways than others that are on the market to measure the same construct; or that this study is the next logical step in a line of programmatic research that will eventually bring an answer to a vexing question.

In the overview, you need to cite some of the most important previous investigations that led you to this particular study. In Chapter 4 of this text, we discuss more about how to determine which articles to cite. This is not a place to do a complete literature review, however; that should be saved for Chapter 2, the literature-review chapter. Here, you simply want to give a glimpse of the literature that has brought you to the place of saying: "This is an important area, and I want to study it." In essence, these are the core articles, theoretical frameworks, or findings that have most significance to the current study. Part of the reason for providing this glimpse is to give the reader an understanding of why you chose to review the specific literature you did in Chapter 2. Readers will have this rationale in mind when they read Chapter 2, and they will be saying, "Yes, I can see why it is important to know about this, given the role it plays in the overall study."

Include Potential Implications for the Study

In the applied areas of psychology and counselor education, theses and dissertations must have implications for both practice and future research. Although you will be highlighting these implications in depth in Chapter 5 of the thesis or dissertation (see Chapter 14 of this book for more details), some discussion of potential implications for this work may help to engage readers and help them see how this particular study has importance for the field. Thus, you should spend some time thinking about what the potential implications are for this investigation. Of course, you need to wait until the data are collected and analyzed to more specifically highlight the implications, but some ideas can be offered at this point, as illustrated in the two examples that follow.

> In addition to providing direction to counselors, a greater understanding of the characteristics of people who have low-flat Holland code profiles compared with the findings of earlier studies of people with differentiated profiles or elevated flat profiles (Gottfredson & Jones, 1993; Swanson & Hansen, 1986) may enhance our understanding of individual differences in the development of interests. If interest patterns are related to developmental issues, it may be possible to suggest ways to integrate some of the existing theories addressing development and gender differences with Holland's theory. The need to extend and integrate theories was noted by Gelso and Fassinger (1992) who concluded that ". . . a great deal remains to be done in integrating personality and developmental psychology more thoroughly into vocational work" (p. 283). Thus, a theory such as the self-efficacy theory of Hackett and Betz (1981) might be used in conjunction with Holland's theory to provide the missing information. (Pusateri, 1995, pp. 2–3)

Note how Pusateri builds a case for the importance of understanding more about low-flat Holland career interest code profiles. She indicates that such an understanding may lead to further integration of personality and developmental psychology with vocational psychology, which she indicates has been called for in the literature.

> This study was designed to expand our understanding of clients and their presenting problems and symptoms by exploring their relationship to personality. In

exploring the linkage between client personality and the types of presenting problems and symptoms reported by clients, it may be possible to gain a clearer understanding of the patterns in client symptoms and problems, in order to facilitate further research. By more clearly articulating the relationship between clients' emotional, interpersonal, experiential, attitudinal, or motivational styles (Costa, 1994) and client presenting symptoms and problems, it should be possible to increase the effectiveness of treatment planning and selection, as well as point out potential determinants of therapeutic outcome that have received little attention in the past. Although approximately 40% of the outcomes from therapy are consistently attributable to the development of the working alliance, little is known about the factors affecting the remaining variance in therapeutic outcome. It has been suggested that personality plays a significant role in this process. As a result, an exploration of the relationship between personality and the presenting symptoms and problems of clients should produce information that would add to the current literature and, possibly, point to new directions for study. (Hammond, 1999, pp. 10–11)

In this example, Hammond is pointing out that one implication of her proposed research is in determining the role personality plays in the development of the working alliance. She suggests that such information would add to the literature in the area as well as provide information to develop future investigations.

Concisely State the Purpose of the Study

One of the most important paragraphs in the overview chapter is a clear and concise statement of the exact purpose of the study. This is a paragraph that readers may go back to several times to make sure they understand exactly what the main purpose is in conducting this particular study. Developing this paragraph often helps the student become much clearer about this purpose as well. Thus, crafting a well-written paragraph of purpose is an essential task of Chapter 1. Following are two examples of statements of purpose from previous theses and dissertations.

The specific purpose of the study focuses on the young adult male children of the Vietnamese who immigrated to the United States in the mid-1970s and early 1980s and who are now an important part of the American society. These men are often more fluent in English than their parents and have adopted many of the American ways and traditions, and yet may have retained certain traditions from their parents' culture. The goal of this study is to develop a further understanding of the psychological impact of biculturalism on shame proneness, gender role conflict, and the psychological well-being of Vietnamese-American men. The study also is designed to examine whether being bicultural leads to personal growth and greater psychological well-being or, inevitably, leads to the type of psychological problems (e.g., ambiguity, identity confusion, and normlessness) suggested by Stonequist (1935) and Park (1928). (Vu, 2000, p. 8)

In his statement of purpose, Vu provides a brief background statement, which describes the sample as being Vietnamese immigrants. He points out that many of these immigrants are bicultural, having adopted parts of the new American culture as well as retaining elements of their Vietnamese culture. He then provides the reader with the central goal, which, in essence, is to study the impact of this biculturalism on a variety of outcome variables. He implies that the study has the potential to determine the positive and negative outcomes that this bicultural role may have.

> The purpose of this study is to understand and describe the reactions of males to two different rape education programs using a phenomenological description of themes found in the participants' written thoughts and reactions to the presentation. These interventions include both an interactive dramatic presentation and a didactic/video presentation. Through the use of the elaboration likelihood model of attitude change (ELM), coding formats were developed to examine the components of central route attitude change, such as personal relevance, involvement in thinking about the message presented, and favorable versus unfavorable evaluations of the program. This study represents an effort to examine the unique ways in which individuals view and experience rape prevention interventions that cannot be discovered through typical quantitative measures. Through the use of participants' written responses to several qualitative measures, this study seeks to examine such questions as: How can we make programs more personally relevant to males? What, if any, material presented tends to increase males' motivation to hear the message? What aspects of the presentations tended to elicit negative or defensive reactions from the males? In what ways are males experiencing these programs differently from females? And, what aspects of the presentations contribute to or hinder males from changing? (Hillenbrand-Gunn, 1995, pp. 7–8)

Note the effective way in which Hillenbrand-Gunn uses her first sentence to describe succinctly the essence of the study. She then goes on to provide more details of the interventions and ways the theory she is using will be tested. She ends her statement of purpose with a series of questions for which she hopes her qualitative data will help to provide answers.

List the Hypotheses and Research Questions

Research questions and hypotheses are critically important to the thesis or dissertation. We think of them as the "motor that drives the study." Generally, the overview is the chapter in which students provide a list of their research questions and hypotheses. Some advisors, however, prefer that hypotheses be listed at the close of Chapter 2. This, like many issues of style, should be explored with your advisor. We prefer to see the hypotheses at the end of the first chapter, as we believe that their placement here sets the stage for the literature that is to come in Chapter 2; that is, from the hypotheses and research questions, readers understand the essential constructs of the study. With this understanding, they are better able to intelligently read Chapter 2 with an understanding of how the literature being reviewed is related to the overall research questions and research hypotheses. Informed readers should be able to discern a great deal about the study simply by reading the hypotheses. For example, readers should be able to see what the major independent and dependent variables are; they will be able to at least guess what types of analyses will be used to test each hypothesis, which also then gives them an idea of what sample size will be needed to adequately test these hypotheses and questions; and they can understand the direction of the predictions and what relationship you believe your major constructs have to one another. Since research questions and hypotheses are so important to the study, we have devoted a chapter solely to their construction (see Chapter 5 of this book). We also discuss how different research questions dictate different types of research designs and statistical analyses in Chapter 5. We recommend that you carefully study this chapter before proceeding to write research questions and hypotheses in this overview chapter.

Provide Needed Definitions, Parameters, Limitations, and Assumptions

The overview chapter may also have a section for definitions, assumptions, delimitations, and limitations. Not all dissertations or theses will need all or perhaps any of these sections, but you should carefully consider whether yours would be strengthened by informing readers about specific parameters of your study (e.g., when you are using very specific terms that may have been used in different ways in previous literature or ones that have a different meaning in layperson terminology than they do in scientific terminology). These sections are also advantageous when you need to make clear from the start that assumptions or delimitations have been made that are important for readers to understand. Although the discussion chapter will provide a section on all of the limitations of the study, you may also want to warn readers in advance so that they are aware of some of the major limitations at this point. Again, these sections are not included in all dissertations or theses. We simply suggest that you consider whether they would be helpful in clarifying certain issues in your study.

Definitions   Conceptual definitions of key constructs are often presented in this overview chapter. Sometimes, operational definitions are also found in a dissertation—often in the methodology section. Think about the key constructs in your investigation. Would they be more easily explained if conceptual definitions were provided in the introduction? Some terms may be so widely known and consistently used that conceptual definitions are not needed. For example, terms like *depression, self-esteem,* and *anger* generally do not need conceptual definitions. Later, in the methods section, you will need to provide operational definitions; for example, "Depression will be operationally defined as the total score on the Beck Depression Inventory, or through interviews using *DSM-IV* criteria." Thus, for every conceptual definition in the introduction, there should be an operational definition in the methods section. The reverse, however, may not be needed.

Assumptions, Limitations, and Delimitations   Sometimes assumptions must be made in the investigation. An *assumption* is something that is thought to be fact but that may have limited evidence to support it. For example, in a methodology in which you may be relying on 12 counselors to exactly reproduce a specific protocol, but, for some reason, are unable to verify that that protocol was executed in the same manner each time, you may want to state an assumption regarding this by saying something like:

> In order to avoid compromising the privacy of participants, a decision was made to not audiotape the sessions. Because of this practice, we must assume that, based on 6 hours of training and pilot testing, the counselors executed the protocol in the manner in which they were trained.

A fine line exists between assumptions and limitations. You should think about how much evidence you have that allows you to make a particular assumption. Statements of *limitation* may be more accurate. For example, let us say a student researcher is conducting focus groups with junior-high and high-school students to determine their perceptions of sexual assault interventions. The researcher has asked for interested participants and is paying the children $20 each for their participation. An assumption about this practice may be:

> It is assumed that the children who volunteer to participate in the focus groups do not differ from the nonvolunteers on any relevant criteria.

Perhaps stating this as a limitation would be more accurate:

> A limitation of the present study is that it is unknown whether the children who participated in the focus groups were the same on all relevant criteria, as children who declined to participate.

A differentiation should be made between *limitations* of a study (which are often methodological issues such as lack of generalizability or lack of psychometrically sound tools to measure constructs) and *delimitations*, which are parameters that the researcher chooses to place on the study. For example, in the preceding case:

> The sample was delimited to students in the age range of 16 to 22, as this is the age range in which the highest number of sexual assaults occurs.

Or,

> The study was delimited to only those students who met the indecisive criteria, since the study was designed to examine only personality correlates of indecisive students.

CONCLUSIONS

Remember that the overview chapter may be short in page length but that it is very important to readers' overall understanding of what is intended in the remaining four chapters. A well-conceptualized and well-written overview engages readers and convinces them that this investigation is worthy of their time and attention and that the writer has carefully thought through the hypotheses and research questions. The overview chapter also sets the stage for Chapter 2, Review of the Literature.

We have prepared a checklist for each of the major chapters in the thesis and dissertation. This chapter includes the checklist for Chapter 1. We strongly encourage you to do a self-critique using these checklists before you give drafts of your chapters to your advisor or others to read. By carefully scrutinizing your own work against these criteria, you will note areas that you have done well as well as areas that may need improvement. Respond as honestly as you can to each of the questions. Then examine the self-assessment to see which areas should be fine-tuned before giving them to the advisor for feedback.

CHECKLIST FOR CHAPTER 1 OF THE THESIS OR DISSERTATION

To what extent do you . . .

1. . . . . engage the reader in the topic?

1	2	3	4	5	6
Not at all				Very much so	

2. . . . . build a rationale for why this study is important to do?

1	2	3	4	5	6
Not at all				Very much so	

3. . . . . concisely state the purpose of the study?

1	2	3	4	5	6
Not at all				Very much so	

4. . . . . *briefly* discuss the methodology?

1	2	3	4	5	6
Not at all				Very much so	

5. . . . . list the hypotheses of the study? [The following statements invite you to examine your research questions and hypotheses that you

construct using skills developed in Chapter 5. We include them here, as your hypotheses will most typically appear in this overview chapter.]

| 1 | 2 | 3 | 4 | 5 | 6 |
Not at all   Very much so

(a) Hypotheses are written as positive assertions; they are not written as null hypotheses.

| 1 | 2 | 3 | 4 | 5 | 6 |
Not at all   Very much so

(b) Only one hypothesis is imbedded in a single statement unless grouping them is less cumbersome (e.g., Career counseling self-efficacy will be positively related to career counseling process variables and outcome variables).

| 1 | 2 | 3 | 4 | 5 | 6 |
Not at all   Very much so

(c) Research questions and hypotheses are combined if appropriate. (Often people use research questions to state the basic area of interest, then spell out the specific questions in subsequent text.)

| 1 | 2 | 3 | 4 | 5 | 6 |
Not at all   Very much so

(d) If a relationship is expected for a specific population, I only state this in the hypotheses (e.g., among inexperienced counselors, in African-American populations).

| 1 | 2 | 3 | 4 | 5 | 6 |
Not at all   Very much so

(e) Hypotheses are as specific as possible yet expressed in a single sentence.

| 1 | 2 | 3 | 4 | 5 | 6 |
Not at all   Very much so

(f) I have eliminated any words or phrases that are not essential.

| 1 | 2 | 3 | 4 | 5 | 6 |
Not at all   Very much so

(g) Hypotheses indicate what will actually be studied, not implications of it.

| 1 | 2 | 3 | 4 | 5 | 6 |
Not at all   Very much so

(h) I have not used two different terms to refer to the same variable; I use parallel construction.

1	2	3	4	5	6
Not at all				Very much so	

6. . . . present any important definitions or parameters?

1	2	3	4	5	6
Not at all				Very much so	

7. . . . have the reader saying: "This is exactly the kind of study that is now needed to extend this area of research in meaningful directions!"

1	2	3	4	5	6
Not at all				Very much so	

SEARCHING AND REVIEWING THE RELEVANT LITERATURE

Finding What Has Come Before

Searching and reviewing the literature are probably the most important aspects of developing a study that adds to the literature in unique and substantive ways. If you do not know what has come before your study, what constructs have already been investigated, what methodologies have proven most effective, and in what ways the research in this field has been criticized, the likelihood of producing a high-quality "next step" in the literature is remote. It has been our experience that many students believe they know how to conduct literature reviews, when, in fact, their skills at doing so are not well developed. Typically, students have already conducted many literature searches during their undergraduate and graduate career. A term paper has required them to go to the library to do a search and briefly summarize their findings. In talking candidly with students about their process for many of these papers, we find that their search has gone something like this:

> Jane B. Swift wanted to look at the role of self-esteem in adolescent delinquency. She went into Psych Info, typed in the key words *self-esteem* and *delinquency,* and crossed them. The search indicated 1,589 articles; she put in adolescent girls to limit the search and got 79 articles. She printed out the abstracts for these articles and found 17 articles in the library that looked most promising. She wrote her review based on the articles and, in some cases, the abstract if she could not find the article. "It really didn't take that long," Jane said.

Although this may seem to some of you like a rather extreme case of a nonrigorous search, there are many variations of this process that lead to much the same result. The purpose of this chapter is to provide an introduction into systematically searching and reviewing the literature for a thesis or dissertation. First, we discuss and normalize the process of conducting a literature search. This is often a nonlinear and, seemingly, trial-and-error process that can sometimes be demoralizing and frustrating to students. Second, we provide a host of resources for conducting a literature search; we emphasize that multiple resources are needed to conduct a thorough literature review. Third, we emphasize the utility of integrating the search for relevant articles with reading and reflecting on the articles as an essential aspect of furthering the search process. To facilitate the process of understanding the literature, we provide several concrete examples of organizing the literature. Literature reviews that are conducted for the thesis or dissertation need to (a) be thorough, (b) be highly specialized to the specific topic that your hypotheses will cover, and (c) involve a high level of conceptual and critical thinking.

The Search Process: A Highly Specialized and Nonlinear Process

Before conducting a thorough review of relevant articles, you need to understand the process of doing a highly specialized search. Students who are conducting their literature reviews often have two complaints: "I did my search and I only found four articles that relate to my topic," or "I did my search and found over 2,000 articles and I downloaded them, but I don't know how I'll have time to read them all." The number of articles identified on a first run can tell you a great deal about the breadth of your topic. Although students frequently ask, "How many references are enough?" with the answer being, "It depends," some global things can be said about numbers. If you are finding fewer than 10 articles that seem relevant to your topic, perhaps your topic is too specialized or you have not conducted the search effectively (e.g., selecting the wrong words for the search engine). If, conversely, you are finding over 200 articles on a "first run," most likely your topic is too broad. The thesis/dissertation literature review is not analogous to a traditional term paper or a report on a broad topic like self-esteem; rather, it is a highly specialized and thorough review that focuses on a very specific area of the professional literature. Consider the following photographic analogy: In conducting a thesis/dissertation literature review, the goal is not to do wide-angle photography of the Grand Canyon, nor is it to focus on one grain of sandstone at the base of the canyon; rather, the goal is to focus on the nuances on a portion of the trail going down into the canyon.

Students often equate thoroughness with number of articles. Thoroughness has little to do with number of articles. You may find hundreds of articles that have something to do with your topic and still not know the literature. To thoroughly examine the literature on a topic, typically you need to find a broad range of high-quality, specific articles, books, government documents, dissertations, critiques, and/or previous reviews that are directly related to your specific topic and then read and reread these articles until you understand the progression of research in this area.

A wide range of literature exists that you may possibly review with any topic. In some cases, books may have been written on just one variable within a topic. Thus, you must identify the most relevant literature that your reader must know to understand your research hypotheses within this topic. A major task is to map the relevant territory for your literature review, identifying relevant studies and discarding irrelevant studies. For example, assume that you are doing a study with three central variables. Think of those variables as three overlapping circles (see Figure 4.1).

The area in the middle where all three circles overlap represents the primary literature. These are studies that have previously been conducted that are likely the most relevant to your study. These studies should be given some prominence in your literature review—more space, more detail of description, more thorough critique. In addition, note the three areas where two of your variables overlap; these studies will most likely be relevant for your study as well. Then there are areas where your variables do not overlap at all. Some of the literature on these variables may be very important if it helps you introduce information that will form the basis for your unique contribution. If this is the case, definitely include this literature as well. However, there is also literature included in this circle that is not relevant to your study. You should not include irrelevant details that detract from your partic-

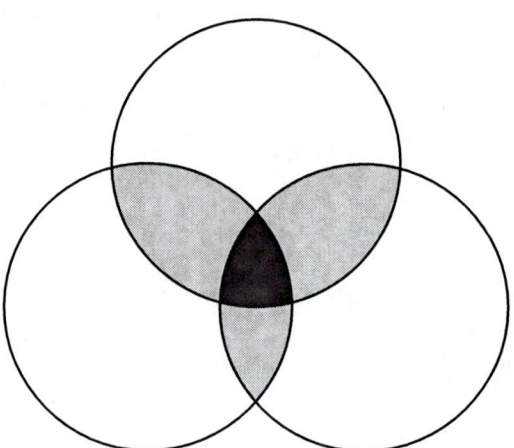

■   *The most relevant literature.* This literature will be reviewed in the most depth as it pertains to the topic.

▨   *The next most relevant literature.* This is literature in which two of the central constructs under investigation in the current study overlap.

▢   *Literature that does not relate directly to the investigation.* This literature pertains to a construct that is included in the investigation but not to the particular aspects of that construct that are important to the current study.

FIGURE **4.1**

Identifying the most relevant literature to present in the literature-review chapter.

ular study. As you are making decisions about what to include in your review, ask yourself these questions: "Why am I including this study or reference?" "Is this investigation needed to build the rationale for my study?" If you can identify only those articles that are relevant to your study, you will avoid the type of review that consists of a huge list of citations, many of which have little to do with your topic.

Typically, as students' schemata become more differentiated about the topic, they begin to find the appropriate focus. In essence, students' level of knowledge about their topic expands and becomes more differentiated as they read and study the relevant literature. During this process, students progress from a rather global or general way of viewing their topic to a highly sophisticated and finely differentiated scheme. They understand more about ways people have conceptualized important constructs within the topic as well as understanding the methodological problems and concerns that affect the topic. This is the process of becoming an expert on a particular topical area. Sometimes, an important part of this process is that students find that some articles are not helpful because they are much too broad or focus on variables not relevant to a particular study; or students realize they need to focus on a particular section within the broader topic to narrow their focus. The latter process or some variation of it is quite common and typically results in discarding some of the previously identified material or conducting additional searches. In essence, this process of differentiating the key constructs within a topic is a very important part of honing an idea and focusing a study. Moreover, differentiation only comes by reading, rereading and analyzing the literature.

Searching the literature in segments is useful when interspersed with reading and thinking about the relevant articles that were found. Rather than trying to find every last article and then sitting down and reading them in a day, a better strategy is to locate those articles that sound like they have the most promise, read and study them and then use those articles to influence the next level of searching. Students who try to find all relevant articles first often find that they use only a fraction of these articles because their study only focuses on one particular aspect of this topic, or the focus of the study may change as they analyze the research. Thus, we recommend that you search, examine and reflect, and then search again with a more refined focus.

An effective literature search is most often nonlinear. Jane Swift's example at the beginning of this chapter is typical of many students' ideas about conducting a literature search. You start with an idea, you search, you narrow, and you write it: a neat, clean, one-directional, linear approach. Our experience is quite the opposite; when students are conducting a thorough and rigorous search, they typically find it to be anything but linear. For example, most students will start their search guided by several rough hypotheses. They may have become interested in a global topic—racial identity development, for example—and have decided to look at the role racial identity development plays in the supervision process. They search the topics *racial identity development* and *supervision* and find articles. As they become immersed in the literature, they observe that several studies have already been conducted on this specific topic; but, in examining the methodology, they find that all have used an analog protocol rather than examining actual supervisory relationships. They also find that gender was never considered as a variable in these studies, and they start hypothesizing that gender role socialization may be another important aspect in supervision outcomes. This hypothesis leads them to search the literature again, more specifically in the gender role literature as it relates to supervision. They also reflect on the advantages and disadvantages of using an analog methodology (see Heppner et al., 1999, for more information about analog designs), and they begin searching for related studies that have used actual supervisory relationships in order to examine the specific methodologies to collect data.

As you can see by this one example, what started out as a linear search for two constructs that were of initial interest quickly changed. Additional searches were necessary to examine other variables, simultaneously weighing the advantages and disadvantages of research methodologies and reconceptualizing the basic research question. We have found that many students become frustrated at this point. From a process perspective, this nonlinear, looping-back process is generally a very good sign that your analysis of your topic is progressing. You may not always feel like you are progressing, but most often that is the case. These kinds of nonlinear processes generally mean that students are (a) critically analyzing a complex topic, (b) refining their conceptualization of their study, (c) developing a far more rigorous methodological approach, and (d) ultimately contributing a great deal more to the field with their research. If you start feeling frustrated in these situations, remind yourself that a thorough literature search takes time to identify articles, time to read and reflect, and more time to repeat the first two steps. As is becoming obvious, conducting a thorough literature search takes a lot of time. Sometimes students defeat themselves by letting themselves believe that they can do it quickly. Be careful! As you plan your time for the literature search, add more time for the nonlinear, looping-back process. Remind yourself that looping back is normal and that you are probably doing the type of learning and analyzing that will greatly improve the quality of your research.

In some instances, students are working hard but not progressing. In essence, they are either stuck or unfocused in their search, going from topic to topic without narrowing their study. If this happens to you, consult knowledgeable peers, your advisor or other faculty. We encourage you not to procrastinate; if you are not making progress, consult with others to clarify both the directions of your search and your feelings about the experience.

Resources to Conduct a Literature Search

Students have found a number of resources useful to identify relevant research for their theses and dissertations.

Handbooks

Handbooks that summarize the important contributions in specific areas of research are published in most fields and can be an excellent place to start your search. These handbooks are typically published every 2 to 5 years on a given topic. Generally, major scholars and researchers are asked to provide a chapter synthesizing the work on a particular topic with which they are very knowledgeable. These chapters are invaluable as they provide extensive references related to the most important research in that specialized area. Examples of handbooks in counseling and clinical psychology are *The Handbook of Psychotherapy and Behavior Change, The Handbook of Counseling Psychology, The Handbook of Multicultural Psychology, The Handbook of Vocational Psychology,* and *The Handbook of Industrial and Organizational Psychology.*

Annual Reviews

Annual reviews are periodic reviews that comprehensively review literature in a particular area. They can be an excellent source if your topic has been reviewed recently. Perhaps the most widely known annual review is the *Annual Review of Psychology.* This annual review has been published each year for the last 50 years. Different topics within the broad field of psychology are reviewed each year. In the career area, the *Journal of Vocational Behavior* also provides annual reviews of the career literature. Similar to the handbooks, most annual reviews are evaluative and include selective reviews of the literature written by experts in the specialty. The advantage of annual reviews is that they are published yearly and can provide specific and current information concerning an area of interest. The reviews and reference lists of articles used in the reviews are excellent places to start your literature review.

Major Review Articles in a Specialized Area

Major review articles are an excellent source of information for a given topic. These review articles are often published as monographs in journals. Some journals rarely publish such reviews, while others such as *Psychological Bulletin* or *The Counseling Psychologist* consistently publish integrative critical reviews on a range of topics. These reviews not only provide comprehensive reviews on a topic but also provide models for how to write a literature review (see Chapter 6 for writing your literature reviews).

People Resources

People can be your very best resource during your literature search. In addition to the librarian we discuss later, knowledgeable faculty—either on your campus, nationally, or internationally—and students who have worked on similar topics can be valuable resources as you search for information. To demonstrate different ways other people can serve as very useful resources, we offer the following four examples:

- I read an article in the most recent *Journal of Counseling Psychology* that a psychologist in Israel had written about the use of "career aspects" (i.e., variables that potentially affect career development). I thought about how interesting it would be to conduct a study that examined religiosity as a potential career-related variable and to examine outcomes that related to this aspect of peoples lives. I emailed the author and he was kind in responding to me about my idea, suggesting a refinement and other literature I should read.
- I saw a conference was being offered in Chicago on Carol Gilligan's work on psychological loss in adolescent girls. All the "biggies" in the field were going to be there presenting their work. I was planning a dissertation on developing a scale to measure the loss these researchers had identified through their qualitative methods. I decided to go to the conference and meet other like-minded people who could suggest other readings to pursue and other ways of conceptualizing my work. It also made me feel like a part of a larger group of scholars and that my work really was important.
- I contacted a woman who had done a dissertation 2 years ago on a very similar topic to what I was thinking about. I called her and we had a great conversation. She had never published her work and said in hindsight she would have done several things differently. She gave me a couple of areas to search for constructs that might be important moderators of the relationship that she explored.
- I became involved in a discussion group on the Internet. These people were very helpful in suggesting sources of information I had not found in my literature searches using the primary search engines in my field.

Note that most researchers are busy people. Thus, you must have done your homework and become knowledgeable about your contact before you request help. In our experience, most people are very willing to help other scholars, especially students. But it can be frustrating to receive calls when the person has not done much thinking about the topic or the questions they are asking. Be sure you have done sufficient work before you call or email, so that you can ask specific questions that result in an efficient use of time.

Informed Use of Search Engines

Many students use search engines to begin their search, which is an appropriate way to start a search; but, for most topics, it is not an appropriate way to *end* a search. The search engines serve a very important function, but many other methods will be important to conduct a thorough search. When using a search engine, be sure you are familiar with the nuances of it. For example, although search engines have become increasingly sophisticated over the years, they cannot think for you. They can search huge volumes of information and can select key words from titles and abstracts, but they cannot read your mind. Search engines will only search what you tell them to search. Thus, the key words that are used for your search are vitally important. Many search engines have an accompanying thesaurus that provides guidance in the selection of words. For example, in doing a search on rape-prevention programming, *rape* may not necessarily be a very useful term. Perhaps better words would be *sexual assault, sexual violence,* and *sexual aggression.* If an author uses the word *sexual assault* instead of *rape* in his or her title or abstract, the search engine is not typically capable of linking the two literatures and will thus identify a much smaller pool of literature than is actually available. In short, although search engines can be very helpful, many times it will take considerable trial and error to determine the most appropriate key terms to use. If students plan to make extensive use of a search engine, it may be useful to schedule an appointment with a librarian and further develop their expertise on using specific search engines.

Interdisciplinary Search Engines

As disciplines have become more specialized, research conducted and cited in one discipline is often not found in the search engine of a second discipline. Thus, for many topics it is simply not a good idea to only use the search engine within your own field of study. In some cases, conducting cross-disciplinary searches can be very exciting and add greatly to the richness of your research. For example, a student in counseling psychology recently conducted a dissertation on racial oppression and specifically developing a scale to examine how different people react to oppression (Howard, 1999). Since the fields of psychology and counseling psychology have traditionally focused on individual differences, this researcher experienced difficulty finding many articles in the psychological literature. By searching in the sociological literature (by using Sociofile, in addition to PsychInfo), she found several articles that were helpful to develop a very rich conceptual base that integrated the environmental context as an antecedent of oppression. Her dissertation became a complex test of a sociological theory and added a great deal more to the literature than had she not used this cross-disciplinary approach.

Thus, students are encouraged to use several search engines besides PsychInfo, such as Sociofile for relevant research in sociology, ERIC (the Educational Resource Information Center) for education-related research,

Index Medline for medically related information, or Business Periodicals Index for industrial and organizational topics. Ask your librarian about appropriate databases and which library has these resources in both print and electronic form.

Librarians

The librarian is your friend! If not, the librarian should fast become your friend! Librarians have a wealth of knowledge and can help make your search much easier. They know what databases may be helpful to you and what resources are available and how to access them. Introduce yourself to your librarian. Many university libraries have people specifically assigned to specialty areas; for example, some librarians are specifically knowledgeable in the behavioral and social sciences. Get to know the person assigned to your discipline. Introduce your topic to the person and ask for the specific help you may need. Many times the library conducts training sessions for students and faculty on using search engines or using the Internet to find government documents. The librarian can be a great help to you when you hit a roadblock or need additional expertise to acquire the information you need.

Not All Articles Are Created Equal

One critical mistake that many students make is to treat all articles the same. When conducting a search and when writing your review (see Chapter 6), you should carefully examine the quality of the articles. Some articles, even though they were published, have serious methodological flaws. Carefully review each article. Is the methodology rigorous? Were adequate numbers of participants used? Were psychometrically sound instruments used? and Were the procedures appropriate? Or were there major methodological flaws such that there are alternative explanations for their findings? You may find important research across many journals; you must examine articles on a case-by-case basis and evaluate each article carefully. High-quality studies should be relied on more heavily than low-quality studies in the literature search and conceptualization of your study. Articles with nonrigorous methodologies can be used, however, to build a case for the more rigorous methodology you are using in your specific investigation.

Work Backward

Once you have located a set of high-quality, relevant articles, examine the references. Note references that you have not found in your searches. This process not only provides an important check regarding the thoroughness of your search but also provides additional articles you may want to examine.

Key Authors

In addition to conducting a topical search, develop a list of authors who have been important contributors to the area. Then, conduct a search of their publication histories. Using a search engine such as PsychInfo and searching by author's name can do this; this procedure will provide a list of all articles published by the author from most recent to least recent. In addition, libraries usually have broader search engines (OVID being one of the most common) that allow you to search by authors as well. These search engines will provide information not only from PsychInfo but also from books and journals not in PsychInfo. Searching publications by key authors may identify additional articles that did not appear in the searches you conducted. For example, they may have published an important policy article in a law journal that relates to your topic or a recent chapter in a text that did not appear on your search.

Social Sciences Citation Index

Another way of finding relevant articles is to use the *Social Sciences Citation Index* (SSCI) to identify articles that have cited some of the most important studies. The *SSCI* is published yearly and consists of citations in the social science literature for a particular year; it is ordered conveniently by author's name. So, for example, perhaps you are doing a thesis or dissertation on the social influence process in counseling. You know that Stanley R. Strong was a major author in this area. In the *SSCI*, find *Strong, S. R.,* and you will find a list of all the authors who have cited his work for a particular year. You can also search specifically for one of his articles that is most central to your research study and examine the citations for that particular article. Many libraries now have the *SSCI* on CD-ROM in addition to book form. This is a time-consuming process but often is useful to identify studies in other disciplines that may be relevant to your study.

Soon-to-Be-Published Sources

Some organizations publish newsletters that are intended to keep their subscribers abreast of the latest developments in the field. For example, *Current Contents: Social and Behavioral Sciences* publishes the upcoming tables of contents for a number of journals. These newsletters, which are published weekly, help keep readers aware of what is being published in numerous related fields. Readers can contact the author and ask for a pre-print of an article not yet published.

Dissertations

Unfortunately, a very small percentage of theses and dissertations is published. This does not mean that these dissertations are unpublishable, only unpublished. That is, many times students do not have the energy or motivation to publish their work. Sometimes a student's advisor does not provide the necessary mentoring to move the investigation from the 200-page dissertation to a 35-page journal article. Whatever the reason, do not equate lack of publication with lack of quality ideas. In some respects, dissertations can be one of the best sources of information for you. For example, the literature reviews in dissertations are substantially longer and sometimes more thorough than those found in published articles. In addition, most dissertations contain appendixes that have copies of the instruments used in the investigation. These can be invaluable as you attempt to identify potential instruments to assess the constructs in your study. Dissertation abstracts can be located through discipline-specific search engines (e.g., Psych-Info) or are available in the *Dissertation Abstracts International* either in written or online form. Entire dissertations can be ordered through Interlibrary Loan; and, although sometimes this can take some time, it may be well worth the wait.

Government Sources

Published journal articles are only one source of information. For example, when writing an article on sexual assault, getting the most up-to-date numbers on prevalence rates is essential. The Bureau of Justice Statistics regularly publishes reports on the rates of violent crime. These government documents represent a massive amount of information that is regularly published but often hard to find without the help of a librarian. Two of the best search tools for government reports are the *Monthly Catalog of Government Documents* and the *Index to U.S. Government Periodicals.* Some libraries may also have the electronic search capabilities of the *Government Documents Index.*

ORGANIZING THE RESULTS OF YOUR SEARCH

You must view the literature search as one of intense critical inquiry rather than one of rote technical activity. Sometimes students gather a pile of articles with the goal of reading them all in one sitting (in no particular order). We also find that students often spend a lot of money copying almost every article they find. We recommend more time actually examining the articles for their usefulness before automatically copying them. In addition, often students' reading is not focused and they are not systematically analyzing the articles.

One tool we have found to be very important when reviewing and critiquing large volumes of articles is a categorization system. The system can be set up using paper, note cards, a computer, a software system specifically designed for this purpose, or whatever works most efficiently for you. The essential issue is that some sort of system is needed that includes a set of criteria that allows reviewers to identify and record important information about each article. After examining several studies, identify the types of information you potentially need to know about the articles. First, ask yourself which types of information you may use in your review; this may vary due to the nature of your topic, the specific variables in question, the methodologies of previous studies, and so on. The following topics are some of the more commonly used criteria for analyzing articles and coding information; some students code on all of these issues, while others may choose a few of the categories:

- Full, APA-style citation
- Research questions
- Dependent and independent variables
- Major hypotheses
- Number of participants
- Race or gender of participants
- Methodological issues/concerns and limitations
- Primary findings
- Wonderful quotes to remember (remember to jot down the page number!)
- Ideas that came to mind that you want to remember from this article
- New references to examine
- Measures used in this article to assess the constructs in this study
- Suggestions the researchers had for improvement of future studies
- Type of research design: prospective, retrospective, between-groups design, and so on

Thinking scientifically is highly important as you critique these studies. You may find, for example, that the measures used to assess constructs in previous studies had very low reliability estimates, or you may find that the construct has been defined in very different ways across studies. You may find that a frequently quoted study used an old version of an instrument that has now been revised and is more commonly used. All of these issues will determine the utility of the article and how much you can rely on the findings when drawing conclusions for your review. Making careful notes about these issues will help immensely as you consolidate and synthesize your thoughts about your topic. Believe us; the more organized and complete your notes, the more time will be saved in the long run.

Similar to searching for relevant literature, coding articles is also not a linear process. For example, one of the authors of this chapter was conducting a comprehensive review of the literature on the impact of psychosocial interventions on cancer patients, specifically in breast cancer patients. He established a coding scheme to record information on a number of variables that seemed important. After about the 20th article, he realized he was not coding on type of cancer; many of the articles were referring to prostate, as opposed to breast cancer, or utilized patients with diverse types of cancer. Since this distinction has implications in terms of gender of the subjects, the prognosis and treatment of the disease, and so on, he needed to recode the studies by cancer type. This is not atypical of the coding process; one can initially carefully identify variables to code, but sometimes a reviewer does not code on even the most obvious distinctions and must recode on new variables. Again, try not to become frustrated or depressed by this seeming retracing of your steps. This is "good"; you are becoming more sophisticated in your knowledge of your topic and are now making finer distinctions about the topic or literature. That you are conceptualizing the literature with more differentiation is a positive sign.

The following is an example of one way of analyzing and organizing a body of literature. One of the authors of this text decided to comprehensively review the social influence literature in counseling. This is a body of literature based on the attitude change literature in social psychology that examined the counselor and client variables related to the change process in counseling (see Heppner & Claiborn, 1989, for more details). The author had been doing research in this area for about 10 years and, thus, had considerable prior knowledge of the literature. He spent several hours organizing a coding system so that he could record a wide range of information on each article; his goal then was to analyze and summarize information across the studies for one or more of the variables at a time. For example, the then pervasive influence models in counseling attributed influence to the counselor, the client, or specific message variables the counselor delivered. Therefore, the author analyzed each article in terms of counselor, client, or message variables.

For example, Table 4.1 depicts the type of working table that was established to record all the studies that included client variables. First, the author and year of publication were recorded in the left column for any study investigating the role of client variables in the influence process. Then, potential client variables that the author thought might be utilized in the previous research were placed horizontally across the top of the page (e.g., client sex, client sex role orientation, client expectations, and client self-concept). Thus, for example, whenever he found a study that examined the role of client sex in the influence process, the results were coded in that category for that particular study. See Table 4.1 for a partial listing of articles. In short, the author developed some systematic way of recording information about a large group of articles that helped him to identify those articles that examined the same client variables; he then was able to examine those specific articles when he analyzed and wrote that particular section of a manuscript (interested readers may examine pages 369–370 in Heppner & Claiborn, 1989, to see the paragraphs written from the more-extensive table referred to in this example).

TABLE 4.1	PARTIAL EXAMPLE OF A TABLE TO RECORD CLIENT VARIABLES IN THE INTERPERSONAL INFLUENCE PROCESS IN COUNSELING			
Author, Year	**Client Sex**	**Sex Role Orientation**	**Client Expectations**	**Client Self-Concept**
McKee & Smouse (1983)	No, sex differences found on perceived counselor expertness, attractiveness, or trustworthiness.			
Banikiotos & Merluzzi (1981)	Yes, sex differences were associated with perceived counselor expertness, attractiveness, and trustworthiness.			
Heppner & Heesacker (1983)			Yes, client precounseling expectations were associated with ratings of perceived counselor expertness, attractiveness, and trustworthiness	

Other tables were developed to record variables related to measurement of the major constructs, external validity, outcomes or major findings, or new ideas that occurred to the researcher. Of course, given the nonlinear nature of this process, the coding scheme was revised several times and some categories did not result in helpful information. The most important outcome of the coding, however, was a systematic analysis of numerous variables across a large body of literature within the social influence area. The outcome was that summarizing certain variables across a number of studies was very easy. For example, the author learned that 37 of the 56 reviewed studies did not meet any of Strong's (1968) "boundary conditions" for external validity and these consisted of what were called noninterview studies. Specifically, these studies would often use videotapes of a counselor and client and then ask viewers to rate the counselor or the influence process on various dimensions. Moreover, these noninterview studies contained an average of only 12 minutes of stimulus materials, which suggested that this specific area of research is based on minimal information and, in essence, initial impressions. For more information about the outcome of the review, see Heppner and Claiborn (1989).

This particular coding scheme was a tool to systematically record a great deal of information, which not only greatly aided retention but also facilitated analysis. Other coding schemes can be used with similar results. What we want to emphasize here is that you need to carefully critique and analyze the studies and summarize your findings in some way. In general, the more you can synthesize your analysis of particular variables across studies, the better. Far too often, students' reviews simply report the results from one study in the first paragraph, another study in the second paragraph, and so on until all the studies have been covered. This type of "reporting" falls short of analyzing, synthesizing, and critiquing the literature.

CONCLUSIONS

In this chapter we discussed the process of conducting a literature search. We suggested that the literature search for a thesis or dissertation needs to be more thorough and extensive than a brief summary of the literature. A thorough literature review cannot be accomplished in a day or a week. We suggested that the process of conducting a thorough literature review is a nonlinear and iterative process such that as the student acquires new information about the topic of study, increased knowledge will result in finer distinctions about the topic, which will often involve recycling and reconceptualizing the study. Typically students will experience an interactive process between searching and studying the literature and the focus of their study, their research hypotheses, and even the methodology of the study. Perhaps most important, we emphasized that the nonlinear and iterative process of the literature search is not only normal but also a positive sign that the student is progressing in understanding the existing literature and increasingly focusing the study. We emphasized that a thorough literature review necessitates not only the use of multiple resources but also the integration of searching the literature and reading, reflecting, and thinking about the literature. At the thesis and, especially, the dissertation level, the literature search is a highly specific search that calls on students to apply many of the skills learned throughout graduate work. The search and eventual literature review will be much stronger if students carefully and critically think about the literature search. Most important, remember to be aware of your own psychological process. If you find yourself getting frustrated or feeling helpless or overwhelmed, take the time to examine your experiences. What do you need to problem solve so that you can continue being productive with your search? You have the skills to do this step. If you are feeling blocked, you must stop and examine what you need to do to keep moving.

RESEARCH HYPOTHESES

The Motor That Drives the Study

In many ways research hypotheses are the driving mechanism of a thesis or dissertation. Thus, sometimes the very first thing a thesis or dissertation committee member reads is the research hypotheses, as these few simple sentences orient the reader to the study quicker than any other part of the thesis or dissertation proposal. The student uses the research hypotheses to succinctly summarize what the focus of the study will be—specifically, the key constructs under investigation and their predicted relationships. The hypotheses are always placed before the methods section and, thus, usually appear at the end of the literature review. Some advisors prefer having the hypotheses at the end of the first chapter in order to orient the reader to the literature that will be reviewed in Chapter 2.

Our purpose in this chapter is to provide specific information about research questions versus research hypotheses and about how students can use research questions to establish the rationale for their research hypotheses. We first define *research questions* and identify key criteria in specifying research questions. We discuss the various criteria by examining examples of research questions, including a series of research questions from a programmatic line of research (problem-solving appraisal). Subsequently we define *research hypotheses* and discuss various elements of good research hypotheses. The last section of this chapter focuses on writing research questions and hypotheses. We provide several examples to illustrate different possible writing styles as well as minor but important nuances involved in writing both research questions and hypotheses. Throughout this chapter we emphasize that writing research hypotheses is not a linear process but, rather, an iterative process as the student develops a particular topic and refines the hypotheses over time. In short, we want to clearly note that, typically, writing the research hypotheses for the thesis or dissertation is not a one-time event but a process that happens over time as students become more knowledgeable about their particular topic.

SPECIFYING RESEARCH QUESTIONS

Typically, as students identify research topics (see Chapter 2) and search the literature (see Chapter 4), they engage in a great deal of thinking about their topic. Subsequently, they think about questions (i.e., research questions) they have about the topic as well as relations they anticipate they might find (i.e., hypotheses). The process of identifying a topic, generating questions and hypotheses, and searching the literature is typically not a systematic, linear process; rather, students often think intermittently about a question or hypothesis within a particular topic, then consider another topic, and vacillate back and forth. As they read the literature in a particular area, they often generate other research topics. Sometimes, when students experience what seems like an unsystematic process of identifying the focus of the research, they become frustrated and demoralized and suspect that they are doing something wrong. Although sometimes what seems like an unsystematic process is the result of not carefully studying the existing literature and clarifying their interests (see Chapter 2), most often students are on the right track of narrowing their topic, which simply takes time and a great deal of thought.

After narrowing the topic, studying the literature, and considering various research questions, you can begin to develop specific research questions. Remember two basic issues in this process. First, take some time to reflect on what you are most interested in learning from your research. We raised this issue in Chapter 2 and suggested that selecting a topic about which you are excited, curious, and passionate can be an important if not essential motivating factor in conducting research. Thus, we encourage you to reflect on your interests and values and focus on research questions that match your values and interests. For many students, clarifying personal and professional interests is an ongoing and iterative process. Thus, as you consider variations of your research questions and hypotheses over time, keep reflecting on what is of most interest to examine at this time in your life. Second, keep in mind that the most useful research in applied professions (like the counseling profession) is research that is helpful to people in some way and, often, responds to some significant societal need. Thus, consider how your research can help the profession to answer relevant and pressing questions, solve problems, or extend theory development. You may find it helpful to ask yourself questions like *So what? What difference can this research make? Why is this research important?* Being passionate about research foci that directly meet a significant societal need is usually a gratifying and meaningful experience. Moreover, researchers in such scenarios typically are intrinsically motivated to investigate their research questions and, in the process, learn more about their research topic with each investigation.

TYPES OF RESEARCH QUESTIONS

Technically, a research question explores the relations among or between constructs (see Heppner, et al., 1999). For example, a research question could be: "Is there a relationship between one's problem-solving style and psychological distress?" Drew (1980) identified three useful, general categories of research questions: descriptive, relationship, and difference. As part of the iterative process of selecting research questions, we recommend that, as you think about the focus of your study, you not only identify the type of research question you are considering but also contemplate alternative questions within all three general areas.

Descriptive Questions

Descriptive questions ask what some phenomena or events are like. With descriptive questions, researchers collect information from interviews, surveys, or inventories; such research can be either qualitative or quantitative in nature. Rarely do descriptive questions involve experimental manipulations. An example of a descriptive question is: What are the coping processes Mexican immigrants use in response to the stressors of acculturation in a rural Midwest community? (For more on this topic, see Suarez-Renaud, 2002.)

Relationship Questions

Relationship questions examine the degree to which two or more constructs are related to each other. The essential feature is some kind of association or correlation between two constructs. In the Suarez-Renaud dissertation, she asked, "Is there a relationship between acculturative stress and psychological distress of Mexican immigrants in a rural Midwest community?"

Difference Questions

Difference questions most often ask if differences exist between groups of people or within individual participants. The essential feature in difference questions is some type of comparison; such questions could be either qualitative or quantitative in nature. Although this was not the focus of Suarez-Renaud's dissertation, an example of a difference question with her topic would be: Are there differences in acculturative stress with Mexican immigrants living in a rural Midwest community as opposed to a southwestern urban environment?

CRITERIA FOR DEVELOPING RESEARCH QUESTIONS

Research questions must (a) ask a question about (b) relationships among two or more constructs (c) that are measurable in some way (see Heppner et al., 1999; Kerlinger, 1986). That is, the constructs identified in the question should be stated clearly and unambiguously in question form. Often the research question inquires about the relationship among two or more constructs; for instance, in the Suarez-Renaud examples, she inquired about a relationship between acculturative stress and psychological distress. In descriptive studies, typically relationships among constructs are not specified because the focus of the study is on collecting or categorizing information. Finally, the constructs need to be measurable in some way. If the construct cannot be measured in a reliable and valid manner, the researcher's ability to adequately answer his or her research questions is greatly weakened (see Heppner et al., 1999, as well as Chapter 7 in this book).

Most important, research questions specify a direction or specific focus for scientific inquiry in the thesis or dissertation. That is, the research questions identify the central constructs of a study and frame the key relationships that are to be examined. Technically, constructs are hypothetical psychological entities (see Kerlinger, 1986) that are unobservable, such as learning styles, problem-solving appraisal, gender role conflict, racial identity, career indecision, counselor credibility, and self-efficacy. Whatever the constructs are that are examined in a study, they must be operationally defined in some measurable way, typically by using an inventory that purports to measure the construct in question. For example, researchers often operationalize gender role conflict with the Gender Role Conflict Scale (O'Neil, 1986). See Heppner et al. (1999) for more details on operationalizing constructs.

Note that all research questions are not created equal! A badly worded research question often will not only lead to ambiguity about the focus of the study but also lead to confusion in the next step, which is developing hypotheses. Consider the following research question: "What type of person is SIGI-Plus (a computerized career information system) most effective for, and how effective is the system in values exploration and clarification for this type of person?" First, the author has combined two questions into one question; generally speaking, this is not a good strategy because the research questions often become confusing because too many constructs are identified. Second, the constructs are ambiguously identified. The author apparently wants to understand how different people find SIGI-Plus (a computerized career information and guidance system) effective, but the words *type of person* and *effective* are too ambiguous. *Type of person* could mean many very different things to different people, such as high or low need for achievement, or, using Holland's (1978) typology, people depicting the six main Holland types, or students in high school versus those in colleges and universities. Likewise, the term *effective* is ambiguous as this could mean the level of client satisfaction or the amount the client learned from SIGI-Plus, or the level of career decidedness. The question is also unclear about whether the study will be a descriptive or difference study.

The aforementioned research question serves to illustrate several key issues about research questions. Readers (especially committee members) should be able to obtain a clear understanding of the constructs central to a study by reading the research questions (and subsequently the research hypotheses). For example, the reader should not be thinking, "I wonder what this student means by 'type of person.' " Readers should be able to identify not just one construct that is being examined in a study but all of the constructs in the study by reading the research questions. The reader should also be able to determine the type of study that will answer the research question (e.g., descriptive, difference, or relationship study). Moreover, the reader should be able to identify the scope of the study, such as if it is a training study that will occur over 6 weeks.

In short, the research question should ask questions about constructs that are of most interest to the student. Moreover, the research question must clearly identify specific and measurable constructs and, if appropriate, identify relationships among the constructs of most interest to the student.

EXAMPLES OF RESEARCH QUESTIONS WITHIN A PROGRAMMATIC LINE OF RESEARCH

Within a given topic, a researcher may generate a wide range of questions. Brainstorming a list of potential research questions often helps students to explore a range of different studies they could conduct within a particular topic. We encourage you to engage in such brainstorming as you examine the research literature within your topic. You can do this alone, with your peers, with your advisor, and with other faculty. Sometimes in the initial stages of examining a research topic, students have difficulty generating even one research question. In this section, we not only provide a list of research questions within one particular construct (problem-solving appraisal) in one research topic (applied problem solving) but also show how adding different constructs or variables in the questions results in very different questions.

In graduate school, one of the authors (Puncky) began to focus on the topic of applied problem solving as one that was consistent with his career aspirations of helping others resolve their personal problems within counseling. His master's advisor, Royce R. Ronning, was instrumental in framing the importance of problem solving for therapists. In essence, he maintained that clients seek help from counselors because they have problems they have been unable to resolve on their own; Puncky very clearly remembers Royce saying, "Counselors ought to know more about problem solving" (Royce R. Ronning, personal communication, 1974). Later, Puncky's doctoral advisor, David N. Dixon, was instrumental in providing more specific guidance to integrate applied problem solving into the counseling process and, particularly, the counseling relationship (see Dixon & Glover, 1984), as well as guiding empirical research in applied problem solving (e.g., Dixon, Heppner, Petersen, & Ronning, 1979).

Since the graduate school days of the mid-1970s, Puncky has developed a programmatic line of research within the topic of applied problem solving. What follows is a list of some of the research questions that Puncky and his colleagues have investigated in various studies. Each study investigates research questions related to applied problem solving and, most specifically, problem-solving appraisal (or sometimes referred to as *perceived effective and ineffective problem solving*). We grouped the research questions by the subsequent research design that was employed to answer the question. To learn more about the details of how the rationale for the research questions was developed in the introduction to the study or how the research questions guided the methods, statistical analyses, and discussion, we refer readers to the actual articles.

Finally, from these examples, we highlight several features of research questions. Again, note that most of the research questions posit some sort of relationship between two or more variables (i.e., Is there a relationship between X and Y?) Other questions posit some sort of differences between groups of people (between-groups design) or even within individual participants (within-groups design). The key feature of between- and within-groups designs is a comparison of some kind. Other questions focus on describing some phenomena or events. In these studies, experimental manipulations are not used; rather, information is collected from inventories, interviews, or surveys. Note that each of these types of designs can answer important questions, but each answers very different questions. Moreover, note how many different questions have been developed in one particular research topic by one researcher and his colleagues; and we could add hundreds more of research questions if we included those by other authors who have researched this particular construct. Finally, note that different types of research questions dictate different types of research designs and even different types of statistical analysis.

Descriptive Designs

- Are problem-solving dimensions underlying the applied problem-solving process consistent with distinct problem-solving stages? (Classification research using factor analysis; see Heppner & Petersen, 1982).
- Does a relationship exist between problem-solving appraisal and depression? Does a relationship exist between problem-solving appraisal

and attritional style? (Correlational research; see Heppner, Baumgardner, & Jackson, 1985).

- Can problem-solving appraisal contribute to identifying different subgroups of undecided college students? (Classification research using cluster analysis; see Larson, Heppner, Ham, & Dugan, 1988).
- Do racial identity statuses of African American college students predict components of problem-solving appraisal and problem-resolution coping on a predominately white campus? (Multiple regression research; see Neville, Heppner, & Wang, 1997).
- How do women breast cancer survivors with lymphedema cope with the obstacles and stressors associated with lymphedema? (Qualitative design using intensive interviews; Heppner, Glauser, et al., 2002).
- Does appraised ineffective problem solving precede or play a causal role in future depressive symptoms? Does the experience of depressive symptoms cause temporary deficits in self-appraisal of problem solving? Does the experience of depressive symptoms predict future deficits in appraised problem-solving effectiveness? (Prospective longitudinal design using structural equation modeling; see Dixon, Heppner, Burnett, Anderson, & Wood, 1993).
- Does hopelessness mediate the relationship between problem-solving appraisal and suicide ideation? (Structure equation modeling; see Dixon, Heppner, & Rudd, 1994).

True Experimental Designs

- Would problem-solving training that emphasized self-management principles be effective? For whom would training be most effective, those who appraise their problem solving effectively or ineffectively? (Between-groups design; see Heppner, Baumgardner, Larson, & Petty, 1988).
- Would differences in perceived effective and ineffective problem solvers be found across intrapersonal and interpersonal problems? (Between- and within-groups design; see Heppner, Hibel, Neal, Weinstein, & Rabinowitz, 1982).

Quasi-Experimental Designs and Time Series

- Would relationships between problem-solving appraisal and psychological distress found in white samples be found in black samples? (Cohort design; see Reeder & Heppner, 1985).
- Do college students with perceived effective and ineffective problem solving engage in different coping activities across time? (Time series; Heppner, Baumgardner, Larson, & Petty, 1988).

- Would mothers and daughters from an incest group (as compared to mothers and daughters from a nonclinical group) differ on amounts of family stress, problem-solving appraisal, coping behaviors, and communication patterns? (Cohort design; see Reis & Heppner, 1993).
- Do clients in counseling with different levels of problem-solving appraisal reach different levels of resolution of their presenting problems over time? (Time series; see Heppner, Cooper, Mulholland, & Wei, 2001).

Conclusion

In sum, we encourage you to reflect on your professional interests and values as well as focus on socially relevant and pressing questions as you develop your research questions. In addition to asking yourself questions about relationships among two or more measurable constructs, we encourage you to consider a wide range of research questions (descriptive, relationship, and difference) across different types of designs and populations. Brainstorming research questions is often particularly helpful in the early phases of developing a research focus, interspersed with studying the relevant research literature, and talking to your advisor and colleagues. As the research questions become more specific and measurable and are honed to match your passion in a way that seems to indicate that a relevant and meaningful contribution can be made from your research, you can then think more seriously about research hypotheses.

SPECIFYING RESEARCH HYPOTHESES

A research hypothesis is more specific than a research question. A research question asks a question about a particular set of events. A research hypothesis goes one more step and predicts an expected relationship between constructs or predicts the results of a set of events. Research hypotheses can be generally grouped into the same three categories as research questions: descriptive, relationship, and difference hypotheses. Similarly, hypotheses should state predicted relationships among constructs, if appropriate, and contain clearly specified and measurable constructs.

Students often ask questions such as *How many hypotheses do I need? Are four hypotheses enough for a dissertation?* If the number of hypotheses is excessively large (e.g., 20 hypotheses), the focus of the study may be too large. Conversely, a single hypothesis is generally too small for most studies, as it does not yield sufficient information. The hypotheses should establish a focused inquiry on a particular topic and usually consist of three to five interrelated hypotheses. Sometimes committee members read a student's hypotheses first because the hypotheses indicate a great deal of information about the study.

Well-written hypotheses provide the knowledgeable reader with a great deal of information. For example, the constructs or variables mentioned in the hypotheses provide a knowledgeable reader with clues not only about what literature should probably be reviewed but also how the literature review will end (e.g., the end of the "funnel"; see Chapter 3 and Chapter 6). Well-written hypotheses identify independent and dependent variables or predictor and criterion variables and whether the focus of a study is descriptive, difference, or relationship oriented. Likewise, well-written hypotheses forecast elements of the methods and results chapters, such as the type of statistical analyses that may be used in the study.

Sometimes writing research hypotheses scares students because they seem to be "sticking their neck out," or "going out on a limb" with their hypothesized predictions. Sometimes students erroneously believe that if they predict a relationship, for example, and it is not supported in their study, then this is really awful and proof that they are not "good" scientists. Keep in mind that the goal of establishing hypotheses is to test your hunches about a particular set of events and that those hunches are based on previous research, theory, and personal and professional experiences. If the hypotheses are not supported, the results provide very important information that something else may be occurring in the predicted relationships, which then helps the research community to examine these phenomena with a new perspective. In short, it is *not* awful and *not* the end of the world if you do not accurately predict expected relationships in the hypothesis. The goal of science is not to prove hypotheses but, rather, to extend the knowledge bases about psychological phenomena. Sometimes the most important knowledge is obtained by not finding expected relationships as initially specified by the hypotheses (see, for example, a thesis and subsequent dissertation by Wright & Heppner, 1991, 1993).

WRITING RESEARCH QUESTIONS AND HYPOTHESES

We begin with a convoluted hypothesis to illustrate several issues about writing research hypotheses. Consider the following "bad" hypothesis:

> There are no significant differences in the mean role expectations white members of predominantly white Greek organizations have for themselves and the mean role expectations they have for members of predominantly black Greek organizations.

This hypothesis is stated as a null hypothesis and, thus, does not predict differences between the two groups. Null hypotheses are statistical hypotheses stating that any difference is attributable to random error. Although the null hypothesis form was previously more commonly reported in theses and dissertations, it is seldom used today as a standard way of stating hypotheses, unless of course the experimenter is predicting no differences between groups. Thus, researchers typically state research hypotheses in which they predict the expected outcome (e.g., one group will score higher than another group, or one variable will correlate positively with another variable).

Hypotheses should be as specific as possible, yet expressed clearly and parsimoniously in a single sentence. The preceding hypothesis uses the terms *significantly* and *mean;* these are statistical terms and are typically assumed. For example, if an experimenter predicts that an avoidant attachment style will be correlated with a measure of psychological distress, it is assumed that the correlation will be statistically significant. Thus, including words such as *significant* or *mean* is generally considered unnecessary. Moreover, the stated hypothesis is excessively wordy. It could be stated more succinctly as, White Greeks will not have different role expectations for members of predominantly white or black Greek organizations.

Students most often write their research questions toward the end of their literature review and typically as part of building a rationale for the particular research hypotheses of their study. In essence, the research questions should flow from the preceding literature review and identify questions that have not been examined previously or that remain unanswered. The typical reader should be able to understand how the author's review of the literature has led to the research questions (and, subsequently, the research hypotheses as well).

The following example is taken from a published article and depicts how the authors used research questions to indicate what was unknown or unanswered in the literature at that time. Note how the authors then developed the purpose of their study to address those research questions, which directly led to their research hypotheses. This study is one of many within what is often referred to as the *social influence literature,* which examined variables related to counselors' ability to influence clients to change a host of attitudes and behaviors (for reviews, see Corrigan, Dell, Lewis, & Schmidt, 1980; Heppner & Dixon, 1981; Heppner & Claiborn, 1989).

Perceived counselor expertness has been reported to be influenced by (a) objective evidence of specialized training, such as diplomas, certificates, and titles, (b) behavioral evidence of expertness, such as rational and knowledgeable arguments and confidence in presentation, and (c) reputation as an expert (Strong, 1968). The presence of a title communicated within an introduction has been found to influence reported source credibility (Hartley, 1969), as well as to influence greater opinion changes within clients (Binderman, Fretz, Scott, & Abrams, 1972). Similarly, it has been reported that information establishing the source's prestige within an introduction has resulted in greater opinion changes for subjects (Browning, 1966; Strong & Schmidt, 1970). In addition, strong evidence exists to support the notion that titles or prestige, when combined with expert-like behavior, does cue greater reported counselor credibility and subsequent opinion change (Atkinson & Carskadden, 1975; Strong & Schmidt, 1970).

There has been an absence of studies, however, investigating the effects of expert counselor behavior alone, prestige alone, or documented objective evidence of competence alone (i.e., diplomas, certificates, awards). The specific question that needs to be answered is this: Do visual, objective indicators influence the client's perceptions of the counselor's expertness?

Similarly, there have been no investigations examining the effects of the sex of the counselor on perceived expertness. Accumulating evidence from social psychology suggests that men and women tend to devalue the performance of professional women (Goldberg, 1968; Lewin & Duchan, 1971). [Note: Although a research question was not explicitly stated here, the preceding sentences implicitly raise questions about sex of the counselor and perceived expertness.]

> The present study examined the effects of environmental cues of competence and the sex of the counselor in terms of perceived expertness. The research hypotheses were as follows:
>
> 1. Clients interviewed in the presence of documented evidence of counselor expertness would perceive those counselors as more expert than those clients interviewed without such cues.
> 2. In both interviewing conditions, the male counselor would be perceived as more expert than the female counselor.
> 3. There would be an interaction effect between the sex of the counselor and the treatment conditions. (Heppner & Pew, 1977, pp. 147–148)

In sum, research questions can be used to highlight questions that are unanswered and, thus, can be used to develop a rationale for conducting a specific study. Authors can then use the unanswered questions to identify the purpose of their study, which directly leads to the specific research hypotheses of the study. Also note in the example that the authors numbered their hypotheses as a way of succinctly summarizing the focus of the study. In this case, the three hypotheses were quite distinct. In other cases where there are a number of related hypotheses, the hypotheses can be subsumed under a general topic and numbered as 1a, 1b, 1c, and so on.

SUMMARIZING THE LITERATURE TO ESTABLISH RESEARCH QUESTIONS AND HYPOTHESES

The next example of writing research questions is drawn from a dissertation on the topic of validating an eating disorders assessment of African American women. The excerpts that we present appeared at the end of the student's literature review. Again, note how the author's analysis of the literature leads to the development of questions or gaps in the literature. We include the preceding two pages before the research questions that nicely summarize the existing literature (see Chapter 6 where we discuss this writing strategy) and what was unknown at that time relative to this particular topic. In essence, Mulholland (1999) aptly builds a rationale by summarizing the literature that leads to the development of her research questions. Again, note how the identification of the research questions formed an essential part of the logic in leading to the author's research hypotheses. In addition, note how Mulholland subsequently enumerated four general research questions that addressed some of the research needs she had identified in the previous section.

SUMMARY OF PROBLEMS REGARDING EATING DISORDER RESEARCH WITH AFRICAN AMERICANS

As stated throughout this chapter, a fundamental problem in the eating disorder field is that too much eating disorder research focuses on middle- to upper-class Caucasian women and too little research examines African American women's unique experiences (Wangsgaard Thompson, 1992). As a result, stereotypes in mental health lead to racism in assessment and treatment. Many medical and mental health professionals do not assess for eating disorders in their African American clientele while they more readily recognize eating disorder symptomology in Caucasian women. Treatment may be delayed, and thus only the most serious cases are seen. Therefore, most case studies on African Americans reflect an inherent treatment bias (Crago et al., 1996).

While three studies with prevalence rates for *DSM-IV* eating disorders and symptoms have been conducted with Caucasian college samples (Brock, 1999; Mintz et al., 1997; Mulholland, 1996), prevalence rates of *DSM-IV* eating disorders and symptoms for African Americans are unstudied. Two studies indicate that African American women at predominantly Caucasian colleges and universities may exhibit greater eating disorder symptomology than African American women at predominantly Black colleges and universities (Gray et al., 1987; Williams, 1994). These studies, supported by Newcomb's (1943) work on reference groups, provide support for conducting a prevalence study at a predominantly Caucasian university. Indeed, prevalence rates for *DSM-IV* eating disorders (anorexia, bulimia, and EDNOS) and symptoms (no bona fide disorder but eating disorder symptoms) would be a contribution to the field. It is possible that EDNOS, which are subclinical syndromes, may more accurately describe African American women's disordered eating than anorexia or bulimia.

In addition, this chapter concluded that only one eating disorder assessment, the Q-EDD, is based on *DSM-IV* criteria and captures the range of *DSM-IV* eating disorders. The Q-EDD differentiates eating disordered from non-eating disordered from symptomatic for asymptomatic participants. All current disorder assessment inventories have been developed on Caucasian women, and only one, the EDI-2, has adequate psychometric properties with a middle-aged African American sample. No instrument's psychometric properties have been examined with exclusively African American college women. Given the particular strengths of the Q-EDD over other inventories, it is the clear choice for psychometric examination with African American college women. Clearly there is a fundamental need in the field for the psychometric properties of inventories to be examined with African American women.

Research Questions and Analyses

The current study addressed the following four general research questions: (a) What are the prevalence rates for the classification of *DSM-IV* eating disordered (anorexia, bulimia, and EDNOS) and symptomatic (no bona fide diagnosis, but eating disordered symptoms) among African American college women?; (b) What are the psychometric properties of the Q-EDD with an African American college sample?; (c) Are there significant differences in the racial composition of reference groups between two classification groups (eating disordered versus non-eating disordered) and three classification groups (eating disordered versus symptomatic versus asymptomatic)?; and (d) Are there significant differences in the body image messages received from parents, other relatives, partner/boyfriend, or peers between two classification groups (eating disordered versus non-eating disordered) and three classification groups (eating disordered versus symptomatic versus asymptomatic)?

For all research questions, respondents needed to meet full criteria for any of the *DSM-IV* eating disorders (e.g., anorexia, bulimia, or the EDNOS diagnoses of subthreshold bulimia, menstruating anorexia, non-bingeing bulimia, or binge eating disorder) to be classified as eating disordered. The classification of symptomatic was used for those respondents who did not meet full criteria for *DSM-IV* eating disorders but nevertheless engaged in behaviors representative of disordered eating. The classification of asymptomatic was used for those respondents who did not endorse any eating disordered behaviors. Data were collected in two Phases to address the four research questions, and the following specific tests were designed to provide evidence relevant to these questions. (Mulholland, 2000, pp. 38–41)

Note how Mulholland also included a paragraph immediately after her research questions to explain how she operationalized some of her variables. This is a common strategy to clarify constructs or variables.

In the subsequent paragraphs, Mulholland then articulated her research hypotheses. Although her hypotheses and discussion consumed 4 1/2 pages in this ambitious study, we only present the first set of hypotheses to illustrate how she integrated her hypotheses within her research questions.

Phase 1

1. The first broad research question concerned the prevalence rates of eating disordered (e.g., anorexia, bulimia and EDNOS) and symptomatic (e.g., no bona fide diagnosis but eating disorder symptoms) classifications among a sample of African American college women. Prevalence rates were calculated as the percentages of the entire sample.

1a. It was hypothesized that the African American sample would have slightly lower prevalence rates for bulimia as compared to the few existing comparable studies with Caucasian samples, which are themselves low (0–3%; Brock, 1999; Mintz et al., 1997; Mulholland, 1996). Previous studies reported that prevalence rates for anorexia are 0%. It was hypothesized that this study would find the same rarity for anorexia and slightly lower prevalence for bulimia in comparison to the non-existent prevalence rates for anorexia and already low rates for bulimia in comparable studies.

1b. Due to the lack of research, no hypotheses were made for the prevalence rates of EDNOS diagnoses among this African American sample as compared to the few existing comparable studies with Caucasian samples (3.6%–5%; Brock, 1999; Mintz et al., 1997; Mulholland, 1996).

1c. Based on both theoretical literature (e.g., Striegel-Moore & Smolak, 1996) and the prevalence of EDNOS versus anorexia and bulimia in comparative Caucasian samples (Brock, 1999; Mintz et al., 1997; Mulholland, 1996), it was hypothesized that among the African American women in this sample, the EDNOS group would be larger than the groups comprised of anorexics or bulimics.

1d. Based on the lack of literature on African Americans regarding the classification as symptomatic (e.g., no bona fide diagnosis but eating disorder symptoms), no hypothesis about this classification was made. (Mulholland, 2000, pp. 41–42)

Note in the hypotheses how Mulholland not only stated her hypothesis in 1a but also included the studies in which the data led her to her hypotheses. Sometimes committee members will want to know why students predicted certain hypotheses, especially if there were any data that led to their hypotheses.

Also note in Hypothesis 1b and 1d that Mulholland did not specify a hypothesis because of the lack of previous research on which to base her hypothesis. On some occasions this is an acceptable strategy, particularly when an author is exploring a relatively new topic. However, avoiding specifying predicted relationships can be problematic in cases such as when an investigator proposes to collect data on a large set of variables and discuss just those that have significant relationships. The disadvantage of reporting only the significant findings is that it tends to capitalize on chance events, which can also create misrepresentations that the relationships among the variables are stronger than they are in reality. Thus, in general, this reporting strategy is problematic and is best to avoid. On other occasions, students will state their best-educated prediction based on even minimal existing data or theoretical writings.

CONCLUSIONS

This chapter focused on the critical central process of developing and writing research questions and hypotheses. In many ways, the research questions and hypotheses are the motor that drives a study. Research questions and hypotheses are pivotal elements in a thesis or dissertation. Research questions highlight information that is lacking and that has been identified in the literature review; such questions in essence establish a rationale for the hypotheses. Likewise, elements of the methods and results chapters, which detail how the study will be conducted, are dependent on the research hypotheses and how the hypotheses are worded. Given the pivotal role of the research questions and hypotheses, they must be very carefully developed in a thesis or dissertation.

Note also that developing the research questions and hypotheses is typically not a simple linear process. Most often students identify potential hypotheses early in the process of selecting a topic; and, as they continue to study the literature (and write their literature review), they modify their hypotheses. That is, as students acquire more knowledge about their topic, they are able to "fine-tune" their hypotheses to reflect their increased level of knowledge. Although sometimes students resist changing their hypotheses, we encourage students to consider a broad range of hypotheses within their topics. This process of "fine-tuning" does not mean the student did not get it right the first time but, rather, usually more accurately denotes that the student's knowledge of a topic is increasing and becoming more differentiated.

WRITING YOUR LITERATURE REVIEW

Integration and Case Building

Writing an engaging, thorough, and compelling literature review for your thesis or dissertation is both a challenging and a creative task. A variety of skills and knowledge are required to do a thorough review. First, you need knowledge about the structure and function of an integrative review. Next, critical thinking skills are required to not only simply review literature but also understand and discuss the literature. Finally, integrative writing skills are required to establish a cogent rationale to build a case for the importance of your unique study that builds on the previous literature in a logical way. This is not a book report with one study reviewed after the other; rather, it is a synthesis, integration, and critique of that literature.

The definition of a review article provided in the *Publication Manual of the American Psychological Association* describes the literature review:

> Review articles . . . are critical evaluations of material that has already been published. By organizing, integrating, and evaluating previously published material, the author of a review article considers the progress of current research toward clarifying a problem. In a sense, a review article is tutorial in that the author (a) defines and clarifies the problem; (b) summarizes previous investigations in order to inform the reader of the state of current research; (c) identifies relations, contradictions, gaps, and inconsistencies in the literature; and (d) suggests the next step or steps in solving the problem. (American Psychological Association, 2001, p. 7)

This definition was written as a guideline for articles that are published in various APA journals. The definition is also appropriate for theses and dissertations, especially because the purpose of the review of the literature chapter is very similar. In addition, some students develop their literature review chapter into a manuscript that is submitted to a journal for publication review. We strongly recommend you consider doing this. You are going to go to a great deal of work reviewing your topic; why not develop this section into a manuscript that may be published and useful to other readers in this area? Each discipline has journals that publish review articles; examples are the *Psychological Bulletin, The Counseling Psychologist* (which publishes integrative reviews, often as a Major Contribution), the *Journal of Counseling Psychology,* the *Journal of Counseling and Development,* and the *Journal of Vocational Behavior.*

At this point you have "mapped out the territory" for your review through your literature search and you are set to begin writing. Writing a paper that reviews a body of literature can be done in different ways. Not only the writing style but also the type of analyses performed on the literature varies among authors. With regard to different types of analyses, authors may focus on treatment outcomes, research design, target populations, or theory construction. The purpose of this chapter is to discuss these areas and to give you examples from existing publications—primarily from previous theses and dissertations—that you can use as models for your own work. In some cases, we present examples from published articles because you may want to examine additional parts of the review as well and these are more readily accessible than theses and dissertations. Specifically, we discuss writing your review and illustrate several (a) structural writing strategies; (b) describing, analyzing, and synthesizing strategies; and (c) stylistic strategies. We begin by providing a structural analysis of several elements of a literature review. These structural elements serve as the building blocks to establish a clear and organized structure for the literature review. The second section of the chapter identifies a number of strategies to describe, analyze, and synthesize groups of specific research studies; these strategies are, in essence, all aimed at integrative writing. The third section focuses on two aspects of the writing process. The first aspect includes several micro, or stylistic, writing elements that are important to incorporate into writing a literature review, such as substantiating assertions and conclusions. The second aspect of the writing process is revising and polishing the first, second, and even third drafts of your paper. Exercise 6.1 at the end of the chapter allows you to practice your integrative writing skills by distilling several pages of what we call "report writing" into one paragraph of integrative writing. You can then compare your paragraph with two other sample paragraphs. Finally, after you have written your first draft of the literature review, we suggest you evaluate yourself using the Checklist for Chapter 2 of the Thesis or Dissertation. In short, this chapter is designed to provide you with a broad range of writing techniques to write a clear and effective literature review. The writing techniques discussed here are by no means exhaustive but are an introductory discussion regarding the mechanics of writing a review of the literature chapter.

STRUCTURAL ELEMENTS IN WRITING A LITERATURE REVIEW

A literature-review chapter requires a number of structural elements, which help guide the reader from one sentence and paragraph to the next in a logical and seamless fashion. Each of these elements serves the function of helping the reader understand what is being covered in this long and rather complex review. The chapter starts with an introductory paragraph that focuses the reader on the topic that will be covered by the review. A road map should be included as an "advanced organizer" of what will be included in the chapter as a whole. The chapter should be divided into sections and subsections, each (depending on its level of complexity) having its own mini–road maps to further guide the reader. Each paragraph should begin with a clear and explicit topic sentence that informs the readers what will comprise that particular paragraph. Each major section should close with a transition that leads the reader into the next topic that will be covered in the review. Finally a summary and concluding section should bring the review together at the end. Thus, instead of the review sounding like a patchwork of bits and pieces with little to connect them to each other, these structural elements help to make it clear how the literature reviewed in the chapter fits together and why you are including the literature you are in the order in which it is presented. The review itself should have the shape of a funnel moving from the broadest issues of why this topic is important to the very narrow issue of your particular research hypotheses. Each of these structural elements is discussed in more depth in the following sections.

The Funnel

In Chapter 3 of this book, we described the funnel in detail and provided a graphic example of how an actual study could be outlined in funnel form. The structure of the funnel is very useful for both the overview chapter and the literature-review chapter, so we mention it again here but refer you back to Chapter 3 for a more thorough description. A literature review for a thesis or dissertation should also be constructed in the shape of a funnel—starting very broadly by introducing the topic; then moving into the focus of the review; continually narrowing the focus to a few selected variables (those that you will include in your study); and, toward the end, developing a rationale for your hypotheses; followed by the hypotheses themsleves. For example, you may start with global statements that help to put your question in the broader sociohistorical context (e.g., the Bureau of Justice Statistics documents that one in four women will experience sexual assault in her lifetime) but then progressively become more and more focused to the particular aspects of the construct you will be studying in your investigation. Within the body of the review, students typically create sections and subsections to review various aspects of the relevant literature. Each section may have mini-funnels in which you start out broadly and then move to a more targeted discussion of the construct as it applies to your study. Keep this funnel shape in mind as you are constructing each section of your literature review, as well as the overall chapter. The end of the review chapter, or the narrowest part of the funnel, typically ends with a summary of the literature review most relevant to building the rationale for examining the specific hypotheses of interest to you. Ideally, by the time readers finish your literature review, they will be saying: "This is exactly the kind of study that will move this area of knowledge a step ahead. . . . Of course, doing this study now makes all the sense in the world."

Introduction and Focus of the Topic

Bem (1995) aptly noted, "A review tells a straightforward tale of a circumscribed question in want of an answer. It is not a novel with subplots and flashbacks but a story with a single, linear line. Let this line stand out and in bold relief" (p. 173). Thus, the chapter should immediately introduce the topic and clearly indicate the purpose of the paper, the scope and/or limitations of the review, and essential definitions if appropriate.

For example, consider a section from Gershuny's (2000) dissertation on trauma, dissociation, and stress. In this section, Gershuny provides the introduction to the focus of her review:

> Recent reviews of relations among trauma, dissociation, and trauma-related distress have focused on important but relatively narrow domains such as the relation between emotional numbing and combat-related post-traumatic stress disorder (Litz, 1992), relations between dissociative phenomena and dissociative disorders (Kihlstrom, Glisky, & Anguiulo, 1994), and relation between trauma and dissociative disorders (Lowenstein, 1991). To help synthesize recent findings, aid in an increased understanding of trauma-dissociation-distress relations, and offer suggestions for future research, the current paper provides a relatively broader review of relations among trauma, dissociative phenomena, and trauma-related distress. In addition, possible explanations of the function of dissociation in relation to trauma are put forth, and suggestions are made that fears about death and losing/lacking control may help account for relations among trauma, dissociation, and post-traumatic distress.
>
> Forms of trauma-related distress included for review consideration in this paper are acute stress disorder (ASD), post-traumatic stress disorder (PTSD), borderline personality disorder (BPD), and bulimia. The inclusion of ASD and PTSD may be obvious; the occurrence of trauma is a necessary precursor for their diagnosis. The inclusion of BPD and bulimia, however, may be less obvious. These were included because both BPD and bulimia have relatively high prevalence of trauma. Leading researchers have posited that traumatic stressors, particularly childhood trauma, may figure significantly in the etiology of borderline personality disorder and bulimia (Chu, 1996; Davidson & Foa, 1993; Bremner, Steinberg, Sothwick, Johnson, & Charney, 1993; Herman & van der Kolk, 1987; Terr, 1995). For example, about 60–93% of adults with BPD and about 65–80% of adults with bulimia, may have experienced some sort of childhood trauma (e.g., Brodsky, Cloitre, & Dulit, 1995; Herman, Perry, & van der Kolk, 1989; Herman & van der Kolk, 1987; Laporte & Guttman, 1996; Ogata, Silk, Goodrich, Lohr, Westen, & Hill, 1990; Root & Fallon, 1988; Sabo, 1991). These prevalence rates of trauma are higher than in related populations such as other AXIS II disorders (Laporte & Guttman, 1996), other eating disorders (Everill & Waller, 1995), anxiety disorders (Mancini, Van Ameringen, &

MacMillan, 1995), mood disorders (Hall, Sachs, Rayens, & Lutenbacher, 1993), alcohol use disorders (Windle, Windle, Scheidt, & Miller, 1995), and in the general community (McCauley, Kern, Kolodner, Dill, et al., 1997). Herman, van der Kolk, and their colleagues (Herman, Perry, & van der Kolk, 1989; van der Kolk, 1996; van der Kolk, Perry, & Herman, 1991) also found a significant relation between childhood sexual abuse and various forms of self-harm in adulthood that are typically found in BPD and bulimia (i.e., self-cutting and bingeing). Such a finding lends further support to the notion that BPD and bulimia are trauma related. Thus, in an attempt to gain greater understanding of the trauma-dissociation-distress relations, acute stress disorder, post-traumatic stress disorder, borderline personality disorder, and bulimia, as well as the traumatic occurrence of childhood abuse, all are included in the literature presented in this paper.

Dissociative disorders, though arguably also trauma-related, are not included in the current review. Because of the relatively low prevalence of dissociative disorders, as compared to the relatively high prevalence of PTSD, BPD, and bulimia, their inclusion was deemed less broadly applicable and thus beyond the scope of the current review. In addition, a thoughtful review of relations between dissociative phenomena and dissociative disorders has already been provided elsewhere (Kihlstrom, Glisky, & Angiulo, 1994). Note also that, in this paper, dissociative phenomena refer to dissociative processes that are not within the diagnostic domains of the dissociative disorders. Rather, dissociative phenomena are conceptualized as reactions to a traumatic event that may, in turn, relate to the occurrence of various forms of trauma-related distress. (For a review of relations between trauma and dissociative disorders, see Loewenstein, 1991). This paper also focuses exclusively on adult populations. Though children and adolescents certainly warrant future work (and have received focus in some empirical studies: e.g., Allwood, Bell-Dolan, & Husain, 1998), their inclusion here is considered beyond the current scope. (Gershuny, 2000, pp. 5–8)

From this opening introduction we get a great deal of information about the focus of Gershuny's review and what will be included and why, as well as what topics will not be included and why. In essence, Gershuny is building a strong rationale for the focus of her research and its place within the existing literature in the field.

Road Maps

A very clear structure of what is to come in the review is required to orient the reader. Although this may seem obvious to you (because you have spent hours and weeks writing this section), for most readers this will be their first exposure to your review. In essence, explain to readers what you are going to discuss in the paper. Road maps, or overview statements, do just that; a road map presents a schema for the reader, a way of communicating what information will follow, and even how the rest of the paper is structured or divided into sections. A road map should be part of the introduction of your literature review. The following example serves to illustrate the forecasting function of a road map:

> There are two primary categories of literature on children of alcoholics. The first research focuses on variables related to being raised in an alcoholic home. These variables range from family violence and behavioral problems to interpersonal skills and coping. The second category consists of descriptive accounts of the dynamics of alcoholic family systems. This literature explores ways in which children in alcoholic homes cope and adapt. This paper will first present a review of the research which has focused on variables related to being raised in an alcoholic home. This will be followed by a survey of descriptive accounts of alcoholic family systems. Finally, therapeutic issues of adult children of alcoholics will be presented. (Wright, 1989, p. 7)

Thus, the road map gives the reader the schema of two major categories of research, what makes up these two categories, in what order these categories will be presented, and what in addition to these two categories will also be covered in the review chapter. In essence, the reader is given an advanced organizer about what to expect when reading the literature review.

Sections and Subsections: Mini–Road Maps

Typically, the review paper is lengthy and contains a great deal of information. The organization of the paper and how different aspects of the literature are related to each other are generally clear to the author but often not as clear to readers. One strategy to facilitate comprehension is to divide the paper into several major sections that follow some natural divisions in the literature. Further divisions or subsections are also advisable within sections. Sections and subsections not only delineate different topics but also ease the transition among different topics. The words you choose to label the sections (the headings or subheadings) can be important to convey the essence of the section. Think about what will be the most effective subheadings to lead the reader along. Sometimes subheadings are simply an introduction of a new concept; other times they can pose a question that the section will subsequently answer. For example: "Why study sex differences?" quickly communicates the essence of the topic of the next section. While subheadings can be important, do not overdo them. Carefully chosen headings move the reader through the text; too many headings can be distracting and disjointive. Worthington and Juntunen (1997), for example, created four major sections in their incisive review of the school-to-work transition literature, which appeared as a Major Contribution in *The Counseling Psychologist*: (a) Youth Labor Market Issues in the School-to-Work Transition, which identified the social needs that merit attention; (b) Potential Strengths, Limitations, and Risks of the School-to-Work Transition Movement, which discussed in great detail the various aspects of the movement; (c) Theoretical Issues, which not only reviewed theoretical issues but advanced new theoretical ideas; and (d) Conclusions and Recommendations, which ended with 12 excellent recommendations for future work in this area.

Occasionally, authors provide an actual outline of the paper, which not only communicates the sections but also the subsections that are to follow. An example of an outline for a review paper published in the *Journal of Counseling Psychology* by Heppner and Claiborn (1989) follows:

Outline: A Review of Recent Social Influence Research
    Stage 1: Establishing a Base for Influence
        Counselor Variables in Analogue Studies
          Expertness
          Attractiveness
          Trustworthiness
        Counselor Variables in Field Studies
        Client Variables
        Client-Counselor Similarity
        Conclusions
    Stage 2: The Influence Process
        Counselor Variables in Analogue Studies
        Counselor Variables in Field Studies
        Client Variables
        Message Variables
        Interactions Among Counselor, Client, and Message Variables
        Conclusions
    Methodological Considerations
        Research Design and External Validity
          Noninterview Analogues
          Interview Analogues and Field Studies
        Procedures in Influence Research
          Realistic and Relevant Variables
          The Focus of Analysis
          Measurement Issues
            The Counselor Rating Form
            Measuring Attitude Change
    Theoretical Considerations
        Extrapolation
        Relevance of Research to a Theory of Influence
        Adequacy of Theory
          Choice of Theory
          Extension of Theory
    Summary and Recommendations (p. 365)

Explicit Topic Sentences

The first line of each paragraph should be a clear, concise topic sentence that introduces the reader to the topic of the paragraph and what is to follow in that paragraph. A reader looking only at the topic sentences of your review should get a very good picture of what your review is about. Sometimes a student provides a very clear topic sentence but what follows in the paragraph is a little bit of the stated topic and a variety of other topics as well. Ask yourself the following two questions: Does each of my topic sentences communicate what is in each paragraph? Do all the sentences that make up that paragraph fit that topic or is there extraneous information in that paragraph?

Note the topic sentences in the following two examples.

> It is important to remember that severe sexual harassment was faced in this country not only by White women workers, but also by Black slaves. (Cohen, 1995, pp. 9–10)

This sentence in Cohen's investigation clearly states that what will be discussed in this paragraph is the sexual harassment faced by Black women who were slaves. The paragraph is then developed around this explicit purpose. It discusses the sexual exploitation of Black women slaves by their "owners" and the lack of protection for Black women slaves.

> Many cross-cultural studies have indicated that Asian (e.g., Taiwanese, Japanese) parents have much higher expectations for their children's achievement than American parents do (Stephenson et al., 1990; Stephenson et al., 1993). (Wang, 1995, p. 3)

From this topic sentence, Wang developed a paragraph that integratively reviews the literature that compares Asian and American expectations for children's achievement, primarily using the work of Stephenson and colleagues as indicated in the topic sentence.

Transitions

Well-worded transitions help the reader get from the last point to the subsequent point. Ask yourself: How do these thoughts fit together, and how can I make this link obvious to the reader? Your reader should not feel lost while going from one paragraph to another or from one section to another. The entire chapter should be seamless, that is, one thought should flow from the last in a constant progression to your ultimate conclusions. Note how Mulholland (1999) provides a transition for the reader from one paragraph to the next as she builds her rationale for examining the prevalence of eating disorders in African American college students:

> Limited data exists on the study of eating disorders with diverse nonclinical samples (Striegel-Moore & Marcus, 1995). The small body of research among African American women indicates that the risk for eating disorders is higher among younger, well educated individuals and those that more closely identify with White, middle-class values (Anderson & Hay, 1985; Hsu, 1987; Lawlor & Rand, 1985; Osvold & Sodowsky, 1993; Pumariega et al., 1994; Rucker & Cash, 1992; Silber, 1986; Thomas & James, 1988). Therefore, a strong case is made for the study of eating disorders among African American women at a predominately White university.

Mulholland seamlessly leads the reader into the next paragraph providing a transition that has the reader expecting what is to come. She continues:

> The study of African American women on predominately White campuses should address some current problems in the field. . . . (p. 37)

Summary and Conclusions

The summary provides the concluding remarks that capture the essential parts of what you want the reader to take away from the section. Common practice is to tell the reader what you are going to do (i.e., provide road maps), do it, and tell them what you did (i.e., provide a good summary). Although the summary may seem very obvious to you, and even unnecessary, a good summary is very informative to readers, especially those who are less familiar with this topic than you are.

You should go beyond just summarizing. As Sternberg (1991), then editor of *Psychological Bulletin,* commented in his editorial message: "Literature reviews are often frustrating because they offer neither a point of view nor a take-home message. One is left with a somewhat undigested scattering of facts but with little with which to put them together. I encourage authors to take a point of view based on theory and to offer readers a take-home message that integrates the review" (p. 3). The conclusions and recommendations that you draw from your review can be the "take-home message." In essence, after you have studied a particular topic or line of research for months, what conclusions can you reach about what is known, and what recommendations can you make to move this work ahead?

Rabinowitz (1984) provided a good example of a summary and conclusion:

> Several problems have hampered supervision research. A major setback has been that empirical investigations have not kept pace with the advancing theoretical literature on the supervision process. Many of the studies performed have investigated variables related to skill acquisition in beginning counselors. Fewer have looked at other needs that beginning counselors have such as gaining self-confidence, becoming aware of personal strengths and weaknesses, and learning to feel comfortable with their own counseling style (Worthington & Roehlke, 1979). Despite the recent developmental emphasis in the supervision literature, there have been very few empirical studies looking at the needs of more advanced counseling trainees.
>
> In terms of relationship variables, supervision research findings are mixed. Analogue studies show that a relationship is not necessary to learn empathy skills. However, real-life studies suggest that over the period of a semester, beginning supervisees expect their supervisors to be available for consultation on cases, support, suggesting approaches to work with clients, and to learn about themselves as counselors (Heppner & Handley, 1981; Johnston & Gysbers, 1967; Worthington & Roehlke, 1979). While analogue studies show that modeling, feedback, and didactic instruction are most important in teaching basic counseling skills, real-life studies have yet to find specific supervisor personalities, styles, behavior, or verbal content that varies consistently with supervisee effectiveness and satisfaction. Perhaps the wide array of instrumentation, subject pools, and research designs distort what is being found. On the other hand, current assessment techniques may not be sensitive enough to the nuances of the supervision process. It may also be possible that the needs of beginning practicum students are so general that any type of guidance or direction is useful.
>
> Developmental theorists in supervision suggest that with advancing experiences come differing needs at various stages of development. It would seem rea-

sonable to hypothesize that more experienced supervisees are more discriminating in their evaluation of supervision and of their supervisor. They are likely more aware of what they would like to get from their supervisors and are probably more assertive in making the relationship work for them. They are also less likely to need direct instruction about counseling techniques or treatment planning except when confronted with more difficult clients. Supervisor feedback at this stage may have more to do with polishing of techniques, discussing client conceptualizations at a higher level, dealing with the feelings that clients elicit in the supervisee, and understanding the supervisory relationship itself. Loganbill et al. (1982) suggest that supervisees at all stages of development cycle through feelings of stagnation, confusion, and integration with the supervisory issues they encounter. While these ideas are intriguing and seem to make intuitive sense, there has been very little systematic research on the developmental stages of the supervision process. The direction of future supervision research may best be established by empirically investigating the developmental frameworks, which have been proposed already. Integrating training techniques, supervisor interventions, and relationship variables with the developmental model may allow investigators to account for discrepant findings and to expand supervision research in a more integrated direction. (pp. 38–40)

Through this summary and conclusion paragraph, Rabinowitz provided not only a summary of the key elements of the literature review but also his point of view (as Sternberg, 1991, emphasized) that the supervision process may differ across supervisee levels of experience. Rabinowitz communicated what he believed to be crucial in this line of research and what would be important next steps to foster greater understanding in this topic. His conclusion became a significant part of his rationale for conducting his dissertation study, which, not surprisingly, examined the process of supervision across different developmental supervisee levels.

DESCRIBING, ANALYZING, AND SYNTHESIZING THE LITERATURE

Perhaps the easiest way to write a review paper is to simply report what each study examined and what was found. This type of review often consists of one paragraph to summarize a study and basically a succession of paragraphs reporting the results of a succession of studies. Each paragraph begins with the author's name and date of the study (e.g., Koss et al., 1987) and then summarizes the study in a paragraph. This type of reporting does distill the existing literature but is more of an annotated summary of the literature than an analysis of the literature.

A good review not only describes the existing literature but also analyzes the literature so that the reader has a greater understanding of that literature. Moreover, a good review synthesizes the overwhelming amount of information in the body or text of the paper so that it is a manageable task to comprehend that literature. One way of synthesizing a group of studies is to identify how individual studies are related to each other, where there is consistency and equivocal findings, and what themes are evident in the literature. We offer a number of strategies to describe, analyze, and synthesize aspects of the literature in the main body of the review.

Prototype or Classic Studies

Sometimes you may find a large number of studies that employ a similar methodology. Other times, you may find a classic study or article that either started a line of research or stimulated a new direction in a line of research. In such cases, you can provide a brief description of the prototypical study or highlight the classic study in some other way. Heppner (1979), in his study of the social influence process in counseling, highlighted a classic study by Strong (1968):

> Perhaps one of the most influential events within the counseling research was Strong's (1968) position paper. Essentially Strong integrated key variables within a counseling relationship (i.e., expertness, attractiveness, trustworthiness, and involvement) into a two-phase model of counseling that stimulated a great deal of research within counseling. In this model the counselor first increases influence potential through enhancement of the key variables and then makes use of the influence power to bring about desired changes in client cognitions and behaviors.
>
> Subsequent research and theoretical efforts labeled the counselor's ability to influence and control another agent's behavior as counselor power (Strong & Matross, 1973). Generally, the greater the perceived power, the greater the persuasive impact and the greater the ability to facilitate change (Jacobsen, 1972). Therapist power (P) has been described as a function of the congruence between the perception of the counselor as a helpful resource (R) and the perceived need by the client (N), which can be symbolized as $P = f (R \ N)$ (Strong & Matross, 1973). It is important to note that power is a function not of the actual resources of the counselor or of the actual needs of the client but, rather, of the client's perceptions of the counselor's resources and the client's needs. Thus, the client's perceptions are seen to be important events in the interpersonal influence process and, subsequently, are highly relevant events for counselors. (Heppner, 1979, pp. 8–9)

Integrating Articles Within a Sociohistorical Context

Sometimes the previous research can be integrated into a chronological perspective that is helpful to the reader's understanding of a phenomenon. Consider the following example by Neville and Heppner (1999):

> Prior to the 1970s research concerning rape focused almost exclusively on the rapist; what was it about his psychological profile that made him more likely than other men to commit rape. Virtually no attention was given to the distress of the rape survivor (Chapell, Geis, & Fogarty, 1974; Frank, Turner, & Duffy, 1979; Kilpatrick, Resick, & Veronen, 1981). The Women's Movement was instrumental in

> shifting the focus of rape research to include an examination of the psychological well-being of the survivors of rape. (p. 41)

In taking a chronological perspective, these authors were able to integrate the previous literature into a larger sociohistorical context. In this case, they highlighted that, until the women's movement brought attention to the welfare of victims, previous research was solely focused on perpetrators.

Quantifying Patterns

Another effective way of summarizing a group of studies is to quantify patterns that you find across several studies. In her dissertation on attitudes toward women in the United Arab Emirates, Al-Darmaki (1998) provided a good example of quantifying patterns in the literature:

> Empirical evidence indicates a relationship between attitudes toward women's roles and a number of demographic factors such as gender, age, social class and religion. . . . Seven studies utilized the AWS as a measure of attitudes. The other studies have either developed their own measures (especially cross-cultural studies) or used other measures such as the Sex-role Orientation Scale (Mullins, 1980) or Sex-Role Scale (Thornton, Alwin, & Camburn, 1983). Thirteen studies out of seventeen that have looked at gender as a contributing variable in attitudes toward women's roles found that women as compared to men revealed more liberal attitudes toward their roles. Nine of these studies have been conducted using samples from other cultures and found gender differences to exist . . . in attitudes toward women's roles. . . . These studies taken together have indicated that gender is the most predictive variable for attitudes toward women's roles. In most of these studies, females compared to males expressed more liberal attitudes toward their roles. (pp. 20–21)

Summarizing Studies on One Variable

One way of analyzing a body of literature is to examine the effects of a single variable across a group of studies. This type of analysis usually requires some way of systematically coding and analyzing the literature, as discussed in Chapter 4 (Searching and Reviewing the Relevant Literature). Thus, in analyzing a group of studies, efficiency and brevity can often be accomplished by making a statement that summarizes several investigations along a common variable. In his dissertation on the supervisory process over time, Rabinowitz (1984) provided a synthesis of the literature on the variable of supervisory feedback:

> Feedback on counseling behavior has been seen by supervisors as a major component of the supervision process (Worthington & Roehlke, 1979). Immediate feedback has been shown to be more impactful than delayed feedback (Carlson, 1974; Silverman & Quin, 1974). Specific performance feedback seems more effective than nonspecific feedback (Carlson, 1974; Payne, Weiss, & Kapp, 1972; Payne, Winter, & Bell, 1972). Greater agreement, more positive content evaluation, and more accurate recall were found to be elicited by supervisory feedback

that was positive and congruent rather than moderate to extremely negative (Bernstein & Lecomte, 1979). Supervisors have been documented giving immediate feedback to counselors in session through the use of light signals (e.g., Canada, 1973), audio signals via wireless transmitters (e.g., Carlson, 1974; Levine & Tinkler, 1964), or in certain instances phoning the therapist in the middle of the session (Haley, 1976). (pp. 20–21)

Tables

In analyzing and coding a large number of studies, a condensed version of some of the variables may be profitably summarized in one or more tables. In essence, a summary table can present some of the raw data of your analysis on a group of studies. For example, we present a portion of the table Croteau, Anderson, Distefano, and Kampa-Kokesch (2000) used to present studies conducted over 16 years that address vocationally related issues of gay, lesbian, and bisexual individuals (Table 6.1). Note how much information can be provided in a concise space using this technique.

Design and Methodological Issues

Each type of research design and subsequent statistical analysis will have certain advantages and disadvantages (see Heppner et al., 1999). In addition, each particular study will have strengths and limitations based on the specific methodology employed. For example, the conclusions from one assertiveness training study may be much stronger than a second study because they contain fewer plausible threats to internal validity. Thus, going beyond the stated conclusions of each study and evaluating the design and methodological issues within each study are almost always thought to be sound practice and can be effective in assessing the quality of the research findings in a particular area. This practice can also build a cogent rationale for the type of design you will be advocating in your own investigation. Gershuny (2000) provides an excellent example of this in her dissertation on psychological trauma, dissociative phenomena, and distress:

> Although a large body of literature has examined and found relations among the occurrence of traumatic events, dissociation, and trauma-related distress, and these findings taken together imply dissociation as a mediator, only one study was identified so far (Everill, Waller, & MacDonald, 1995) that has examined the potential mediating role of dissociation to the relation between trauma and distress. Given the recent theoretical and empirical focus on the roles of dissociation in trauma-related distress, it seems imperative to examine dissociation as a potential mediator of the trauma-distress relation. If the presence and degree of dissociative phenomena do not explain at least some of the relation between trauma and distress (i.e., do not at least partially account for the relation between trauma and distress above and beyond that which is accounted for by trauma alone), then a focus on the role of dissociation in the psychological aftermath of trauma becomes suspect. (p. 2)

TABLE
6.1

CONTENT AND FOCUS OF JOURNAL ARTICLES IN LGB VOCATIONAL PSYCHOLOGY 1980–1996

Reference	LGB Identity Development	Discrimination and Climate	Managing Sexual Identity	Societal Messages and Interests	Practitioner Interventions	Lesbian, Gay, or Bisexual	Exploration, Choice, and Implementation	Type of Article	Stated Focus
Belz, 1993					✓	G	CI	P	Case study analysis
Bieschke & Matthews, 1996					✓	LGB	N/A	R	A study of career counselor behaviors that are LGB client affirming
Boatwright et al., 1996	✓		✓			L	EC	R	A study of lesbian identity development and effects on career trajectory
Chojnacki & Gelberg, 1994	✓	✓			✓	LGB	CI	T	Suggested person–environment career counseling be applied with LGB clients
Chung, 1995		✓		✓		LGB	C	T	Suggested person–environment framework be applied to LGB career design making
Chung & Harmon, 1994				✓		G	C	R	A study of "the career interests and aspirations of gay men" (p. 224)
Croteau, 1996		✓	✓			LGB	I		Review "of nine published studies on the workplace experiences of LGB people" (p. 195)
Croteau & Bieschke, 1996						LGB	N/A		Overview of existing literature; advocates a move "beyond pioneering" (p. 119)
Croteau & Hedstrom, 1993		✓	✓		✓	LG	CI	P	Case study analysis
Croteau & Lark, 1995		✓	✓			LGB	I	R	A study of work experiences of LGB student affairs professionals
Croteau & Thiel, 1993	✓				✓	LGB	CI	P	Examined need to integrate sexual orientation into career counseling through case examples

Source: Croteau, J. M., Anderson, M. Z., Distefano, T. M., & Kampa-Kokesch, S. (2000). Lesbian, gay, and bisexual vocational psychology: Reviewing foundations and planning construction. In R. M. Perez, K. A. DeBord & et. al (Eds.), *Handbook of counseling and psychotherapy with lesbian, gay, and bisexual clients* (pp. 383–408). Washington, DC: American Psychological Association. Used with permission.

In essence, Gershuny is highlighting an important gap in the literature and advocating an examination of the potential mediational role of dissociation to the relation between trauma and distress. In doing so, she is utilizing her analysis of this area to provide a rationale for her dissertation study.

Identify Problems

Often, helping readers understand what the obstacles are in a particular line of research is useful. Thus, you may identify and list criticisms; deficiencies or limitations in the literature; and/or design, methodological, and theoretical problems with the past research. Sometimes students feel a bit timid about criticizing previous researchers or well-known scholars. Although exercising diplomacy may be prudent, fresh perspectives can provide insight by identifying obstacles and limitations. For example, note how Perez (1993) identified significant gaps in the literature in the following paragraph:

> Research on problem-solving appraisal has increased with the emergence of the PSI and Heppner and Krauskopf's (1987) information processing perspective. . . . However, little, if any, attention to research has focused on the actual process of real-life problem solving in delinquents. Larson and Heppner (1989) cite major methodological limitations regarding restricted populations (e.g., college students) and the need to extend research to other populations. . . . Additionally, the use of the PSI with children, adolescents, and special populations (e.g., learning disabled youth, adjudicated adolescents) is noticeably absent. (pp. 31–32)

Drawing Conclusions

Another way to summarize studies is to draw a broad conclusion based on a group of studies. Broad conclusions may be made about the efficacy of a particular counseling intervention like counselor self-disclosure or about the effectiveness of a particular type of training like assertiveness training. The following example is a concluding paragraph in a literature review published in the *Journal of Applied and Preventive Psychology* by Neville and Heppner (1999):

> In analyzing the combined results of studies conducted over the last 15 years, a pattern of postrape reaction and recovery has become evident. It appears that the vast majority of rape survivors suffer an intense psychological reaction immediately following the assault and for many this acute reaction phase lasts as long as 3 months. This acute reaction has been characterized as consisting of significant levels of fear, anxiety, depression, self-esteem issues, and sexual dysfunction (Frazier, 1990; Hanson, 1990; Kilpatrick et al., 1992; Resick, 1993). (p. 42).

In short, by providing this conclusion, the authors are reviewing 15 years of research on psychological consequences of rape and integrating it for the reader. They identify a theme or pattern in the data that indicates a common acute reaction to sexual assault, and they provide a number of studies to support the statement cited earlier in their review.

Conversely, when the empirical findings do not support one view and there is, in fact, some disagreement in the literature, these equivocal findings should be noted. We provide two examples of handling this type of pattern. The first example is from the Neville and Heppner (1999) review of psychological sequelae of rape. It specifically examines the empirical findings related to the role of social support in the adjustment of rape survivors:

> Research on the relationship between various aspects of social support and adjustment is equivocal. Several studies suggest that greater social support and understanding are associated with few initial (Atekeson et al., 1982; Norris & Feldman-Summers, 1981; Ruch & Chandler, 1980; Sales et al., 1984) and long-term effects (Burgess & Holstrom, 1979; Emm, 1985; Kimerling & Calhoun, 1994), whereas others have found that social support is not related to either initial (Popiel & Susskind, 1985) or long-term adjustment (Golding et al., 1997; Neville & Clark, 1997; Wyatt et al., 1990); no study to date has found a positive relationship between social support and negative adjustment. (p. 55)

In discussing equivocal findings, you must not only present the studies representing the contradictory findings but also use your expert knowledge of the field to offer explanations for these findings. In her examination of the role of gender-related personality traits in predicting process and outcome variables in supervision, Warner (1996) provides our second example:

> One characteristic that has received mixed support in the literature is sex of the supervisor. Differential results have been reported regarding whether or not female supervisors are seen as having more impact than male supervisors. Putney et al. (1992) found that female supervisors are seen as being more effective than male supervisors. However, Kennard, Stewart, and Gluck (1987) found the opposite to be true, and Worthington and Stern (1985) found there to be no perceived differences in the quality of the supervisory relationship based on supervisor sex. Further, Nelson and Holloway (1990) found that sex differences along this dimension are overshadowed by the power inherent in the supervision role. Thus, the results of studies examining whether male or female supervisors are more effective are inconclusive. (pp. 1–2)

Rather than leaving the reader with this inconclusive summary, however, Warner uses her expert knowledge of this area to offer a possible reason for these equivocal findings. She continues:

> These contradictory results evident in the area of biological sex and supervision may be explained by the failure of these studies to obtain more specific measures of gender as opposed to the more global variable of sex. There is a tremendous amount of within group variance within each sex. It follows that finer distinctions of the variable sex are necessary to understand these results, as called for in the literature (Mintz & O'Neil, 1990; Marecek, 1995). (p. 2)

Future Research Directions

The other side of identifying obstacles and limitations is to identify and/or suggest potential solutions for future lines of research. What type of studies could future research conduct that would answer some major questions in this area?

Such observations can be made throughout the main body of the review and/or synthesized within a final *conclusions and recommendations* section. Following are two examples of the way students have written this section. Note how both Davis (1996) and Kasai (1997) provide very specific suggestions for future researchers. This is a very important section as it provides the reader with a sense of what needs to be done next.

> A number of opportunities for future research are evident on the design and results of this study. Perhaps the most obvious opportunity for future research is to conduct a similar study utilizing time series with data gathered over at least 20 sessions of psychotherapy. Such a study would provide a more straightforward time-series analysis, without the potential loss of information or risk of alpha inflation from averaging cross correlations.
>
> Future research might also investigate the contribution that internalization makes to outcome. The unique contribution of the internalization process to outcome has not been empirically investigated. Additionally, researchers might investigate the interactions between the alliance and internalization as they impact therapeutic outcome. Techniques such as hierarchical linear modeling might be considered for this purpose.
>
> Greenberg (1994) and Gelso and Carter (1994) have described differing patterns of the working alliance over the course of therapy. Kivlighan and Shaughnessy (1995b) found that these patterns varied in their contribution to therapeutic relationship and the working alliance may vary depending on the pattern of the alliance over therapy. How each of these patterns might be related to internalization of therapy is unknown.
>
> The degree to which the representations of the therapy experience actually affected intersession client behavior in this study is unknown. Recall that some ongoing influence on behavior is necessary to assert that internalization has taken place. Thus, future research may examine ways in which intrapsychic representations of the therapy experience influence client behavior outside of the therapy setting. (Davis, 1996, pp. 17–18)
>
> Future research must begin to examine the generalizability and stability of the Japanese Grandiosity Scale through confirmatory analyses with other samples that consist of equal numbers of males and females. Independence from social desirability of this scale is also in need of investigation in order to detect distortions. An attempt to include a wider range of items might be necessary to increase variance accounted for by the GDG and GAG factors.
>
> Research that assesses the relationships between the Grandiosity Scale and other grandiosity scales, such as the Pseudo-autonomy Scale (Lapan & Patton, 1986), the Superiority Scale (Robbins & Patton, 1985), the NPI (Raskin & Hall, 1979), and between the Grandiosity Scale and other personality and psychological well-being variables are needed in order to investigate the construct validity of the scale.
>
> The applicability of the Japanese Grandiosity Scale to different age groups and in different environments, such as people from rural areas or Japanese people who are in different countries, may be needed in order to investigate differences based on developmental and environmental variables. This is also applicable to the measures of independent self- and interdependent self-construals.
>
> Another crucial area for future research is examination of the construct of self-construals. As discussed in the limitations of this study, the independent self-

and interdependent self-construals seemed not to be two dichotomous categories but rather four cluster categories. Results of this study indicated that a decrease in interdependence does not necessarily mean an increase in independence. Further theoretical work is necessary for the adequate development of this construct. Finally, it may be useful in future research to examine an even broader range of variables with which to operationalize these constructs. In particular, other instruments might be developed in order to assess the cultural impact of the West on the Japanese. (Kasai, 1997, pp. 91–92)

WRITING STYLE AND PROCESS

Revising and Polishing

Perhaps the most important message regarding writing style is to write in a clear and concise manner. As Bem (1995) noted, "A review tells a straightforward tale. . . . Clear any underbrush that entangles your prose by obeying Strunk and White's (1979) famous dictum 'omit needless words' and by extending that dictum to needless concepts, topics, anecdotes, asides and footnotes" (p. 173). One strategy to enhance clarity and conciseness is to revise and rewrite earlier drafts, preferably a few days after the first writing. Our observation is that very few people write excellent first drafts. Our suggestion is to let the draft "cool" a bit and give yourself some distance from it, then return to revise and polish the writing, keeping in mind clarity and conciseness. Specifically, look for ways to eliminate unnecessary words. For example, we typically polish manuscripts at least twice before we ask a colleague for feedback, which is another useful strategy to polish your writing. Our suggestion here is to select one or preferably two colleagues who are willing and able to provide both detailed editorial feedback on writing style and specific comments about more conceptual and methodological issues related to the content of the review itself. The clearer the writing, the more likely the reader will stay engaged and understand the point of view you are trying to communicate.

Anticipating Questions

Part of writing with clarity is anticipating questions of readers and then revising the writing to answer those questions. Try to think about your advisor or committee members reading your review as you yourself reread it. What reactions will they have? What questions will they have? Common questions that advisors have are: What evidence do you have to support this statement? What is the point of this paragraph? Or, So what; what does this all add up to, and why is it important? How is this construct defined (i.e., the meaning of a word is unclear, usually a jargon-related word that makes sense only to those very familiar with the area)? What are some studies to support this conclusion? Trying to anticipate and respond to these potential questions in your writing is very helpful in producing writing that is clear and understandable.

Having a Voice in the Review

As Sternberg (1991) noted, taking a perspective in your review can be useful. In developing your point of view, do not limit your own voice in the process. After studying the literature for weeks, you most likely will have many observations that could affect future research on this topic. So include your observations, or hunches about hypotheses, or what you believe really needs to happen next (which can also formally be in the form of recommendations at the end of your paper).

Substantiating Claims and Plagiarism

Cite others when appropriate, and give credit where credit is due. Note in the following example that Baker (1998) not only cites the original source of a definition of a construct in the leadership literature but also acknowledges an earlier conclusion of a previous reviewer (Riggio):

> Consideration is the degree to which the leader shows concern for the group members and his/her orientation toward participatory management (Fleishman & Harris, 1962). On the other hand, initiating structure is the extent to which the leader organizes, defines and structures the subordinates' jobs (Fleishman & Harris, 1960). When summarizing the Ohio State studies, Riggio (1996) stated that these two dimensions have been consistently shown to be independent of each other. (p. 18)

Basically, researchers have a responsibility to acknowledge the original contributions of others, as well as to clearly distinguish their own scholarly insights (Heppner et al., 1999). Reviewers should use quotations and proper citation form when quoting a verbatim passage of another author; paraphrasing sentences from other articles should include a citation (see Heppner et al., 1999, for a more thorough discussion of ethical issues involved in plagiarism).

You also have a responsibility to substantiate claims or conclusions, preferably with empirically supported research as in the following example:

> Generally, studies have supported predictions made by the third part of Fiedler's theory (Peters, Hartke, & Pohlmann, 1985; Strube & Garcia, 1981), although some have not (Graen, Alvares, Orris, & Martella, 1970; Vecchio, 1977). Likewise, according to Peters et al. (1985), Fiedler's predictions are supported more consistently in laboratory settings than in studies conducted in real world settings (Baker, 1998, pp. 35–36).

Conversely, do not make claims like the following without providing supporting references: "Research supports the effectiveness of the ABC intervention, or the XYZ theory has received very strong empirical support." The scientific community will want to know what data supports such assertions.

It is important, however, that you know what statements need to be cited versus what is common knowledge and does not require citations. For example, if you are making a statement like "Stress is a factor in the lives of many adults," this probably does not require a citation to support it. If, however, you say something like "Biofeedback has been found to be effective in treating stress," that assertion merits documentation. The first statement can be thought of as general and common knowledge that has been well documented for many years. The second statement is more specific, is discussing a specific relationship, and is in need of citations to support the claim.

Using Professional Jargon

Specialized terminology within a field is termed *jargon*. Webster's Collegiate Dictionary (tenth edition) defines jargon as "the technical or characteristic idiom of a special activity or group." However, Webster also defines jargon as a language of "obscure and often pretentious language marked by circumlocutions and long words." These two contrasting definitions are important in that they communicate both the central advantage and disadvantage of using professional jargon. Because jargon is technical and specific to one's discipline, it can at times provide a highly specialized meaning, essential to the understanding of a construct. This specialized language is capable of making fine nuances and conceptual differentiations that more colloquial language is not designed to communicate. For example, many lay persons would use the terms gender and sex interchangeably. Within psychology, however, sex is the term used for biological differences between men and women and gender is a cultural term used to describe a social construction. However, when jargon is used indiscriminately, it can be confusing and introduce vague or mentalistic constructs that are not easily measurable. You must ask yourself whether the use of a specialized term will help clarify a conceptual distinction that is important for the understanding of your study. If so, professional jargon is probably appropriate.

Using Colloquial Language

One important aspect of writing scientifically is being able to differentiate colloquial terminology from scientific terminology. Colloquial language is used commonly in conversation; it is unstudied and familiar. Colloquial language tends to be appropriate in ordinary conversation but not in scientific written discourse. The following examples contrast frequently encountered colloquial terminology and an appropriate scientific version:

- "The instrument taps into" as opposed to "The instrument assesses"
- "Participants filled out the instruments" as opposed to "Participants completed the instruments"

- "We were able to get participants from . . ." as opposed to "We were able to obtain participants from"

Although these differentiations may seem unimportant, colloquial writing tends to compromise the scientific credibility of the writing as it tends to be less specific and does not conform to expectations of the scientific community. A review paper necessitates scientific writing, not creative writing. Often the psychological constructs in the review are complex and do not benefit by adding a creative twinge to your writing style.

Using Repetition and Parallel Construction

Using repetition and parallel forms can enhance comprehension. For example, consider the following two sentences.

- Beginning counseling trainees may be seeking greater support from their supervisors early on in their training period, but later on in their supervisory sessions they may want to be more independent of support from their supervisor.
- Beginning counselor trainees may seek more support from their supervisors early in their training and less support later in their training.

The latter is preferred. Thus, we suggest that you hold the grammatical structure of clauses parallel when you are writing about parallel types of events or constructs. This tends to make for clearer, more understandable writing. Sometimes less-experienced writers attempt to add variety to their sentences as in the first example, with loss in comprehension and clarity.

CONCLUSIONS

The purpose of this chapter was to provide a wide range of writing techniques, which aid in developing a clear and informative literature review. The review of the literature is a critical step in understanding what research has come before the investigation you are planning and how that previous literature can inform your own investigation. You can integratively present this previous literature while simultaneously constructing a case for the study you are about to undertake. We end this chapter with a writing exercise that allows you to practice integrative writing. Use this exercise to practice and hone your writing skills. Following the exercise is the "Checklist for Chapter 2 of the Thesis or Dissertation," which you can use to assess and revise your literature review.

EXERCISE 6.1: SYNTHESIZING INFORMATION ACROSS STUDIES

This exercise will provide you with practice in synthesizing information across studies, which is an important aspect of writing a review paper. A brief document follows that is written in "report-writing style." The document discusses six studies in six paragraphs, or one study per paragraph. The focus of the document is the fundamental attribution error (which has been widely researched in social psychology) as it has been investigated in professional helpers.

Your task is to synthesize the information in the document into one—maximum—concluding paragraph, much like you may commonly find in published review papers. As you examine the following document, first identify a common theme among all the studies. Next, reflect on what can be concluded from these studies, both what the data suggest and what we do not know about this area. After you have written a concluding paragraph, compare your paragraph to the examples provided.

THE FUNDAMENTAL ATTRIBUTION ERROR AND PROFESSIONAL HELPERS

Within an attributional perspective, the professional helper, or any helper for that matter, is in an observer role. From this vantage point, one of the most important tasks for the professional helper is the identification and definition of the causes for the client's presenting problem. As with any observer, the primary danger for the psychologist or counselor in the helper role is susceptibility to the fundamental attribution error. Even worse, there is evidence that professional helpers are more susceptible to this type of distortion than the ordinary observer.

Batson (1975) investigated professional and nonprofessional helpers in a simulated referral agency. Subjects were asked to make attributions about the locus of a client's problem. In general, those in the helper role attributed the client's behavior to personal dispositions even though the clients attributed their behavior to situational factors. Furthermore, nonprofessional helpers made more situational attributions (40%) than professional helpers (23%). Thus, the professional helpers seemed even more willing than the nonprofessional helpers to make personal attributions.

With a similar intent, Innes and Braendler (1978) studied the likelihood that professional training might exaggerate the susceptibility of helpers to overestimate the contribution of personal factors to behavior problems. In this study, subjects were teachers, teacher trainees, and nonteachers. A videotape interview of a school counselor and a high-school girl discussing an actual problem was shown. The subjects were asked to judge the situational versus personal factors in the problem. Results showed that teachers were no more likely to attribute personal factors as causing the problem. Of course, the generality of these results to psychologists as well as other problem situations is unclear.

Snyder, Shenkel, and Schmidt (1976) had subjects (female undergraduates) listen to a taped therapy interview in which the client claimed her problems were due to her situation. Half the subjects were told the client was chronic while the other half were told this was the first interview for the client. Experimental subjects were instructed to assume either the role of the client or the role of the counselor. In essence, they were asked to empathize with one of the individuals on the tape. Control subjects were given no instructions regarding the roles. Overall, counselor-role subjects rated the client's problem as significantly more personality based than either the client-role or control subjects. In absolute terms, client-role and control subjects rated the client's problem as about equally due to personal and situational factors; counselor-role subjects rated the client's problems as more personal than situational. These results suggest that the counselor role exaggerated the usual observer bias (fundamental attribution error) as compared to the control group. Diagnostic labels also had an effect on the attributions made. Clients labeled as chronic were judged by subjects to have problems significantly more personality based than clients described as "first time in therapy."

Rubenstein and Bloch (1978) compared the perceptions of social workers and social work clients. They found that social workers regarded 39 of the 50 clients in the sample as having intrapersonal problems. In contrast, only 21 of the clients regarded themselves as having this kind of problem. The authors concluded that this divergence in attribution was caused by a disagreement between the social workers and their clients over the nature of the clients' problems.

Sherrard and Batson (1979) conducted the only research that has analyzed the attributions of counselors and clients in an actual interview. Using an intake interview as the basis for interaction, the discrepancies between client and counselor assessment of the client's problems were investigated. Counselors were expected to view client problems as more personally caused than clients would view them. However, results indicated that both counselors and clients perceived problems as personally caused. Despite this unexpected finding for the clients, predictions for counselor perceptions were as anticipated. Counselors did favor personal factors in explaining client problems.

Additional direct and indirect evidence of an overattribution effect by counselors comes from a review by Wills (1978) of the perceptions professional helpers have about clients (exclusive of diagnostic judgments). After surveying a portion of the research on attributional factors in helping relationships, Wills concludes that there is a distinct tendency by professional helpers to see clients as the cause of their problems. In summation, he asserts,

> A tendency toward personalistic attributions has been observed among both lay persons and professionally trained therapists, and there is evidence that in several settings, helpers are not sensitized to the situational constraints that influence clients' behavior. (pp. 988–989)

The overattribution of clients' problems to personal factors is one process that contributes to a general negative perception of clients. It has been shown that professional helpers have unfavorable perceptions of clients on many dimensions (see Wills, 1978). Clearly, one component of the overall negative perception by professional helpers is the operation of the fundamental attribution error.

As instructed, write a one-paragraph concluding statement. Use references to document your conclusions or assertions.

Following are two different concluding paragraphs. Examine these paragraphs, and compare them with your paragraph. Note how Example #1 tells the reader that three of the studies were analogue studies and, thus, raises the issue of generalizability. Note how both reviews identify the same recommendations for future research. Note how the first review quantifies the number of studies supporting a similar conclusion.

Example #1

Counselors who are engaged in identifying and defining client presenting problems appear to be susceptible to the fundamental attribution error. Specifically, in four of five studies (including three analogue studies) subjects in helper roles were more likely to attribute client problems to personal causes than to situational causes (Batson, 1975; Innes & Braendler, 1978; Synder et al., 1976; Rubenstein & Bloch, 1978). Those subjects in client roles however tended to attribute problems to situational causes. In contrast to results obtained in the analog studies, the data in the one in vivo study indicates that both counselor and client perceived problems to be personally caused (Sherrard & Batson, 1979). In view of the discrepancy between results of the analog studies and the in vivo study, further research using actual counseling situations appears to be warranted to further examine the fundamental attribution error with professional helpers.

Example #2

In summary, some evidence exists that there is attributional error, or at least attributional discrepancies, between the subjects in professional helper roles and subjects in a client role (Batton, 1975; Innes & Braendler, 1978; Snyder et al., 1976; Rubenstein & Block, 1978). Specifically, there seems to be a tendency for helpers to make attributions to personal rather than situational factors of the client, whereas individuals in the client role may tend to make more situational attributions. This phenomenon seems to have been demonstrated most clearly in analogue studies, and the naturalistic studies provide some support for the professional helper's attributional tendency (Rubenstein & Bloch, 1978) but the results are less conclusive (see Sherrard & Batson, 1979). The discrepancy between counselor and client attributions seems less clear in the actual counseling studies. More naturalistic studies are needed to explore this phenomenon.

CHECKLIST FOR CHAPTER 2 OF THE THESIS OR DISSERTATION

In this section we provide a scale to assess key elements we have discussed as being important in writing a literature-review chapter. We encourage you to use this scale when you have written a first draft of your literature review but before you have given it to your advisor or to a peer for review. By honestly assessing how well you have utilized these skills, you will be able to identify areas where your literature review could be strengthened. In short, we encourage you to critically evaluate the strengths and weaknesses of the writing of your literature review as you continue to work on refining it.

To What Extent Did You . . .

1. . . . Define and clarify the parameters of the topic that you are addressing?

1	2	3	4	5	6
Not at all				Very much so	

2. . . . Integratively summarize previous literature?

1	2	3	4	5	6
Not at all				Very much so	

3. . . . Identify and discuss relations, contradictions, gaps, and inconsistencies in the literature?

1	2	3	4	5	6
Not at all				Very much so	

4. . . . Discuss an appropriate scope of literature, with the most prominence on literature most closely related to the current investigation?

1	2	3	4	5	6
Not at all				Very much so	

5. . . . Take your own unique point of view in writing the literature review?

1	2	3	4	5	6
Not at all				Very much so	

6. . . . Provide a "take-home message" to the literature review?

1	2	3	4	5	6
Not at all				Very much so	

7. . . . Write clearly and concisely? (Extraneous words and phrases are not used. Studies with little direct bearing of the current topic are not reviewed.)

1	2	3	4	5	6
Not at all				Very much so	

8. . . . Include a good writing structure evidenced by the following?
   a. Road maps to point out the structure of the review

1	2	3	4	5	6
Not at all				Very much so	

   b. Explicit topic sentences that communicate what is in each paragraph

1	2	3	4	5	6
Not at all				Very much so	

    c. Transitions that carry the reader to the next thought

1	2	3	4	5	6
Not at all				Very much so	

    d. Appropriate subheadings that serve to clarify major sections

1	2	3	4	5	6
Not at all				Very much so	

    e. Summaries that provide closure to major sections and the review as a whole

1	2	3	4	5	6
Not at all				Very much so	

9. . . . End the review with conclusions?

1	2	3	4	5	6
Not at all				Very much so	

10. . . . Eliminate colloquial language?

1	2	3	4	5	6
Not at all				Very much so	

11. . . . Use jargon only as necessary?

1	2	3	4	5	6
Not at all				Very much so	

QUANTITATIVE METHODS

Mapping Your Research Plan

The methods chapter of your thesis or dissertation is the map of exactly what you are going to do and how you are going to do it. This chapter is often the most scrutinized section of your proposal, because your committee will spend most of its review time thinking about your methods and trying to think of ways of making each part of your methods as strong as it can possibly be. Flaws in methodology can lead to weak, invalid, unreliable, and unusable results. Although actually writing the methods chapter is perhaps the easiest of all chapters, the thinking you will need to do before you actually begin writing is critically important. The goal of your methods chapter is to describe the exact steps you will take to conduct your study. The guiding principle is to provide enough detail so that even a fairly naïve reader could replicate your study. This chapter is a place to provide a specific set of instructions about conducting the study but not a place to replicate information already in the literature review.

Typical sections in methods chapters are (a) Participants, (b) Instruments, (c) Procedures, and (d) Statistical Analyses. These sections generally appear in the order presented here, although they can be varied if necessary to more adequately describe your study. The purpose of this chapter is to provide the specific information needed in the aforementioned four sections. In addition, we briefly discuss the introductory preface that often appears in this chapter. We provide several examples of the different sections and encourage students to carefully study these examples as they could serve as exemplars. We also highlight and discuss several issues contained in the examples that commonly occur in methods chapters. Finally, we provide the Checklist for Chapter 3 of the Thesis or Dissertation for you to rate yourself on how well you accomplished each main aspect of writing a methods chapter.

WHERE TO BEGIN: THE CHAPTER ROAD MAP

The first one or two paragraphs in the methods chapter should provide a road map, or overview, of the chapter. This overview can be quite concise, simply providing the reader with a good idea of what will be found in each section.

Following is a brief example of a road map that was used at the beginning of Wei's methods chapter.

> This Methods Chapter will be divided into four subsections. First, the characteristics of the participants will be described. Second, the psychometric properties of each instrument will be described. The Inventory of Adult Attachment Scale (AAS) will be used to measure attachment. The Problem-Solving Inventory–Form B (PSI) and the Problem-Focused Styles of Coping (PF-SOC) will be used to measure coping styles; the Ambivalence Over Expressing Emotion Questionnaire (AEQ) will be used to measure conflicted emotions. Finally, the Beck Depression Inventory (BDI), State-Trait Anxiety Inventory-Trait Form (STAI-T), Hopelessness Scale (HS), and State-Trait Anger Inventory (STAXI-T) will be used to measure intrapersonal distress; the Inventory of Interpersonal Problem-Short Circumplex Form (IIP-SC) will be used to measure interpersonal distress. Third, procedures will be described about how data was collected. Finally, the structural equation model with latent variables will be discussed to analyze the data. (Wei, 2000, p. 40)

With this brief road map, Wei provides the reader with the structure for the chapter. She also gives the reader an advanced organizer concerning which constructs she will be measuring and, specifically, which instruments will be used. She mentions that she will be using structural equation modeling to analyze her data.

PARTICIPANTS

The purpose of this section is not only to indicate who will be the participants in your investigation but also to describe how many, their characteristics (e.g., age, sex, race/ethnicity), and how they were selected. The term *participant* is used in lieu of the previously used term *subjects* to communicate the active and consensual relationship the participant has in the investigation. Probably one of the most frequent errors made in the participant section is describing the procedures used to actually collect data from the participants. This information is typically presented later in the procedures section. The participants section is focused only on issues of where you will obtain the participants, how many there will be, and if they are representative of the population to which you want to generalize. Thus, after reading this section of your proposal, reviewers should be able to ascertain

1. Who the participants are and where you will obtain them
2. The number of participants
3. The representativeness of your sample and thus its external validity or generalizability

Who Are the Participants, and Where Will You Obtain Them?

The issue of obtaining your sample is an important one. The basic issue is utilizing a sample that is representative of the population to which you want to generalize your findings—your target population. It could be college students, fraternity college students, high-school teachers, prostate cancer survivors, African American adolescents, counseling center clients, or Catholic children. After defining the target population, you need to identify a group of people who fit this definition and are accessible; this group is technically called the *participant pool*. The third step is to select participants from that pool. A critical issue is to select participants in such a way that they are representative of the participant pool and the larger target population. Ideally, random selection of participants from the participant pool increases the odds of obtaining a representative sample (for more details, see Heppner et al., 1999). In short, the generalizability of the results of your study will be directly related to your target population, the representativeness of your participant pool, and the selection of your participants. In general, the more you can use random selection from a large heterogeneous target pool, the stronger the generalizability of your findings to the target population. However, using random selection and large participant pools is not always possible. Obviously, there are trade-offs in the choice of a sample, typically relating to ease of data collection and generalizability of the results.

In thinking about your intended target population, think about specific parameters that may be of interest for your study. Are there demographic considerations of importance? Does the age or developmental stage of the person matter? Does your study need to assume a certain level of psychological health or illness; do people need to be distressed at a certain level to make appropriate participants? If you are doing your research in a business, do years of experience matter or does the particular culture of the organization matter? In a prison, does the amount of time already served or the type of crime the person committed affect your study in any way?

For example, if you want to generalize your results to college students, are your participant pool and subsequent sample broad enough that you can make this claim? Is your sample obtained through random selection, or is it restricted to enrollment in a particular class? Are the participant pool and sample representative of key factors such as year in school, sex, age, and race? For example, if it is collected at one college in the Midwest, are there aspects of that particular campus that are unique, special, and perhaps nonrepresentative of campuses in the East or in the country as a whole? If you are investigating a controversial topic like abortion or homosexuality, are the views represented on the campus from which you are collecting representative of campuses throughout the United States?

The field of psychology has been criticized for an over-reliance on college-age samples—introductory psychology students in particular—and the practice of generalizing the findings to people in general from this restricted sample. For some types of studies, this sample may be very appropriate. We know, for example, that 18–22 year olds are involved in date rape to a much higher degree than other age groups (Koss, Gidycz, & Wisniewski, 1987). Using a college-age population for this topic is very appropriate. We also know that, in the United States, a broader range of all university students take introductory psychology courses than other introductory courses, such as introduction to economics. Thus, using this population for some studies is amply justified. However, be aware that too often researchers select "convenience" samples and then have great difficulty generalizing their results in any meaningful manner.

As you consider various issues related to selecting your sample, jot down the limitations of your sample. You will typically need to discuss these limitations in your discussion chapter. How could you lessen these limitations? How could you obtain a more heterogeneous pool? Could you possibly randomly select participants without creating major difficulties? Brainstorm options with your peers and advisor. Now is the time to be creative. Sometimes combining a community sample with a college sample for greater heterogeneity is a possibility. You may be able to collect data at a historically black college or university and add that sample to one that you collected at a predominately white university in order to increase the generalizability of your results.

The important point is to examine the pros and cons of your potential participant pool and subsequent sample and evaluate what this sample will mean in terms of generalizability of the findings. Too often when students are asked where they are going to obtain their sample, the response is: "I know somebody who works for Easy Digit, and she said I could easily survey 200 co-workers during their lunch hour." Although this type of practical and functional consideration is important and obtaining participants is a crucial part of conducting your thesis or dissertation, using time and care to determine who comprises the target population, participant pool, and sample is vitally important to the contribution of your study (for more details, see Heppner et al., 1999).

In this section and the next (The Sampling Method . . .) are four examples of descriptions of participants from past students' theses/dissertations to further illustrate issues pertaining to selecting and describing participants.

DESCRIPTION OF PARTICIPANTS FROM A SURVEY STUDY

Participants

The total sample of this study consisted of 345 students attending a small Midwestern liberal arts college. Students in their fifth year of study and those who reported having transferred to Westminster from another college were eliminated, leaving a final sample of 306 students. The sample included 236 males (mean age = 19.7 years) and 70 females (mean age = 19.6 years); 90 freshmen, 100 sophomores, 73 juniors, and 43 seniors. The sample comprises 54.7 percent of the eligible (nontransfer and non-fifth-year) students enrolled during the semester in which the investigation took place. The subjects were kept naïve as to the nature of the experiment, being told only that the study investigated how they solved problems and interacted with their environment. (Neal, 1983, p. 48)

Neal was interested in examining students' awareness and utilization of campus helping resources and whether variables such as problem-solving style and student's year in school affected students' awareness and utilization. Thus, he reported his sample by class level as this was one of his independent variables, one that was obviously necessary for readers to understand the sample. He eliminated transfer students because they would not have the same background and knowledge of the campus helping resources, which might confound the results. A small number of fifth-year students would complicate some of the intended statistical analysis and, thus, were also eliminated from the study. Note that he reported that the obtained sample was comprised of almost 55% of the eligible students at that college, which provides some useful information to the reader about the generalizability of the results. Also note the disparity between 236 males and 70 females; in most instances, such a disparity would cause concern about the adequacy of the sample. However, Neal collected his data at an institution that was historically all male and, during the transition to a co-ed institution, these numbers reflected the population at that time. Nonetheless, the gender disparity would be a limitation in generalizing the results to other college campuses. Finally, Neal reported what participants were told so that readers could evaluate whether any sort of bias or demand characteristics might have affected the results (see Heppner et al., 1999, for a discussion of participant bias).

Typically, describing your participants in much detail is difficult prior to actually conducting the study. However, your thesis/dissertation committee usually wants some information about the intended participants so they can evaluate this aspect of the study. In the next two examples, we present participants sections from both the thesis proposal and the completed thesis of Meifen Wei (1998) to illustrate differences between the two time periods.

DESCRIPTION OF PARTICIPANTS
FROM A THESIS PROPOSAL AND A COMPLETED THESIS

Participants (Thesis Proposal)

Based on power analysis (moderate level of intercorrelation among the three independent variables, anticipated regression weights, and desired power), participants will be approximately 40–50 counseling dyads at Youth Counseling Centers in Taiwan. The counselor demographic information will include sex, age, and previous counseling experience.

There are sixteen Youth Counseling Centers in Taiwan. Nine centers have a face-to-face interview service. The counselors are screened from a three-stage, 6-month pre-training. The counselors of the Youth Counseling Centers are volunteer counselors, primarily female, in ages ranging between 21–50 years old. Some of the counselors have counseling-related majors, but some do not; their educational levels include bachelor degree and above. The counselors are supervised by senior counselors in the Youth Counseling Centers and also participate in regular job training; they typically work at least 8 hours in individual counseling services each week.

Participants (Completed Thesis)

Participants were 30 counseling dyads from the (a) Youth Counseling Center (n = 24, 80%) and (b) College Counseling Center (n = 6, 20%) in Taiwan in 1996 (from January to December). Counselors consisted of 10 (33.3%) male and 20 (66.7%) female; 21 bachelor level, 7 master level, and 2 doctoral level. Half of the counselors received training in a counseling-related major; half had a non-related major. Ages ranged from 21–50 years of age (M = 32.21, SD = 8.15). The counselor counseling experience ranged from 5 months to 15 years (M = 3.8 years, SD = 4.6 years). Clients consisted of 5 (16.7%) males and 25 (83.3%) females; 6 (21.4%) had prior counseling experience and 22 (78.6%) had no counseling experience. Ages ranged from 14–47 years old (M = 25.46, SD = 9.40). (Wei, 1998, p. 13)

In this study, Wei focused on variables that would be associated with the working alliance in counseling dyads in Taiwan. Note that Wei simply indicated in her proposal the type of demographic characteristics for which she would collect information for both counselors and clients; subsequently, in the completed thesis, she reported the actual demographic data (e.g., the actual number of male and female counselors who participated in the study). Also note that she anticipated that her committee members probably would be unfamiliar with the participant pool (Youth Counseling Centers and their counselors in Taiwan), so she briefly described that pool within the participant sections in her proposal. Subsequently, in the completed thesis, she described the counselors' training background and experience level to inform readers about this context. Thus, as this example illustrates, the participant descriptions will be quite general at the proposal stage but very specific at the defense stage.

The Sampling Method: Random or Nonrandom?

As we indicated earlier, many issues can arise regarding how you can obtain a representative sample from a larger population (see Heppner et al., 1999). In the methods chapter, however, your purpose is not to discuss all the sampling design issues but, rather, to describe what method you are using to obtain your sample. Consider the following examples:

RANDOM SELECTION OF PARTICIPANTS

A systematic random sample will be drawn from a list of all psychologists who have been licensed in the state of Missouri for ten years or more. The sample will be obtained from a research center specializing in the distribution of selected sampling lists. A table of random numbers will be used to locate the initial sampling pool. Every 25th person will be selected such that an initial group of 450 will be obtained. These persons will be mailed the questionnaires. (Shoyer, 1997, proposal)

NONRANDOM SELECTION

A nonrandom sample of 200 participants derived from asking professors at two universities for permission to recruit in their classes will be used in the current investigation. The battery of instruments will be administered to select undergraduate and graduate level classes at the University of Missouri, which is a predominately White institution, and at Lincoln University, which is a historically Black institution. Approximately equal numbers of participants will be solicited at the two institutions. (Browne, 1997, proposal)

The strength of random selection is that it tends to reduce sampling biases and thus increases the generalizability of the results to the larger population. There is no easy way of assuring that the obtained random sample indeed will be representative of the target pool or larger population. Note that obtaining randomly selected samples is difficult and often not accomplished. Conversely, the distinct disadvantage of nonrandom selection, as in the latter example, is that it is difficult to know how representative the obtained sample is of the participant pool and target population. For example, if the professors who were asked to recruit in their classes all taught advanced courses in ceramics, the sample might well not be representative of the larger university population. Subsequently, in nonrandom selection, be careful how you select participants and take steps to increase representativeness of the sample. The latter example does attempt to sample both African American students and White students in order to generalize to these two groups. In general, you should attend to both race/ethnicity and gender in sampling whenever possible (see Ponterotto & Casas, 1991).

Sample Homogeneity versus Heterogeneity

Heterogeneous populations have advantages because they contain great variability of characteristics, whereas homogeneous populations are limited in the extent to which they can be generalized. But heterogeneous populations have problems too, such as the extent the results can safely generalize to the subgroups within the population. For example, perhaps you want to examine the role of collective self-esteem in predicting psychological distress in African Americans. The person wants a diverse sample of college students and adults. She is able to collect from a historically Black college, a Black Baptist church in the community, and the local minimum-security prison. Thus, there is great heterogeneity: socioeconomic status, social class, education, religiosity, gender, age, and a host of other factors vary in this population. However, the various subgroups (e.g., prison inmates) may be too small (n = 15) to adequately allow separate analysis on these subgroups.

Representing Underrepresented Groups

Racial and ethnic minorities and other underrepresented groups have not been included in studies in substantial enough numbers to be able to generalize about them in any meaningful way. The vast majority of the previous research in counseling and clinical psychology is based on White participants or participants of otherwise unspecified race/ethnicity. Whether our findings can generalize to members of racial and ethnic minority populations remains an unanswered question in many areas of research. Remember that you are now contributing to the knowledge base of your profession, and you can contribute to enhancing its generalizability to help clarify where there are similarities and differences related to racial and ethnic status. Additional steps are often required to enhance the ethnic and racial diversity of a sample, such as oversampling of racial and ethnic minority group members to achieve representativeness; this takes time, energy, and commitment and, in some areas of the United States, may be difficult, although not impossible, to do. Given the growing numbers of racial and ethnic minorities, as well as other underrepresented groups in the United States (e.g., gay, lesbian, bisexual, different religious orientations, persons with disabilities, etc.), our research must be generalized to these groups. We encourage you to consider how your study can be made more representative of diverse individuals to which you want to generalize your results. Brainstorm with your peers and advisor concerning how you might gain access to diverse individuals. You may need to form new connections with people in order to be able to access nondominant populations. Also be thinking about ways of giving back to these communities so that they can experience some direct benefits of your research.

Number of Participants: How Many Do I Need?

Perhaps the most asked question when students are planning their theses or dissertations is: "How many participants will I need?" More specifically, the question is: "How many participants will I need to find an effect if indeed a true effect exists?" People use three primary ways of making this decision: general rules of thumb, past studies, and power analysis.

For certain types of statistical analysis, *rules of thumb* have developed that can serve as a very rough guide (e.g., 15 participants to a cell in a factorial design, 10 participants for each variable in multiple regression). You can find these sorts of guidelines in research design and statistical textbooks. However, these are really rough estimates and, given the intricacies of your specific research question, these rules may indicate far too many or far too few participants for your particular study. A major determinant of how many participants you will need is the strength of the relationship between the variables of interest in your study. When a treatment is extraordinarily effective, the effect of the treatment is easy to detect. For example, if a cognitive treatment of depression reduces self-deprecating statements from an average of 20 an hour to zero, achieving a statistically significant finding with a small number of participants is likely. If, however, the treatment reduces self-deprecating statements from 20 to 18 an hour, finding a treatment effect will be more difficult (if a treatment effect really exists) and you will need many more participants. Thus, using the general rules of thumb can provide some general guidelines but they have limited effectiveness.

Another way of determining an appropriate sample size is by examining *past studies* that are similar to the one you will be doing and examining the number of participants in those studies. This is particularly useful if you have coded your articles (see Chapter 4) and are able to find studies that used similar constructs to the one you are proposing. The following is an excerpt from a dissertation proposal that uses previous research for determining the sample size.

> The number of participants needed for this study will be determined by comparing this study's sample size to past sample sizes used in similar research studies. Among research studies whose sample sizes will be compared include studies (a) that examined session impact events and working alliance ratings, (b) with adolescents and (c) that utilized hierarchical linear modeling and time-series analysis as the primary statistical analysis. . . . Given these comparative studies it appears that a moderate sample size of 45 to 60 over a moderate time frame of 4 to 10 sessions would provide sufficient power to test the current hypotheses. (Ji, 1998, proposal)

A third and more precise method of determining the necessary number of participants is by doing a statistical procedure called a *power analysis*. The purpose of a power analysis is to determine how many participants will be needed to detect the effects due to the independent variable, if differences in fact exist. In order to conduct a power analysis, you need to know the (a) effect size of the variables of interest achieved in previous studies similar to your own (the effect size is typically categorized as small, medium, or large); (b) type of statistical analyses you will utilize; and (c) alpha level, or statistical significance level, you will be using in your study. In general, the more participants you use, the more power you have to find an effect (if it is indeed present). The level of power, which is expressed as a probability (e.g., .80), means that with a certain sample size, you will be able to detect differences, if they in fact exist, 80% of the time. Obviously you do not want to conduct your study if the probability is small (e.g., 10%) that you will find any differences (if they really do exist).

Unfortunately, in applied research, the chance of finding a true effect is often very small; if the results are not statistically significant, the researcher is in a quandary, not knowing if the lack of significant findings was the result of reality (no differences really exist) or was due to insufficient power to detect the effect. So the process is to search the previous literature on your topic and obtain estimates of the effect size of your independent variable; the effect size is basically how much variance is accounted for by the independent variable on the dependent variable, or strength of association. Then, select the alpha level, as well as the type of statistical analysis, using various tables (e.g., Cohen, 1988) to determine how many participants will provide varying levels of power. A power level of .8 is customarily used, although it is arbitrary (see Heppner et al., 1999, for more details). A power analysis is typically presented as in the following example:

> On the basis of earlier research by Heppner, Good, et al. (1995) and Heppner, Humphrey, et al. (1995), the effect sizes for the interventions were estimated and used to determine the number of participants needed for a moderate effect size for each group to attain an adequate power level of .80. Through this analysis, it was estimated that approximately 14–16 participants were needed per group to retain an adequate level of power of 80. (Heppner et al., 1999)

Computer programs are available that can help to simplify power analysis procedures. However, the more complex your hypotheses and statistical analyses, the more difficult it will be to effectively conduct a power analysis.

INSTRUMENTS

At this point, you have most likely identified the constructs of interest for your study and you have operationalized the constructs by selecting specific variables and specific instruments that best assess those variables. In the instrumentation section, the basic task is to describe the psychometric adequacy of the instruments in your study. Typically, 11 points should be included in the description of each instrument, roughly in the following order: (a) instrument name, (b) acronym, (c) author(s), (d) key reference(s), (e) a brief description of the construct the instrument assesses, (f) number of items, (g) type of items (e.g., Likert format), (h) factors or subscales and their definitions, (i) indication of the direction of scoring and what a high score means, (j) reliability estimates, and (k) validity estimates. These 11 points are the essential elements of an inventory. In a proposal meeting, your thesis or dissertation committee will examine this information to evaluate the strengths and weaknesses of each instrument.

Although all 11 points provide useful information, the estimates of reliability and validity are perhaps the most critical. If an instrument has poor estimates of reliability and validity, then the operationalization of the construct is likely to be inadequate (see Heppner et al., 1999, for more technical information about reliability and validity). Basically, *reliability* pertains to consistency between measurements at different time intervals; more technically, reliability is the variance in scores due to true differences among individuals. The two primary ways of reporting reliability are alpha coefficients (for internal consistency estimates) and test-retest correlations (for stability estimates). Internal consistency refers to the homogeneity of items. How well do items that are designed to measure the same construct hold together in a scale? Generally speaking, alpha coefficients should be above .7 at a minimum. The alpha coefficient is the most used measure of internal consistency. Split-half reliability correlation coefficients can also be used where the scores derived from one-half of the items are correlated with the scores derived from the other half of the items. When scores are dichotomous (correct/incorrect, true/false) then the Kuder-Richardson-20 is most often used and reported. Test-retest correlations reflect the stability of a person's scores on the same inventory over time. If a construct is expected to remain stable over a period of time, then test-retest correlations should be high. Test-retest reliability is most often collected over a period of 2 to 3 weeks on a sample size of at least 40 participants. In all cases, you should report the time interval to inform the reader of the time frame. Whereas a test-retest correlation of .6 over 2 weeks is problematic, a correlation of .6 over two years is impressive. If possible, report estimates of reliability from samples demographically similar to the population you are studying (e.g., adolescents).

Validity pertains to accurately assessing the construct that the inventory purports to measure (see Heppner et al., 1999, for more details). Of the many types of validity, probably the most important is construct validity, or the degree to which the scores reflect the construct you are trying to measure. We briefly note three strategies to establish construct validity. One strategy is to correlate two instruments that are intended to measure very similar things; if there is a high correlation, that is *convergent validity*. Instruments that are intended to measure quite different constructs should not relate to each other; if small correlations are found, then this information provides an estimate of *discriminant validity*. Another way to establish the construct validity of a scale is through the statistical procedure called *factor analysis*. Items that measure the same constructs will group together or load on the same factors. The factors are then interpreted as constructs. If the measure you are using for your thesis or dissertation has not been validated with the same population proposed in your study, factor analysis may be suggested to ensure that the factor structure is the same for your unique sample. A related issue is whether the instrument you are planning to use for your study has cultural validity for the specific group of people you are using. Some constructs or items may be perceived quite differently because of the sociocultural differences in various groups, particularly racial and ethnic minority groups. If you think this may be the case for your sample, you may also try using pilot groups in which you receive feedback on the scale, or items in the scale, before administering it to your entire sample.

Examine the following examples of instrument descriptions from several students' theses and dissertations. As you read, compare and contrast the descriptions, as each of them has a slightly different style.

DESCRIPTIONS OF INSTRUMENTS

The Collective Self-Esteem Scale

Collective self-esteem was measured by the race-specific version of the Collective Self-Esteem Scale (Luhtanen & Crocker, 1991). This scale consists of 16 Likert items that are represented on a 7-point continuum (1 = strongly disagree, 7 = strongly agree) with higher scores indicating greater CSE. The CSES includes four subscales: (a) Membership Esteem, which assesses an individual's belief about how worthy [he or she is] as a member of [his or her] social group, (b) Private Esteem, which assesses one's personal belief about how good one's social group is, (c) Public Esteem, which assesses one's judgment of how positively others evaluate one's social group, and (d) Importance to Identity, which assesses the importance of one's social group to one's self-concept. Each of these subscales contains four items. Coefficient alphas for the race-specific version were .75 for the Membership subscale, .72 for the Private subscale, .88 for the Public subscale, and .84 for the Identity subscale (Crocker et al., 1994).

The Collective Self-Esteem Scale has been found to correlate with several other measures. These include (a) a moderate positive correlation with the Individualism-Collectivism Scale (Hui, 1988), and (b) a small positive correlation with the personal, collective, and social aspects of the Aspects of Identity Questionnaire III (Cheek, Underwood, & Cutler, 1985). In addition, all of the subscales except Identity were found to be moderately correlated with internal and environmental orientation (Internal Orientation Scale; Sampson, 1978), and with the Individualization Scale, (Maslach, Stapp, & Santee, 1985). When correlating this measure with the Social Desirability Scale (Crowne & Marlowe, 1964) no correlation was found. Although no test-retest data has been cited for the race-specific version of the CSES, test-retest data for the general version was reported as .68 over a 6-week period (Luhtanen & Crocker, 1992). (Browne, 1997, proposal)

The Problem-Solving Inventory

[The Problem-Solving Inventory] (PSI; Heppner & Peterson, 1982; see Appendix A) is an instrument that assesses individuals' perceptions of their problem-solving behavior. It consists of 32 six-point Likert scale items, where low scores indicate behaviors and attitudes typically associated with "effective" problem solving. Since the PSI is a self-rating questionnaire, scores should not be considered synonymous with subjects' actual level of problem-solving skills (Heppner, 1988). Factor analysis has revealed three distinct constructs: problem-solving confidence (11 items), approach-avoidance style (16 items), and personal control (5 items). Reliability estimates revealed that the constructs were internally consistent (.72–.90; N = 150) and stable over a 2-week period (.83–.89; N = 31). In addition to the three factor scores, a total PSI score is used as a single, general index of problem-solving appraisal. Initial estimates of validity suggested the instrument is measuring constructs that are (a) amenable to change through specific skill training in problem solving, (b) related to general self-perceptions of problem solving, (c) related to personality variables, most notably locus of control, (d) unrelated to conceptualizing the means to solving a hypothetical problem situation, and (e) unrelated to intelligence or social desirability (Heppner & Petersen, 1982). Research has indicated that high PSI scorers (self-appraised "ineffective" problem solvers) and low PSI scorers (self-appraised "effective" problem solvers) differ significantly on self-ratings of motivation to solve problems, expectations of success, the importance of ability and effort, avoidance, systematicity, and interpersonal trust (Heppner et al., 1982). Interviewers (who were blind to subjects' PSI scores) rated the two groups as significantly different in terms of effort, awareness social skills, anxiety, and insightfulness, and correctly identified subjects as either high or low PSI scorers in 33 out of 40 cases (Heppner et al., 1982). (Neal, 1983, pp. 49–50)

The Reynolds Adolescent Depression Scale

The RADS (Reynolds, 1986) is a 30-item measure with a 4-point Likert-type response format that measures the severity of depressive symptoms in adolescents in four domains: cognitive, motoric-vegetative, somatic, and interpersonal. The response choices are Almost Never, Hardly Ever, Sometimes, or Most of the Time, with higher scores indicating greater endorsement of depression symptoms. A sample item reads, "I feel that no one cares about me." Seven items are inconsistent with depression and are reverse-scored. Internal reliability coefficients range from .91 to .94. Internal reliability in the current study is .88. Test-retest reliability coefficients, expected to be moderate for a state construct, were .80 and .79 after 6 weeks and 3 months respectively, and .63 after 1 year. Extensive validation of the RADS is presented by Reynolds (1986), including content validity; criterion-related validity in the form of concurrent validity; construct validity as evaluated by convergent, discriminant, and factorial validity; and clinical validity. For example, the RADS has been shown to have high positive correlations (most greater than .70) with measures of adult depression such as the Beck Depression Inventory and the Center for Epidemiological Studies Depression Scale. (Llorens, 1998, pp. 65–66)

First, note how efficiently some of the descriptions provide information about all 11 of the key points, such as the Collective Self-Esteem Scale by Browne. Also note the difference in length between what was a new inventory described by Neal in 1982—the PSI—and a well-established scale—the RADS—described by Llorens. With a well-developed and widely used scale (e.g., the MMPI), referring readers to sources that have compiled psychometric information about the scale is more appropriate than trying to summarize 100 or more investigations. However, with a newer scale, providing considerably more details for readers is often helpful.

Also note that students often include the inventories in an appendix. This is often very helpful for members of the committee to study the items of the inventories. We strongly recommend this practice for proposal meetings and for inclusion in the final thesis or dissertation.

PROCEDURES

Data Collection

The procedures section should describe chronologically the exact steps for all phases of the study, from preliminary pilot testing to contacting participants and administering the instruments or the interventions. Note any ethical issues and how you will deal with them. Typically, the procedures section should have a great deal of detail, although the length will vary depending on the type of study. Some of the needed protocols or manualized interventions can be referred to in the appendixes, but basically the procedures should be carefully described in the procedures section. When your procedures are complex, a time-line chart might be useful in describing them. For example, describe how the sample was derived, what participants were told about the study, the manner in which the participants will be protected from harm and informed about their rights, if any incentives or rewards were offered, any interventions that were used, how data were collected, the order that instruments were administered, what time periods elapsed between events, any training of experimenters or assistants, or any pilot or preliminary work that was conducted. In essence, all aspects of the study need to be documented so that another investigator could replicate the procedures of the study in the same chronological order.

The following excerpts from four procedures sections from students' theses or dissertations not only serve as concrete examples but also highlight issues commonly encountered with different types of procedures. The first example provides a model of a procedures section from a survey study:

PROCEDURE
Data Collection
A roster of 163 masters and doctoral level practicing psychologists and their employment addresses in the Columbia and Jefferson City areas was compiled to serve as a list of potential participants. Compilation of this list occurred through combining information from area phone books, referral guides, telephone calls, and Internet search. Potential participants were mailed a letter of inquiry. This letter of inquiry (a) described the study and its potential benefits to the profession, (b) clearly stated that responses would be anonymous, (c) described what participation would entail, and (d) requested the recipients' participation in the study. In addition, the letter described an expression of appreciation and incentive for participation consisting of a $100 raffle for all participants who returned a raffle entry card separate from their completed data packet. A copy of this letter can be found in Appendix F.

Respondents were asked to call or email the principal investigator within 1 week of receiving the letter of inquiry if they were not willing to participate in the study. This method was chosen because of the potential expense of mailing a study packet to all potential participants regardless of their willingness to participate. Six letters of inquiry were returned marked "address unknown," and six people were not eligible for participation, bringing the potential sample size down to 151. Fifteen of these potential participants declined to participate in the study and were immediately taken off the mailing list.

The remaining 137 potential participants were mailed a study packet consisting of a cover letter (Appendix G), a consent form (Appendix H), the study measures, a postage-paid return postcard for participation in the raffle, and a request to return the completed packet within 2 weeks of receipt. Again, potential participants were assured that their participation would be anonymous. A reminder letter was sent to potential participants at approximately weeks 2 and 4 following the mailing of the study packet. A copy of this letter is found in Appendix I. Included in the reminder letter was a request to call the principle investigator if there were any questions and/or if a second study packet was needed. After two reminder letters, 89 eligible study packets were returned to the principle investigator representing 59% of the total eligible sample of potential participants. (Shoyer, 1998, pp. 63–64)

This description by Shoyer (1998) aptly captures many relevant details, and the actual letters in the appendixes allow the readers to examine them for additional details if necessary. One major problem with conducting a survey study is difficulty in obtaining a response from the majority of the participants; if for example, only 25% of the sample respond, the generalizability of the results is questionable because the vast majority of the sample did not respond. Typically, approximately 30% of the sample responds to a well-developed survey during the first mailing (see Heppner et al., 1999, for more details on conducting survey studies). Note that the use of follow-up reminder letters typically boosts the return rate approximately 10% with each reminder.

The following is a procedure section from a correlational study using counterbalancing; the primary activity involved data collection from groups of African American college students from two universities.

Procedure

Permission was secured from both universities to use their students as human participants in the investigation. The various independent and dependent measures previously described were counterbalanced in order to decrease the possibility of order effects.

Data collection was conducted in two methods. In method 1, used at the predominately African American university, instructors of undergraduate courses were asked to allow data to be collected in their classes. Following their approval, a female research assistant attended these classes to collect the data. Upon arriving at the classes, the research assistant informed the students that they had the option of participating in the study but they were not required to do so. If the students agreed to participate in the study, they were asked to complete a consent form. After this they were told (a) that they would be completing measures that dealt with how they felt about themselves, others, and how this affected their psychological functioning, (b) who would be conducting the study, and (c) approximately how long it would take (20–30 minutes). If they did not have any questions, they then received a packet from the researcher and were instructed to begin.

In method 2, used at the predominately White university, students from general psychology classes voluntarily signed up to be participants in the investigation and were given credit from their instructors. Upon arriving at the research site at the appointed time, they were then given the same instructions as the students from the other university.

Upon collection of these scales, the previously signed consent form was collected from the participants. Following this, they received a debriefing form stating a more detailed description of the study (See Appendix B). (Browne, 1997, proposal)

Note in this example the counterbalancing of the instruments used by Browne. This is a good strategy for later checking if the order of presenting the instruments affected participants' responses, particularly due to participant fatigue if a number of instruments were being used. Also note that Browne provided a debriefing form to enhance the educational experience of participating in the study.

The following extract is from a procedure section of a study that focused on developing a new inventory to assess expectations of Taiwanese parents as perceived by college students. A critical aspect of a psychometric study is the development of the items, which is the focus of this excerpt.

INSTRUMENT CONSTRUCTION

Item Development

The following criteria guided the construction of the items. All items had to be related to Chinese/Taiwanese parental expectations. Each item had to focus on the current college students' experience of perceived parental expectations. The development of the items consisted of at least four different activities, all of which resulted in deletions of, additions to, and refinements of the items: (a) identification of domains and initial items, (b) a small pilot study to examine basic testing procedures and items in general, (c) a back translation to test the face validity of the items' relationship to the domains, and (d) an intensive pilot procedure to assess item performance and specific wording. In order to develop items, the author reviewed previous studies on this topic, discussed the topic with other international students from Taiwan, and then identified the following five domains of parental expectation for further examination: dating/marriage, character training, academic achievement, responsibility for parents, and responsibility for family. Fifteen items were developed for each domain. In total, 75 items were placed in random order to minimize response set biases.

Dawis (1987) recommended the use of a small pilot study before the primary data collection procedures to determine how easily the directions are followed, how long the instrument takes to complete, and, especially, how appropriate the items are for the target population. The 75 items were tested with eight international undergraduate students from Taiwan who not only responded to each item but also provided feedback indicating whether each item was related to their personal experience and whether there was any confusion in the wording.

Finally, in order to clarify semantic issues, simplify wording, and improve the validity of the inventory, as suggested by Dawis (1987), an intensive pilot study with a large group was conducted. One hundred ten undergraduate students (48.2% male; 51.8% female) in Taiwan participated in this pilot study. Before completing the pilot inventory, participants were asked to write down three of the most frequently perceived parental expectations; after completing the pilot items, participants were asked to provide their feedback to revise the inventory. Coefficient alphas indicated very good internal consistency for the three subscales (alphas ranged from .93 to .94). In addition, the mean of the items was examined. Items were omitted if their means were extreme (over 5.0 or less than 2.0); if the item-total correlation was below .20, or if their omission caused alpha to increase (Meir & Gati, 1981). Subsequently, 62 items were selected and included in the final version of the Discrepancy of Parental Expectation Inventory (DPEI).

Data-Collection Procedures

College students in Taiwan were recruited to complete the 62-item DPEI. The personal information solicited on the instruction sheet included gender, age, years in college, and type of college. Specifically, in order to represent college student populations in Taiwan, college students from three different types of college/university settings in mid-Taiwan were recruited: medical college/university, teacher college/university, and general university. Four class instructors following written instructions administered the inventory. Specifically, the instructor read a brief introduction of the research procedure and verbally requested students' consent to be in the study. In reading the instructions, the instructor stressed the voluntary nature of the study. After verbally agreeing to be in the study, participants were told that they were participating in a study regarding perceived parental expectations and their self-performance. The participants took about 30–45 minutes to complete the questionnaires. When all participants finished the questionnaire, they were informed as to the purpose of the study, invited to ask questions, and given credits toward fulfilling their course requirement. (Wang, 1995, pp. 37–40)

Note that Wang carefully specified the criteria she used in developing the items to define the parameters of the items; specifying such criteria helps readers understand the parameters of the items. Next she described the activities she engaged in to develop the items; developing good items takes a great deal of time and usually is enhanced by obtaining feedback from colleagues, as well as piloting the items to polish the wording, identify confusing items, and clarify instructions. The back translation is an excellent check for the face validity of each item and coverage of the intended domain. Wang also engaged in an excellent step of conducting a large pilot study with a sample from her intended population, not only to see if all instructions and items were clear but also to do a preliminary examination of how the items perform. Note that Wang subsequently omitted some items because they failed to differentiate respondents. Sometimes researchers will substitute additional items at this stage. Note that it takes a great deal of time and energy to develop good items, and, generally speaking, it is hard to be overly obsessive at this point. With regard to Wang's data collection, note her strategy to obtain data from three types of universities in Taiwan, which would tend to increase the generalizability of her results to the target population of Taiwanese college students. Sometimes problems can arise if different instructions are given to different groups, so Wang prepared written instructions that were read to students in all groups, thereby increasing the probability that students received the same instructions.

Conducting research on actual counseling presents a number of challenges. The following excerpt of a procedure section details the anticipated procedures for a counseling process study conducted across multiple sites.

PROCEDURE

The investigator will send the research proposal and a cover letter (see Appendix F) to the director of the Department of Counseling, Youth Counseling Centers, to explain the purpose of this study. The director of the Research Division of the Department of Counseling will help the investigator encourage three to four centers to participate in this study and explain the purpose and procedure of this study (see Appendix G) to the full-time counselor at each center. Following agreement, the full-time counselor of these centers will explain the general purpose of the study to their volunteer-counselors, specifically exploring the process of counseling. Ten to twenty counselors will be encouraged to voluntarily participate in this study at each counseling center. Counselors who agree to participate will be asked to sign the consent form (see Appendix H), provide some demographic information, and complete the PSI inventory before or after their first interview. It will take about 10–15 minutes.

When the clients come to the counseling center, the full-time counselor will inform clients about the purpose of the study and encourage clients to participate in the intake interview. Clients who agree to participate will be asked to sign the consent form (see Appendix I), provide some demographic information, and complete EAC-B, CRF-S, and WAI-S inventories. Clients will complete the EAC-B (pretest) in the interview room before the first session. The procedure will take about 5–10 minutes. After the first session, the full-time counselor will give the client EAC-B (posttest), CRF-S, and WAI-S questionnaires to be completed in the interview room. This will take about 15–25 minutes. All assessment protocols will be administered and collected by the full-time counselors, sent to the director of the Research Division of the Department of Counseling, and finally forwarded to the researcher. A code number written on the outside of the questionnaire package will identify clients and counselors. The clients' code numbers will be the same as their counselors'. All information that is collected will remain confidential; it will clearly state that neither member of the counseling dyad will share the information nor will they be used in the counseling session in any way. Both counselors and clients will receive a debriefing sheet (see Appendix J) and will be thanked for their participation after they complete the inventories. They can leave their name and address if they are interested in knowing the results. The researcher will send a "research abstract" to them after the research is finished. (Wei, 1997, proposal)

Note how Wei arranged to have a person at each participating center assume major responsibility for supervising the data collection. Having someone overseeing data collection at the site is very important because many things can and do go wrong in data collection during a process study [believe us!!]. Note also that Wei utilized code numbers to identify clients and counselors so as to maintain anonymity of people's responses should an accident occur and the questionnaires be lost. Finally, note that Wei used the future tense, which is the norm on proposal drafts of theses and dissertations.

Internet Data-Collection Procedures

The last decade has seen the advent of the possibility for students to conduct their thesis or dissertation data collection on the Internet. Several important advantages to this type of data collection are (a) access to a much larger, more diverse sample; (b) data collection can be completed online, coded, and saved to data files greatly saving on researcher time; (c) greater potential inclusion of difficult-to-access samples through specialized Web sites; (d) data can be collected at any time day or night; (e) increased access to cross-cultural samples that may reside in other countries where actual travel may be prohibited.

Some special concerns with Internet-based data collection include participants who respond multiple times. Internet data collection is not feasible for studies that require actual contact (intervention studies). In addition, a much greater likelihood of self-selection bias exists in Internet samples. Also, Internet data-collection methodologies may be particularly susceptible to participants who supply incorrect data in order to sabotage the research (Schmidt, 1997). Nonetheless, Internet research has been steadily growing since its inception in 1995. As more techniques become refined and more researchers learn this methodology, the research grows in rigor. While a description of how to conduct Internet-based data collection is beyond the scope of this book, some good references include Birnbaum (2000, 2001) and Schmidt (1997).

When data collection has occurred on the Internet this should be discussed specifically in the methods chapter. Following is the methods section from a recent investigation that used the Internet to collect data on attitudes toward bisexuality (Mohr & Rochlen, 1999). Note how Mohr and Rochlen take the reader step by step through their procedures from the initial email message through how they attempted to control for nonvalid responding.

PROCEDURE

The study was announced in an electronic-mail (email) message that was sent to lesbian and gay student organizations at 26 universities in the United States and Canada. The message described the study as an investigation of lesbians' and gay men's attitudes toward bisexual women and men. Individuals interested in participating were directed to an address on the World Wide Web (WWW) where they could access the online survey. Participants were first given an informed consent sheet that explained that transmission of survey data via the Internet is not secure and that complete confidentiality of the data could therefore not be ensured. Participants were told, however, that confidentiality was guaranteed once the data had been received by the researchers. Participants who agreed with the informed consent statement (agreement was indicated by clicking on text reading "I have read this page, and I would like to take the survey") were given the survey, which included the original pool of 80 ARBS items and a short demographic information form. No identifying information was collected, but participants were given the option of including their email address if they wished to receive a summary of the research findings. Participants who wished to receive a summary of the findings but who did not want to disclose their email address were given a WWW address on which the summary would be posted. After completing the survey, participants were given a debriefing sheet that explained the hypotheses of the study. They were also given contact information for Jonathan Mohr.

A total of 276 individuals completed the survey. Three of these individuals submitted their completed surveys twice. As recommended by Schmidt (1997) and Smith and Leigh (1997), duplicate surveys were identified using the date, time, and origin of submission; the email address of the respondent; and inspection of the survey data for identical responses. One survey from each pair of duplicate surveys was eliminated from the data set. Because of the focus on lesbian and gay male participants, we analyzed data from only those participants who identified themselves as being "mostly homosexual" or "exclusively homosexual" on a 5-point scale of sexual orientation identity (1 = *exclusively heterosexual*, 2 = *mostly heterosexual*, 3 = *bisexual*, 4 = *mostly homosexual*, 5 = *exclusively homosexual*). Thus, data from 21 bisexual-identified individuals were not included in our analyses.

Schmidt (1997) noted that WWW-based survey methodologies are particularly susceptible to respondents who intentionally supply incorrect survey data to undermine the research. This danger may be especially great when conducting lesbian, gay, and bisexual (LGB) research because of the pervasive societal intolerance about LGB issues. Furthermore, because the survey-taking environments of WWW users are highly variable, respondents may supply incorrect data because of inattentiveness and distractions. We used two strategies to reduce the chances of including incorrect data in our analyses. First, we limited the announcement of the study to a venue in which hostile antigay individuals would not be expected to learn of the study. Second, we included a "validity check" item in the WWW surveys designed to identify individuals who were either inattentive or randomly responding to survey items. The item was "Please do not respond to this item." Data from four participants who incorrectly responded to this item were not analyzed. (pp. 355–356, with permission from American Psychological Association.)

STATISTICAL ANALYSES

The methods chapter of a thesis or dissertation proposal typically contains a section that describes the data analyses that will be used to test the hypotheses. This information is only in the methods chapter of the proposal; in your final dissertation or thesis, this information will be contained in the results chapter. You should carefully consider each of the hypotheses and the respective statistical analyses. Doing so can save you the pain of collecting data that are subsequently not useful or at least cumbersome because the form of the data does not match the hypotheses.

This may be an anxiety-producing activity for you; even though you may have done well in your statistics courses, you may find it much more difficult to apply what you have learned to your own research. This is a critical time to become aware of and cope with your fears. Too many students avoid thinking specifically about their analyses at the proposal stage and subsequently have much more difficulty after their data are collected and they are ready to actually conduct their data analyses. Just remember that even though many students in the social and behavioral sciences have fears and anxieties related to the statistical analyses portions of their thesis or dissertation, numerous ways are available to get help in this arena. Having a clear plan of action for analyzing your data may help you to feel calmer and in control. Conversely, avoiding a clear plan often adds to the stress. We encourage you to monitor your feelings and thoughts during this part of your study. If you hear yourself saying, "I am never going to be able to figure this out" or "I am going to try to avoid putting anything in my proposal about my analyses and hope no one notices," stop and change those self-defeating messages. Do some more reading; talk with your advisor, other faculty, and peers who have knowledge of statistics. From our experience, most all graduate students are capable of mastering the statistical aspects of their thesis or dissertation.

At the point of writing your proposal, carefully write each of your hypotheses (see Chapter 5) and then determine the statistical analysis that would be most appropriate to test each of them. A number of tools can help you do this. For example, most textbooks include charts that help you determine what might be the most appropriate statistical technique for different types of data. One such chart from the Tabachnik and Fidell (1989) text is shown in Table 7.1 (see pages 130–131). Once you have determined your independent and dependent variables for each hypothesis, you can use the chart to guide your decisions for appropriate statistical analyses. This is also a good time to consult with your advisor about ways of analyzing your data. You may also find it helpful to consult with statistically minded peers for additional help and suggestions. If you have conducted a thorough literature review and coded the articles by type of statistical analysis, you will be able to use the articles as models as you develop your own statistical analysis section.

Remember, however, that, like many other sections of a thesis or dissertation, the data analysis portion is rarely a linear activity. Although you may have a very clear plan of what statistical analyses you will use to test each hypothesis, the reality is that many times data are analyzed in a number of different ways to try to understand the underlying relationships among them. Sometimes, for example, the number of participants you propose in your thesis or dissertation is different from what you will actually obtain. For example, one of our students found that she had sufficient numbers of participants to split her sample in half in order to be able to conduct not only an exploratory factor analysis (EFA) on one half of the participants but also a confirmatory factor analysis (CFA) on the other half of the participants; this addition of the CFA greatly added to the validity of the scale she was developing. Another student was able to obtain more African American participants than expected, so she was able to run separate subgroup analyses. Other times, the numbers of participants are less than anticipated and, thus, may dictate a change in the proposed statistical analyses. Other factors such as the distribution of scores (e.g., skewness) or the correlation among variables may affect your decisions about the type of statistical analyses needed. For example, other analyses may be helpful to conduct that you did not propose originally. Many times students will conduct their stated analyses and then think of other questions they want to examine. Sometimes when a hypothesis is not confirmed, students want to conduct additional analyses to more completely understand the data. Thus, although having a clear plan to guide your analyses is important, sometimes factors evolve that alter this original plan. Should this happen, be sure to consult with your advisor and members of your committee about the appropriateness of any changes you make in your analyses plan. Their major concern will probably be whether you have good conceptual, theoretical, or statistical reasons for doing alternative statistical analyses. Do not simply conduct more analyses in the hopes of getting significant findings. This practice seriously jeopardizes the scientific rigor and validity of your study.

Thus, for the proposal, a concise statement of how each of your primary hypotheses will be analyzed is sufficient. Unless you are using a nontraditional form of analysis with which your committee members may be unfamiliar, including a lengthy description of the analysis technique is not necessary. Following are examples of three analysis sections from thesis or dissertation proposals. Note the level of detail presented.

Example 1 of Analysis Section

For the four research questions and corresponding hypotheses, the research design was a 2 × 2 factorial multiple analysis of variance (MANOVA). The independent variable, personality type, was measured by the PSI and crossed extroversion-introversion with stability-change creating four categories, or personality types. Separate MANOVAs were run for Alcohol Expectancies (four dependent variables), Alcohol Consequences (three dependent variables), and Drinking Situations (two dependent variables).

In addition to the planned analyses, exploratory analyses were also conducted. Separate MANOVAs were run using the following independent variables with alcohol-related variables on the dependent measures, gender, race, year in school, residence, GPA, and parental drinking. (Towle, 1992, pp. 52–53)

Example 2 of Analysis Section

The research design was a descriptive survey design, intended to provide information about the nature of session impacts and the working alliance formed by veterans with and without PTSD. To describe the sample, continuous demographic variables were analyzed using t-tests. In addition, categorical demographic variables were analyzed using chi-square analyses. To test the significance of differences among means, a series of multivariate analyses of variance (MANOVAs) were performed. When significant differences were found between group means, univariate ANOVAs were performed to further define the differences. In addition, a correlation matrix was created to determine the relationships among dependent variables.

There were two levels of the single independent variable, namely PTSD and non-PTSD. There were 12 dependent variables. Three of these were measured by

TABLE 7.1 CHOOSING AMONG STATISTICAL TECHNIQUES

Major Research Question	Number of Dependent Variables	Number of Independent Variables	Covariates	Analytic Technique	Goal of Analysis
Degree of relationship among variables	One	One		Bivariate r	
		Multiple	None	Multiple R	Create a linear Combination of IVs to optimally predict DV
			Some	Hierarchical multiple R	
	Multiple	Multiple		Canonical R	Maximally correlate a linear combination of DVs with a linear combination of IVs
	None	Multiple [discrete]		Multiway frequency analysis	Create a loglinear combination of IVs to optimally predict category frequencies
	One [discrete]	Multiple [discrete]		Multiway frequency analysis [logit]	Create a loglinear combination of IVs to optimally predict DV

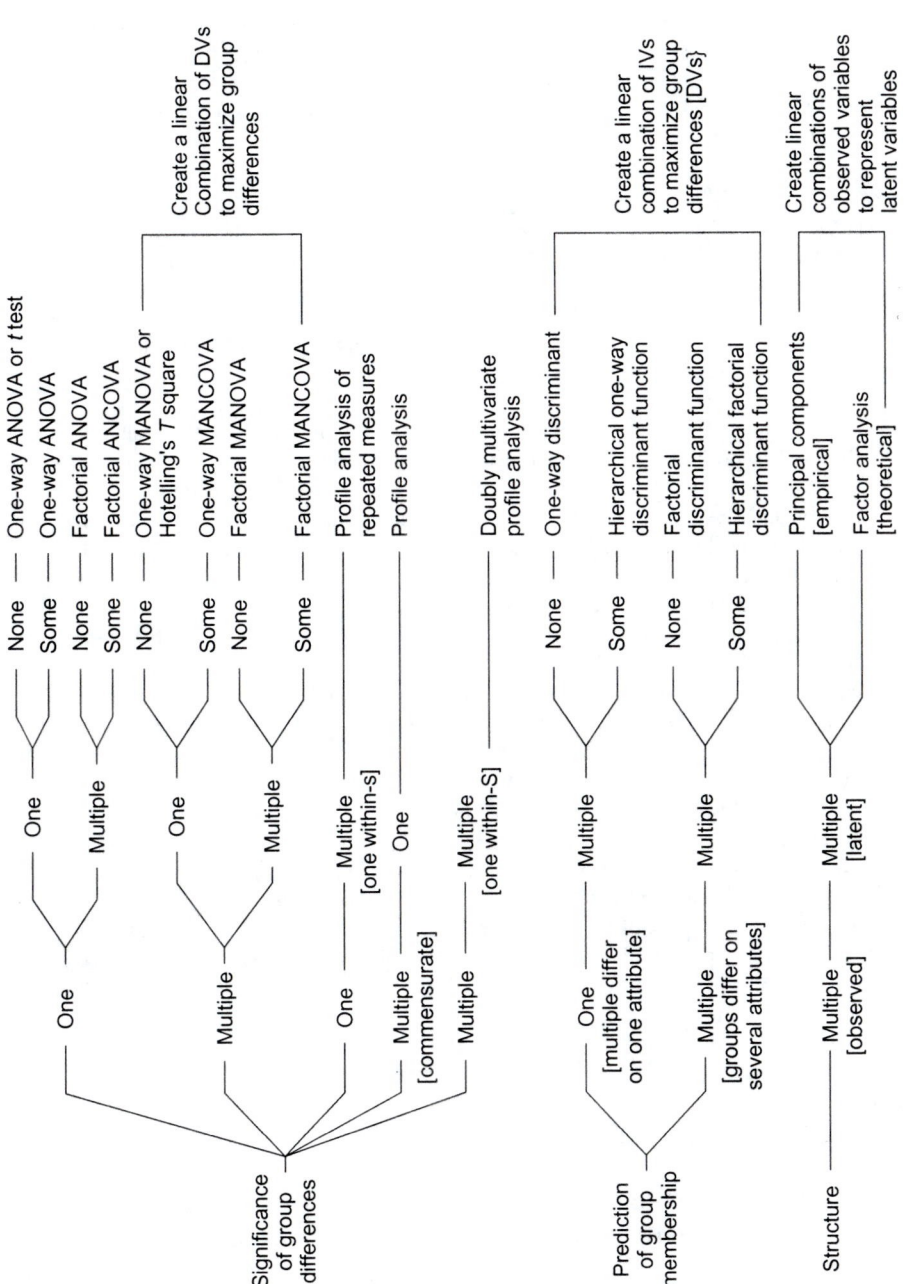

the SIS: Task Impacts, Relationship Impacts, and Hindering Impacts. Three were measured by the WAI-S: Tasks, Goals, and Bond. The remaining six were measured by the SDS: Realistic, Investigative, Artistic, Social, Enterprising, and Conventional.

Additional analyses consisted of two steps. First, Cronbach's alpha was computed to estimate the internal consistency of the SIS and the WAI-S for this population. Secondly, to determine the effects of key demographic variables on client responses, a series of chi-square analyses was conducted using Holland code and each of the following pieces of demographic information: race, marital status, work status, income level, previous education or training, disability rating, job tenure, job satisfaction, and PTSD. (Murray, 1997, p. 94)

Example 3 of Analysis Section

Preliminary data analyses were performed to estimate sample size for power, test for normality, and to obtain descriptive statistics on demographic information and each of the research variables. Preliminary analyses also employed a 2×2 multivariate analysis of variance (MANOVA) to test for significant differences in scores between questionnaire form (Form A vs. Form B), and location (learning center vs. detention). The dependent variables were total scores for the PSI, PGD, PA, SP, LOC, and the BDI.

Three major analyses were then performed in order to test the three research hypotheses. First, a canonical analysis was performed to test the hypothesis that measures of narcissistic vulnerability, locus of control, and depression are significantly related to scores of problem-solving appraisal in delinquents. PSI factor scores (control, approach-avoidance, problem-solving confidence) were used as one set of variables and the total scores on PGD, PA, SP, LOC, and the BDI were used as the other set of variables.

Second, Hotelling's T2 was used to test the hypothesis that repeat offenders score significantly higher than first-time offenders on measures of problem-solving appraisal, narcissistic vulnerability, locus of control, and depression. Hotelling's T2 is the analysis of choice for a one-way multivariate analysis of variance with two groups (Cohen, 1988). Offense status (repeat offenders vs. first-time offenders) was used as the independent variable and total scores on the PSI, PA, PGD, LOC, and the BDI were used as dependent variables.

Third, hierarchical regression analyses were employed to test the hypothesis that measures of narcissistic vulnerability (PA, PGD, SP), locus of control, and depression, respectively, significantly predict problem-solving appraisal in both first-time and repeat offenders. Separate analyses were employed for first-time offenders and repeat offenders. The total PSI score was used as the criterion variable and total scores on PGD, PA, SP, LOC and the BDI were used as predictor variables. (Perez, 1993, p. 51)

CONCLUSIONS

The methods chapter typically contains numerous details about exactly what students either propose to do or actually did in conducting their study. These details are important to understand how the study will be or was conducted, or to evaluate the instruments chosen for the study. Thus, faculty involved in the student's thesis or dissertation committee typically will attend to this chapter very carefully and almost always will ask questions about some aspect of the methods during the student's proposal meeting. It is therefore very functional for you to carefully think about the methods of your study and carefully write this section. Most important, the methods chapter communicates the essential details to evaluate, in part, the scientific rigor of the study.

CHECKLIST FOR CHAPTER 3 OF THE THESIS OR DISSERTATION

In this section we provide a scale to assess key elements we have discussed as being important in writing a methods chapter. We encourage you to use this scale when you have written a first draft of your methods chapter but before you have given it to your advisor or to a peer for review. By honestly assessing how well you have utilized these skills, you will be able to identify areas where your methods chapter could be strengthened. In short, we encourage you to critically evaluate the strengths and weaknesses of the writing of your methods chapter as you continue to work on refining it.

To What Extent Did You . . .

1. . . . Provide a basic road map to guide the reader through the methods?

1	2	3	4	5	6
Not at all				Very Much So	

2. . . . Include sections on participants, instruments, procedures, and analyses?

1	2	3	4	5	6
Not at all				Very much so	

3. . . . Cover the following issues in the participants section?
    a. Source of participants

1	2	3	4	5	6
Not at all				Very much so	

   b. Number of participants

1	2	3	4	5	6
Not at all				Very much so	

   c. How you arrived at the number of participants

1	2	3	4	5	6
Not at all				Very much so	

d. Information provided about whether this number will provide adequate power for the proposed analysis

1	2	3	4	5	6
Not at all				Very much so	

e. Information about attempts to improve the representiveness of the sample and thus its generalizability

1	2	3	4	5	6
Not at all				Very much so	

4. . . . Provide information on each of the following in the instrument description?

a. Name

1	2	3	4	5	6
Not at all				Very much so	

b. Acronym

1	2	3	4	5	6
Not at all				Very much so	

c. Authors

1	2	3	4	5	6
Not at all				Very much so	

d. Publication date

1	2	3	4	5	6
Not at all				Very much so	

e. What is measured

1	2	3	4	5	6
Not at all				Very much so	

f. Number of items

1	2	3	4	5	6
Not at all				Very much so	

g. Type of items (Likert)

1	2	3	4	5	6
Not at all				Very much so	

h. Factors and subscales

1	2	3	4	5	6
Not at all				Very much so	

    i. What a high score means

1	2	3	4	5	6
Not at all				Very much so	

    j. Reliability of the scale

1	2	3	4	5	6
Not at all				Very much so	

    k. Validity

1	2	3	4	5	6
Not at all				Very much so	

5. . . . Clearly describe the procedures used to conduct the study?

1	2	3	4	5	6
Not at all				Very much so	

6. . . . Use an appropriate level of specificity so that the study could be replicated?

1	2	3	4	5	6
Not at all				Very much so	

7. . . . Provide a concise description of the data analyses you will be using to test your hypotheses?

1	2	3	4	5	6
Not at all				Very much so	

QUALITATIVE METHODS

8

On the Road to Exploring the Unknown*

> Within the last century, Western science and physics have made a startling discovery. We are part of the world we view. The very process of our observation changes the things we observe . . . And the observer participates in that event by the very process of his or her observation. There is no way to avoid this interaction. Eastern science has recognized this basic principle for a very long time. The mind is a set of events, and the observer participates in those events every time he or she looks inward. Meditation is participatory observation. What you are looking at responds to the process of looking. What you are looking at is you, and what you see depends on how you look. (Mahathera, 1990, p. 22)

You may be wondering why the opening of this chapter talks about meditation. You are not reading the wrong chapter! This chapter discusses qualitative research methods. One of the common techniques utilized by some qualitative researchers is "participant observation." The quotation perfectly depicts the process of conducting participant observation and qualitative research. Why? When you meditate, you look into your own mind; therefore, you are playing the role of observer. At the same time, you also participate in the process of looking inward; if you are attached to and cling to certain thoughts, those thoughts will be what you see. Using an analogy, conducting qualitative research is a very similar process to meditation; that is, "what you see depends on how you look." The questions you ask your participants and the methods you utilize to observe certain phenomena are all "filtered" through the lenses of knowledge, language, values, and worldviews. Thus, as a qualitative researcher, you have to be aware of your own assumptions and biases that you bring into the research. Yet, just as in meditating, you do not "push away" your thoughts or try to convince yourself

*This chapter co-authored with Yu-Wei Wang.

that they do not exist; instead, you note their existence as the thoughts rise and fall and still focus on looking at your mind. Therefore, as a qualitative researcher, you "bracket" your assumptions, take field notes, write reflexive journals, and tell your readers what your "filters" are. The lived experiences of the participants are what you focus on, and researchers are the instruments in this discovery process with the awareness that your worldviews shape your understanding and interpretations of the phenomena under analysis and the stories you narrate.

This interpretive practice also involves a great deal of exploration. Use traveling as an another analogy; all researchers are travelers on the road to explore the unknown in the process of conducting qualitative research. In the meantime, things you pack in your bags and directions you choose all influence what you will see on this journey. As Denzin and Lincoln (1998) pointed out, "research is an interactive process shaped by his or her personal history, biography, gender, social class, race and ethnicity, and those of the people in the settings" (p. 4). Therefore, who you are, whom you meet in the journey, and how you interact with each other all influence the storytelling process.

With this brief description of the nature of qualitative research, you may sense that qualitative methodology is different from most of the quantitative studies that you may have been exposed to in research design classes. Although students may use some similar strategies in conducting qualitative and quantitative dissertations/theses, those who are interested in doing qualitative research may face additional challenges such as the overwhelming complexity of various strategies of inquiry, lack of training, and mentor/committee members who are not knowledgeable about qualitative paradigms. At the same time, some students may also misunderstand the nature of qualitative research and inappropriately present their study as a qualitative one while only including several open-ended questions in their research design. Therefore, this chapter discusses issues uniquely pertaining to writing the methods chapter for a qualitative dissertation/thesis. First of all, the definition of qualitative research and key myths and facts about qualitative research are presented. Then, the approaches to structure the methods section of a qualitative thesis or dissertation are described. Most important, the ways to write the paradigms and various strategies of inquiry (i.e., grounded theory, consensual qualitative research, or phenomenology/hermeneutics) of a qualitative thesis or dissertation are illustrated with examples. Please note that the studies cited in this chapter are good examples of qualitative research but not the "only correct" ways to conduct qualitative research. Furthermore, the ways to evaluate the rigor of the methodology are briefly described. Finally, conclusions are provided at the end of this chapter.

BEFORE TELLING YOU THE STORY: WHAT IS QUALITATIVE RESEARCH?

In this section, the definition of qualitative research is presented. Second, we discuss some common myths regarding the nature of qualitative research. Subsequently, some basic facts about qualitative research are delineated.

Definition of Qualitative Research

Before you can start writing the methods chapter for a qualitative dissertation or thesis, you need to have a clear understanding of the definition of qualitative research. Because qualitative methodology is utilized across various disciplines (e.g., anthropology, education, nursing, and sociology) with numerous methods (e.g., open-ended and quasistructured interviews, participant observation and documentary methods), definitions vary. Though you may feel confused about and overwhelmed by the variation of terminology, as well as the philosophical and procedural diversity of qualitative research, it can be concluded that qualitative research has the following characteristics, as summarized by Denzin and Lincoln (2000):

> Qualitative research is a situated activity that locates the observer in the world. It consists of a set of interpretive, material practices that make the world visible. These practices transform the world. They turn the world into a series of representations, including field notes, interviews, conversations, photographs, recordings, and memos to the self. At this level, qualitative research involves an interpretive, naturalistic approach to the world. This means that qualitative researchers study things in their natual settings, attempting to make sense of, or to interpret, phenomena in terms of the meanings people bring to them. Qualitative research involves the studied use and collection of a variety of empirical materials—case study; personal experience; introspection; life story; interview; artifacts; cultural texts and productions; observational, historical, interactional, and visual texts—that describe routine and meanings in individuals' lives. Accordingly, qualitative researchers deploy a wide range of interconnected interpretive methods, hoping always to get a better understanding of the subject matter at hand. It is understood, however, that each practice makes the world visible in a different way. Hence, there is frequently a commitment to using more than one interpretive practice in any study. (pp. 3–4)

Influenced by the interpretivist-constructivist tradition, qualitative researchers believe that objective reality can never be fully understood or discovered and that there exist many possible ways of looking at realities. Qualitative researchers are devoted to understanding specifics of particular cases and embedding their research findings in an ever-changing world. They value rich descriptions of the phenomena under analysis and attempt to represent individuals' lived experience through writing and interpretations. They use different methods to "add rigor, breadth, and depth to any investigation" (Flick, 1992, p. 194). Qualitative researchers are interested in capturing the individual's point of view through multiple strategies such as interviewing and observation, instead of deploying etic and nomothetic approaches that emphasize the goal of discovering and describing universal principles by quantifying the observed phenomena. Qualitative researchers choose from various research tools in accordance with their research questions and contexts to better understand the phenomenon of interest (Nelson, Treichler, & Grossberg, 1992), instead of verifying or falsifying a priori hypothesis through experimental designs and statistical analysis.

Myths and Facts About Qualitative Research

Due to insufficient understanding of the definition and characteristics of qualitative research, several common myths exist about this form of inquiry. First of all, many students have a mistaken belief that qualitative research only consists of asking people open-ended questions and analyzing participants' answers. Second, some people think that only one kind of qualitative methodology exists and are unaware that qualitative research has a variety of traditions, such as phenomenology, grounded theory, and so on. Third, some people believe that qualitative research should only be used in areas where not enough information is available to do quantitative studies. These perspectives overlook how qualitative research can add to the depth of understanding about certain phenomena.

Finally, some students choose to conduct qualitative studies because they think it is easier than conducting quantitative ones. They believe that qualitative research is less rigorous than quantitative research and ignore the fact that qualitative research is very time-consuming. Conducting qualitative research, in fact, is a highly self-reflective and introspective journey in which the researcher listens to other people's stories, retells the stories in the way that she/he understands them, or even reconstructs the story with the participants. Creswell (1998) indicated that qualitative researchers should be willing to (1) "commit to extensive time in the field"; (2) "engage in the complex, time-consuming process of data analysis—the ambitious task of sorting through large amounts of data and reducing them to a few themes or categories"; (3) "write long passages, because the evidence must substantiate claims and the writer needs to show multiple perspectives"; and (4) "participate in a form of social and human science research that does not have firm guidelines or specific procedures and is evolving and changing constantly" (pp. 16–17). Therefore, those who opt for doing qualitative research because of their fear of statistics should be reminded that qualitative research is not the "easy way out" (Craig Rooney, personal communication, 2001). Although qualitative procedures may not be as clearly delineated as quantitative procedures, researchers must obtain highly specialized knowledge and demonstrate rigorous endeavors, as is evidenced in this chapter.

Therefore, before you decide to commit to qualitative research, you are strongly encouraged to think: *Are the kinds of questions I have best answered through qualitative inquiry? Am I conducting a qualitative thesis/dissertation for authentic reasons? Am I using this methodology to avoid conducting statistical analysis or, rather, to approach a more appropriate methodology? How have I equipped myself with the knowledge on the basic ontology, epistemology, and methodology of qualitative research? Do I have the kind of course work and research experience to conduct a quality investigation? Do I have advisors and/or committee members who can provide the kind of expertise I need to conduct a qualitative investigation? Am I psychologically ready to go through this journey?* You should spend time thinking about and discussing these questions with your dissertation advisor and committee.

Where Does This Story Start?

After you obtain appropriate training and decide to conduct a qualitative study, the methods chapter of a thesis or dissertation is the place to articulate your plans for a rigorous, credible, and trustworthy qualitative study. As was stated in the quantitative methods chapter, "The methods chapter of your thesis or dissertation is the map of exactly what you are going to do and how you are going to do it." Particularly for qualitative research, the following dimensions are typically included in the methods chapter: (a) paradigms (e.g., assumptions and rationale for using an interpretive research design); (b) strategies of inquiry (e.g., what hermeneutics is and how one uses hermeneutics to study the lived experience of adopted adolescents); (c) participants (e.g., the sampling procedure and a detailed description of the participants); (d) instrument (which will be you, the researcher); (e) data collection and analysis procedure (pertaining to trustworthiness and credibility issues).

Although the outline of the methods chapter can be constructed in different ways, all of the aforementioned dimensions should be included. Following are the tables of contents from two previous students' dissertations:

METHODS SECTION IN A GROUNDED THEORY DISSERTATION (SCHAEFER, 1997)

III. Methodology
    Research Methodology
    Setting
    Sample Selection
      Purposeful Sampling
      Maximum Variation Sampling

Making Initial Contact With Respondents
Characteristics of the Sample
   Rachael
   Janet
   Louisa
   Victoria
   Miko
   Judith
   Elaine
   Gerda
   Brenda
Data-Collection Techniques
  Unstructured Depth Interview
   The Interview Guide
   Probing
  Field Notes
  Recording Data
Establishing and Building Trustworthiness
  Credibility
   Prolonged Engagement
   Peer Debriefing
   Negative Case Analysis
  Member Checking
  Transferability
  Dependability
  Confirmability
  Reflexive Journal
Data Analysis
  Grounded Theory
  Researcher Qualifications
Summary

METHODS SECTION IN A PHENOMENOLOGICAL DISSERTATION (ADAMS, 1997)

Chapter III. Design of the Study
     Overview
     Introduction of Case Study Research Methods
     Researcher as the Instrument
     Participants
     Ethical Considerations
     Data-Collection Methods
      Access and Contact
      In-Depth Interviews
      Interview Procedure
      Field Notes
     Data-Analysis Methods
      Triangulation
      Profiles
     Making Thematic Connections
      The Researcher as Analyst

The Qualitative Software Program
Summary

Notice in these two examples that the authors communicated that they would present their rationale for selecting a particular paradigm and strategy of inquiry (e.g., grounded theory) and told the readers that they would explain the participants and instruments of the study, as well as the data analytic procedures.

AS THE STORY UNFOLDS . . .

PARADIGMS: THE GROUND RULES

Clearly articulating the paradigm that will be utilized is the most appropriate way to begin a methods chapter. To conduct a qualitative thesis or dissertation, you must first understand the basic tenets and philosophy of a particular paradigm. This is important for several reasons. First, after gaining this knowledge through reading and coursework that discuss the philosophical foundations of qualitative paradigms, you will be better equipped to conduct a qualitative thesis/dissertation. Second, this knowledge will help you to think about your research question(s), purpose(s) and methods. Third, it will also prepare you to defend your thesis or dissertation by providing a strong rationale for utilizing your particular qualitative methodology. Fourth, as introduced later in this chapter, qualitative research has many different strategies of inquiry (e.g., phenomenology, grounded theory) and each inquiry has somewhat different philosophical underpinnings and is related to various paradigms (e.g., interpretivism/constructivism/hermeneutics, postmordernism/feminism/critical theory, participatory/collaborative paradigm, pragmatism); therefore, understanding the basic tenets and philosophy of qualitative research will help you select a particular paradigm that may best address your particular area of inquiry.

Another critical part of the methods chapter is a discussion of the basic philosophical issues of qualitative research, such as ontology (the nature of reality), epistemology (the relationship between the inquirer and the known), and methodologies (the methods of gaining knowledge of the world). Table 8.1 (adopted from Denzin & Lincoln, 2000, p. 168) contrasts the philosophical foundations of positivism and postpositivism (on which quantitative research is based) with the philosophical foundations of critical theory, constructionism, and participatory paradigm (which constitute the philosophical underpinnings of qualitative research). In general, all qualitative paradigms assume relativist ontology (multiple realities are socially and individually constructed) and transactional epistemology (the knower and

TABLE

8.1

BASIC BELIEFS OF ALTERNATIVE INQUIRY PARADIGM—UPDATED

Issue	Positivism	Postpositivism	Critical Theory et al.	Constructivism	Participatory
Ontology	Naïve realism—"Real" reality but apprehendable	Critical realism—"Real" reality but only imperfectly and probabilistically apprehendable	Historical realism—Virtual reality shaped by social, political, cultural, economic, ethnic, and gender values crystallized over time	Relativism—Local and specific constructed realities	Participative reality—Subjective-objective reality, cocreated by mind and given cosmos
Epistemology	Dualist/objectivist; findings true	Modified dualist/objectivist; critical tradition/community; findings probably true	Transactional/subjectivist; value-mediated findings	Transactional/subjectivist; created findings	Critical subjectivity in participatory transaction with cosmos; extended epistemology of experiential, prepositional, and practical knowing; cocreated findings
Methodology	Experimental/manipulative; verification of hypotheses; chiefly quantitative methods	Modified experimental/manipulative; critical multiplism; falsification of hypotheses; may include qualitative methods	Dialogic/dialectic	Hermeneutic/dialectic	Political participation in collaborative action inquiry; primacy of the practical; use of language grounded in shared experiential context

Note. Table 8.1 was adopted from Denzin and Lincoln (2000, p. 168).

the known are inextricably intertwined), as well as dialogic/intrepretive methodology (Guba & Lincoln, 1998). If you are interested in enhancing your knowledge of the philosophical underpinnings of these paradigms, some excellent introductions and discussions can be found in *The Handbook of Qualitative Research* (e.g., Lincoln & Guba, 2000; Schwandt, 2000), the *Handbook of Counseling Psychology* (e.g., Morrow & Smith, 2000), and the *Handbook of Multicultural Counseling* (e.g., Morrow, Rakhasha, & Castañeda, 2001).

After you understand the various paradigms, you will need to choose one of them for your thesis or dissertation. Morrow, Rakhasha, and Castañeda (2001) made recommendations on how to select paradigms (also including positivist and postpositivist paradigms) in accordance with the individual's personal and mental models, research question, and discipline. Consider, for example, the compatibility of a particular paradigm with your own personal values, beliefs, personality, previous research experience, and research interest. Morrow et al. also emphasized the importance of having a "wise mentor," especially when the dissertation committee is not supportive of qualitative research. In addition, they strongly recommend consulting other qualitative researchers and your committee members before making this critical decision.

Following is a description of a particular paradigm from a grounded theory study (Holmes, 1999). The author briefly articulated the philosophical foundation of a qualitative paradigm in the beginning of the methods chapter. Please also note that the author used the term *interpretive research* instead of *qualitative research* in order to emphasize the importance of fundamental philosophy in qualitative research.

> This study used an interpretive approach to research based on grounded theory (Glazer & Strauss, 1967; Strauss, 1987; Strauss & Corbin, 1990) and dimensional analysis (Schatzman, 1987).
>
> Underlying the grounded theory approach to research is an alternative epistemology that offers a new model on which to base systematic inquiry. "Interpretivism" seems to be emerging as a broadly acceptable umbrella term for the confusing number of philosophical labels associated with this alternative research paradigm (Ferguson, 1993). These include "postmodern" (Gergen, 1994), "narrative" (Rennie & Touknanian, 1992), "social constructionism" (Berger & Luckman, 1967), and "naturalistic inquiry" (Lincoln & Guba, 1985).
>
> Interpretivism holds that facts are not discovered by objective investigation but, rather, are the social constructions of humans who understand the world through interpretive activity (Ferguson, 1993). It calls for a new approach to the acquisition of knowledge based on the assumptions that the observer and the observed are inseparable, that the nature of meaning is relative rather than absolute, that phenomena are dependent upon context, and that the process of understanding is inductive, constructive, and qualitative (Rennie & Toukmanian, 1992).
>
> Lincoln and Guba (1985) concisely summarized the differences between positivist and naturalist paradigms in the following table (p. 37):

Axioms About	Positivist Paradigm	Naturalistic Paradigm
The nature of reality	Reality is single, tangible, and fragmentable	Realities are multiple, constructed, and holistic
The relationship of knower and known	Knower and known are independent, a dualism	Knower and known are interactive and inseparable
The possibility of generalization	Time- and context-free generalizations are possible	Only time- and context-hypotheses are possible
The possibility of causal linkages	There are real causes temporally precedent to or simultaneous with their effects	All entities are in a state of mutual simultaneous shaping, so that it is impossible to distinguish causes from effects
The role of values	Inquiry is value free	Inquiry is value bound

Interpretivism invites a multiplicity of accounts of reality and a multiplicity of self-accounts. It, for example, encourages individuals to explore a variety of means of understanding the self but discourages a commitment to any one of these accounts as the "true self." It encourages an acceptance of the ever-changing nature of reality.

Underlying the interpretivist view is the idea that people understand the world through narratives or stories. These narratives are reconstructed and new meaning is generated through interaction and through discourse. People constitute and are constituted by the stories that they live and the stories that they tell.

> I want to claim much more than the comfortable platitude that stories are a good thing and should be attended to.
>
> Stories are habitations. We live in and through stories. They conjure worlds. We do not know the world other than as a story world. Stories inform life. They hold us together and keep us apart.
>
> We inhabit the great stories of our culture. We live through stories. We are lived by the stories of our race and place. It is this enveloping and constituting function of stories that is especially important to sense more fully. (Mair, 1988, p. 107).

And yet none of these personal stories can claim to be the one "truth" or the one "reality." It is impossible to develop a narrative, a system of principles, a theoretical framework that can be applied in any context. Gergen (1992, p. 181) quoted Heinz von Foerster as saying: "We are blind until we can see that we cannot see." This is the basis of the interpretivist perspective. There is no absolute truth, there is no absolute reality, and humans are active agents in creating meaning through action and discourse.

Research in an interpretivist framework takes on a radically different form to that of traditional objectivist research. Instead of relying on the testing of hypotheses of causal relationships, interpretivist research is interested in individual perceptions and meaning structures. "Its goal would be the articulation of deeply personal meanings and the construction of possible worlds through imaginative participation in conversation with the client" (Neimeyer, 1993, p. 225). The central concern is to understand what is happening through the eyes and minds of the people involved in the situation under study. This requires that the researcher attempt to approach a study with an open mind and with awareness of personal bias or attachment. This is far from the traditional approach to research where the focus is on testing of a causal hypothesis generated through theoretical arguments.

Clearly, interpretivist research is a far more radical departure from the traditional positivist research paradigm than simply moving from quantitative to qualitative methodology. Interpretivist research generally uses qualitative methods of inquiry such as participant observation and in-depth interviews, but using qualitative research methodology is not synonymous with interpretivist research. There is a clear distinction between using qualitative methods and doing interpretive research. Interpretivism refers to a set of fundamental beliefs about the nature of our knowledge, whereas qualitative methodology simply refers to a set of methodological techniques and strategies that can be used in either paradigm. (pp. 41–44)

STRATEGIES OF INQUIRY: GETTING YOUR ROAD MAP

Each qualitative paradigm is connected to specific research designs and strategies of inquiry. You need to be clear about the differences among various strategies of inquiry in order to make informed decisions regarding what qualitative approaches to use and when to use them (Creswell, 1998) and, subsequently, design your thesis/dissertation according to the guidelines of a particular chosen strategy (e.g., grounded theory).

After you choose a specific strategy of inquiry, you may choose a model to follow (e.g., a journal article that utilizes certain strategies of inquiry) when designing your thesis/dissertation. Then, in the methods chapter, describe the rationale of using the specific paradigm and strategy of inquiry and illustrate how those methods relate to the phenomenon of interest and purpose of the thesis/dissertation.

Following is an example from a grounded theory study (Stoddart, 1999). In the methods chapter of this dissertation, the author clearly stated which strategy of inquiry was selected for her study and the reason that it was an appropriate strategy of inquiry for her research question on learning about White racial identity. Please also note that the author clearly identified which grounded theory approach was chosen for the research project. Finally, she clearly addressed the advantages and disadvantages of using the particular approach:

> Grounded theory was chosen as a methodology because of its emergent design; reliance upon induction; and emphasis upon not bringing preconceptions into the study. Concepts and theory emerge in relation to the voices that create them. Also, since so much theory has been created by the White male power structure, I think it is very important to listen to and build theory from those outside the established paradigm. Grounded theory facilitates this through its ongoing and close connection between the participants, data collection, and analysis as theory is being built.
>
> Grounded theory is also well suited to investigate process and change, an integral aspect of the learning that occurs for White women as they become aware

of their racial identity. From its pragmatic and symbolic interactionist roots, grounded theory has emphasized studying transformation.

> Since phenomena are not conceived of as static but as continually changing in response to evolving conditions, an important component of the method is to build change, through process, into the method . . . . Grounded theory seeks not only to uncover relevant conditions but also to determine how the actors respond to changing conditions and to the consequence of their actions. It is the researcher's responsibility to catch this interplay. (Corbin & Strauss, 1990, p. 5).

The constant comparative method also ensures ongoing verification of the work; this vehicle allows any biases of the researcher to be discovered, aerated, and broken through. The constant comparative method also allows for the further contributions of respondents in the development of the theory. Concepts can be "checked" with those affected by the work. Grounded theory methods empower the respondents as well as the researcher.

Grounded theory has other principles in common with feminist work. Wuest (1995) pointed out grounded theory's ongoing reflexivity facilitates its feminist nature. Other tenets of feminist theory like the knowledge being produced be useful for lay and academic communities and that the research not be oppressive can easily be integrated into a grounded theory study. This dissertation is well within the bounds of a feminist study and it is important that the methodology honor this tradition.

This project used the grounded theory methodology outlined by Glaser (1978; 1992; 1993; 1994; 1995). It was chosen over the approach advocated by Strauss and Corbin because it seems better able to synthesize narratives into its research procedures. It also seemed the most open to integrating the holistic processes that occur for White women as they learn about their racial identity.

It is important that cognitive, affective, and kinesthetic factors be incorporated into a grounded theory study, if these phenomena are important concepts to the emerging theory. These aspects are crucial because they may be influential in the development of a White racial identity. Any methodology that would limit looking into cognitive, affective, or kinesthetic aspects would greatly inhibit the effectiveness of the emerging theory. Glaserean grounded theory seems best at incorporating these phenomena.

Another advantage of the grounded theory method, especially the approach advocated by Glaser, is that researchers can concentrate upon examining the data, not mastering certain techniques. If one is focusing upon how to do a certain procedure, it could be easy to lose sight of what is happening in the data. Creativity and insight could be lost.

The disadvantages of using the grounded theory approach promoted by Glaser is that there are less procedures for novice researchers to rely upon. The theoretical sensitivity, so important to Glaserean grounded theory, is limited in new researchers.

As a novice researcher, these are critical issues for me to address. I relied extensively on Glaser's methods, with input from my dissertation committee. I also leaned on my excellent support system: family, friends, and colleagues who have some experience in theoretical principles and research techniques. I also continued to read theory in other fields, as Glaser suggested, for building my own theoretical sensitivity. (Stoddart, 1999, pp. 44–45)

You may feel confused at this stage because of the variety of strategies of inquiry and because qualitative researchers in various disciplines have identified and labeled qualitative inquiries differently. For example, Strauss and Corbin (1990), whose fields were sociology and nursing, mentioned five strategies of inquiry (i.e., grounded theory, phenomenology, life history, ethnography, and conversational analysis); conversely, Moustakas (1994), whose field was psychology, listed six qualitative traditions (i.e., grounded theory, hermeneutics, empirical phenomenological research, ethnography, heuristic research, and transcendental phenomenology).

Based on the relevance to the field of psychology and the clarity of their connection to specific paradigms and procedure, three strategies of inquiry are presented in this chapter: grounded theory, consensual qualitative research, and phenomenology/hermeneutics (Creswell, 1998; Denzin & Lincoln, 2000; Morrow & Smith, 2000; Richardson, 1996). The basic principles of these qualitative methods along with examples of written qualitative thesis/dissertations will not only help you understand how to conduct certain studies but also provide guidelines for evaluating the quality of a particular qualitative research study.

Grounded Theory

In this section, grounded theory is defined and its various features are introduced: (a) theory is grounded in data, (b) constant comparative method, (c) memo writing, and (d) theoretical sampling. Typically, all of these features would be described in the methods chapter of a grounded theory thesis/dissertation.

Definition and Purpose   Grounded theory has its roots in the Chicago school of sociology and the tradition of symbolic interactionism. According to Creswell (1998), "In this type of study, the researcher generates an abstract analytical schema of a phenomenon, a theory that explains some action, interaction, or process" (p. 241). This strategy of inquiry is appropriate for studying "the local interactions and meanings as related to the social context in which they actually occur" and, therefore, is particularly attractive to psychologists (Pidgeon, 1996, p. 75).

Theory Is Grounded in the Data   Grounded theorists argue that theories should be developed from the data collected in the field. Unlike quantitative researchers, grounded theorists neither test existing theory nor try to fit their data into preconceived concepts. Instead, all of the theoretical concepts should be derived from the data analysis and account for the variation in the studied phenomenon (Charmaz, 2000). Following is a brief overview of the grounded theory method in a doctoral dissertation (Holmes, 1999). Notice how the author emphasizes the necessity for the theory to be grounded in the data.

> Grounded theory provides an organized systematic method of conducting inter-
> pretivist research that is relatively well documented. Strauss and Corbin (1990)
> summarized the goals of grounded theory methodology as follows:
> The analytic procedures of grounded theory are designed to
>
> 1. Build rather than test theory.
> 2. Give the research process the rigor necessary to make the theory "good
>   science."
> 3. Help the analyst to break through biases and assumptions brought to, and
>   that can develop during, the research process.
> 4. Provide the grounding, build the density, and develop sensitivity and inte-
>   gration needed to generate a rich, tightly woven, explanatory theory that
>   closely approximates the reality it represents (p. 57).
>
> A grounded theory is one that is inductively derived from the study of a par-
> ticular phenomenon. It develops out of the process of systematic data collection
> and analysis of data pertaining to that phenomenon. The grounded researcher
> does not begin with a theory and then attempt to prove it but rather begins with
> an area of study and allows the theory to emerge (Strauss & Corbin, 1990).
> Research operations and conceptual work are not distinct activities but comprise
> a continuous and integrated process. As the data collection (in this case inter-
> views) proceeds, the emerging theory is fed back into the interview process and
> guides the direction of inquiry and the selection of subjects (Bowers, 1984).
> "Memoing" is used to record the development of the emerging theory and to
> record methodological decisions. (Holmes, 1999, pp. 51–52)

Since the theory is grounded in the data collected from the field, the sources of the data must be clearly presented. The data sources of grounded theory research could include a combination of data types (e.g., archival/textual mate-rials, participant observation, autobiographies, participants' journals); interviews with the participants are a primary data source (Pidgeon & Henwood, 1996).

Following is an excerpt from a journal article that clearly describes the data sources of a grounded theory study:

Data Sources

Each of the 11 survivors of sexual abuse participated in a 60- to 90-minute in-depth, open-ended interview, during which two questions were asked: "Tell me, as much as you are comfortable sharing with me right now, what happened to you when you were sexually abused," and "what are the primary ways in which you survived?" Morrow's responses included active listening, empathic reflection, and minimal encouragers.

After the initial interviews, 7 of the 11 interviewees became focus-group par-ticipants. Four were excluded from the group: 2 who were interviewed after the group had started and 2 who had other commitments. The group provided an interactive environment (Morgan, 1988) that focused on survival and coping. In the initial meeting, participants brainstormed about the words *victim, survivor,* and *coping.* Subsequent group sessions built on the first, with participants explor-ing emerging categories from the data analysis and their own research questions, which had been invited by Morrow. Morrow took a participant-observer role, moving from less active involvement in the beginning to a more fully participatory role toward the end (Adler & Adler, 1987).

A central feature of the analysis was Morrow's self-reflectivity (Peshkin, 1988; Strauss, 1987). Morrow's own subjective experiences were logged, examined for tacit biases and assumptions, and subsequently analyzed.

Documentary evidence completed the data set. These data consisted of participants' journals kept both in conjunction with and independent of the project, artistic productions, and personal writings from earlier periods of participants' lives. (Morrow & Smith, 1995, p. 25)

Constant Comparative Method   The hallmark of the grounded theory research, constant comparative method, is "an aspect of axial coding and the formation of the visual theory, model, or paradigm" (Creswell, 1998, p. 239). The purpose of comparative method is to develop "many categories, properties, and hypotheses about general problems" instead of to "ascertain either the universality or the proof of suggested causes or other properties" (p. 104). Glaser and Strauss (1967) designed this method to generate a theory "that is integrated, consistent, plausible, close to the data" (p. 103). This method sets grounded theory apart from content/thematic analysis, which uses reliability and validity as criteria and emphasizes "the counting of instances within a predefined set of mutually exclusive and jointly exhaustive categories" (see Pidgeon, 1996, p. 78).

According to Glaser and Strauss (1967), the four stages that constitute the constant comparative method are (a) comparing incidents applicable to each category, (b) integrating categories and their properties, (c) delimiting the theory, and (d) writing the theory (p. 105). They also emphasized that although one stage leads to another, some earlier stages will continue operating simultaneously until the termination of the data analysis.

Pidgeon and Henwood (1996) emphasized the importance of documenting this analytical process fully while conducting ground theory research, which helps to track the procedures and helps the researchers become aware of the implicit, a prior assumptions that they hold. They described the analytic process as shown in Figure 8.1 (p. 88). As depicted in the figure, this data-collection procedure was described as a "zigzag" process by Creswell (1998)—"out to the field to gather information, analyze the data, back to the field to gather more information, analyze the data, and so forth" (p. 57). In other words, data collection and data analysis are not discrete stages in grounded theory research.

Since Glaser and Strauss published *The Discovery of Grounded Theory* (1967), grounded theorists (including Glaser and Strauss) have been advocating different "proper" ways of analyzing data and presenting the findings, such as Glaser's comparative approach (1992); the dimensionalizing, axial coding, and conditional matrix strategies suggested by Strauss and Corbin (1990); and dimensional analysis formulated by Schatzman (1991). No matter which data-analysis method you decide to utilize, you should review the key literature,

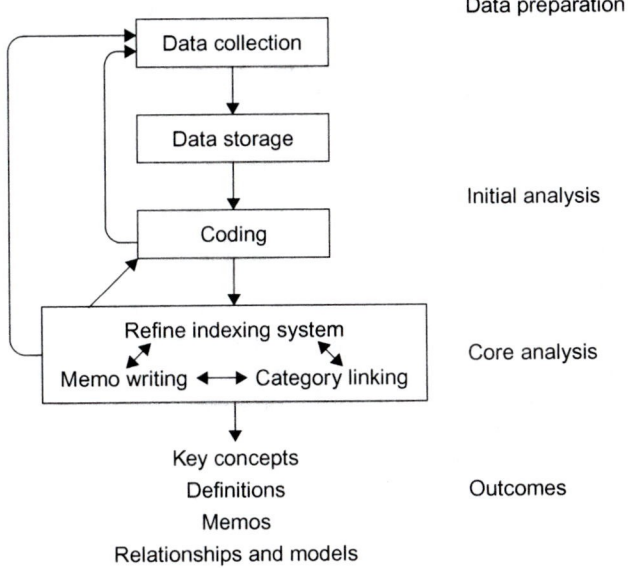

FIGURE **8.1**

Analytic Process of Grounded theory approach.

From "Grounded Theory: Practical Implementation" by Pidgeon and Henwood in Handbook of Qualitative Research Methods for Psychology and The Social Sciences, Richardson (ed.), 1996. Used by permission of Blackwell Publishing.

understand the data-analysis method, and discuss your choices with your advisors and committee members because this will greatly influence the ways data is collected, prepared, analyzed, and presented.

Consider the following examples from two grounded theory studies.

DESCRIPTION OF CONSTANT COMPARATIVE METHOD

The details of data collection and analysis pertaining to this study revealed themselves as the research was conducted. The responsibility of this study was to produce grounded theory concerning the mother-daughter relationships of women leaders and their mothers. The constant comparative method was utilized to do this. As recommended by Lincoln and Guba (1985) the first step in analyzing the interviews was to examine the data and identify units or incidents on a "looks right, feels right" basis. These units were then placed on colored coded cards (one color for each participant). The units were identified by codes to designate which participant (coded #) and which interview (I, II, or III) and which page of that interview from which the unit was drawn. This process of coding was useful in establishing the audit trail. The cards were classified by the researcher into 45 categories (See Appendix E). The units or incidents were compared to others in the same category and this process of constant comparison led to theories about the characteristics of each grouping. This process was followed with the interviews from each participant and the continual coding and categorizing led to common classifications. Existing categories were refined and redefined as new information was added.

During this process, the explanatory theory began to take shape. The categories were classified into three major themes and these were used to formulate the grounded theory of this study. Gradually, the categories were filled and the researcher realized economy (fewest possible categories) and meaning in the research interpretation. At this point data collection was terminated and the final stage of writing the theory began (Schaefer, pp. 89–90)

DESCRIPTION OF ANALYTIC METHOD

The analytic process was based on immersion in the data and repeated sortings, codings, and comparisons that characterize the grounded theory approach. Analysis began with open coding, which is the examination of minute sections of text made up of individual words, phrases, and sentences. Strauss and Corbin (1990) described open coding as that which "fractures the data and allows one to identify some categories, their properties, and dimensional locations" (p. 97). The language of the participants guided the development of code and category labels, which were identified with short descriptors, known as *in vivo codes*, for survival and coping strategies. These codes and categories were systematically compared and contrasted, yielding increasingly complex and inclusive categories. . . .

Open coding was followed by axial coding, which puts data *"back together in new ways by making connections between a category and its subcategories"* (italics in original, Strauss & Corbin, 1990, p. 97). From this process, categories emerged and were assigned in vivo category labels. Finally, selective coding ensued. Selective coding was the integrative process of "selecting the core category, systematically relating it to other categories, validating those relationships [by searching for confirming and disconforming examples], and filling in categories that need[ed] further refinement and development" (Strauss & Corbin, 1990, p. 116).

Codes and categories were sorted, compared, and contrasted until saturated—that is, until analysis produced no new codes or categories and when all of the data were accounted for in the core categories of the grounded theory paradigm model. Criteria for core status were (a) a category's centrality in relation to other categories, (b) frequency of a category's occurrence in the data, (c) its inclusiveness and the ease with which it related to other categories, (d) clarity of its implications for a more general theory, (e) its movement toward theoretical power as details of the category were worked out, and (f) its allowance for maximum variation in terms of dimensions, properties, conditions, consequences, and strategies (Strauss, 1987). (Morrow & Smith, 1995, pp. 25–26)

In the first example, the author gave a brief account of constant comparative method. In the second example, the coding procedure is briefly described. You need to provide more detailed accounts of this data analytical procedure in your thesis/dissertation. For example, Holmes (1999) and Rooney (2000) used five to six pages to describe open coding, axial coding, selective coding, conditional matrix, and core category selection.

Memo Writing   In addition to "theory is grounded in the data" and "constant comparative method," "memo writing" is the third primary feature of grounded theory. It is defined as a process to record "hunches; comments on new samples to be checked out, explanations of modifications to categories; emerging theoretical reflections; and links to the literature"

(Pidgeon & Henwood, 1996, p. 95). Charmaz (2000) indicated, "Memo writing is the intermediate step between coding and the first draft of the completed analysis. . . . It can help us to define leads for collecting data—both for further initial coding and later theoretical sampling. Through memo writing, we elaborate processes, assumptions, and actions that are subsumed under our codes" (p. 517). Pidgeon and Henwood (1996) also warned that researchers should "write a memo as soon as the thought has occurred, for, if left unrecorded, it is likely to be forgotten" (p. 95). In a word, memo writing is an important technique for grounded theorists. It not only facilitates the constant comparative method, theoretical sampling, and theory development but also helps with the later writing of the results and final paper.

Following is a description of memo writing from the methods section of a doctoral dissertation:

> Throughout the entire open and axial coding processes, the investigator maintained an audit trail, in addition to the construction of narrative and story summaries, that documented the ongoing process of the research and that marked the evolution of categories and their suspected relationship. This audit trail contains "memos" written by the investigator (Bowers, 1990). Keeping the audit trail is another function of trustworthiness for the current study (Lincoln & Guba, 1985).
>
> . . . Memos written in the study included 73 pages of single-spaced type and were forwarded to the five members of the investigator's doctoral dissertation committee for their review and feedback. Memos for this study included all of the areas suggested by scholars of qualitative research: pre-entry memos containing the investigator's beliefs about the phenomenon under study, coding of raw data, data analysis and reduction, and process notes (Lincoln & Guba, 1985). (Rooney, 2000, pp. 92–93)

In this example, the author not only explained how he used memo writing to strengthen his research finding but also delineated the length of his memos as well as the types of memos included in his writing.

Following is an example of a memo that was written after the author reviewed several interviews in a study on "dual self." Note how the author described her comprehension of the data, refined the relationships among categories, and grappled with the emerging theory when writing her memos. (You could include your actual memos in the appendix of your thesis or dissertation.)

> The dual self in this case is the *contrast* between the *sick self* and the *monitoring self* (actually *physical* self might be a better term [than *sick self*] since some of these people try to see themselves as "well" but still feel they must constantly monitor in order to maintain status—they also rather easily sink into self-blame when the monitoring doesn't work).
>
> With Sara S. we see definite conversations held between the physical and monitoring self. Through her learning time or body education, self-taught and self-validated she has not only developed a sense of what her body "*needs*"; she has developed a finely honed *sense of timing* about how to handle those needs.

With the dual self, the monitoring self *externalizes* the internal messages from the physical self and makes them concrete. It is as if dialogue and negotiation with ultimate validation of the physical self take place between the two dimensions of the dual self. Consequently, the competent monitoring self must be able to attend to the messages given by the physical self. The learning time is the necessary amount of concentration, trial and error to become an effective monitoring self.

Mark R., for example, illustrated the kind of dialogue that takes place between the monitoring and physical selves when he talks about person to kidney talks and what is needed to sustain that new transplanted kidney in his body.

The dual self in many ways is analogous to the dialogue that Mead describes between the I and the me. The me monitors and attends to the I, which is creating, experiencing, feeling. The monitoring me defines those feelings, impulses and sensations. It evaluates them and develops a line of action so that what is defined as needed is taken care of. The physical self here is then taken as an object held up to view, which can be compared with past physical (or for that matter, psychological) selves, with perceived statuses of others, with a defined level of health or well-being, with signals of potential crises, etc. (Charmaz, p. 517)

Theoretical Sampling   The last basic feature of grounded theory study, theoretical sampling is used by grounded theorists to "select a sample of individuals to study based on their contribution to the development of the theory. Often, this process begins with a homogeneous sample of individuals who are similar, and, as the data collection proceeds and the categories emerge, the researcher turns to a heterogeneous sample to see under what conditions the categories hold true" (Creswell, 1998, p. 243). It characterizes the ongoing analytic process in the field and a theory-driven way of sampling. It is also referred to as *purposeful sampling* (Patton, 1990, p. 169) and *purposive sampling* (Lincoln & Guba, 1985). Theoretical sampling helps researchers target new data that would facilitate the emergence of theory after the initial analysis of the data at hand. Theoretical sampling differs from the sampling method in quantitative research, in which researchers are expected to obtain a representative sample in order to enhance generalizability of the research finding. "Theoretical saturation" occurs when "the new data fit into the categories already devised" (Charmaz, 2000, p. 520), and it indicates the end of the data-collection process.

Following is an example of theoretical (purposeful) sampling in the study conducted by Schaefer (1997) that focused on mother-daughter relationships in female leaders:

Purposeful Sampling

In utilizing the constructivist paradigm to conduct the proposed study, the method of sampling was "purposeful sampling" (Patton, 1990, p. 169). This is also called "purposive sampling" (Lincoln & Guba, 1985) and "theoretical sampling" (Glaser & Strauss, 1967). In qualitative research the logic and strength of purposive sampling lies in choosing cases which abound in data for thorough investigation. Information-rich cases are those which provide the investigator with copious information about issues of pivotal importance to the direction of the research (Patton, 1990).

Maximum Variation Sampling

In order to reach the objective of purposeful sampling, maximum-variation sampling was used. This is described by Morse (1994) as "the process of deliberately selecting a heterogeneous sample and observing commonalities in their experiences" (p. 228). She refers to Patton (1990) who noted that "two types of data are obtained using this technique. The first is high-quality case descriptions, useful for documenting uniqueness; second, significant shared patterns of commonalities existing across participants may be identified" (Morse, 1994, p. 229). Lincoln and Guba (1985) stress that "the object of the game is not to focus on the similarities that can be developed into generalization but to detail the many specifics that give the context its unique flavor" (p. 201).

Making Initial Contact With Respondents

In order to obtain a heterogeneous (i.e., complex) sample, it was necessary to use serial selection of participants. Maximum heterogeneity demanded a range of ages (30 to late 50s); a range of work orientations (not-for-profit, business, government, the professions, and volunteer); some participants who are married, divorced, or single; and some participants who have children and some who do not. An effort was made to choose participants from various areas of New Jersey. Other selection criteria, which presented themselves as the data from the unstructured depth interviews were analyzed, were birth order and unique life experiences. Therefore, in this study each new participant was selected after the previous participant had been interviewed and the data analyzed.

A letter from the researcher and a consent form were sent to 132 female members of LNJ from Classes 1987 to 1994, advising them of the purpose of this study and inviting them to participate (see Appendix A). If they had an initial interest in the study, they were asked to complete a demographic form (see Appendix B) and return it to the researcher. Within 2 months of the mailing, 38 women had returned the demographic form and indicated their interest in participating in the study. Eight letters were returned due to the addressees having moved. Six women wrote to offer regrets that they were not able to give the time to participate; they expressed their interest in, and support of, this research.

The initial participant in the study was the woman who first returned the demographic form. The researcher contacted her by telephone and made an appointment for the first meeting. The interview was conducted in the participant's home (as were the other interviews with two exceptions) as a natural setting is considered to be important in qualitative research. It also gave the researcher an opportunity to see the participant's taste and style in furnishing and decorating her home. At that meeting, the first participant was given information about the study; and after review, she then signed the consent form, which included a statement regarding the confidentiality of the participants (see Appendix C). The first interview was conducted following this, and it lasted one and one-half hours. The next interview was scheduled for the following week and lasted approximately the same amount of time. The same schedule and format was adhered to with all participants. Each interview was tape-recorded. Data were collected and analyzed and successive participants were chosen on the basis of their potential to provide new information to enrich the sample. A summary of each respondent's interviews was prepared by the researcher, and at the third interview this was presented to her orally; the participant had the opportunity to confirm the data and to make any changes or additions. Unlike quantitative research, in qualitative inquiry the size of the sample is not determined in advance of the study. . . .

Lincoln and Guba (1985) suggest that "sample selection continues to the point of redundancy" (p. 22). When no new themes or patterns become apparent, when no additional information is forthcoming, sample selection and data collection may end. In many respects this is a judgment made by the researcher subject to review by the peer debriefer. The use of peer debriefer is important in establishing credibility. The researcher exposes herself to a disinterested peer (although interested enough to be an important part of the process) in a similar way to an analysand revealing herself to her analyst. The debriefer functions as a "devil's advocate" and keeps the researcher "honest." The debriefer helps the researcher maintain awareness of her posture and her values.

My peer debriefer was a Counseling Psychologist who received her Ph.D. from Seton Hall University. She had completed a qualitative study of the factors that influenced married women's choice to work or not after the birth of their first child. The peer debriefer is currently in private practice and has many years of clinical experience. (Schaefer, 1998, pp. 62–71)

In this example, the author articulated her sampling method and data-collection procedure so that the readers can examine the rigor of the research design. Note that she used multiple interviews to collect richer data. She also provided detailed descriptions of the sample and summarized the limitations of the sample in the end (due to limited space in this chapter, they were not included here; readers can read the original dissertation for more details). Furthermore, the author also stressed how she decided when theoretical saturation occurred and described how she used a peer debriefer to enhance the credibility of the study. Finally, a description of the peer debriefer was provided so that the readers could assess the qualifications of the peer debriefer.

Consensual Qualitative Research

In this section, a relatively newly developed strategy of inquiry, consensual qualitative research (CQR), is briefly introduced followed by examples. CQR is a systematic way of examining the representativeness of results across cases through the process of reaching consensus of multiple researchers (Hill, Thompson, & Williams, 1997).

The CQR has been utilized in several counseling psychology studies (e.g., Juntunen et al., 2001; Knox, Hess, Petersen, & Hill, 1997; Ladany et al., 1997; Williams, Judge, Hill, & Hoffman, 1997). Hill, Thompson, and Williams (1997) developed CQR to conduct qualitative research and analyze data based on grounded theory (Glaser & Strauss, 1967; Strauss & Corbin, 1990), comprehensive process analysis (CPA; Elliott, 1989, 1993), phenomenological approach (Giorgi, 1970, 1985), and feminist theories (e.g., Fine, 1992; Harding, 1991). There are many common premises and differences between the

CQR and these other qualitative approaches (see Hill et al., 1997; Hoshmand, 1997, for a review). However, as Hoshmand noted, Hill et al. "did not articulate the implicit philosophical perspective on which the communal processes of CQR are based" (p. 601). Therefore, students who decide to use CQR must specify the philosophical underpinning of qualitative research and paradigm in order to account for this shortcoming and link the gaps among the ontology, epistemology, methodology, and methods.

The primary components of CQR include gathering data through interviews and open-ended questions, describing the phenomenon of interests by words (not numbers), using a criterion-based sampling method, and understanding the parts of the experiences in the context of the whole. Furthermore, the data analytic process involves inductively analyzing narratives of participants' experiences and identifying domains and core ideas (abstracts) from the data. Categories are developed by cross-analyzing the consistencies in the core ideas within domains. Usually, a small number of cases (8 to 15) are studied and a primary team of three to five researchers form consensus on ways to interpret the data after they independently analyze the data so that multiple perspectives are included in the decisions. One or two auditors examine the consensual judgments on the domains, core ideas, and categories to ensure that important data are not overlooked. Raw data are examined to see whether the findings and interpretations accurately reflect the data (for more details, see Hill et al., 1997).

Following is an example of the table of contents for the methods chapter of a typical CQR study:

Participants
    Interviewees
    Research Team
    Researcher Biases and Expectations
Measures
    Demographic Questionnaire
    Interview Protocol
Procedures
    Pilot of the Protocol
    Selecting Participants
    Contacting the Participants
    The Phone Interview
    Transcribing the Interviews
    Training of the Research Team
    Data Analysis (Williams, 1997)

The methods chapter describing CQR should include the following key sections: (a) researchers and researchers' biases and expectations, (b) interviewees and participants selection, (c) interview protocols and pilot of the protocol, (d) training of the research team, (e) interview (data collection), (f) transcribing, and (g) data analytic procedure. Actual examples utilizing CQR as the strategy of inquiry are used to illustrate how authors have written the various steps of the methods chapter.

Researchers and Researchers' Biases Clearly describing the researchers is very important because the data analyses of the CQR rely on the consensual process of members of the research team. Although the composition and the dynamics of the team are important, there is no absolute right type of team composition (e.g., faculty members, senior therapists, graduate or undergraduate students). You need to clearly consider the various possibilities of the team composition and be very careful in selecting the team members, considering possible power differences among the group members and types of expertise, as well as level of commitment needed from the team members.

In addition to the basic information and tasks of the team members, the authors of a CQR study should also document researchers' biases and expectations about the research findings because their personal opinions may greatly affect the data analytical outcomes. Following is an excerpt from a CQR study that illustrates both of these issues:

> The primary researchers for this study were three White doctoral-level counseling psychologists (Nicholas Ladany, Karen O'Brien, and Clara E. Hill); three White graduate students (Deborah S. Melincoff, Sarah Knox, and David A. Petersen) in doctoral programs in counseling psychology served as the interviewers. All six served as judges for the coding tasks.
>
> Prior to collecting data, we noted our biases and expectations regarding the potential findings of the study. We discussed these biases and expectations to increase awareness and to minimize their impact on the data analysis. Four of us believed that most trainees would admit that they had been sexually attracted to a client and that shame, guilt, and embarrassment would accompany the sexual attraction. One of us expected that the sexual attraction would not be extremely intense. Three believed that the guilt and shame might inhibit disclosure of the sexual attraction to the participant's supervisor. Four of us agreed that the trainee would be more likely to disclose to a supervisor if the supervisor was supportive, open, and caring and if there was a strong working alliance between them. One of us suspected that most of the trainees would disclose the sexual attraction to their supervisors, whereas another expected that the supervisor would need to broach the topic if it was to be discussed at all. Two of us believed that the participants would have received less than adequate training in this area. In sum, we were quite interested in the topic and reported some range of expectations about it. None of us reported particularly traumatic experiences having to do with sexual attraction to clients, and all of us indicated an openness to discovering what was to be found in the data. (Ladany et al., 1997, p. 415)

Following is another example from a study conducted by Juntunen et al. (2001). The authors clearly described the expertise and the experiences of the researchers composing the CQR analysis team. Although the authors did not articulate the researchers' biases and expectations, they documented the specific steps they took to decrease the effects of researchers' assumptions on the data analytic procedures and the ways they monitored the group dynamics.

Analysis Team

Because a diverse analysis team interpreted the data, it is important to briefly describe the members of the team. Cheryl Broneck is an advanced doctoral student of Asian and European descent. She has several years of counseling experience and interests in multicultural psychology and gender issues. Cindy Juntunen is a faculty member of European descent. Her interests are in career psychology, social action, and multicultural relationships. Paula Morin is an advanced doctoral student from the Turtle Mountain Chippewa tribe. She has worked with American Indian people in several settings and has interest in multiculturalism and resiliency. Gennea Seibel is an advanced doctoral student from the Mandan and Hidatsa tribes. She has also worked with American Indian people in many social service settings and is pursuing research related to diabetes and American Indians. Scott Winrow is an advanced doctoral student of European descent. He has several years of experience in counseling centers and is currently completing a study of success strategies among American Indian college students. Four members of the analysis team were also interviewers in the data collection. One interviewer was unable to participate in the analysis portion of the study, and one member of the research team joined the study after the interviews had been completed.

At the beginning of the analysis phase of the study, each member of the team had conducted and/or read some segment of the interviews. We recognized that we had already developed assumptions about the data prior to beginning the group coding. In an attempt to limit the effect of these assumptions, each of us recorded our assumptions in written form. In an early analysis session, each of us discussed the assumptions or biases we had identified. These assumptions fell into two broad categories: assumptions based on knowledge of career development theory and assumptions based on preconceived ideas of American Indians and their cultural norms. The intent of the discussion was to make biases explicit so that the group would be better able to avoid finding preconceived categories and themes within the transcripts.

The analysis team met weekly to discuss individual interpretations of the data, moving toward consensus about the meaning of the data. Although it was impossible to quantify the consensus process in a meaningful way, we took care to seek input from every group member as equitably as possible. On a few occasions, we audiotaped our group analysis meetings, and a review of those tapes indicated that we all shared opinions and that we had many involved and extensive discussions before we reached consensus, particularly early in the analysis process. (Juntunen et al., 2001, p. 277, with permission from American Psychological Association.)

Interviewees and Participant Selection   The sample of participants should be carefully identified in the methods chapter as well because participants' background will help the readers to understand the context of the data. The CQR adopts the criterion-based sampling method (Goetz & LeCompte, 1984, as cited in Hill et al., 1997), in which the criteria should be clearly stated. This method will ensure that the participants have had some depth of experiences with the phenomenon of interest and can provide meaningful information for the purpose of the study. Usually, 8 to 15 cases are studied intensively

by using CQR because (a) this sample size, albeit small, will provide a sufficient number of cases for the researchers to examine variability and consistencies across cases, and (b) additional cases typically add minimal new information (Hill et al., 1997).

Following is an example from Juntunen's study on American Indian perspectives on the career journey (2001). The authors delineated the important information of the participants as related to the phenomenon under
investigation (e.g., their tribe of origins, educational level). Also, the authors
separated the descriptions of two groups of participants because the data
analytic results were different for participants who attended college and
those who did not.

Participants

Pilot interviews were conducted with two adults, one man and one woman. The
woman was an upper-level college student from the First Nations of Canada, and
the man was a member of the Mandan–Hidatsa tribe, who was employed and who
had a high-school education. Following analysis and revision to the interview procedure (as described below), 18 American Indian adults were recruited to participate in the primary study.

The 18 participants, ages 21 to 59 years, were interviewed as part of a larger
study of 40 participants, ranging in age from 6 to 59 years. In the adult participant
group 11 (61%) were female and 7 (39%) were male, with a mean age of 46.3
years, with one person not reporting age. Ten of the participants were from a single Northern Plains state, and the remaining participants were from three other
north central and northwestern states. Educational achievement ranged from
some high school to some graduate education: 1 participant (6%) had completed
10th grade, 5 participants (31%) were high school graduates (including 2 with
General Equivalency Diplomas), 7 participants (44%) had completed some college, 1 participant (6%) had completed an associate's degree, and 2 participants
(13%) had completed baccalaureate degrees and some graduate work.

After charting the results of the analysis (described later in the *Procedures*
section), differences were noted between those who had completed some college
education and those who had not. Therefore, the remaining participant descriptions are provided separately for the two groups.

Among participants who had completed some or all of their high-school education, there were five women and two men. They ranged in age from 35 to 61
years, with a mean age of 51.2 years, with one person not reporting age. These
seven adults were members of the Sioux (3), Nez Pierce (1), Chippewa (1), Mandan–Hidatsa (1) and Hidatsa–Arikara (1) tribes. They were employed in parapro-
fessional teaching (2), babysitting (1), and unskilled labor (1). Two members of
this group were retired, one because of disability, and one member of the group
reported she was not working.

Among those who had completed some postsecondary education, there were
five men and six women. These participants were affiliated with the Chippewa
(4), Sioux and Lakota (3), Manda–Dakota–Hidatsa–Crow (1), Crow (1), Mandan–
Hidatsa (1), and Arikara (1) tribes. Among this group, there were five current college students, two nurses, one affiliated health service provider, two tribal government officers, and one train conductor. In addition, two of the students were
part-time employees in service and retail positions. The students were planning

to seek careers in teaching (2), mental health services (1), law (1), and accounting (1). (Juntunen et al, 2001, pp. 275–276)

Following is an excerpt cited from a CQR study to illustrate how to write the procedures of recruiting the participants. The authors not only described the criteria of selecting the clients to be interviewed but also documented, step by step, how they obtained access to the participants, which will help the readers to understand how the data were gathered and to replicate the study if needed.

Procedures: Recruiting Clients

Twenty-one experienced therapists, all Ph.D. psychologists known to or by the counseling psychology faculty at a large mid-Atlantic U.S. university, were contacted by phone and asked to invite their clients to participate. They were informed that the study would examine clients' perceptions of the effects of therapist self-disclosure. The 14 who agreed to participate were asked to give a research packet to no more than 5 of their adult (at least 18 years old) long-term clients. These clients must have already had at least 10 sessions with the therapist, must have had no planned termination in sight, and must have otherwise been appropriate for participation as determined by their therapist. Each therapist received between two and five packets, for a total of 57 packets. Of these 57, therapists reported that they actually distributed 40 packets.

The first contact between the primary researcher (Sarah Knox) and the potential participants occurred through the research packet, which was distributed by the therapists to those clients who met the above criteria. The packet included a letter to the client containing information about the nature of the study and assuring confidentiality, the client consent form, a demographic form, and a list of the questions that would be asked in the first interview. Clients were informed in the letter that the study was examining clients' inner experience of therapist self-disclosure in psychotherapy, and they were provided with the definition of therapist self-disclosure used in this study as well as examples of therapist self-disclosure. They were told that their consent meant that they would be volunteering to participate in two audiotaped phone interviews and that their therapist would know of their participation only if they chose to tell him or her. Potential participants were then asked to choose whether to continue their participation. For those who refused, their involvement was at an end. Those who agreed to participate completed and returned the consent form and the demographic form. Materials were returned by 20 clients, who were then scheduled for an interview (Knox et al., 1997, pp. 276–277).

Interview Protocols and Pilot of the Protocol

In a CQR study, participants are usually interviewed by phone or in person. An interview protocol is often developed through reviewing the existing literature and after conducting pilot interviews to evaluate its adequacy. Yet, it is important at a point later that the researchers bracket (i.e., set aside) the information gained from the literature so that data could be approached from a fresh perspective and could "speak" for themselves.

The Interview Protocol section from a CQR study follows:

The purpose of the interview was to examine the career choices of prominent female counseling psychologists in light of any serendipitous events they may have experienced. Because Patton (1990) has suggested starting the interview with a focus on the present before asking about background factors, we began the interviews with a warm-up question about current job activities (i.e., "Please tell me a little about what you do in your career and the various activities you take part in" and "How much time do you spend in academic activities and in practice activities?"). The interview then moved to asking about the participants' past in terms of their career path (see Appendix B for a copy of the full protocol). For example, the participants were asked how they decided to become a counseling psychologist, why they chose academia, who their role models or mentors were, and what some of their past career aspirations were. We believed this information would provide a context in which to place the impact of the chance events on their career choices.

Open-ended questions were then used to help facilitate participants' recall of the chance event. First participants were asked about their own personal definition of chance and whether they could identify any chance events that they had encountered that had affected their own career paths. Then they were asked to describe their most salient chance event. Other questions about the chance event included information about the event itself (e.g., what happened, when it happened, who was involved) and about the significance of the event (e.g., how it changed or impacted their career path or career choices). Next, the participants were asked to describe the context surrounding the event (e.g., stage of their career development, involvement of family or significant others, demographic issues, any barriers they encountered) and what they believed helped them take advantage of the chance event. Emphasis was placed on the collaborative nature of the interview and the importance of the participants conveying how they saw and made meaning of the events in their lives. (Williams, 1997, pp. 39–40)

In the beginning of this interview protocol description, the author first stated the purpose of the entire interview. Then, she explained the reason for starting her interview with certain warm-up questions and listed those questions. Subsequently, she described the types of questions she focused on ("the participants' past in terms of their career path") after the warm-up question and the purpose for asking those questions ("provide a context in which to place the impact of the chance events on their career choices"). Instead of listing all of the interview questions, the author asked the readers to refer to her appendix for a copy of the full protocol and provided some examples of the questions. In the second paragraph, the author described how she utilized interview questions to gather data on the participants' perceptions of the chance events that had an impact on their career paths. The author not only described the flow of the interview questions but also clearly identified the dimensions of the phenomena that interested her (e.g., participants' definition of chance, the significance and the context of the chance event, how they took advantage of the chance event in their career development). Finally, the author stated her efforts to understand the participants' perspective of the investigated phenomenon. These descriptions of the interview protocol helped the readers to understand the contents of the interviews as well as the rationale of having those questions in the interview.

After the protocol is developed, one or two pilot interviews are recommended by Hill et al. (1997) to test the protocol. A description of the procedure of piloting the interview follows:

> The interview questions were first piloted with two female counseling psychology professors. Both were White, married, and had one child. One was age 34 and the other age 35. One of the women had been in her career for 3 years post-Ph.D. and the other for 4 years. The two women participated in an audiotaped pilot phone interview. Results from this pilot helped determine the final form of the interview. The interview questions were revised for the protocol based on the participant's comments. The transcriptions of the pilot interviews were also used to help train the research team in the qualitative methods and data analytic strategies. (Williams, 1997, p. 41).

In the preceding example, the author described the number of interviewees and how she used the pilot results for her research (i.e., to revise the protocol and to train the research team members). The pilot of the protocol is important in CQR research because the interviews are more structured than the ones in other types of qualitative research (e.g., phenomenology), and CQR researchers use the pilot to examine the appropriateness and relevance of the interview questions from the participant's perspective or uncovering any important concepts that are unexpected by the researchers. Therefore, you must clearly identify who was interviewed in the pilot so that the readers can assess the credibility of the pilot interviews; you must also specify how you utilized the results of the pilot interviews instead of saying *only* that the protocol was piloted.

Training of the Research Team   Before the interview is conducted and the data are analyzed, the primary researcher of the CQR study needs to ensure that the research team members receive appropriate training in conducting interviews and data analyses. Following are two examples; one describes the training pertaining to conducting interviews, and the other one documents the training process for performing CQR data analyses.

TRAINING INTEVIEWING SKILLS

The interviews were semistructured, wherein each of the specific questions was asked but the interviewer was also encouraged to follow up on important ideas that fell outside the realm of those questions. The principal investigator and one of the American Indian scholar consultants trained the research team members to conduct the interviews. All of the interviewers had at least 1 year of experience providing counseling services, had completed at least some didactic training in career counseling, and had completed at least one multicultural counseling course. In a 90-minute training session, the interviewers read the questions, role-played a brief interview, and discussed ways in which they could best follow up on responses to the questions. (Juntunen et al., 2001, p. 276)

Because the interviewers are the instruments of the research, their interview skills will affect the quality and quantity of the data collected during the interview. In the preceding example, the author not only used interviewers who already had expertise and knowledge on content area of the study but also conducted training sessions for practicing interview skills.

TRAINING DATA ANALYSIS SKILLS
FROM A CQR DISSERTATION PROPOSAL

Training involved several weeks of meetings where feminist qualitative paradigms, consensual qualitative methods as well as research team members' expectations were discussed. The primary researcher also gave the research team members readings on rape, coping, qualitative research methodology as well as a copy of the dissertation proposal. The transcripts from the pilot interviews were used as practice for consensual qualitative research method as well as a springboard for further discussion. Since it is essential that all members would feel free to assertively state their opinions with each other in consensual qualitative research (CQR), power dynamics and team cohesiveness were emphasized. The team was encouraged to raise issues and questions about the project and readings throughout the research project. Finally, researchers may experience difficulties of "the stress, the deep personal involvement, the role conflicts, the physical and mental effort, the drudgery and discomfort—and even the danger—of observational studies" (Punch, 1998). The team members were reminded that it is essential for them to be aware of the possibilities of these stressors, to support each other throughout the research project, to process their emotions and document how their affective reactions may influence their research endeavors and interpretations of the events in their reflexive journals. The total number hours of this training ranged from 15–20 hours. (Wang, 2002, pp. 77–78)

In this example, the author described the length, the content, the purpose, and the process of the training section in her dissertation proposal. In particular, the emotional aspect of conducting research was emphasized in the research training process. Certain research topics (e.g., sexual assault, child abuse) may arouse lots of emotions in the researchers during the reading, interviewing, transcription, or data analysis process. Thus, the author delineated how she is going to tackle this issue in the research team training section. All of this information communicates the various aspects of data analysis utilized in this particular study.

Interview (Data Collection) The actual interviews can be conducted on the phone or face to face. Furthermore, immediately following the interviews, you should record memos (e.g., impression of the interviewee, comments about the flow of the session) that are often used later in understanding the data. Two examples are provided to illustrate the process of conducting interviews. The first example is a phone interview, and the second is a face-to-face interview.

In the first example, participants for the study were notified that the purpose of the study was to understand their sexual attraction to clients during the past 2 years of doing therapy and that the format of interviews would be two phone interviews over the period of 2 weeks. The participants were required to complete a survey containing their basic demographic information, whether or not they were sexually attracted to a client, their willingness to participate in the study, and their contact information. The participants were also informed that they would receive a book as a small token of appreciation. The author then described the entire phone interview process:

> We randomly assigned participants to interviewers. The assigned interviewer called the participant to arrange a time for the interview. Only the first name of the participant was used to set up and conduct the interviews. We informed participants that the interview would be taped and that their responses would be kept anonymous. At the end of the first 30–45 minute interview, the interviewer and participant set up a time for a 10–15 minute follow-up interview. During the time between the two interviews, another researcher on the team listened to the initial interview and gave suggestions for further probing during the follow-up interview. Also, the follow-up interview gave interviewers a chance to think of areas to probe further and provided participants with an opportunity to reflect on the initial interview and provide additional information. After the follow-up interview, interviewers asked participants to send their names and addresses on a postcard to one of the graduate students on the research team so that the participants could receive the book that served as the research incentive. Thus, there was no way to link the name of the intern to a specific interview. Following the interviews, we assigned each participant a code number, which was subsequently used to ensure anonymity. (Ladany et al., 1997, pp. 415–416)

Notice in this first example that the authors described how they ensured the confidentiality of the interview content, as well as how they utilized the second interview to gather richer data. In the second example, which follows, the author described specifically how she will conduct the face-to-face interviews. When the interview topics are sensitive (e.g., sexual assault experience in this case), some participants are likely to need referrals to counseling services, which needs to be specified in the methods chapter.

> During the interview, the researcher will first introduce herself and use responses such as active listening, minimal encouragement and emotional support. She will make sure that the participants have adequate space to convey the way they conceptualize their experiences without the researcher's view being imposed on them (for example, the participants will be encouraged to give their own definition of rape). Although all of the questions in the protocol should be asked at some point of the interview, the interviewer will leave the question open-ended and vary the order of the questions in accordance to the flow of the interview. Participants will have the freedom to answer the questions in an unstructured fashion. Probes will be used to obtain more in-depth and complete information or to clarify a response. In the end of the interviews, the researcher will ask each interviewee whether she wants to add anything else, how the interview process is for her, and if she has any feedback on the project. When necessary, referrals will be made to counseling services with the interviewees' consent. After the interview, the primary researcher will ask the interviewees whether they would like to review the transcripts and how they would like the transcripts to be sent to them so that confidentiality will not be breached. The participants will also be provided the opportunity to review a summary of the findings. Following these procedures will

ensure the reciprocity of the research relationship as well as the collaborative emphasis in feminist qualitative research. (Wang, 2002, pp. 76–77)

Transcribing the Interviews   According to Hill et al. (1997), once the interview is completed, it should be transcribed verbatim with identifying information omitted and unnecessary nonlanguage utterances ("um," "ah") and fillers ("you know") deleted. Copies of the transcripts should also be reviewed by the interviewees for additions, corrections, or clarifications. This step is called "member check," which enhances the credibility of the data (Lincoln & Guba, 1985). Consider, in the following example, the steps taken by the author to ensure the accuracy and anonymity of the transcripts:

> After the interview, the research team members transcribed the audiotapes (the primary researcher conducted all of the interviews and each of the three other team members transcribed 4–5 interviews). Then the primary researcher listened to each tape and matched it against the transcript and made corrections. The transcripts were then assigned a code number (1–13) and were sent to the participants for corrections and/or additions. This allowed the participants an opportunity to highlight any information they wanted to be "masked" in the final analysis (so as to protect confidentiality). When the transcript was returned to the primary researcher, she made the necessary corrections although there were not many requested. (Williams, 1997, p. 44)

Data Analytic Procedure   Hill et al. (1997) delineated the step-by-step data analytic procedure. Basically, the four stages of data analysis—(a) identification of domains, (b) core ideas, (c) audit of core ideas, and (d) cross-analysis—should all be briefly described in the thesis or dissertation. Following is a good example of how to write the data analysis section of the methods chapter:

Identification of Domains

Each transcript was individually read and coded for domains, or primary topic areas. Original domains were assumed by the questions asked in the interview. These were refined and new domains were added as new data were analyzed. As domains were identified, each team member identified data blocks (participant statements). The assignment of data to different domains was done within each transcript that reflected the various domains. We then brought our individual assignment of data to the team meeting and discussed our interpretations until we reached consensus. The final set of domains included the following: the meaning of career, definitions of success, supportive factors, obstacles, and living in two worlds.

Core ideas

Once the domains for individual transcripts had been discussed and agreed on, core ideas within each domain were then identified (see Hill et al., 1997, for a complete discussion of the analysis process). We recorded these sets of domains and ideas in graphic form, with each domain serving as the center of an axial diagram. This process allowed us to see how individual core ideas might be represented in more than one domain and also to better identify other relationships between domains, to determine that domains and core ideas had been defined clearly enough to be meaningful. Some appropriate overlap was observed. However, in a few cases, it became apparent that two or more domains were better collapsed into one or that one domain was too inclusive. For example, discrimination was originally an idea addressed under the domain of living in two worlds. However, additional discussion, particularly in the cross-case analysis, resulted in the decision that discrimination was being discussed as a separate obstacle in the career journey, rather than as an aspect of living in two worlds. Examples of emerging core ideas included benefit to others, rejection of materialism, concern for the future, and obstacles and barriers.

Audit of Core Ideas

After each of the transcripts had been analyzed using this individual and group technique, a master list of the domains was constructed and all of the core ideas from the 18 transcripts were listed and categorized within domains. An auditor then reviewed the set of domains and core ideas. The auditor, Dominic Barraclough, was a member of the research team who had completed interviews but did not participate in the analysis portion of the project. He is of European descent and was completing a predoctoral internship in a counseling center setting while the analysis was being conducted. The auditing resulted in verification and clarification of several domains identified by the team as the team responded to the auditor's feedback.

Cross-Analysis

The audit was followed by cross-analyses, during which domains and core ideas were compared across the individual transcripts to determine a set of categories. During this process, the group looked at the domains and core ideas with an emphasis on discovery (Hill et al., 1997), looking for new ideas to emerge from the data. Domains and core ideas were combined into new categories. The team then went through the original transcripts again with the new set of categories to investigate whether any important information had been overlooked and to identify descriptive quotes for each category and core idea. Following the cross-analyses, the auditor again reviewed the work of the team and provided feedback on the categories. The team reviewed the auditor's feedback, discussed the points raised, and made some modifications to the cross analyses. (Juntunen et al., 2001, p. 277)

In this example, the authors clearly summarized the steps they took at each stage of data analysis. Also, following the description of each procedure, they provided examples of domains and core ideas that emerged from the data analysis. Moreover, in the core idea section, the authors explained the axial diagrams, which were used to facilitate their data analyses and to decide whether there was a need to revise the domains and core ideas. After the domains and core ideas are constructed, a master list of the domains and core ideas, as well as the original transcripts, should be given to the auditors. According to Hill et al. (1997), the auditor(s) should be outside of the data analysis team in order to bring in a fresh perspective. Therefore, you should clarify your background when you write your methods chapter. In short, these steps should be clearly documented so that the readers can evaluate the rigor of the research method.

Phenomenology/Hermeneutics

Phenomenology study "describes the meaning of experiences of a phenomenon (or topic or concept) for several individuals. In this type of qualitative method, the researcher reduces the experiences to a central meaning or the 'essence' of the experience (Moustakas, 1994)" (Creswell, 1998, p. 236). In the following paragraphs, the major procedures of a phenomenology study are introduced along with examples of how to write the various sections of the methods chapter.

Phenomenology has its roots in the works of Wilhelm Dilthey, F. D. E. Schleiermacher, Hans-Georg Gadamer, Martin Heidegger, and Edmund Husserl on phenomenological and hermeneutic philosophy. Since then, many individuals in social science fields, especially sociology and psychology, followed its tenets and implemented its philosophy in their research. Different approaches to phenomenology were developed (e.g., psychological phenomenology, hermeneutic phenomenology, existential phenomenology, social phenomenology, reflective/transcendental phenomenology, and dialogical phenomenology). (For a review, see Creswell, 1998.)

Phenomenological researchers need to design their studies to be ideally suited to understand the phenomenon under investigation (Polkinghorne, 1989). Phenomenological researchers follow some general guidelines in developing their studies. These guidelines for conducting a phenomenological study were summarized by Creswell (1998) into five areas: (a) philosophical perspectives and epoche; (b) research questions and lived experiences; (c) sampling and data collection; (d) phenomenological data analysis; and (e) essential, invariant structure (or essence) of the lived experience. These five dimensions of the guidelines are key concepts of the approach and should be included in a phenomenological thesis or dissertation. Each is illustrated with examples in the following sections.

Philosophical Perspectives and Epoche   You need to understand the philosophical perspectives of phenomenology and/or hermeneutics prior to conducting a phenomenological thesis or dissertation because its philosophy influences the ways to approach your research topic and the ways to study how people experience a phenomenon (Creswell, 1998). In the beginning of the methods chapter of a thesis or dissertation, you need to briefly summarize the philosophical perspectives of phenomenological research so that the readers will know the tenets embraced by the researchers when the study is conducted.

Consider the following example from a hermeneutic phenomenological study of adopted adolescents. The author first stated that the purpose of his study was to investigate the lived experience and philosophical view of adopted adolescents and to understand "the meaning of being adopted, the process coming to understand adoption in their lives, concerns and psychological problems they have experienced related to adoption, and the relationship of adoption to the understanding they have developed about what it means to be a human being" (Abbott, 1999, p. 51). Then, the author pinpointed that his study is grounded in the ontological hermeneutics of Martin Heidegger and Hans-Georg Gadamer and its methodology is based on the strategy developed by Donald Polkinghorne, Patricia Bénner, Karen Plager, and Victoria Leonard. Following is part of his description of the philosophical view of the ontological hermeneutics. Notice that the author not only described the philosophical tenets but also illustrated how he integrated the philosophical thinking into the formulation of his research.

PHILOSOPHICAL PERSPECTIVES FROM A HERMENEUTIC PHENOMENOLOGICAL DISSERTATION

This hermeneutic and phenomenological study acknowledges at the outset then that its object is different than that of a statistical or empirical study, that what it has produced is interpretation, and that criteria other than those of a Cartesian and objectivist science will have to be adduced to evaluate the worth or accuracy of its results. Such a study, as Taylor (1985b) remarks, is hermeneutical in the sense that

> . . . its most primitive data would be the readings of meanings, and its object would have the three properties mentioned above: the meanings are for a subject in a field or fields; they are moreover meanings which are partially constituted by self-definitions, which are in this sense already interpretations, and can thus be re-expressed or made explicit by a science of politics. (p. 52)

Thus, as Taylor convincingly argues, it follows that the empirical ideals of the natural sciences do not apply here, and hence the interpretations produced by this type of study will never be verifiable by appeal to an ultimate criterion beyond any and all possible differences in interpretations (see Taylor, 1985b, p. 53). In fact, Taylor asserts that ultimately, the criterion or what counts as a superior interpretation in a hermeneutical science is that, '. . . from the more adequate position one can understand one's own stand and that of one's opponent, but not the other way around' (p. 53). Or, as Anthony Stigliano has asserted (class lecture, CSPP, 1997) in considering the nursing studies of Patricia Benner (1984), the plausibility of an interpretation lies in its ability to stand up to competing alternative explanations, its consistency with implications of the text or phenomena being studied, and in that it can be used to ground successful innovations or improvements in the lives or practices of those concerned with the phenomena.

Therefore, in light of this hermeneutic perspective, rather than attempting to utilize an "Archimedean" or transcendent point of view in which one discovers foundational knowledge based on a prior principles established by "judgments which could be anchored in a certainty beyond subjective intuition" (Taylor, 1985b, p. 19), this inquiry utilized a somewhat different method. Specially, I sought to construct, through an interpretive dialogue with the adopted subjects, a plausible reading of the meaning of some of the psychological problems frequently experienced by adopted teenagers. This is a reading or interpretation that takes into account both the adopted person's alienation and estrangement from social and hence individual reality, and the interaction of this phenomenon with aspects of our dominant culture's current understanding of what it is to be human, have a self, and belong to a family and a society.

Based on the hypothesis that adopted individuals may have some unformulated philosophical insight into what Heidegger, among others, has called the "interpretive" nature of human Being, the study sought to make explicit these possible aspects of adoption and the perspective on the nature of human being embodied in the lived understandings, problems, and practices of these particular subjects. It attempted to develop a possible way of conceiving of an "ontology of adoption" set against the larger cultural background of notions of selfhood, identity, autonomy, and agency; what Charles Taylor has referred to as a culture's shared inter-subjective understandings about human beings and our practices which form the social matrix within which individuals live and act (Taylor, 1985b, p. 34).

This method, as has been said, differs radically from the tenets of standard quantitative research and is based largely on Martin Heidegger's understanding of Being/human Being, and on Gadamer's exegesis of the process by which we pursue understanding in general. That this method is appropriate to psychological inquiry has been well established. Taylor (1985b, pp. 3–4), for example, contends that

> A being who exists only in self-interpretation cannot be understood absolutely; and one who can only be understood against the background of distinctions of worth cannot be captured by a scientific language that essentially aspires to neutrality. Our personhood cannot be treated scientifically in exactly the same way we approach our organic being. What it is to possess a liver or a heart is something I can define quite independently of the space of questions in which I exist for myself, but not what it is to have a self or be a person.

Thus, the human sciences must have as their object meanings and the lived understandings of individuals-in-context; an object that can only be rendered intelligible via the interpretations of persons who, like everyone else, are embedded in a particular social and historical context. Furthermore, it is an assumption of this study that our understandings of world and self are not derived in a realm of privatized subjectivity from an a priori set of principles or consciously held beliefs which can be exhaustively and objectively spelled out by studying the isolated subject. Our self-interpretations have a more public and, paradoxically, a more concealed origin. . . . (Abbott, 1999, pp. 54–56)

Furthermore, before conducting a phenomenological research, you need to bracket your assumptions and judgments about the phenomenon in order to understand the phenomenon through the informants. This strategy was termed *epoche* by Husserl. You need to document these presuppositions in the methods chapter. Following is an example of how the researcher delineates his/her assumptions about the phenomenon under investigation. The excerpt is from a phenomenological study on the perspectives of elderly people on resilience across the life span. In particular, notice that the author included his biographical sketch in the appendix so that the readers could obtain more understanding on the author's stance and his lens through which he interpreted the phenomenon under study.

The researcher maintains balance between freeing participants to tell their stories openly while retaining the focus that allows the specific information of interest to surface (McCracken, 1988). Essentially, in the qualitative method the researcher gathers and transmits information from the participants to the audience in the least interfering fashion. This promotes empirically grounded findings. The researcher must keep participants and their subjective worlds at the center of attention throughout the research (Gubrium, 1992).

Researchers who study subjective experiential meanings aim to use techniques which inhibit their perspectives from influencing the participants' words (Jacobs, 1994). The goal is for the participants to naturally articulate their perspectives free of researcher bias (Kaufman, 1986). In qualitative inquiry, clarifying the worldview, assumptions, and theoretical orientation of the researcher offers readers the context of the researcher as the instrument (Merriam, 1988). Merriam suggests that one's disciplinary orientation may determine how phenomena are defined.

The researcher's role in this study was to draw out, organize, and transmit participant's meanings relative to resilience, in the least interfering way. To allow insight into the researcher's cultural background, worldview, assumptions, and theoretical orientation, a biographical sketch is provided as Appendix C. (Adams, 1997, pp. 56–58).

Research Questions and Lived Experiences   The research questions for a phenomenological/hermeneutic study are developed in order to understand the everyday lived experiences of individuals and to explore what those experiences mean for them (Creswell, 1998). These research questions could guide the development of the interview questions and generate dialogue about the phenomenon under study between the researcher and the participant. Consider the following example of the research questions for a hermeneutic phenomenological study on adopted adolescents:

> This study attempted to address the following general questions about the experience and problems of adopted adolescents using specific questions organized in a semi-structured interview schedule (see Appendix A). The general research questions as well as the specific questions found in the interview schedule were developed through a process of extensive readings of both the psychological literature on adoption, and the works of philosophical and hermeneutic thinkers such as Martin Heidegger and Hans-Georg Gadamer. These two seemingly disparate domains of thought began to become integrated for me during my clinical experience in using philosophy in the counseling process with adopted teenagers in residential treatment. In general, this study investigated the following issues:
>
> 1. Was there a sense of "not-at-homeness" or of being "out of everydayness" in relation to one's family, environment, or self to be found in the discourse of adopted adolescents?
> 2. How did this sense of being dislocated or not-at-home show up in the discourse? For example, was it conveyed as a sense of "not belonging" or not "fitting in"?
> 3. If so, was it related to adoption? In what ways?
> 4. Did the fact of adoption, or of having been told of one's adoption, change things significantly for the adolescent; i.e., in their development or sense of

self, family relationships, friendships, orientation toward work and life goals, etc.?

5. Could we better understand this change, or the differences in these adolescents' experience using the hermeneutics of Heidegger and Gadamer? How did these thinkers help us to interpret what was conveyed by adopted adolescents?

6. If adopted adolescents had a sense of not being at-home or unproblematically immersed in their everyday contest, and if this perception was related to adoption, then why was it important to investigate it?
   - Why was it important to them?
   - Why was it important for others (therapists) to understand?
   - What were the effects the adolescents perceived this feeling or perspective to have had on their life?
   - Were they negative? Pervasive? What domains of functioning did this perception effect most, and why?
   - Were they positive? In what ways had this perception helped the adolescents?

7. If it existed in some form, did the adopted adolescent's perception of the problematic and contingent nature of our "selves" and relationships offer knowledge or a valuable perspective to persons who were not adopted; i.e., insights into the general condition of human being?

8. What, if anything, did these adolescents' insights into the nature of human being and selfhood reveal about our current cultural configuration of the self and its attendant discontents or illnesses?

9. What implications for treatment could be drawn from adopted adolescents' self-interpretations of their existence in general, or of their specific psychological problems which resulted in their seeking therapeutic assistance? (Abbott, 1999, pp. 58–60)

In this example, notice that the author first clearly stated how he formulated the research questions and then delineated the questions he raised about the phenomenon of interest. He emphasized the importance of grounding the interpretations in the discourse (e.g., How did this sense of being dislocated or not-at-home show up in the discourse?) and attempted to use the philosophical tenets of hermeneutics to interpret lived experiences of the adopted adolescents. Furthermore, in accordance with the guidelines of conducting a phenomenological study, the author is interested in how the participants' perception of the phenomenon is related to their everyday context. Finally, the last three research questions also contribute to understanding the implications of this study for nonadopted people, revealing cultural configuration of self as well as formulating treatment for the psychological problems of adopted adolescents.

Sampling and Data Collection   In the following paragraphs, the sampling method (criterion-based sampling) and data-collection method (e.g., long interviews) of phenomenology is illustrated with examples.

Criterion-based sampling is used in a phenomenological study to select participants who meet the following criteria: (a) they experienced the phenomenon under study, and (b) they can articulate their lived experiences (Creswell, 1998). Following is an example of participant selection section of a phenomenological study on the resilience of the elderly. Notice that the author first described the criterion-based sampling method and clearly stated the criteria for selecting the participants for his study. Then, he presented his rationale for choosing those criteria.

> Purposeful sampling (Patton, 1980 & 1989), also defined as criterion-based sampling (Goetz & LeCompte, 1984), was used in selecting the participants. The following criteria were used to guide purposive sampling: participants were unknown to the researcher and each other, they were few in number, and they were culturally contrasted (McCracken, 1988).
>
> Ethnocultural representation is an especially important consideration with the oldest-old. Due to the morality rate among many minority cultures, there is a significant lack of representation in this age group (U.S. Bureau of the Census, 1993, 88, table 113). As of 1990, the ethnocultural divisions in the United States were 80.3% White (includes Anglo-Saxons, White ethnics, and socioreligous ethnics), 12.1% Black (includes African Americans, West Indians, and Haitians), 9% of Hispanic origin (includes Mexicans, Puerto Ricans, Cubans, Spaniards, and other Central and South Americans), 2.9% Asian (includes Chinese, Filipino, Japanese, Koreans, Indochinese, Pacific Islanders, and Middle Eastern Asians), and 0.8% Native Americans (includes American Indians, Eskimos, and Aleutes) (Axelson, 1993).
>
> Qualitative researchers mention a point in their inquiry when the same information is reported where little new is being learned (Bertauz, 1981; Douglas, 1976; Glasser & Strauss, 1967; Lincoln & Guba, 1985). A diverse sample of participants who reflect the same dimensions, known as information saturation, demonstrate that enough exploration has occurred (Seidman, 1991).
>
> Saturation with consistent themes and patterns between cases occurred in this study by the seventh participant. Ten individuals were interviewed to attain three male participants to match the gender census of the oldest-old and maintain contrast between the cases. The Statistical Abstract of the United States reported that as of 1990 there were 980,000 males (28%) and 2,542,000 females (72%) that were aged 85 and over. Including cases beyond the saturation point strengthens confidence in the findings.
>
> The participants were volunteers who were 85 years old and over (the oldest-old age group). They were cognitively and physically capable of participating in retrospective life-review. Contrast was high between participants, including the following cultural variables: ethnicity, gender, sexual orientation, education, spiritual and religious perspectives, socioeconomic status, and personal history. A highly contrastive sample with likeness of surfacing themes strengthens characteristics consideration. This research purposefully included culturally contrastive older adults, to increase the cultural richness represented in the data. (Adams, 1997, pp. 58–60)

After presenting the sampling method, you should describe your data-collection method. Typically, data are collected via in-depth (e.g., 2 hours) interviews with 5 to 25 individuals. In addition, self-reflection of the researchers during and after the interview process, as well as depiction of the phenomenon from art works (e.g., poems, paintings, and novels), could be included as part of the data (Moustakas, 1994; Polkinghorne, 1989). In the following example, the author utilized interviews as the way to collect data; thus, the interview protocol was presented in the methods chapter.

INTERVIEW SCHEDULE FOR A HERMENEUTIC PHENOMENOLOGICAL DISSERTATION

The data for this were the narratives and insights of adopted adolescents collected individually using semi-structured, face-to-face interviews. The interview data were recorded by audio tape and handwritten notes, and later organized thematically for interpretation (See Data analysis, p. 68). The interviews were structured to some degree by the schedule in Appendix A, though the schedule was intended to serve more as a guide and reminder to the interviewer to inquire about specific domains rather than to set up a strict "question and answer" interview format. The schedule served as a prompt to help elicit and stimulate the adoptees' stories about salient events and insights concerning their sense of self, the vicissitudes of adoption, family relationships.

The interview schedule was divided into the following sections; each related to the overall research questions but which addressed somewhat different aspects of the participant's experience, history and functioning. These sections were:

- General Information and Family History
- Childhood and Adoption Discourse
- Current Functioning and Understanding About Adoption
- Philosophy and Worldview (Abbott, 1999, pp. 65–66)

The author generated the interview protocol from his research questions. He stated the structure and purposes of the interview schedule, as well as the primary dimensions of the phenomenon under study. Due to limited space, he presented the entire protocol in the appendix. In the actual protocol, he avoided using any jargon (e.g., "not-at-homeness" for adopted adolescents); instead, he wrote his interview questions in common language (e.g., "How did you feel about growing up in your adopted parents' home? Did you feel you fit in?") so that they could be easily understood by the participants. The interview protocol should cover many dimensions of the everyday lived experience and create an open space for the participants to freely retell their life stories.

Data Analysis   Two examples of the data analytic procedures of phenomenological studies follows. Phenomenological and hermeneutic researchers have proposed slightly different analytic techniques. You need to decide whose model you are going to follow when conducting you analyses and clearly state the sources, as well as the steps of the analytic method, as in the following examples:

DATA ANALYTIC PROCEDURE IN A PHENOMENOLOGICAL STUDY

The procedure proposed by Colaizzi (1978) was used as the means for analyzing the interview protocols:

1. Sense of the Whole—The analysis team read each protocol to "acquire a feeling . . . (make) sense out of them" (p. 59).

2. Extracting Significant Statements—From each protocol the analysis team extracted statements that were directly related to the phenomenon under study.
3. Formulating Meanings—The analysis team assigned meaning to the extracted significant statements, deriving meanings that "should never sever all connection with the original protocol . . ." (p. 59).
4. Clustering Themes—The analysis team organized the formulated meanings into clusters of themes and validated them by referring back to the original protocols to ensure their existence.
5. Exhaustive Description—The emergent themes were compiled into an exhaustive description of the investigated phenomenon as the analysis team attempted to achieve . . ." as unequivocal a statement of identification of its fundamental structure as possible . . ." (p. 61).
6. Final Validation—The investigator invited the participants in the study to review the exhaustive description to verify whether or not it was congruent with their experience. Any corrections, addition, and deletion that the participants indicated were needed, were made. Each participant was provided an explanation of the thematic structure derived from the interview protocols. (Webb, 1996, pp. 28–29)

DATA ANALYTIC PROCEDURE IN A HERMENEUTIC STUDY

According to Leonard, then, the process of data analysis begins when the research recognizes, personally, the three components of this forestructure. These three components are, briefly:

1. The "fore-having," which is an a prior sense of the totality of all the elements which make up a given phenomena.
2. The "fore-sight," which is essentially the interpretive or theoretical "lens" through which the research is inclined to view the phenomena.
3. The "fore-conception," which are criteria, derived from the above elements of understanding, for what counts as an appropriate question in the study, and what would constitute an answer to such a question.

In a hermeneutic study the object in recognizing these elements of bias is not to attempt to remove them entirely or somehow transcend them to arrive at an objective stance. Rather, the exigencies of a hermeneutic approach demand that the researcher constantly remains aware of these foreground understandings and be firmly committed to allowing them to be challenged, expanded, and re-worked by the discourse of the actual subjects . . . .

The next step in the interpretive process may be seen as the attempt to organize the data coherently. Here again I will borrow from Leonard's concise summary of the method developed by hermeneutic researchers such as Polkinghorne, Benner, and Plager under the guidance of the philosophers Hubert Dreyfus and Charles Taylor. Leonard (1994, p. 59, in Benner, 1985) suggests three general steps in the interpretive process:

1. Thematic analysis, in which all of the collected data is read carefully, in order to get a global sense of the material. Lines of the inquiry concerned with these themes are then established via the theoretical forestructure which has been identified as grounding the study. From these lines of inquiry, one identifies an overall interpretive framework, and then re-reads

the participants' responses and stories with this plan in mind. From this re-reading will emerge categories of meaning, or types of understandings which will constitute the foundation of the study's results.

2. The researchers analyzes specific events, happenings, or situations that the participant discusses. The researcher looks for "exemplars" or stories that may be interpreted to make explicit a meaning or perspective which can be seen to be essential in other events in the participant's narrative, even though the specific circumstances of the two events will differ.

3. The researcher identifies "paradigm cases," that is, cases in which strong patterns of meaning and practice emerge, and through which clear inter-pretations can be developed to show how a participant's actions or atti-tudes have emerged from his or her context, concerns, and implicit understandings.

In this study, the adoptee's stories, remarks, and answers were organized along these lines. Instead of using step three as outlined above, I substituted a section including contextual data which appeared significant and was not other-wise included in the previous results sections. Furthermore, to these interpretive components I added an organizational step which fell roughly between steps one and two above: the narratives of the participants where thematically organized into Thematice Research Prepositions, discussed in the Results Section as TRPs. (Abbott, 1999, pp. 71–73).

From these two preceding examples, the readers would know the model and the exact procedures that were followed by the author in analyzing the data. This also set the stage for presenting the results chapter that follows. In other words, the readers then would expect to see the various interpretive results (e.g., themes, exhaustive descriptions) generated in the analytic procedure.

Essence of the Experiences   The exhaustive descriptions were con-structed through extracting the significant statements, formulating meanings, and clustering themes of the original data. The exhaustive descriptions could provide the readers an understanding of the essence of the lived experiences and represent a unifying structure of a phenomenon. The examples of how to write the exhaustive descriptions are provided in Chapter 13.

TRUSTWORTHINESS OF QUALITATIVE RESEARCH

After presenting the paradigm and strategy of inquiry in the methods chapter, you should address the rigor of the qualitative research design. Some researchers have argued for alternative ways to evaluate the rigor of data col-lection and analytic procedure in qualitative research (Pidgeon, 1996). For example, comparing to the criteria used by quantitative research for evaluat-ing a quantitative study (e.g., internal validity, external validity/generalizability, reliability and objectivity), a different set of criteria (i.e., credibility, transfer-ability, dependability and confirmability) were proposed by Lincoln and Guba

(1985) to evaluate the scientific worth of the qualitative research. Many of the techniques for establishing good scholarship (trustworthiness) of qualitative research were mentioned in the earlier section on Strategies of Inquiry. Lincoln and Guba (1985) summarized the methods utilized by qualitative researcher groups who follow different paradigms and strategies of inquiry and indicated how these methods would address the same questions asked by quantitative researchers regarding the rigor of the research endeavors. Many qualitative researchers have since followed Lincoln and Guba's suggestions in conducting qualitative research; you may refer to Lincoln and Guba's (1985) book for more details.

Following is a brief example on how to describe trustworthiness of the methods:

> In qualitative inquiry the interviewer is the research instrument. Patton (1990) emphasizes that the worth of an interview depends to a great extent on the qualities of the interviewer. It is crucial that the interviewer depends to a great extent on the qualities of the interviewer. It is crucial that the interviewer be trustworthy if the study is to be successful. Trustworthiness must be established with the participants, but equally important, the credibility of the work must be demonstrated to the scholarly community, which has a long tradition of support for quantitative methodology and statistical findings. Lincoln and Guba (1985) also emphasize the importance of trustworthiness. The research must persuade the receivers of her work that the results of the inquiry are worthwhile. It is the responsibility of the researcher to determine what arguments, criteria, what questions asked and answered would be persuasive on this issue.
>
> Lincoln and Guba (1985) note that in quantitative inquiry the criteria for judging trustworthiness are internal validity, external validity, reliability, and objectivity. In qualitative inquiry, the analogous criteria are credibility, transferability, dependability, and confirmability. . . .

Credibility

The naturalistic inquirer strives to present the "multiple constructed realities" (Lincoln & Guba, 1985, p. 295) of the participants and the credibility of these presentations is measured by their acceptance by those same participants. To reach the goal of utmost credibility in this study four techniques were utilized to insure that the findings are trustworthy. There are prolonged engagement, peer debriefing, negative case analysis and member checks. We shall discuss each of these in relation to the study.

Prolonged Engagement

In order to produce credible findings it was essential for me to spend sufficient time with each participant to get to know her well enough to be trusted with the details of one of her most intimate relationships. It was important to see each participant in her home and to learn the formation of her present family or individual lifestyle. The exception in this study was a participant who asked to be seen in her office because of the presence of her young children, which she felt, would be distracting. I agreed to that request, but was invited to the participant's home for the third interview. Her children were not at home.

. . . The process of building trust between this researcher and the participants extended over several months as the interviews progressed. Lincoln and Guba (1985) refer to trust as a growing process. The researcher must show participants that their trust will not be betrayed; that anonymity will be maintained; that the reasons for the study have been honestly portrayed, and most importantly that the interests of respondents and the investigators will be equally respected. It is essential that the participants influence and inform the inquiry process. . . . (Schaefer, 1997, pp. 76–79)

Note in this example that the author described the criteria for evaluating trustworthiness first and then presented the specific steps that were taken to meet those criteria in this particular study. She went on to use another eight pages to describe how she strove to establish credibility, transferability, dependability, and confirmability of her study.

CONCLUSIONS

This chapter addressed a wide range of issues related to the methods chapter of a qualitative thesis or dissertation. The nature and definition of qualitative studies were initially discussed, followed by the clarification of the key myths and facts regarding this type of methodology. You were encouraged to have a clear understanding of qualitative research before deciding to use this methodology. The next sections focused on the various paradigms and strategies of inquiry for qualitative inquiry. Three strategies of inquiry (namely, grounded theory, consensual qualitative research, and phenomenology/ hermeneutics) were introduced with excerpts from dissertations and journal articles. We maintained that you need to attend to the different philosophical underpinnings and data-collection procedures as well as analytic approaches for each strategy of inquiry. The examples cited in this chapter can serve as models to follow when you write your methods chapter. Finally, the ways to evaluate the rigor of qualitative research methodology were briefly described.

EXCLUSION IS EASIER, INCLUSION IS BETTER

Diversifying Samples*

This is a particularly exciting time in the development of research in applied psychology, both within the United States and abroad. Within the United States, society is increasing in diversity along a host of dimensions. For example, the total U.S. population has increased by 13.2% over the last decade (U.S. Census Bureau, 2001). During this time the number of White individuals in the United States has decreased and the number of racial and ethnic group members has increased and is projected to continue to rise; this is but one example of the increased diversity of the U.S. population. In addition, given the Internet and greater global mobility, the same limitations no longer exist to studying cross-cultural samples. Studying psychological phenomena from a cross-cultural perspective can add a great deal to existing knowledge bases. Moreover, there is a growing appreciation for the importance of studying psychological phenomena from a culture-specific perspective.

Previous contributions to the applied psychology literature have been skewed toward studying primarily White, middle-class, highly educated, freshman and sophomore college students (Buboltz, Miller, & Williams, 1999; Dawis, 1987; Evans & Donnerstein, 1974). This is true in part because it was easier and more convenient. Often times these samples were collected in introductory psychology classes, where students were required to participate in a certain amount of research as a requirement of the class and, thus, the data were much more convenient to collect. Although this research has provided a great deal of important information about psychological phenomena, greater diversity of samples is needed to be able to more accurately generalize findings to the broader population. Thus, although a college student population may be very appropriate to answer certain research questions (e.g., acquaintance rape on college campuses, binge drinking in the fraternity system, first-year career indecision), the type of diversity within the samples used for these college studies needs to be examined. For example, do the samples include the diversity of

*This chapter co-authored with M. Meghan Davidson.

179

college students currently on campuses? Are they reflective of the growing trend of more adult learners; more first-generation college students; greater racial and ethnic diversity; greater numbers of international students; or "out" gay, lesbian, bisexual, and transgendered individuals? If the samples of college students are not reflective of populations on campuses, then the results of a particular study may or may not generalize to all students. For example, does acquaintance rape happen at the same rate for international students on college campuses and are the underlying attitudes toward sexual violence the same for this group?

Thus, generalizability is a key issue in considering what type of sample is most appropriate for your thesis or dissertation. We strongly encourage you to ask yourself: To what population do I want to be able to generalize my results? Although researchers often want to generalize to the world's population, in reality researchers should identify the most important and realistic populations to which they want to generalize given their particular topic. Once you have answered the question of generalizability, then you will be more clear about where a sample will need to be obtained.

In addition to diversifying samples on college campuses, going outside of college samples into communities where the vast majority of the populace lives is also important. Fitzgerald and Betz (1994) note that although only 20% of the U.S. population is college educated, 70% of psychological research is conducted with college samples. Munley (1974) noted many years ago that a more active research agenda focused on populations other than college students was necessary in order to provide services for people across the life span and for individuals outside of the academic setting. Though stated over 25 years ago, this observation remains true today and may even be a more urgent call to heed. Today's society has numerous pressing social problems, all of which can benefit from scientific inquiry. Psychologists and counselor educators can make a contribution to enhancing the quality of life for many diverse populations through research.

There are vast numbers of understudied or unstudied populations. The tendency is to think first about racial and ethnic minority populations, because these groups have been understudied in the professional literature. Their plight has been more severe than many other groups in that they often experience prejudice and oppression from living in a racist society. Thus, diversifying samples along racial and ethnic lines is critical. Other groups that have been underrepresented in the literature also could greatly benefit from study—for example, people who live in rural areas; the aged; women; individuals with physical disabilities; members of particular religious groups; gay, lesbian, bisexual, or transgendered individuals; and individuals with learning disabilities. Thus, in this chapter, we define diversity broadly. Most important, we encourage you to consider how you can impact the knowledge base in applied psychology with people from these and other understudied groups.

Sometimes when students are at the thesis or dissertation level, they have difficulty understanding how important building a knowledge base that can be useful in solving a social problem is, but students' research can do just that! While one research study will not bring a cure for breast cancer, it may discover psychosocial interventions that greatly ease the psychological pain of coping with the disease. Although one research study will not stop sexual violence, it may find critically important interventions to alter attitudes and behaviors related to rape. Although a true cure for eating disorders is beyond the reach of a single thesis or dissertation, a study may help to validate an instrument, for example, on an African American population; because of a single study, diagnosis and treatment of African Americans with eating disorders can be enhanced. In short, many important questions are yet to be answered and many diverse samples are in need of research.

Although conducting a study that examines previously underrepresented groups is appealing, sometimes students encounter obstacles in collecting their data or finding appropriate participants. Collecting data from college students in large introductory courses is often faster and more convenient. Rosie Bingham (2000) coined the following phrase in her presidential address to Division 17 (Counseling Psychology) of the APA: "Exclusion is easier, but inclusion is better." She further challenged organizations to greater inclusion by urging them to "draw the circle bigger." Although Rosie was referring to inclusion and exclusion of racial and ethnic minorities in professional organizations such as the Division of Counseling Psychology, her phrase aptly applies to inclusion and exclusion of various subgroups in the research conducted in applied psychology.

If the focus of your research is on diverse, non-college-student populations, then the question becomes: How do you get access to these more diverse populations? The purpose of this chapter is to provide you with information about conducting research with diverse samples. This chapter begins with a discussion of both the benefits and drawbacks of conducting research with diverse samples. In preparing this chapter, six interviews were conducted with students who conducted research for their theses or dissertations with noncollege samples. Four of the interviewees were women and two were men. One was a Latina and the remaining five were White. One individual interviewed was an "out" gay man. On average, each interview was 1 hour in length. Topics addressed included advantages and disadvantages, lessons learned, advice, and ethical dilemmas. Examples from other students that were not interviewed also appear in the chapter. The students' thesis and dissertation topics were diverse, such as career development of Latinas and Latinos, stress and coping behaviors of staff who work in shelters for battered women, evaluating a program aimed at increasing adolescent girls' interest in math and science, examining the experience of lesbian and gay counselors in supervision, and a scale development project focused on organizational change in businesses. Although these investigations studied a wide variety of research questions, many common themes, advice, and suggestions emerged throughout the interviews. Subsequently, the next section of the chapter summarizes the most important pieces of advice gleaned from these interviews: (a) Determine what sample is most appropriate for the topic of study, (b) Do not be afraid to work outside familiar settings, (c) Seek out supportive people, (d) Research a topic where you feel deep and abiding passion, (e) Develop and use your networks, (f) Determine how your research can benefit others, (g) Demonstrate respect for research allies, (h) Be explicit about what you need from the research, (i) Give back to people who have given to you, (j) Expect that things will go wrong and take five times longer than you would logically think. The chapter closes with a summary and some additional comments regarding personal qualities.

ADVANTAGES OF DIVERSIFYING SAMPLES

In interviewing students who have conducted theses and dissertations with non-college samples, several advantages were emphasized time and time again. We briefly highlight seven advantages of using diverse samples in research.

Reaping Intrinsic Rewards

Each individual that was interviewed commented on both the personal and professional meaning derived from doing work with non-college samples. For example, the student who conducted the program evaluation of a curriculum designed to increase adolescent girls' interest in math and science stated this: "I know that my study is making a real impact. My investigation will sustain and improve this program and, in turn, help more girls." Another student who examined the career development of Mexican American girls discussed the personal meaning and rewards for herself by sharing the following: "As a Latina from their own community who has succeeded educationally, I can be a role model to this group of girls. Through my work, I could show these girls that they too can succeed." As another example, the student who studied stress and coping behaviors in a population of shelter workers shared the following: "It is important to do applied research to give to the community, to do something *they can use*. The best way to do that is to include the community as the actual sample rather than a college sample. This is much more meaningful and makes more of a difference."

These are immensely powerful statements regarding the work that these students have done. Pursuing work that is personally and professionally meaningful can be very fulfilling and, therefore, represents a significant benefit to diversifying samples.

Investigating Underserved and Understudied Populations

"Their experiences have never been in the literature, their voices have been left out. My research has allowed their voices to be heard." This is how one interviewee who conducted his study on the training experiences of gay and lesbian counselors described an important advantage of doing research on diverse samples. Another student interviewed described the population she studied as an "unacknowledged sample." Too often the professional literature in various disciplines does not contain a broad representation of voices; consequently, many voices are unheard. Numerous groups of people are underserved and underresearched. Knowing about these groups who have historically been ignored in science is essential. As researchers, you have the ability to give voice to those who have been omitted in the professional literature, thereby providing a more comprehensive and accurate knowledge base.

Acquiring New Opportunities and Research Projects

Many of the individuals interviewed discussed numerous opportunities and further research ideas that developed from their work on their theses or dissertations. These opportunities were not expected and seemed to come as a pleasant surprise. For example, the student who evaluated the math and science program for girls was asked to work on future projects with that organization. The student who investigated training experiences of lesbian and gay counselors discovered career-development issues throughout his qualitative coding and thus has another research question to pursue. The student who examined shelter workers found herself naturally networking for possible future jobs in public policy and expanding her career options. The student who focused his dissertation on organizational change made many contacts to begin his future in consulting.

Clarifying and Enhancing One's Research Self-Efficacy

Sometimes students view themselves as simply in training and are not fully aware of their research expertise and proficiency in many areas. Students who diversified their samples discovered their own unique talents and skills. For example, one student discussed how valued and needed she felt in working on her interdisciplinary dissertation. Because she had a background in psychology and the organization with whom she worked was rooted in math and physics, her work involved two very different perspectives. In working with this group, she realized she had skills that the individuals in math and physics did not have. She was frequently called by the organization while conducting her statistical analyses and asked what she had discovered. Such interactions led her to understand more clearly that she had real expertise to offer this organization. Another student who studied organizational change reported that the businesses with whom he worked were very eager to know the results of his study. The executives of the various companies in the study were very interested in how the employees were coping with change within the work environment. Thus, significant interest from company administrators was very empowering and affirming for the student!

Enhancing the Generalizability of the Research

For many research questions, a college sample does not utilize the most appropriate population. Consider the following study. A researcher is interested in examining how individuals cope with change within their work environment, specifically if the work environment is going through "downsizing" or "rightsizing." The researcher is constructing a scale to measure various coping strategies in light of organizational change. In many ways, conducting an analogue study using college students as participants where they would simulate actual employees in a given organization or company would be easier. The students would be told to "act as if you are an employee in a company that is preparing to 'downsize' and let go of some of its employees." Given this hypothetical scenario, the students would be asked to respond to the questionnaire. Although analogue research has many advantages (see Heppner, Kivlighan, & Wampold, 1999), would it be the most appropriate given the research question? In this case, actual employees provide a sample in which stronger conclusions can be drawn about employee coping behavior. Thus, consider the research question, the type of possible conclusions, and to what populations the researcher wants to generalize the results. In many cases, a community sample or a more diverse sample provides a stronger and more generalizable research outcome.

Increasing One's Personal Knowledge

By using diverse samples, students often increase their knowledge base. Many of the interviewees discussed gaining a broader perspective by conducting research with non-college samples. They reported feeling more "connected to the real world." For example, one student discussed working with shelter workers: "This is an important group of people who do important work. Learning how they cope with tremendous stress in their real lives is meaningful." Another student indicated that examining the psychological theories commonly used in academic settings to determine whether these theories were relevant and appropriate for other environments was helpful. The student who examined the ways in which individuals respond to organizational change highlighted the need to be in a true-life setting: "I need to be with people who are *really* going through organizational change, so college students would never be true-to-life." By investigating samples outside of academic settings, students gain important information and are able to see aspects of the "real world" that others often miss.

Bridging the Gap Between Academia and the Community

Sometimes a gap exists between academia and the communities where the educational institutions are located. That is, the academic institutions and communities have limited interactions, which sometimes can create misunderstandings or even suspicion between these two groups. For example, sometimes community groups have felt they have been "used" as a researcher collected data for a thesis or dissertation, and that was the end of the "collaboration." Students indicated it was meaningful to work in close collaboration with and even for the community. By doing so, they reported that they were in fact creating a bridge between what sometimes appears to be two separate worlds—academia and the community. One student described her experiencing by reporting: "It is important to do applied research, to give to the community, to do something *they* can use. This bridges the gap between academia and the community. The best way to do that is to use them as an actual sample, rather than college students." By incorporating individuals and organizations from the larger community in various research projects, it is possible to not only build bridges from seemingly different environments but also help make the world a better place one step at a time.

DRAWBACKS TO DIVERSIFYING SAMPLES

Although using nontraditional samples has many benefits and advantages, some possible drawbacks are also important to discuss.

Time Demands

The vast majority of individuals with whom we spoke discussed the time commitment involved with using diverse samples as the number one disadvantage. When using noncollege samples, the luxuries of one-shot data collection and less preparation time are lost. Utilizing diverse samples entails contacting many people, organizing and attending meetings to get people on board with your study, travel, phone calls back and forth, faxing, and so on. Inherent additional work comes with using a noncollege population for research. Recruitment is simply harder than going into a psychology course and administering surveys.

Financial Costs

In addition to the extra time commitment, diversifying samples often entails more financial costs. Many of the individuals interviewed discussed costs in terms of travel expenses such as lodging, as well as long-distance phone calls, faxing costs, and so on. Consequently, you may need to pursue funding sources for this type of research. Some of the individuals interviewed discussed applying for and receiving fellowships such as the American Psychological Association Division 35 Hyde Fellowship, the American Association of University Women Fellowship, and various research awards at their institutional affiliations (see Chapter 2 for Web sites with information on financial support for research). The point here is that conducting research with samples outside the confines of a college or university will likely entail greater financial resources, and you may need to seek support to conduct such research.

Students' Time Lines Versus Agency Operations

Earlier in this chapter, we discussed the potential lack of control that students often encounter while researching diverse populations. Our interviewees shared with us the disadvantage in competing time lines. Often students have their time line for completing their thesis or dissertation in order to graduate. However, students' completion or graduation dates are typically not high priorities for agencies or organizations. Agencies or other organizations have normal operating procedures in place that have often been developed over many years and for specific reasons. Thus, administrators from these outside agencies/organizations often make the decisions concerning when data can be collected, from whom the data will be collected, and what kind and how much data can be collected. If, for example, the study is a program evaluation and the organization decides to postpone the program for 2 months because of their internal needs, the researcher's time line can be dramatically affected. When considered in light of a student working to complete her or his master's thesis or dissertation within a year, such a 2-month delay can be very difficult and pose numerous problems.

Different Levels of Understanding of Research Methodologies and Agency Procedures

Students in higher education are familiar and often comfortable with research designs and methodologies. Individuals outside this setting may be less knowledgeable about various aspects of research. In addition, often the student is an outsider to the organization and may not understand the typical operations of the organization and the rationale underlying its procedures. Thus, many of the individuals interviewed discussed the difficulty in communicating about the most optimal research methodologies and in understanding how the various organizations operated.

One student discussed her frustration in collecting data from various shelters. The directors of the shelters wanted to collect the surveys directly from the employees and, subsequently, send the data to the student. The student, cognizant of the importance of return rates, believed that this would reduce the return rate if employees questioned the confidentiality of their responses by returning the surveys to the directors. Although the student communicated this information with the directors, they were very firm in how the data were to be collected. Thus, different ways of approaching the research project may necessitate negotiations that may prove difficult.

Psychometric Concerns

Because of the overreliance on college samples, most of the instruments used in research have been developed and normed with college populations. Thus, whether the measures are reliable and valid when used with noncollege samples is unclear. This is an obvious drawback in conducting research with diverse samples and one that can only be remedied as researchers examine measures with more diverse populations.

ADVICE FOR "DRAWING THE CIRCLE BIGGER"

Determine What Sample Is Most Appropriate for the Topic

The first step in deciding if and how to diversify your sample is to carefully examine your chosen topic and to think carefully about what sample is most appropriate. Ask yourself the question: Once I have completed this investigation, who will be the most important sample to which I want to generalize my findings? This question is equally important if the sample is a more traditional collegiate sample or a more diverse community sample. For example, a student conducting a prevalence study of eating disorders on college campuses may want to generalize to sorority women, or to women who are in collegiate sports, or to a more random sample of all college women. She may be interested in studying the prevalence of eating disorders among African American college students. She may be interested in generalizing to both men and women who are suffering from eating disorders. An effective way to understand the most appropriate populations to be able to generalize your findings to is reading the literature to determine where data already exist on samples and where there are underrepresented or totally unrepresented groups. For example, in the area of eating disorders, prevalence studies have been conducted on college campuses in general and in sorority populations. Up until very recently, however, no prevalence studies had been reported on African American college women. Thus, one of our students (Mulholland, 2000) determined that, although replication studies of existing campus samples would certainly add to the literature, it seemed like it would add significantly more information if she were to conduct the first prevalence study with an African American collegiate sample. Because of this study, now some initial data exist concerning prevalence rates for various eating disorders in African American college women.

Thus, as you are conducting your reviews of the literature, monitor (and even record) the sample that was used in each investigation. In fact, we encourage you to develop a form to record this information and other relevant facts (see Chapter 4 for more information). Through this process, you will be able to determine with which samples your constructs have already been studied and what type of populations are underrepresented.

Do Not Be Afraid to Work Outside Familiar Settings

The fear of going outside the most typical data-collection methods with college students seems to be a factor for many people considering research with diverse samples. The notion of uncharted territory can be threatening and can elicit different types of fear. Maybe people will not understand what you want to do. Maybe they will not think it is important. Maybe they will not even want to talk to you about your ideas. These are all fears many of the people we interviewed had as they began to think of research questions that involved populations outside of the typical college student population. One student who examined the career development of Mexican American girls discussed two of her fears: studying a Latina population when she herself was White and obtaining a sample from high-school settings. Her method to overcome these fears was to "generate courage by practicing again and again what I was going to say." Another student explained overcoming her fears by continually reflecting on her reasons for choosing the population to be examined; she reminded herself of the importance of investigating a sample that had been previously overlooked in the literature. Through tactics such as these, you can be more comfortable going beyond common data-collection methods and typical populations.

Seek Out Supportive People

In anything that is new or novel, there will always be those people who will tell you it is a bad idea, that you should not pursue something different, that you should stick with the conventional. Likewise, in pursuing research that is non-traditional and incorporates diverse samples, students often encounter resistance to their ideas. Every one of the individuals interviewed for this chapter spoke of naysayers; they shared with us their experiences of faculty members or friends who discouraged them and their research topics. They related experiences with people who expressed the following sentiments: "Getting that sample will be too hard," "You'll never get the return rates you need," "It will take too much time," "Organizations outside university settings do not want people coming and doing research." One student, whose eventual career goal was academia, was told by a faculty member that, if he was going to study a nontraditional population (in this case, a gay and lesbian population) or take a nontraditional slant (e.g., feminist), he should couple this with more traditional approaches or traditional constructs (e.g., depression) so that the "old guard" at a given institution would have some way to connect with his research. This student shared with us that he believed that the advice of this faculty member was not naysaying but that its intent was protective. Although this individual probably had the student's best interests in mind, receiving this kind of feedback is still discouraging. Some comments from the "naysayers" may be valid. For example, the sample may be very difficult to obtain. It may indeed take more time. But we emphasize that these facts should not necessarily be the deciding factors. We encourage you to think carefully about the feedback offered and determine how valid it is in your unique situation but also to realize that sometimes you will need to follow your own dreams, even when others do not think it is the best idea for you.

For many reasons, the students and professionals we interviewed persevered with their ideas and pursued the topics they wanted to research in the manner they wanted to research them—and they all did so successfully. They told us how they deliberately sought out those faculty and friends who would support them and their less-than-traditional ideas. For example, one student wanted to investigate postpartum depression in women. Clearly, this is an area that would not be easily studied in an academic setting. Through contacting agencies like Planned Parenthood and local hospitals, this student was able to connect with individuals who recognized the importance of her research and were interested in the information she could provide to them from her study. Thus, the individuals at these agencies supported and encouraged this student to reach women experiencing postpartum depression. Another student interested in qualitative research for his dissertation received some protective comments from his advisor that qualitative research is a time-intensive methodology and perhaps not the best choice for a dissertation. However, this student connected with another faculty member who had a strong interest and much experience in this type of research. Through this faculty member's support, the student successfully employed a qualitative design. Overall, those interviewed said this: If the idea is important to you and you think it is meaningful for the knowledge base of the field, then pursue it. And, most important, seek out those who believe in your idea.

Research Your Deep and Abiding Passion

Probably the single piece of advice that was heard the most times in our interviews pertained to selecting a topic for which the student feels passion. This advice further highlights the discussion in Chapter 2 on factors to consider when choosing a topic. One student who conducted a program evaluation of a curriculum aimed to increase adolescent girls' interest in math and science stated: "Choose a topic and population that you are really passionate about and you will stick with it and care more about it." This student believed that her passion for her dissertation kept her motivated and ultimately made her all the more determined to persevere in the face of obstacles and obtain her sample and complete the project. Another student studying the career development of high-school Latinas said that she was passionate about her topic; she believed the population was understudied, and she was committed to the need for empirical work and knowledge in this area. Her passion carried her through her dissertation despite some telling her that getting a large enough sample of high-school Latinas was nearly impossible. Thus, although conducting research with samples other than college students can be difficult, having a sense of passion and commitment to your ideas can often help you persevere and stay motivated through the obstacles that are a normal part of the process.

Develop and Use Your Networks

Another frequently offered piece of advice was to encourage students to use their social and professional networks. Two important pieces here are (a) who you know in your own circle and (b) interpersonal connections with others. One student interviewed said, "Who you know is so important." Students often think, "I do not know that many people; I just moved here for my master's or my Ph.D. work, and I have no connections in this community." However, students have often made more connections than they give themselves credit for. We encourage you to not limit your thinking to only the people that you personally know. Draw the circle bigger; think of all the people that you know and then all the people that they know. Expand on the ideas and networks of faculty and students at your home institution. As one interviewee stated: "Communicate with faculty members whenever you can. Let them know what areas you are interested in, and check in periodically to see what they are doing. They will remember your interests and can often hook you up with people."

An important observation offered by several interviewees was that the better your relationship is with faculty, students, and others, the more likely they will be willing to refer you to someone who may help you. For example, one of our students was talking with a faculty member about her interests. The faculty member had a very good impression of the student. She was positive, professional, had demonstrated excellent initiative in the past, and had developed excellent skills as a researcher. Because of his positive relations with this student, he recommended her to another faculty member in another discipline who had a large National Science Foundation grant. Through this grant, the student was able to work on an interdisciplinary team and collect data on a diverse sample. That this faculty member felt strongly about the student's skills so that he could confidently refer her to another faculty member across campus is a tribute to the student. Thus, building good relationships throughout your graduate programs is critical.

The student who wanted to do her dissertation on career development and high-school Latinas grew up in an area where there is a large population of Mexican Americans. Rather than geographically limiting her data collection to where she attended graduate school, she called a former Spanish teacher who was able to help her with the connections to collect data in her high school. Because of this connection, the student went on to collect a very large sample of Mexican American adolescent girls. The career development of Mexican American girls is one of the most underrepresented in all of the career literature. Because the student was able to collect this large sample, she was able to conduct structural equation modeling to examine the fit of career counseling theories to this population. Thus, consider the bridges you built in years past to potentially help in current research.

Helen was interested in examining the role of religiosity on the formation of career values and choices. She was interested in using a diverse sample of community adults who would describe themselves as religious. She had moved to the community 3 years earlier to attend graduate school; and, while she was involved in a church herself, she had not become involved in the community as a whole and indicated that she did not know where to start in trying to solicit a diverse sample. As we brainstormed with her as part of a research class she was taking, many ideas and potential contacts emerged. Over half of the class were members of a church, and half of them knew the pastor well enough to be able to introduce Helen, thus helping to get the process moving. Other students indicated that they had weekly meetings where various speakers came in and presented on topics of interest to the congregation. Some felt that a topic like the "Relationship of Faith and Work" would be well received as a program and that many of the members would be willing to complete the questionnaires Helen needed prior to her presenting a program. Still other students suggested peers who were not in the class but who they knew were very involved in community churches and could provide a point of entry for Helen. These and many more ideas were generated, and Helen started realizing that her network was much larger than she had appreciated. Helen methodically began making connections with fellow students over coffee, explaining her research and asking whether they would provide an introduction to someone within their church who could be helpful to her.

Thus, we encourage you to develop and use your connections in order to obtain diverse samples. Although you may think you do not have connections, you may be surprised at how many people are in your circle who can be of help to you.

Determine How Your Research Can Benefit Others

Although sometimes people offer to help collect data for a student's research simply because the student is a nice person, most often people need to be convinced of the benefits of the research to them or their organization. In contacting individuals for assistance, you often have one and only one opportunity to make a good impression; thus, it is critically important that you reflect on how your research may benefit the individual or organization from whom you are seeking assistance. Although the advantages are highly dependent on the specific research you are proposing, the following list may include some ways that your research may benefit the organizations or individuals you are approaching. Research collaboration:

1. Can provide a connection with an academic institution. Sometimes community organizations, businesses, or schools are looking for ways they can have associations with a university. Such associations can enhance the credibility of their agency's goals and are often seen as positive public relations.

2. Can provide data that can be used for future grant writing. Oftentimes community agencies or organizations do not have the time or expertise to collect data that can serve as the rationale for obtaining local, state, or federal monies.

3. Can provide a means to engage in cutting-edge research in a given area. For example, your research, especially if the study is published or presented, can help an agency fulfill one of its goals, such as producing research on certain topics. The agency may take some degree of ownership as well and co-present your research at one of its professional meetings or work to publish it in a journal within its field.

4. Can help solve a problem or answer a question organizations or individuals have. Thus, your research can help an organization directly to deal with a pressing concern. For example, the student who conducted the evaluation on a program designed to enhance girls' interest and pursuit of math and science directly assisted that program by determining what was effective and what needed improvement in the curriculum.

5. Can help agencies serve their mission or role. Perhaps you are interested in understanding the stressors and coping mechanisms of international students on a college campus. Approaching the International Student Office Director and helping him/her to understand that your research can provide valuable information on what international students are experiencing as stressful and what effective coping strategies are being

used could be very informative to the director. This is clearly within the mission of the International Student Office, which may not have the time or expertise to conduct such an investigation.

6. Can help fulfill the mandates of a current grant. Sometimes individuals are awarded grants based on a specific content area but have less experience to evaluate a broad range of grant outcomes. For example, a team of chemistry professors was awarded a grant to help adolescent Native American girls into science-related occupations. Although team members knew a great deal about conducting research in the basic sciences, they knew relatively little about evaluating the program's impact on the science self-efficacy of these girls. Thus, in cases such as this, your training and expertise can be highly valued across disciplines.

These are but a few of the possible benefits to others of a student's thesis or dissertation research. Think about your audience; what benefits or functions can the research serve to this audience? Several benefits can usually be identified; however, talking with people more familiar with the population to identify a full range of benefits is sometimes helpful. Exploring other potential benefits with the agency using a more general approach may even be helpful: "I want to determine how we can make this a win-win situation. In what other ways might this research be of benefit to you?" Through probing, offering suggestions, and brainstorming together, additional benefits may become obvious that had not occurred to you earlier.

Demonstrate Respect for Research Allies

Although you may bring many skills to your thesis or dissertation, you must approach people with the utmost respect, regardless of educational background, job title, or research experience. Most of the individuals we interviewed commented on this topic as important to note, even though it may sound like common sense.

First, when you have your initial meeting with the contact person (or at any point along the way), do so with respect for the work that the organization does and for the knowledge that the organization has. In some instances, it may become apparent that you know more about research than the people with whom you are working. However, the individuals in the organization likely know more than you do about the specific population that you are seeking to recruit. Those interviewed highlighted the importance of never losing sight of the knowledge and unique expertise of organization members or the fact that *you* are the one that is asking for *their* help.

Second, our interviewees stressed the importance of not "talking like an academic" or using professional terminology as if you were talking to a professor. Many of the people we interviewed experienced a situation in which they were talking on a "different" plane than their audience; that is, they used language that was appropriate for use in academic circles but that came off as overly intellectual or even ostentatious to others. This can be rather off-putting and may turn someone off to both you and your research idea. At the same time, be careful to not "talk down" to people, which suggests a lack of respect. Although you should not overuse professional jargon, you should speak in a manner that reflects your intelligence and knowledge. Because our interviewees stressed that this may be a hard balance for many students, particularly since professional jargon becomes so well ingrained, they suggested that students may want to practice giving their presentation to someone who can provide them with feedback.

Be Explicit About What You Need From the Research

You must be completely clear with the contact person about what your needs are and the ramifications if those needs are not met. Many individuals who are not connected with academic institutions may have no idea how important deadlines are and getting as many participants as you need to conduct statistical analyses. You will need to clearly communicate these specific needs to the contact person. For example, one student worked for a year establishing a project, all the while being assured that a particular summer program had 100 students. As data collection was soon to begin, she was informed that the program would only have 40 students that particular summer. The student's hypotheses and subsequent data analyses were predicated on having a sample size of 100, all of which was approved by her committee. The contact person's response was, "Can't you just run some other kind of analysis?" Another student was given assurances that in the course of one semester she would be able to collect data on 75 counselor-and-client pairs from a community agency. Three quarters of the way through the semester she had two client-and-counselor dyads. The agency response was simply, "I am not sure what happened, we generally have more clients than this." Both of these incidents highlight that the contact persons were not clear on how important it was for the student to obtain a particular number of participants by a particular date. In one other example, a student had carefully developed a battery of instruments to test his research hypotheses. The agency he was working with had approved these instruments, as had his thesis committee. When the project was about to commence, the agency contact person insisted that the instruments would take too much time and that the student needed to cut the number of items in half. Doing so would have dramatic impact on the student's ability to test his proposed hypotheses. Although these kinds of problems can happen in field settings regardless of the clarity with which the student describes her or his needs, making every attempt to clearly communicate with the contact person about the potential ramifications of such problems may help to limit their occurrence.

Give Back to People Who Have Given to You

Every individual we interviewed spoke about giving back to those who are giving to the student's research. Whatever organization, institution, agency, or business is allowing you to conduct research with its group is doing you a favor. In the past, researchers have been criticized for "using" diverse samples without giving anything in return. In some cases, people already struggling with their life circumstances were "used" in a study, with no benefit ever coming back to them or their communities. Thus, you must consider how you can give back to those individuals and institutions who are kind enough to help in your data collection.

The individuals we interviewed provided some examples of ways to contribute something to the group with which the student is working. The student who did her research on career development and high-school Latinas provided presentations for the school administrators and teachers. By doing so, these individuals had a wealth of information that they could personally use in the future regarding helping to foster Latinas' career development. The student who investigated individuals' responses to organizational change for his dissertation also prepared presentations to members of the companies' executive boards and included specific information regarding their employees and their reactions, fear, stress, and coping in response to major changes and reorganization happening in the company. Another student who did her thesis on stress and coping behaviors in a population of shelter workers provided written reports of her research findings to the workers. Additionally, she made a presentation to this group and allowed time for questions from the participants (i.e., what can they do to better cope with stress?) Other students provided more personal gifts to research allies who had gone out of their way to be helpful in the data-collection process. For example, one student who was allowed into mathematics classes in the public schools gave small presents to the teachers, along with a personal note of thanks.

One of the best outcomes regarding giving back to those that have given to the student is that the organization, institution, or agency comes away from the research project feeling positive. They have something tangible as a result of allowing the student to conduct research. They feel like they have benefited from the process rather than possibly feeling taken advantage of or "used"; and, perhaps, if someone in the future asks to conduct research with them again, they will remember the good experience and allow someone else to conduct another study, increasing the knowledge base that much more.

Expect Things to Go Wrong

Our interviewees noted that things often went wrong. No matter how well the student plans, how detail-oriented the student is, things will still go wrong.

Although this is true in all kinds of research, it is often more likely in field set-tings where there is less experimental control than in research done in a class-room for experimental credit or in a laboratory environment with students who are familiar to the research process. Thus, be cognizant of the fact that most likely things will not happen the way you have planned. It happens to all researchers, and it is simply part of the process of research, but particularly field research. Knowing and expecting that things often do go wrong will allow you to not be so hard on yourself when things do go wrong. You simply learn from your mistakes and move on. For example, one student shared her story of making a mistake in using an instrument. She used a 5-point scale when in fact the instrument used a 14-point scale. Although at first this felt devastating to her, she realized that there was nothing she could do about it at that point and moved on with the next steps of her project. However, she has learned how critical it is to double-check details such as the instruments. Another stu-dent collected data, but forgot to reverse-score a number of items on an essen-tial screening instrument. Participants were put into two groups and then interviewed as a result of their incorrect scores. By the time the mistake was discovered, a tremendous amount of time and energy had been expended on the project. Thus, many interviewees stressed the importance of double-checking everything in the research process.

Other things that can go wrong will be out of your control. For example, the Institutional Review Board (IRB; see Heppner, Kivlighan, & Wampold, 1999, for more information) could take longer than expected to review your application, causing you to miss that window of time to collect data or causing you to wait until the next semester to collect data. You could be set to collect data at a high school on a certain day, but a large snowfall could cause the school to be closed and, thus, not allow you to collect your data (that has hap-pened to one of the authors!) Or maybe an agency promises that 100 people are going to attend a given program, and, for whatever reasons, only 35 actu-ally attend. Your ability to conduct specific analyses or to have enough statisti-cal power can be drastically reduced by such an event. One of our students had painstakingly worked to develop a project designed to study undocumented workers. She had worked with community leaders and had been assured she would be able to obtain data from at least 100 undocumented workers. The day after her proposal meeting, where she had convincingly assured her com-mittee that she would be able to secure her sample, an INS raid in the com-munity removed her sample overnight!

These things happen to even seasoned researchers. You can plan as well as possible, but at times things will happen and will need to be dealt with as best you can. In fact, making mistakes along the way is often necessary to truly learn the procedural details associated with collecting data. As many told us in their interviews, expect everything to take five times longer than you thought it would take. Because mistakes happen, because things go wrong, we encourage you to not only expect things to take longer than you originally planned but also add extra time for the various steps along the way. In addition, we encourage you to be hypervigilant of what may and can go wrong and then monitor those events closely to quickly identify any problematic situations and intervene as quickly as possible.

CONCLUSIONS

The individuals we interviewed stressed the importance of four personal qualities: persistence, proactivity, assertiveness, and attention to detail. Whereas these personal attributes are important in all types of research, we believe that they are even more critical when conducting research with diverse samples. We encourage you to strengthen these significant attributes within yourself to be more prepared to successfully diversify your samples.

In essence, we hope to have provided inspiration and encouragement for you to draw your circle bigger. Expanding knowledge bases and examining populations other than those that have been typically studied are essential. As psychologist Rosie Bingham said, "Exclusion is easier, but inclusion is better."

WORKING WITH YOUR ADVISOR AND COMMITTEE

The student, the advisor, and the thesis or dissertation committee form a team whose goal is to ensure a high-quality thesis or dissertation that contributes to the existing literature. The student is the person who conceptualizes, proposes, and conducts the actual project; but the advisor, in particular, and, to a lesser extent, the committees are crucial team members. Working well with this team is vital to the success of the project. A number of nuances and issues of protocol are important to understand if these relationships are to flow smoothly. This chapter is focused on helping you work well with your advisor and committee throughout the thesis or dissertation process. Specifically, we discuss (a) working with the advisor, (b) choosing a committee, (c) contacting the committee, (d) working with committee members after the proposal meeting, (e) providing the committee with the proposal and scheduling the meeting, (f) important ways to prepare for the committee meeting itself, (g) feeling confident and nondefensive, (h) updating the committee periodically during data collection and analysis, and (i) scheduling and presenting the defense.

WORKING WITH THE ADVISOR

Your working relationship with your advisor is often the most important relationship you will have as you work on your thesis or dissertation. The most important thing you can do is to work closely with your advisor on numerous drafts of your thesis or dissertation before the proposal or defense meeting gets scheduled. Thus, for the best outcome, you should work with your advisor at every step of the process from conceptualizing your ideas to developing your committees to proposing and defending your work. The advisor is the person who is ultimately responsible for saying, "This is ready to go to committee." Thus, the student and the advisor generally exchange several drafts of the manuscript, with the advisor providing feedback about needed changes and ways to strengthen the draft. By the time the advisor is willing to say, "This is ready to go to committee," you should be able to rest assured that at least one faculty member, the advisor, approves of the study and will support your proposal or defense. In this section we discuss three important points about working with your advisor: (a) understanding the advisor's role, (b) keeping the advisor informed, and (c) allowing ample time for the advisor to read and respond to multiple drafts of your work.

Understanding the Advisor's Role

Probably one of the most important things for students to understand is how the advisor views his or her role. Advisors vary in terms of what they think about their role in working with students on their theses or dissertations. Some advisors view their role as a working partner, helping the students think through all aspects of their projects. Others see theses or dissertations as much more independent projects where students need to demonstrate their ability to conduct large, independent research projects. You will be greatly helped if you know how your advisor views this role and what you can expect from your advisor in all phases of the process. Differences in how advisors perceive their role can be seen at all stages of the thesis or dissertation process but perhaps most publicly in your proposal or defense meetings. For example, some advisors view their role as helping students through difficult problems that may be highlighted in committee meetings while others see students as needing to demonstrate their own ability to handle such issues.

This relationship, however, works both ways and you have the right to ask your advisors for things you need. For example, you may ask for regular meeting times as your thesis or dissertation is conceptualized. Thus, in some respects, a negotiation process exists between the student and the advisor regarding the role of each and the parameters of the working relationship between them. One of the most important issues in working with the advisor is finding appropriate ways of keeping the advisor informed about issues and progress related to the thesis or dissertation.

Keeping the Advisor Informed

The advisor will have difficulty advocating for the student if the student does not communicate thoroughly with the advisor. Thus, at any point in the thesis or dissertation phases in which the student is making decisions and moving ahead, the student must communicate these decisions with the advisor. In addition, after the advisor and student have agreed upon various aspects of the design or methodology of the project, the student must communicate any intended changes to the advisor. Not doing so can make both the student and faculty look bad in the process. For example, a student and his advisor had worked through numerous drafts of the student's dissertation proposal. They had many long discussions about various aspects of the methodology including the number of participants to be used in the analysis. The student wanted to collect data on a much smaller number of participants than the advisor thought necessary for an effective test; but, eventually, they had agreed on the methods, including the greater number of participants, and the advisor had agreed that the proposal was ready to go to committee. Then, unbeknownst to the advisor, the student had reduced the number of participants that he would be using in the final draft that went to the committee. When the committee met, several members raised a concern about the small number of participants being proposed. The advisor responded that that had been changed and in fact the student would be collecting the larger number. The committee members responded that that was not what was indicated in the actual proposal.

This made the student look bad in that the committee felt he had not done sufficient research to determine an appropriate number of participants. It also made the advisor look as if she had not read the final draft of the proposal and, in general, called into question the thought and rigor that had gone into other aspects of the proposal as well. Thus, the advisor and advisee must work as a team and the student must keep the advisor informed at all stages of the process.

Allowing Ample Time for the Advisor to Read and Respond to Multiple Drafts

The student and advisor must plan a timetable for the proposal to be completed. Having a realistic and firm timetable will help both the student and the advisor feel more confident about the proposal before it goes to the committee. Thus, think realistically about how long it will take to prepare the proposal and then go through a series of three or four versions with the advisor. Allow sufficient time for making the revision and returning it to the advisor. Often times, when students have decided what they want to propose, they do not allow enough time for this feedback and refinement process. They expect the advisor to drop everything and turn the proposal drafts back to them immediately, not realizing at that moment that the advisor has many other responsibilities to take care of in addition to students' proposals. This does not set the stage for a good working relationship between the student and advisor. A key to feeling prepared to have a proposal go to the committee is allowing ample time for drafts to pass between student and advisor.

Understanding the advisor's role and negotiating changes if the student needs for that role to be different, keeping the advisor fully informed, and developing appropriate time lines for drafts are three critical areas in the advisor/advisee relationship. As this chapter proceeds through the various stages from forming a committee to defending the thesis or dissertation, many other critical advisor and advisee roles will become clear. Perhaps the first major issue is the formation of the student's committee.

FORMATION OF THE COMMITTEE

The constellation of committee members can be very important to the quality of the finished thesis or dissertation. Committee members can be extremely helpful in suggesting resources and providing expert technical assistance and support in this process. You should work with your chair or advisor in determining what the best group of faculty would be given the unique skills both you and your advisor bring to the process, as well as unique needs that the project requires that a committee member could assist with. For example, perhaps the thesis or dissertation topic is one involving scale development and validation on the construct of internalized racism. Having at least one committee member who is well versed in the multicultural literature—ideally, in that portion of the literature that involves the impact of racism on the person—may be most helpful. Similarly, having another member who has scale development expertise may be helpful. Thus, having faculty who could advise on specific literature to be examined in the multicultural area, as well as a faculty member who could consult as needed on the intricacies of factor analysis, would strengthen the committee and eventual project.

Particularly in the case of dissertation research, many universities require the inclusion of an "outside member," that is, a faculty member outside the student's home academic department. This provides an important opportunity to include a cross-disciplinary perspective on the topic you have selected. For example, by including a committee member from sociology, religion, nursing, or statistics, you can be exposed to other theoretical perspectives that can inform the project or can identify a particular area of expertise that may be helpful to the overall project. One student, for example, was interested in examining an issue related to organizational change. Her selection of a faculty member from the College of Business not only provided expertise on the topic of organizational change but also provided contacts for data collection within business settings. Another student was interested in studying stress and coping related to various kinds of trauma and identified a faculty member in anthropology who was an expert on assessing stress levels and especially knowledgeable in using biophysical assessments. Both of these outside members dramatically strengthened these students' eventual products.

Finding the appropriate outside committee member may take additional work on the part of the student. Often times students are familiar with faculty research expertise within their own departments and, sometimes, colleges but often have few contacts in other departments on campus. To find appropriate outside members, you may first consult with advisors and other faculty who may have contacts on the campus. Usually, some faculty within each department have been more involved at the college and university level and have thus been able to meet faculty from other disciplines through their committee work or other activities. Talking with such faculty members can be a very useful starting place. In addition, many departments now have Web sites where faculty research interests are noted. Spending some time researching Web sites for disciplines that may help inform the project is another good source of information. If you have been active on the campus yourself, you may have a host of connections with other graduate students who can refer you to faculty within their respective departments who may be helpful outside members. The important point here is that the outside member can be a very useful addition to your committee. By taking some time and researching an appropriate member, you may be adding a great deal of expertise not found in your home department.

Once you and your advisor have determined what specific needs you have and have selected specific faculty members with those areas of expertise, the other members of the committee may be generalists who can give a wide range of feedback and suggestions. Other faculty members who are not selected to be on the committee can also help, but be wary of using too much of their time. It is generally assumed in most departments that, if the student needs extensive consultation from a faculty person, that faculty member would be asked to be on the formal committee.

Three common mistakes we have often seen students make when choosing a committee are (a) choosing only supportive people, (b) avoiding a potential committee member whom the rumor mill has labeled "difficult," (c) stereotyping faculty members' interests too narrowly, and (d) not consulting sufficiently with the advisor to determine if the constellation of committee members is appropriate before inviting them to serve on the committee. We examine each of these in turn.

Although everyone wants as much support as they can get during this potentially stressful time, you should be wary of inviting faculty to be on your committee just because they have the reputation of being easy or nice. You may like them and they may like you, but they may not offer a lot to help to strengthen your thesis or dissertation. Some faculty members are invited to join a great number of student committees because they are seen as more approachable. Be careful though; if faculty members are on too many committees, they could be overwhelmed and spend little time reading and studying your particular project. You really need committee members who will take the responsibility of being on the committee seriously and help to ensure an excellent product.

In addition, beware of the rumor mill. A faculty member can get labeled amazingly quickly as difficult or as someone to avoid inviting to be on a committee. While consulting with peers who have experience with various potential members is good, be careful to assess whether students' own insecurities or issues may have them catastrophizing about mild suggestions a faculty member made that were meant in a helpful manner. Your own perceptions may have been quite different than those of the individual you are consulting, given differences in maturity, psychological adjustment, and skill level. We are struck in our own experience how long a reputation can persist. In one situation, an advisor suggested a potential committee member. The student responded that he had heard that this particular faculty member was very unreasonable and that students did not want him on their committees. When the original incident that had triggered this rumor was tracked down, it was discovered that it was almost 10 years earlier and it involved a student who had done a particularly poor thesis. The committee member was probably justified in suggesting major revisions to help the student develop an acceptable proposal. But in the 10 ensuing years, all of the details about the situation have been lost and only the core message lived on—that this faculty member is unreasonable and should be avoided. Remember that the faculty member who commits the needed time to think through potential problems and to offer suggestions for change is really the supportive member and the one who has your best interests in mind.

In addition, be careful not to stereotype what expertise faculty members would have to offer too narrowly along only their research areas. For example, sometimes racial and ethnic minority faculty are only invited to serve on committees when the student is doing a project that involves some type of diversity related issue. As one of our students recently said: "My thesis has nothing to do with racial and ethnic minorities, so why would I invite Dr. White to be on my committee?" Remember that faculty have a broad range of training and skills and could provide helpful feedback for aspects of a student's work going well beyond their own research agendas.

Unfortunately, political conflicts exist in most academic departments. In most departments, some faculty do not get along well with other faculty for a host of reasons. Most of the time these personality conflicts or philosophical differences are kept under control and do not surface in inappropriate settings like a student's committee meetings. However, consult with your advisor to determine the particular constellation of committee members who will work well together. The last thing you want to have happen is for two faculty to take out their own issues with one another by fighting about some issue related to your work.

CONTACTING POTENTIAL COMMITTEE MEMBERS

After you and your advisor have decided on appropriate committee members, you should also consult with the advisor about the appropriate protocol to use in contacting them to serve on the committee. In some departments, this is handled quite informally with a phone call or even email; in other departments, the expectation is that students will make appointments and talk with potential members about their topic and about the faculty members' willingness to serve. Especially with members whose academic homes are outside of your department, scheduling an appointment is a good idea as you may have had limited contact with this member previously and in this way can introduce yourself and what the expectations would be for the outside faculty member. For all potential committee members, give them an idea of when you expect the majority of the work for them to occur (i.e., reading the proposal and finished thesis/dissertation). This allows faculty members to plan their schedules for how many committees they will agree to serve on at that time. You may also mention to potential committee members if they are being asked specifically because of their expertise in a particular area. You should be careful not to be offensive, however, with such statements as "I wanted to ask you because I would like to have a woman on my committee," as the comment diminishes what the faculty member has to offer over and above her gender.

It is particularly important to have in-depth discussions with committee members if there is anything unusual or out of the ordinary about some aspect of your proposal. For example, in some cases students have access to existing data sets and are interested in using these for their thesis or dissertation rather than collecting their own data. In cases like this, potential faculty members must understand that this is what the student will be proposing in order to decide whether or not they want to be on the student's committee under these special circumstances.

LEVEL OF CONTACT WITH COMMITTEE MEMBERS OUTSIDE OF MEETINGS

Depending on protocol in your department or with a specific advisor, you may have no contact, a small amount of contact, or a great deal of contact with other committee members before the actual committee meeting. For example, some advisors prefer that the student work only with them up until the point of the committee meeting; others prefer that the student consult with other committee members as the student's ideas are further developed. Especially when a committee member has been asked to join the committee because of his or her particular expertise in an area, that committee member should be consulted as the investigation is developed. Thus, you should ask the advisor about the preferred protocol regarding your level of contact with committee members.

PROVIDING COPIES OF THE PROPOSAL TO THE COMMITTEE AND SCHEDULING THE MEETING

You should schedule your proposal meeting at least a couple weeks in advance of the meeting and also provide each committee member with a copy of the entire proposal prior to the meeting. The amount of time that the committee members should have the proposal varies from department to department, so you should consult with your advisor about what is appropriate protocol within your department. Generally speaking, 1 week is probably the most typical length of time. The delivery of the proposal to the committee members should occur, if possible, in hard-copy form. It is becoming more commonplace to email attachments of various documents; however, the thesis, or dissertation proposal, or completed project tends to be quite long and faculty members should not have to spend the time and their resources printing out the entire document.

PREPARING FOR THE PROPOSAL MEETING

In preparing for the proposal meeting, you can take a number of important steps to help ensure a successful outcome: (a) making sure you believe that the project is feasible; (b) understanding the culture of proposal meetings; (c) anticipating the hardest, most critical question; (d) practicing with a peer or advisor; (e) preparing a visual presentation; (f) preparing a table of research questions and proposed analyses; (g) studying the proposed type of analysis and the research design; (h) approaching committee members who may have concerns; and (i) breathing, relaxing, or meditating.

Do You Believe the Project Is Feasible?

The purpose of the proposal meeting is for your committee members to thoroughly understand and have confidence in your ability to carry out the proposed work, such that they feel comfortable signing their names indicating they have approved your proposal. Thus, a prime question in your mind should be: "How can I prepare myself and my proposal in such a way that not only do I feel confident but my committee also feels confident in my ability to carry this work out successfully?" This is a very important philosophical point. In our experience, we find that sometimes students get in the mindset that they need to convince or persuade their committee that they can do what they are proposing. Although this is true, a much more important goal is to convince yourself that this is a feasible project. That is, it is possible to use persuasive skills to make your committee believe something is possible; the ultimate question, however, is, do *you*, given your thoughtful planning, think it is highly likely that you will be able to carry out the proposed work?

What Is the Departmental Culture Like During Committee Meetings?

The cultures of proposal meetings vary from institution to institution and can vary depending on the unique composition of committees. Some are characterized as *adversarial*, in which you are, in fact, "defending" your ideas and methods when challenged by committee members; others are more collegial and take the form of *problem-solving or idea-generating sessions*, in which committee members are simply providing suggestions for strengthening aspects of your proposal. You should obtain information from peers that are more senior who have already proposed their theses or dissertations and from your advisor about their predictions of what the experience will be like. Having this type of information can help you prepare psychologically and functionally for the proposal meeting.

Anticipate the Hardest, Most Critical Question

Most of the time students avoid thinking of what is the hardest, most critical question or concern that will likely be raised by the committee. If, instead, they would embrace the question and do everything they can to evaluate the seriousness of the issue, they would be doing themselves a great service. Thus, we encourage you to anticipate the most difficult question. This can be done in consultation with the advisor and with peers who may help critique the proposal. Next, evaluate how serious this problem is to the overall design of the study. In this section, we discuss (a) what committee members will be looking for in each chapter of the proposal; (b) specific ways to prepare for defending your methodology, including providing a number of student examples; and (c) an important caveat.

Committee members will examine all aspects of a proposal carefully. In Chapter 1, they will be particularly interested in whether you are building a cogent argument for the study being conducted. Does it make sense to them that this is an important and worthwhile next step in the research? In Chapter 2, they will be examining the thoroughness and care with which you present the literature that has come before. Although committee members commonly suggest a reference or two that have not been included, the literature review should not have gaping holes. If you have consulted with faculty members about appropriate literature they would suggest to review, either that literature should be cited or you should be able to provide a rationale for why it is not included.

Although Chapter 1 and Chapter 2 are important, committee members will probably spend the majority of their time and attention on Chapter 3, the methods. Being well prepared in this area is very important because this chapter represents the blueprint, or exact steps you plan to take, for carrying out your project. In many ways, when committee members sign the papers saying that they support the proposal they are primarily saying that they approve of the methodology and believe it will provide an adequate test of the research questions and hypotheses being proposed.

Thus, you should do as much as possible to be prepared to defend your choice of methodology. This preparation can take many forms, including (a) making initial contacts with resource people who can help you obtain the appropriate number of participants, (b) conducting pilot tests or focus groups to test some aspect of the protocol, (c) conducting a power analysis to determine the number of participants that will be needed to find differences or relationships should they exist, (d) consulting with Institutional Review Board staff to determine if there is a way to ensure human subjects' protection given the methods of the study, or (e) consulting with seasoned researchers in the field about the most appropriate instrumentation.

We must, however, add a caveat here: In doing these preparatory activities, a delicate balance must be achieved. There is a danger if committee members perceive that you have moved ahead with the study without their approval. Thus, you should consult with your advisor about these preparation steps. The preparatory work should be described as steps being taken at the initial stages to decide if the idea is feasible. Any contact people should be clearly told that you do not have committee approval at this time. Thus, you need to achieve that delicate balance between gathering information that will help give you and your committee confidence and not doing so much that committee members perceive that they have little room for input into the design or methodology.

To illustrate the use of these preparatory activities, we present the following examples:

- A student was interested in conducting a large-scale study using Hispanic adolescents. Given that the student was currently living in an area where the percentage of Hispanics was very small, she realized that this might be of concern to her committee members. In order to increase her (and her committee's) confidence that she would be able to obtain the needed sample size, she talked with a counselor in a predominately Hispanic school about the possibility of collecting data in her school. She asked the counselor to help her realistically assess how many participants might be possible, logistically how and when this project might be conducted (time of year, in classes, study halls, or as a take-home instrument), any problems the guidance counselor saw that may occur in the data-collection process, what human subjects' approvals would be needed, whether active consent would be required from parents, ways that she might be able to "give back" to the participants in exchange for their cooperation, and so on. The student made it clear to the counselor that she was exploring the feasibility of the project but that she had not yet received approval from her committee to conduct the project. Being able to provide this very specific information to the committee was a crucial step in helping the student feel confident about her ability to conduct the proposed research and, ultimately, in gaining the committee's approval of the proposal.

- A student was planning to conduct a study that required a very large battery of assessment measures to be administered to a group of elderly women living in a retirement community. The student understood that a predictable concern on the part of the committee might be the time such a battery would take and whether it was feasible and humane to put elderly individuals through such a procedure. The student decided to conduct a pilot study. He recruited a small group of elderly women to not only take the instruments but to provide feedback from their perspective concerning the feasibility of other peers taking this number of instruments and ways of making it a more comfortable process for them. This type of information was critical in helping the student and his committee decide if the number or type of instruments needed to be reduced.

One last example of preparation involves being sure that students have adequate statistical skills if they are planning to conduct complex forms of data analysis. For example, if you plan to use structural equation modeling as the primary analysis in your project, you should be prepared for this through coursework, reading, or working with a faculty member on a project prior to conducting your own independent project. Similarly, if you plan to conduct a primarily qualitative investigation, a series of courses will be necessary to prepare yourself for such an undertaking. Being able to describe to your committee your own skill level and past experience in various aspects of this type of project is helpful in increasing both your own and the committee's confidence in your ability to conduct the project.

Practice With Peers or Advisor

You may also feel more confident if you have previously presented your ideas to a group of peers, to your advisor, or in a class. In most proposal meetings, students are asked to prepare 10- to 15-minute presentations of the main points of their investigations. An excellent idea is to practice this presentation by yourself, as well as in front of your advisor or peers. A very common problem is that students do not actually practice or time the talk, and they generally have considerably more information to present than can be accommodated in a 10- to 15-minute frame. Then they find themselves going over the allotted time and rushing through their presentations as they start getting cues from their advisors or other committee members that the typical time for such presentations has elapsed. Thus, practicing and timing this presentation are vitally important.

In addition to practicing the brief presentation, you may have friends ask questions to which you may practice responding. Although the types of questions that are asked by committee members vary greatly depending on the department, the individual member, and the topic and methodology being proposed, the following list is provided to give you some idea of the range of questions that may be asked. You may practice responses to these questions or similar ones that you can generate that may be more specific to your unique study.

1. Can you explain to me specifically what type of analysis you plan to conduct to test each of your hypotheses?
2. How are you planning to get this many participants to cooperate with your study when it appears that they will have no incentive to do so?
3. How will you deal statistically with attrition?
4. Can you clarify what theoretical framework you are using to guide this investigation?
5. What was your rationale for selecting this instrument instead of some of the others that are widely used in this area of research?
6. How can you justify using solely a student sample for this study?
7. What ways have you thought of to increase the likelihood of getting a good representation of racial and ethnic minority participants in your sample?
8. What is your rationale for departing from the previous methodology that has been used in similar studies?
9. How did you arrive at this sample size?
10. What have you done to try to increase the internal validity of this research?

Prepare a Concise Visual Presentation of the Main Points

Having a brief visual presentation of the primary points you want to make in your presentation is often helpful to the student and to the committee. This can take the form of a handout, overhead transparencies, or a PowerPoint presentation. Whichever form it takes, you should keep it short and concise, presenting only your most important points. Remember that committee members have read the proposal; the purpose of this brief presentation is to allow you to highlight some of the most important aspects of your investigation. Think about what the most helpful information for the committee would be and what the best way to present that information would be. One good example from a recent committee meeting was a person who was proposing to conduct a study examining various constructs related to the male gender role and physical and psychological distress. The student was using structural equation modeling and had a quite complex model to test. He was primarily concerned about how to explain the various paths he was proposing to test. For his proposal, he used several layers of overhead transparencies to present the model in stages, with each new transparency laid over the previous, integrating more paths that would be tested. This was very useful in that it deconstructed the complex idea into steps that could be more easily understood.

Provide a Table That Indicates Each Research Question and Each Corresponding Type of Analysis

For students in the behavioral and social sciences, the statistical analysis section often causes the most concern. Students are concerned they will be asked questions for which they are unprepared regarding their analysis plan. The more prepared you can be concerning what types of analyses you are proposing to use in your investigation, the more confident you will be. Especially if you have a number of research questions and hypotheses, you may find it useful to prepare a table indicating on the left each of your hypotheses or research questions, then columns indicating the independent and dependent variables and, specifically, what scale score is being used to operationalize these variables. For example, is a total score being used, a subscale score, or a single item? Finally, indicate what type of analysis will be used for each of the hypotheses. This strategy is also helpful when developing and validating a measure, as depicted in Table 10.1. Here Chen (2001) lists the instruments she will be using to validate an Attachment-to-God measure she is developing. She lists the individual measures in the left column and then indicates whether subscale scores will be used; what types of analysis will be done (in this case all correlations); whether she predicts this scale will be positively, negatively, or nonsignificantly correlated with her new measure; and, finally, what type of validity estimate these analyses will provide (convergent, divergent, predictive, etc.) Developing this type of table not only gives you confidence that you have carefully considered the intricacies of your analyses but also helps a committee member quickly see what you are proposing to do in your analyses.

Study the Type of Analysis and the Research Design

The committee will expect the student to be knowledgeable concerning both the proposed research design and statistical analysis. While it is generally not expected that students are totally familiar with all research design and all forms of statistical analysis, it is reasonable to assume that the particular designs and analyses being used in students' theses or dissertations are ones they know a good deal about.

Although students are more commonly using statistical consultants to assist in performing their analyses, they are still responsible for understanding conceptually what is being done statistically and for being able to respond to committee members' questions. Thus, responding to a committee member's query with "I don't know why I ran an oblique rotation; my statistics consultant said it would be a good idea" is not acceptable. If a student is using a statistical consultant, that student still must understand *why* various analyses are being proposed. To prepare yourself in this area, we suggest that you read and reread the sections from a research design book that describes the design

VALIDITY HYPOTHESIS
LEVEL OF ANXIETY DIMENSION IN SPIRITUAL ATTACHMENT MEASURE

Scale	Subscale	Predicted Relation	Hypothesis	Validity
MC-Social Desirability Scale		correlation	not significant	discriminate
Experience in Close Relationships Scale	Anxiety	correlation	positive	convergent
	Avoidance	correlation	not significant	discriminate
The Intrinsic Religious Motivation Scale		correlation	negative	discriminate
The God Image Scale	Influence	correlation	negative	discriminate
	Providence	correlation	negative	discriminate
	Presence	correlation	negative	discriminate
	Challenging	correlation	positive	convergent
	Acceptance	correlation	negative	discriminate
	Benevolence	correlation	negative	discriminate
The Spiritual Assessment Inventory	Awareness	correlation	negative	discriminate
	Defensiveness/Disappointment	correlation	positive	convergent
	Realistic Acceptance	correlation	negative	discriminate
	Instability	correlation	positive	convergent
The Outcome Questionnaire	Subjective Distress	correlation	positive	predictive
	Interpersonal Relationships (conflicts)	correlation	positive	predictive
	Social Role(dysfunctional)	correlation	positive	predictive
The scale itself	level of avoidance	independent		

TABLE
10.1

VALIDITY HYPOTHESIS
LEVEL OF AVOIDANCE DIMENSION IN SPIRITUAL ATTACHMENT MEASURE

Scale	Subscale	Predicted Relation	Hypothesis	Validity
MC-Social Desirability Scale		correlation	not significant	discriminate
Experience in Close Relationships Scale	Anxiety	correlation	not significant	discriminate
	Avoidance	correlation	positive	convergent
The Intrinsic Religious Motivation Scale		correlation	negative	discriminate
The God Image Scale	Influence	correlation	negative	discriminate
	Providence	correlation	negative	discriminate
	Presence	correlation	negative	discriminate
	Challenging	correlation	positive	convergent
	Acceptance	correlation	negative	discriminate
	Benevolence	correlation	negative	discriminate
The Spiritual Assessment Inventory	Awareness	correlation	negative	discriminate
	Defensiveness/Disappointment	correlation	positive	convergent
	Realistic Acceptance	correlation	negative	discriminate
	Instability	correlation	positive	convergent
The Outcome Questionnaire	Subjective Distress	correlation	positive	predictive
	Interpersonal Relationships (conflicts)	correlation	positive	predictive
	Social Role (dysfunctional)	correlation	positive	predictive
The scale itself	level of anxiety	independent		

being used in the current investigation. The text by Heppner, Kivlighan, and Wampold (1999), for example, provides in-depth chapters on each of the major research designs and describes the advantages and disadvantages of each. Refreshing your memory about the intricacies of the particular design you have chosen can help you feel much more confident in responding to questions related to design issues.

Similarly, refresh your memory concerning the primary statistical analysis being planned for the investigation. You can read the chapter in a prominent and current textbook about this type of analysis; ask statistics professors when they will be covering the particular type of analysis in their courses, and inquiring whether you can sit in on those lectures; consult with your advisor or another faculty member with particular expertise in the type of analysis proposed; and schedule a session with your statistical consultant to carefully review all aspects of the analysis. By preparing in these ways, you will feel a great deal more confident about your ability to respond to questions related to your design or analyses.

Approach Committee Members Who May Have Concerns

We have found that sometimes students will have one committee member who they fear will have concerns that might derail their proposal meeting. The students tend to ruminate about this potential concern and, in some cases, catastrophize about how the concern will destroy the proposal meeting. If a student has such a concern, the best strategy is to approach the committee member prior to the meeting, ask the committee member directly if he or she sees any problems with the design of the investigation, involve him or her in the process, and seek his or her advice and suggestions. Often, students find that the faculty member thinks the proposal is fine, but knowing that ahead of time can make a tremendous difference in going into a meeting with confidence. Conversely, if the committee member does have concerns, the student can have time to think about and problem-solve the concerns prior to the meeting.

In addition to these tangible preparatory activities that students can do, a number of psychological and attitudinal issues bear thinking about in preparing for the proposal meeting. Perhaps the most important of these are being relaxed and presenting an appropriate level of confidence and nondefensiveness.

Breathe, Meditate, Relax

Prior to the meeting, do the kinds of things that you know help to calm you. Exercise, meditation, thinking about past successes, giving yourself positive self-statements, and breathing deeply and fully can help relax you so that your anxiety does not diminish your confidence in the proposal meeting. Whatever you can do to help yourself feel relaxed and at your best should be the goal.

Feeling and Presenting a Confident Image

If you want your committee to have confidence in you, you need to portray confidence in yourself. The committee meeting is not a time to self-disclose inadequacies. Most students have feelings of inadequacy about their skills in some areas that will be required for their projects, but the proposal meeting is not the time to be verbalizing these feelings of inadequacy. Avoid comments like these (that we have heard at meetings we have attended):

- I am not very good with research design issues, and I avoided taking that class as part of my doctoral work, so I am not sure what you are asking.
- I don't know why I did a MANCOVA there; my statistics consultant told me it was the thing to do.
- These meetings make me so anxious; I really hope you all will be nice to me.
- I really don't want to do research in the future; I just want to get this approved, get it done, and graduate.
- I was hoping my old guidance counselor would let me in to collect in his school. I don't know; it might be a long shot.

All of these statements share the common result of putting doubt in a committee member's mind about the student's ability to conduct the proposed research. This is the exact opposite result students want to have following a proposal meeting. Instead, the proposal meeting should be a time when the student can demonstrate competence consistent with his or her level of graduate education. Thus, students should prepare themselves psychologically and through careful study to become as confident and comfortable as they can before proposing their thesis or dissertation.

Practice Nondefensiveness

Imagine this scene: A student is proposing her thesis. A senior faculty member is on her committee. He asks a question related to her methodology. The student does not understand what the faculty member is suggesting but responds with an answer nonetheless. The faculty member rephrases the question. The student responds, "I don't know *what* your problem is with this, but this is what I am planning to do."

This scene from a recent committee meeting is a stark example of how *not* to respond during a proposal meeting. As you might guess, the student's response served to escalate this interpersonal interaction. The lack of respect shown to the senior faculty member caused him to get more rigid and resentful. The student became more entrenched in her perspective, and what could have been an amicable discussion about a potentially useful way of strengthening the methodology became a mini-battle.

Thus, understanding the role of the faculty member and the role of the student in proposal meetings is very important. Faculty members view their role as offering suggestions and raising concerns with the eventual goal of strengthening the thesis or dissertation. The student's role is not only to provide information about his or her thinking and rationale for making particular decisions but also to listen to the faculty members' suggestions respectfully and try to determine if the suggestions will indeed *be* helpful in strengthening the thesis or dissertation. Thus, in the preceding scenario, it would have been more facilitative if the student had first asked for clarification about the concern being raised. "I am not sure I am understanding exactly the point you are making," or "Can you tell me more about what you are suggesting there?" or trying to paraphrase what the student understood the faculty member to be suggesting and then asking if that was accurate. Once the concern is understood, the student should describe the rationale or thought process used in making the decision he or she did; for example, "Here was my rationale for selecting that particular instrument—let me know if this doesn't match your experience with it." Here the student is trying to walk that delicate line between letting the committee know he or she has done a lot of thoughtful reflection at all the various choice points in the project and communicating an openness to committee suggestions and modifications where appropriate.

In responding to faculty concerns or suggestions, do not give up too soon on your original strategies. Sometimes faculty members are simply suggesting an idea that they thought of but are not adamant about. They may simply be asking you to consider an alternative. You will have read and studied this area for a number of months, examined other articles in this area, critiqued methodologies, and become somewhat of an expert in the area. Thus, you may have a great deal of specific information that faculty members do not have regarding why a particular decision was made. So, be open to hearing suggestions but also ready to provide rationales for your decisions. Giving up too quickly may call into question the rigor and thoughtfulness with which the original decisions were made. For example, another recent committee meeting had the following interaction: The student had presented her proposal. A committee member raised a question about the choice of independent variable being used in the study. The student immediately agreed with the committee member saying that she was happy to change that variable and asked the faculty member to suggest a better variable to investigate. This response called into question the student's thought and care in selecting the original variables. Were these variables not selected using theoretical and empirical guidance from past studies? Was there not a clear rationale for selecting this variable rather than a thousand others that could have been examined? By being so quick to agree, the student gave the committee the impression that these variables were not very important, which caused the committee to start questioning the whole theoretical rationale for the investigation. Thus, listen openly and nondefensively to faculty suggestions but you do not need to agree to every suggestion.

Sometimes in committee meetings, a committee member will offer suggestions that imply a different study than the one you are proposing. Thus, the committee member is not merely suggesting a small modification but, rather, a major overhaul in a way that dramatically changes the focus of the study. You must be able to provide a rationale for the importance of doing the original study and perhaps indicate that you believe that the suggestion would make a very good next study in this field. In this situation, the advisor would typically help you respond to this type of concern.

DATA COLLECTION AND ANALYSIS

After you have your proposal approved and have received human subjects' clearance, you are then ready to conduct data collection and analysis. During this time there is generally little contact between you and the committee if everything is proceeding according to the plan outlined in the proposal. You may simply update committee members periodically via email or in casual meetings as to how you are progressing. If, however, any aspects of the investigation change during data collection or analysis that alter what was initially proposed in substantial ways, you should first consult with the advisor and then communicate with committee members and seek their approval of the changes that were necessary. This is important because when committee members sign their approval to your proposal, they are in essence signing a contract with you. You are agreeing to do what has been described in the methods section, and committee members are saying, "We agree that this is an appropriate plan." This approval request can happen through a joint letter from you and your advisor to the committee in which the rationale for making changes to the original plan is described. This procedure helps to protect you and the advisor from the possibility that a committee member will not approve the final thesis or dissertation because it deviated in some way from the original contract that the committee member signed.

SCHEDULING AND PRESENTING THE DEFENSE

Much of what was communicated in the first part of this chapter regarding scheduling and presenting the proposal applies here. You should consult with your advisor about the appropriate protocol to be used in scheduling and preparing for the meeting. How far in advance should faculty members be contacted to schedule the meeting? How far in advance should the committee members receive the draft of the thesis or dissertation? How long and what type of presentation should be made?

Generally, similar to the proposal meeting, you will be asked to present a 10- to 15-minute overview of the project. In this meeting, you will tend to focus less on the rationale for the study, the previous literature, or the methods and provide a great deal more information on the results and discussion. It is often helpful to use the presentation time to remind committee members of the results of each of the major hypotheses or research questions. What the study found and what the implications are for those findings will probably be the main overarching concerns during the defense meeting.

As with the proposal meeting, you should prepare and practice the 10- to 15-minute overview, as well as ways of responding to questions the committee might ask. Again, the questions committee members ask vary greatly depending on the members and the topic of the study. However, the following questions are provided to help you practice answering some standard questions that are often asked during a defense:

1. How do these findings support previous research and theory in this field?
2. If some of the results were not consistent with previous research or theory, how would these be accounted for?
3. What do you see as the most important implications of this research for future researchers?
4. What do you see as the most important implications of this research for practitioners?
5. How would you very briefly describe, in laypersons' terms, the most important things you found in your investigation?
6. What, in hindsight, would you do differently were you to design this study again?

Through preparation of this kind and following the other forms of preparation recommended for proposal meetings discussed earlier in this chapter, you will feel more confident going into your defense meetings. Generally, if the thesis or dissertation is well prepared, the defense can become a conversation with colleagues. This is often a time of very positive and affirming feelings, as you successfully complete the last requirement on your way to earning the master's or doctoral degree.

CONCLUSIONS

Your relationships with your advisor and your committee are critical to a successful thesis or dissertation. When these relationships are working well, they can be a source of tremendous productive feedback that will help you strengthen your research and produce a rigorous and thorough thesis or dissertation. Good working relationships can also foster a great deal of emotional support during an often-stressful process. We hope that through the kind of preparation discussed in this chapter, you will have positive and professionally rewarding relationships with your advisors and committees.

DEMONSTRATING INTEGRITY AND PROFESSIONALISM IN YOUR RESEARCH

In the sometimes chaotic energy that is involved in completing a dissertation or thesis, losing sight of the *process* is all too easy, that is, how students are conducting themselves in the process of doing this work. Sometimes researchers can get into an arrogant stance of "the ends justify the means." Getting the data and getting the project done seem tantamount, and the process of how it gets done pales in significance. The purpose of this chapter is to focus on the importance of conducting research in a way that reflects your own integrity and the integrity of your profession. We want to help you think about ways of conducting research in a manner that is mindful of the trust that your research assistants, allies, and participants have in you and of the tremendous honor it is to be able to investigate your passions and write about your findings in respectful ways. We want to emphasize that we are all part of a professional community and the actions of one member can influence the perceptions of many people about our fields. Being a thoughtful, caring, respectful professional can dramatically influence how people think about educators, counselors, and psychologists.

This is not a chapter on research ethics, per se, although we certainly discuss behaviors that embody the highest standards of our professions' ethical codes. [For a more thorough discussion of how the ethical guidelines specifically apply to the research endeavor, we refer you to the text *Research Design in Counseling*, which has a chapter on Ethical Issues in Counseling Research (Heppner, Kivlighan, & Wampold, 1999, pp. 79–117), which has broad applicability to the social sciences and includes a copy of the American Psychological Association ethical guidelines.] Much of what we describe here is about conducting yourself with professionalism and integrity in each step of the research process. We assert that there are important considerations even from the very beginning, when you are just beginning to plan your research project. At each step of the way from topic selection to methodology (selecting participants, instruments, and procedures), all the way through data analyses and reporting and interpreting the results of the study, there are important issues that you need to be thinking about in order to embody high standards of professionalism and personal integrity. By providing numerous personal examples, we hope that you will be able to reflect on ways your own dissertation or thesis can be conducted that personify the best values of your profession.

This chapter first discusses attitudes toward research and specifically toward the thesis or dissertation. Next, we discuss the role of professionalism and integrity at each of the various stages of research. Specifically, we provide examples and discussion of potentially problematic areas at the following seven major stages of thesis or dissertation development: (a) topic selection considerations; (b) working with various research allies; (c) conducting a literature review; (d) methodological issues such as selecting participants, instruments, and procedures for the investigation; (e) issues specific to conducting qualitative, observational studies; (f) analyzing and reporting results; and (g) discussing the findings.

While we do not intend for this to be an exhaustive list of the myriad of situations that may arise at each of these stages, we do hope that it provides sufficient examples from real-life research projects. Sometimes our students tell us that it seems to them as if ethical issues happen to other people, that the ethical examples that are in textbooks seem to them to be quite extreme and unlikely to affect them. In this chapter, we provide many examples that have happened to colleagues, students, and us. We do this to help students understand that issues related to ethics and professional integrity are everywhere, in every research project, and that every student will have ample opportunity to grapple with their own issues during their thesis and dissertation research.

ATTITUDES TOWARD CONDUCTING RESEARCH

Arguably, the most important issue related to conducting research in a manner that reflects professional integrity is the student's own attitude about conducting research. We have seen a whole continuum of attitudes in students preparing to conduct their thesis or dissertation research. Some students are thoroughly engaged in their project; their passion for it is obvious, and they can barely wait to get their committee's approval to start the data-collection process. They see their work as potentially contributing important findings to both practitioners and researchers. On the other end of the continuum are students who see the thesis or dissertation as a means to an end: graduating. Students' attitudes about research and science have developed from a variety of sources such as the media or stereotypes and messages received from previous teachers. Some students simply dislike science and see it as an esoteric activity best left to White men with black-rimmed glasses working in isolated labs.

In addition, some students have received messages that they are not good at math or science, which has led them to avoid research activities. We have often heard these students say, "I really don't care how this turns out, I just want to get this done." We refer to this as *divorcing* oneself from the research project by paying more attention to the outcome than to the process. We, too, want every student to graduate; we also want every student to begin this developmental process as a scientist, which has important personal and professional implications. We believe it is essential for students to think about their attitudes toward research, prior conceptions, stereotypes, fears, and expectations for the research process. Through an awareness of their attitudes, students can more clearly understand their own behaviors in the research process. Although we can appreciate that research may not be the first love of everyone in applied psychology or counselor education, it is important to understand how attitude affects all aspects of the research process, from working with research allies to interpreting results.

REFLECTING ON EACH PHASE OF THE RESEARCH PROCESS

Topic Selection

Chapter 2 provided a host of issues for students to consider when choosing a topic for their thesis or dissertation research. We discussed the importance of choosing topics for which the student has a deep and abiding passion and ones that help contribute to solving major social issues. Thus, the act of choosing the topic for the thesis or dissertation is in fact an act that reflects on your sense of personal integrity and professionalism. Consider the following two scenarios of students we have interacted with recently:

- I think I can get access to this big data set where I work. I would need to see what instruments they have already collected and see if I can come up with some research questions that seem plausible based on what they already have in the files. I hope I can come up with something my committee will approve, because that would save me having to collect all my own data, which could burn up another couple semesters.
- My advisor told me I could tag on to a project that he is doing. I really have no interest in it, in fact, I think he is really on the wrong wavelength with this research, but I guess it doesn't matter all that much . . . is just a requirement after all, one more hurdle they are making us jump.

Both of these students have clearly divorced themselves from their topic selection. Because of increased efficiency, they are willing to sacrifice their own passions to complete their projects quickly. In the first example, the student seems oblivious to the need to select topics and research questions that will actually contribute to the professional knowledge base. He is much more interested in being able to construe a research question that can be answered by the data that have already been collected by the agency where he works. In the second example, the student is implying that, in her professional judgment, her advisor's research may not be headed in a fruitful or promising direction but that she is willing to overlook these flaws in order to jump the hurdle of a thesis. Thus, even at this very early stage in the thesis or dissertation process, professionalism and integrity can be compromised.

Another important place where ethical judgment and professionalism are required in the selection of a topic relates to using care to not select ones that are too close to emotional issues that students are experiencing in their own lives. A very fine line exists between selecting topics for which a student has passion and selecting topics that are too emotionally charged for the student to maintain scientific objectivity. Two recent examples come to mind. One student, who had struggled with an eating disorder for years, decided to write her dissertation on this topic. At times she overidentified with her participants, had frequent debilitating emotional reactions to her research, and recapitulated some of her own issues, all of which impeded the success of her project. Similarly, a student who had recently lost a child to sudden infant death syndrome (SIDS) wanted to investigate how other parents with SIDS experience psychologically reacted to the loss. Given his own recent trauma, this research was very painful for him. In addition, he was less able to maintain a sense of objectivity in his research. Thus, we urge students to find topics they find personally meaningful, yet ones that do not involve issues with which they are currently struggling.

Conducting a Literature Review

Although it is sometimes hard for students to see themselves as experts when they are at this stage of their thesis or dissertation research, they will indeed be experts on their topic. They will know a great deal about a narrowly defined topic. In being an expert it is critical that students do the work that that role implies. Carefully reading and critiquing the literature, as we discuss in Chapter 4 and Chapter 6, are critical aspects of professional integrity. The profession needs to have confidence that the researcher has read and understood the critical related literature of a field and is basing his or her current investigation on that knowledge. Thus, the researcher should read and study a great deal about the topic and have an understanding of the methodological problems and recommendations that have been made by previous researchers. Presenting this knowledge objectively and scientifically in the literature review demonstrates the researcher's integrity in this process. We have been on student committees in which students have clearly not read the literature. They may be proposing a project that has already been conducted with limited importance. They may be proposing a methodology that has been severely criticized in the literature. They might also have simply read a chapter that integrated results from previous investigations without going back to those original sources to really understand what was found. Although all researchers at times use secondary sources for some of their literature review, the majority of articles that are core to the student's study should be read and cited from the original source. Unfortunately, when students rely on a couple sentences that may be published in a handbook on the topic, the essential meaning of the findings may be lost and, thus, may compromise the current study. However the absence of information occurs, this lack of accurate knowledge of what has come before may have the result of involving participants in an investigation that does not have a meaningful purpose and, thus, may compromise the integrity of the researcher and the research process.

Working With Research Allies and Assistants

Another early venue where issues of professional integrity can be evident is in working with research assistants. As we indicated in Chapter 1, the thesis or dissertation project does not have to be done in isolation. Master's and doctoral students often provide experiences for undergraduates who are interested in research by allowing them to participate in some of the tasks involved in the thesis or dissertation. Think about the experiences that are provided to these research assistants and work with them in a way that communicates the values and ethics of your profession. Contrast these two scenarios, which were presented to us by two different undergraduate research assistants:

- I met with the researcher once at the very beginning, he gave me a huge stack of data to enter. He showed me how to enter it and told me if I had any problems to call him, but I was basically on my own. All I did for the whole semester was data entry—all numbers that had no meaning to me. I think the project had something to do with adolescent depression, but I am really not sure. I didn't even get to see him at the end of the semester. He just emailed me that he would turn in a grade.
- When the researcher first met with me, he asked me about myself and my own career aspirations. I told him I wanted to go on to graduate school. He told me the kind of experience I would be getting working on this project would be very helpful. His team was made up of undergraduates and graduate students, and he, as well as the other graduate students, could provide me with a lot of information about graduate school. He told me all about the project; it was on the role of gender role identity in predicting health outcomes. He encouraged me to take all the instruments they give to their subjects, so I would have a better idea about what data I was entering. He actually sat down and went over the instruments with me, which was such a neat experience. Most of what I did was data entry, which is kind of dull, but he also tried to vary my tasks by teaching me how to do library searches for him and developing reference lists in APA style. The part I enjoyed the most was when our team had its weekly meeting. He made us feel like what we were each contributing was important and that each of our opinions was valued on the team. It was a really good experience, and he said he would write me a strong letter of recommendation for graduate school.

Undergraduate students are often seeking research experience to test out their interests in doing research and to be more competitive for graduate school admissions. These students can be very helpful in conducting thesis or dissertation research. Undergraduates can be trained to do a range of tasks, which takes some of the burden off the student who is conducting the thesis or dissertation and can, as in the second scenario, provide an excellent learning experience for the undergraduate assistant as well.

Unfortunately, we hear of too many situations in which undergraduates are simply used as unpaid labor, with little or no attention to making it a good learning experience for them. If you plan to utilize research assistants, carefully consider how to make this an experience that enables them to grow, to become excited about the research process, and to feel that they learned something about themselves or conducting research as a result. The experience they will have as a research assistant may very well help them decide if they want to go on to graduate school, and you can be a powerful role model of a graduate student within applied psychology whom they can emulate.

This same philosophy applies to anyone students are working with during their research. For example, perhaps mental health counselors are helping to collect data for the project. How can you help them feel appreciated for the extra effort they are donating to the project? Going to a weekly staff meeting, updating them on the data-collection progress, thanking them for their work in helping collect the data, and perhaps, bringing treats to the staff meeting are all ways of demonstrating respect and appreciation for these research allies. In addition, you can further demonstrate professionalism through being organized when meeting with allies; being considerate of their time or lives—for example, asking them what's convenient for them; and building relationships with them over time. Building strong relationships with research allies takes time and work but is often a highly rewarding professional experience. Your level of professionalism and integrity in this process communicates a great deal about the values of the profession.

Methods

Selecting Participants   In Chapter 9, we discuss the issue of selecting samples that are representative of the populations to which you would like to generalize your findings. Thus, you must carefully assess what populations are most important to generalize the findings to. While participant selection is often seen as a functional decision, it is also an ethical one. Simply obtaining conveniently available participants without regard to whether they are the most appropriate participants to answer the research questions of the study is an important professional consideration. Historically, in applied psychology, the tendency has been to study first-year psychology students, as they are easy and convenient to access for research purposes. For some studies they may be appropriate; for many studies, however, this practice compromises the generalizability of the study. Using the convenience sample approach often undermines the ultimate contribution of the investigation to the literature.

Designing a methodologically strong and meaningful investigation takes on even greater import when students are interested in investigating samples from small or hard-to-access populations. These participant pools are not inexhaustible, and individuals can only be expected to participate in a finite number of investigations. Thus, make sure whenever you request participation, particularly from a difficult-to-access sample, that you have a study that has the potential to actually contribute to the literature. For example, recently, many individuals are attempting to conduct research on racial and ethnic minorities. This is very important, as so many previous studies have not included minority group members in their samples (see Chapter 9). Thus, racial and ethnic minority group members may be receiving requests to contribute data to numerous investigations. Understandably, in all likelihood they will choose not to participate in studies if they feel barraged with requests. Similar remarks can be made about a host of other groups such as supervisees, experienced therapists, or trainees within a graduate program. A few years ago, one of the authors was a committee member for a master's student who was conducting his very first piece of research. Given his inexperience, his study was not well designed. He was planning to administer his questionnaires to 200 racial ethnic minority trainees in psychology across the nation. Because of the mediocre design of the study, which was basically a correlational study testing constructs that had already been demonstrated to relate, the likelihood of this research ever being published and contributing to the knowledge base in applied psychology was very small. Thus, he was in effect proposing to exhaust a hard-to-access sample with a study that had little promise of making a contribution.

This was perhaps an extreme example; however, it behooves us all to work to design the type of study that will have a high probability of contributing to the literature. In our view, conducting a thesis or dissertation is not simply practice in doing research although that is part of the function. A much larger goal is a shared responsibility for doing the kind of work that will make a contribution that eventually benefits people's lives.

Soliciting Participants   In attempting to involve people as participants in research, the methods of solicitation should be carefully considered. Particularly important is that potential participants must be fully apprised of their rights (see Heppner, Kivlighan, & Wampold, 1999). These rights include the right to voluntary involvement without any form of coercion. Sometimes when student are under pressure to obtain the number of participants needed to answer their questions, drifting over the line between solicitation and coercion is easy. For example, in one study a student needed to obtain participants from fraternity houses; he met with the presidents of the fraternities to solicit their help in recruiting participants. Even though he stressed that participation should be voluntary, he noted that some fraternity houses had sent all their pledges. Upon closer examination, he found that presidents had made this participation a pledge requirement. Thus, the participants were not really voluntary. In another case African American women were needed for a study that was being conducted on a predominately White campus. The student researcher obtained a list of all African American women on campus and called them to solicit their participation. However, if she was unable to reach the potential participants and they did not call her back in response to the message she left, she called again and again, up to 12 times a day, and even late into the night. Clearly this practice could be perceived as harassing potential participants. Thus, it is very important to treat human participants with the utmost respect, to fully inform them of their rights as research participants, and to not engage in activities that could be perceived as harassment.

Procedures Used in the Investigation   Should individuals agree to participate in an investigation, you still need to think about all aspects of the research protocol and be sure that they are treated with respect and that their participation is educational and helpful to them. For example, in one situation of which we are aware, participants were asked to complete 3 hours of questionnaires without a break in a non-air-conditioned auditorium in the heat of the summer. Clearly this type of treatment is a breach of professionalism and ethics, as well as violating simple human kindness. Keep protocols brief, and provide comfortable accommodations and breaks when necessary to facilitate the process.

Sometimes research protocols become overly lengthy as a result of the practice of "throwing in an instrument" to see what you will find. When designing protocols, you should only include instruments for which you have a clear theoretical need, that is, instruments that will help to answer the theory-based questions that are driving the investigation. Sometimes, however, the student, or even a faculty member, thinks it might be interesting to "throw in another measure to see what you will get." This practice generally has limited scientific merit and can cause undue fatigue for participants. Although the comfort of all participants must be protected, this issue becomes especially important when conducting research on vulnerable populations such as the elderly or mentally or physically ill participants.

Vulnerable participants may also be ones that have suffered particular trauma in the past, and the practice of asking them about the trauma may feel like retraumatization. For example, a student was conducting her thesis on the issue of partner violence and was interviewing women who had been beaten by their husbands or partners. In this situation, particular care was taken to utilize highly skilled interviewers who were experts in partner violence and highly sensitive to the needs of these women.

You must also recognize the needs of individuals who may be assisting with the investigation in other ways than by being participants. For example, in another situation, a student was developing a protocol for rape prevention that utilized previous rape survivors on a panel discussing the impact of the assault on their lives. Two important lessons related to professionalism were evident from this dissertation investigation. First, the student had read and studied the rape-prevention literature and knew that a previous study had demonstrated that when rape survivors spoke about the rape itself, men's attitudes toward sexual violence actually became worse as a result of the intervention. Thus, the student researcher knew that it would be important to limit the comments of the panelists to the physical and psychological sequelae of the assault and not the graphic details of the assault itself, which evidence suggests had a negative impact on participants. This example highlights the need for you to be highly knowledgeable about the topic you are investigating. Lack of knowledge and expertise can, in fact, do harm to participants. The second important lesson of this particular project was the need for the panel to meet and discuss the parameters and boundaries of what they were and were not willing to discuss on the panel. Thus, the investigator arranged for a meeting prior to the intervention so that panelists could discuss such issues as whether they were willing to take questions from the audience, how they wanted to be introduced, and any other parameters that would help them feel more safe and comfortable in the situation. The investigator also provided a time for debriefing following the intervention so those panelists could have time to share their thoughts and feelings about the experience.

Carefully thinking about the protocol for data collection can avoid many unfortunate situations. For example, one student was conducting her dissertation on adult children of alcoholics (ACOA). For this research she needed to screen a large number of students to obtain a much smaller sample of ACOAs. She was allowed to insert a small screening questionnaire into the protocol of a mass screening that was conducted each fall in an introductory education class. She then contacted those students whose screening instruments indicated they considered themselves ACOAs. She then asked them to participate in the next phase of the study, which she had scheduled in a group format for the following week. She communicated that all data that would be collected would be strictly confidential and that even the participants' names would not be physically connected with their data. She did not, however, communicate to willing participants that the next phase would be in a group format. When several participants had arrived for the next phase, she overheard one saying to the other, "Hey, I had no idea your parents were alcoholic." Thus, the confidentiality she had promised in her verbal and written consent form was not respected given the procedures she had developed to collect the data. Although hindsight is 20/20, when one is in the throes of conducting research, overlooking a procedure that could seriously jeopardize ethical practice is very easy. Institutional Review Boards (see Heppner, Kivlighan, & Wampold, 1999) review and attempt to help the researcher foresee these kinds of ethical compromises; but, even with these boards in place, problematic procedures often go unnoticed. Thus, you must think through as carefully as possible what all the ramifications may be of any procedures being planned in the investigation.

Instrumentation   When selecting instrumentation, not only the length of the assessment protocol but also the validity and reliability of the instruments are critical. Instruments should be selected that are appropriate for answering the questions that are posed by your thesis or dissertation. If instruments are used that have poor psychometric properties (see Chapter 7), this can make the results of the investigation uninterpretable, thus putting participants through unnecessary work for no good reason. In addition, you need to examine whether the type of instrument used has been validated for the sample that you want to obtain. For example, consider the story about a man who was studying Eskimos in Alaska. The participants were difficult to access, and it took him 6 months to obtain the number of participants he needed for his investigation. His data collection involved completing several instruments all using Likert scales that ranged from *strongly agree* to *strongly disagree*. On the last day of his data collection, when he was feeling very good about obtaining the numbers he needed, his host took him aside and said, "Likert scales do not capture the way Eskimos think; we have a quite different way of thinking about ourselves and the world than can be communicated in this format." Boom! With that statement, the researcher had the validity of his study seriously called into question. If the scales, in fact, did not capture the worldview and thinking patterns of this group, then how valid and meaningful were his findings? This example also highlights the importance of having cultural informants assist with the research process. Although only researching those groups that the investigator knows intimately is undesirable, the investigation must be informed by individuals who are experts on the cultural group under study.

Qualitative and Observational Studies

Although much of this chapter relates to both quantitative and qualitative studies, a number of critical issues within qualitative research need to be addressed separately. When conducting a qualitative investigation, the proximity, length of connection, and type of connection with the "participant" can be considerably different than when conducting a quantitative investigation. This poses a number of ethical issues for the researcher to consider. In the genre of observational/ethnographic studies, the researcher becomes his or her own research instrument and this often is a very different stance than that taken in quantitative research methods. Scholars of observational/ ethnographic research often argue for a total immersion in the field, which often places researchers in situations where conventional definitions of informed consent or confidentiality are much more complex. In most typical psychological studies using a qualitative methodology, the researcher becomes much more intimately involved with the participant, often conducting lengthy interviews and having multiple contacts with the participant. In these cases, it is often necessary to build trust and camaraderie between the researcher and the participant. A whole line of feminist scholarship has argued that researchers should be co-creators of knowledge with their participants, that it is critical to "rescue emotion from its discarded role in the creation of knowledge" (Fonow & Cook, 1991, p. 11). Thus, as qualitative investigations become more common within psychology, there will no doubt be more integration of the unique issues qualitative researchers face within existing ethical codes. Until then, however, it is critically important when conducting qualitative research to carefully consider the unique issues presented by the methodology employed and to maintain the highest possible integrity and ethics in designing the methodology.

Data Analysis and Presenting Results

After data have been collected, the data-analysis phase begins. You may think, given that this phase represents the end of contact with human participants, that it is free of ethical and professional issues; but, you will find that issues related to professionalism and integrity are part of all aspects and phases of the research project. For example, at the data-analysis stage, you must demonstrate a high degree of competence in analyzing and interpreting your results. If data analyses are conducted poorly or without adequate competency, serious misinformation can become part of the knowledge base. The chapters in this text on presenting quantitative and qualitative results are a good reference, as well as the numerous references provided in those chapters to statistical-analysis and qualitative-analysis texts. If you do not feel confident in analyzing and interpreting results, seek consultation from experts. In doing so, however, you must understand what is being done and why it is being done; this is part of maintaining the integrity of the research. We have had a number of students over time who have made use of statistical consultants. Many of these consultations are very appropriate. Students have stayed with the process and understood why certain analyses were appropriate for their research questions. They have understood the results that were generated from these analyses and could explain them to their committee and to us. In contrast, we have also heard of students who paid a consultant not only to conduct to all of their analyses independently but also to write their results chapter. These students then came to their committee meetings with little understanding of why their analyses were conducted and what they meant. This type of behavior seriously compromises the integrity of the thesis or dissertation.

There are many ways to lie with statistics. Some would contend that with enough data manipulation a person can get interesting or publishable results. The integrity of the scientific process requires that researchers have research hypotheses that they are analyzing and that they remain true to the research questions that guided their project. *Dustbowl empiricism* is a term used for the practice of continuing to conduct analyses until finding significance. Since much research, especially at the data-analysis stage, is a private matter, researchers must use professional integrity in conducting such analyses in line with the scientific method.

Discussing Your Results

Discussing your results also requires a high level of professionalism and integrity. You should be well versed in the instruments and literature used in your investigations. For example, one of our students was examining participants at a historically Hispanic college and found them to be more depressed than an adult norm sample. His first interpretation of these results was that the context of the historically Hispanic college must in some way create an atmosphere that was not positive for these individuals and that subsequently created greater depression. Not until it was suggested that he find a normative study of college students did he find his sample to be very similar to other students on their level of depression. Thus, you must examine and interpret results very carefully so that accurate statements are presented related to the results. This is especially important when results could be construed to be detrimental to persons of specific groups such as disabled persons; racial and ethnic minority group members; and members of particular social classes, sexual orientations, or religious preferences. Many of these groups have a long history of having the data they contribute to investigations come back to hurt them in various ways. Thus, be sure to carefully examine the interpretations that are being made, alternative explanations for the findings, and what impact such interpretations may have on the community from which the sample was obtained.

You must also clearly document the limitations of the investigation. Sometimes students tend to gloss over limitations in their research. Note that all research, by definition, has limitations. Stating clearly what those limitations are in theses and dissertations will aid readers in understanding more about possible confounds in the study and will aid future researchers in building on and improving what has been contributed in the current project.

The discussion chapter is also a place to discuss alternative hypotheses that may be important to the integrity of the contribution. Helping the reader understand what may have caused the results is an important role for the researcher. Do not take leaps from the data with statements that overgeneralize the findings. Trying to remain as clear and objective as possible in presenting and discussing results is an important ethical responsibility.

CONCLUSIONS

The purpose of this chapter has been to help you reflect on the myriad of ways you can exhibit the highest levels of professionalism and integrity while conducting your thesis or dissertation research. Professional ethics are said to be "expressions of our values and a guide for achieving them" (Diener & Crandall, 1978, p. 14). In the sometimes hectic world of researchers, it is easy to lose sight of the process of how they conduct themselves as researchers and the values and ethics they communicate about themselves and their professions. This chapter should help you reflect about each stage of the research process and how to integrate professionalism throughout your project.

CONDUCTING QUANTITATIVE ANALYSES AND PRESENTING YOUR RESULTS[*]

The results chapter of your thesis or dissertation provides the answers to your research questions and hypotheses discussed earlier in Chapter 5. The style of writing in this chapter is quite different according to the methodology you chose (i.e., quantitative versus qualitative methodologies). This chapter covers how to present results obtained by quantitative statistical analyses; presenting results utilizing qualitative analyses are discussed in Chapter 13.

We have witnessed that writing the results from quantitative analyses can be one of the most anxiety-provoking tasks for students who are writing a thesis or a dissertation. It can be the most fearful for students who consider themselves "math phobic." Students commonly "get stuck" in this stage of the task even though they have the printed outputs from statistical programs in their hands. We have seen two types of difficulties that students encounter most frequently. One is that students have little knowledge of how to interpret the results from the printed outputs; the other is that students have difficulties in effectively summarizing and writing the results of their study. The former is beyond the focus of this chapter; thus, students are encouraged to refer to the manuals of the statistical programs or related books (e.g., for SPSS users, see Green, Salkind, & Akey, 2000; for SAS users, see Hatcher & Stepanski, 1994). Note that the purpose of this chapter is not to provide details in computing statistical techniques (e.g., *t* test, ANOVA, cluster analysis, etc.); instead, we place our main focus on providing a practical guide on how to write the results chapter properly and effectively. Thus, we only briefly discuss the basics of each statistical technique; for more details on understanding various statistical techniques, please refer to the suggested references in each section. Also note that covering all the broad array of statistical analyses is impossible; thus, we select the most widely used statistical techniques and offer ways to present these analyses in counseling and related mental health fields.

[*]This chapter co-authored with Dong-gwi Lee and Hyun-joo Park.

The purpose of this chapter is to provide a wide range of writing techniques to describe a variety of quantitative statistical analyses often used to answer research questions or hypotheses. In particular, we provide two levels of suggestions. First, we discuss three structural elements often used to establish a clear and organized structure for the results section: (a) road maps, (b) writing results of preliminary analyses (e.g., data screening, descriptive analyses), and (c) writing results of main analyses using a variety of statistical techniques. Second, we divide the various statistical techniques into two categories on the basis of the numbers of dependent variables involved: (a) univariate analyses when researchers have one dependent variable (e.g., chi-square test, t test, several types of analysis of variances, ANCOVA, three types of multiple regressions), and (b) multivariate analyses when researchers have more than one dependent variable (e.g., MANOVA, cluster analysis, two types of factor analyses, structural equation modeling). Each statistical technique is explained with three subsections: (a) general introduction and brief discussion of when to use the specific statistical technique, (b) common components in writing the results of that statistical analysis, and (c) actual writing examples from previous students' theses or dissertations and/or published research articles with our commentary notes about the examples.

We end this chapter with the "Checklist for Chapter 4 of the Thesis or Dissertation," which allows researchers to check whether they followed the appropriate procedure or included components in writing results using a variety of statistical techniques. "Useful References for Other Statistical Techniques" suggests references often used in social science such as hierarchical linear modeling (HLM), discriminant function analysis, and canonical correlation analysis.

We recommend that you read and follow the specific analysis techniques related to your specific research questions. For example, if you are interested in classifying different types of people using multiple measures, you can refer to the cluster analysis section. Again, note that the main purpose of this chapter is not providing detailed statistical information but providing useful guidelines for writing results using the variety of statistical techniques. Thus, we strongly encourage you to refer to useful statistical textbooks we have suggested for the specific sections for more details.

WHERE TO BEGIN: THE CHAPTER ROAD MAP

Like other chapters, the first one or two paragraphs in the results chapter should provide a clear road map to serve as a guide for committee members or others who are reading this chapter. The road map serves as an advanced organizer, telling the reader what to expect in the chapter.

Following is a brief example of a road map for the results chapter from the beginning of Jones (2000):

> This chapter describes and summarizes the statistical analyses used to evaluate the research questions and hypotheses established in the previous chapters. Subsequent to the data screening process, this chapter reports the results of the screening for co-morbidity in the sample and the procedural check on the instruments used. Next, the results of the clustering solutions for both the personality and clinical syndrome and the level of functioning/self-efficacy are reported along with the results of the multivariate follow-up analysis. For both solutions, the clusters will be named and their relationship with major demographic variables will be reported. The overlap of the clustering solutions will be described. Finally, the relationship between the cluster solutions and the post-treatment outcomes (recidivism to drug use or criminal behavior) will be reported. (p. 61)

In this example, Jones was careful to identify each section of her results chapter. Note that each of the sections (except for the preliminary analyses) specifically addresses each of her research questions or hypotheses. In a quantitative study, the results sections should be consistent in addressing the research questions or hypotheses previously identified in the earlier chapters, preferably in the same order. Through this road map, Jones provides her readers with a clear sense of what will follow in the results chapter.

COMMON PRELIMINARY COMPONENTS OF THE RESULTS CHAPTER

Data Screening

Typically, entering data into a computer file prior to beginning the actual data-analysis stage is very time-consuming and laborious. Especially with a large data set, students often feel a great deal of relief to have all of the data entered onto a file; amen! However, please keep in mind that, even if the data set has been scanned by computer rather than entered by hand, inaccurate data can still occur due to respondents' random marking on the scantrons, and so on. Thus, the importance of checking the accuracy and relevance of the data cannot be overemphasized. We first want to underscore that errors often occur during data entry. Probably because of the multitude of numbers and the tediousness of the task, even the most conscientious researchers make mistakes. Note especially that sometimes the data-entry errors create dramatically different results in the subsequent data analyses. Students commonly report odd or inconsistent findings in their results chapters due to errors in data entry, overlooking assumptions of normality, and underestimation of influential observations, sometimes referred to as *outliers*. We have also found that students have a tendency to jump immediately into their main statistical analyses after completing their data entry without taking the time and care to ensure that they have clean, accurate data. We understand data screening or cleaning procedures are often time and energy consuming, but they are highly critical steps.

Following are five steps typically involved in data screening, as well as some associated examples:

Step 1 *Check the accuracy of the data entry.* This is crucial, as finding mistakes in data entry is quite common. For example, in one of the author's previous studies, 13 participants were found who were coded as females, but only 10 females were actually in the study; in a career research data set, one client was coded with an age of 1, but all clients were actually adults; and in another data set, several of the items on the Problem-Solving Inventory (PSI: Heppner & Petersen, 1982; Heppner, 1988) were entered as 7, but the PSI item scores only range from 1 to 6. Statistical analyses based on such errors in the data-entry stage obviously provide misleading results and often make critical differences in determining the statistical significance of the results.

We recommend that students conduct the following two strategies to effectively check the accuracy of their data entry. First, if the data set contains a small numbers of participants, review the data file on the computer screen to determine if any visually inconsistent (or improbable) scores appear on any of the variables. However, with a larger data set, this process is often too time-consuming and carefully checking all of the data points is difficult. Thus, for a larger data set, we typically recommend that students print frequency tables and use graphic methods (i.e., histograms, box plots) to find improbable scores across all variables (e.g., demographics, variables of interest) considering the possible score ranges for each variable. Students can easily obtain these outputs by using popular statistical programs. If this review process identifies improbable scores, we recommend that students examine the original responses from participants and insert the correct numbers in the data file. After removing erroneous data and inserting the correct numbers, repeat a second step of conducting frequency tables to once again check the adequacy of the entered scores (repeat this process until you are confident that the data have been entered properly).

Step 2 *Check missing data.* Missing data is one of the most common problems in data analysis. This problem typically occurs when some participants did not complete one or more instruments or did not respond to some items on an inventory for a variety of reasons (e.g., fatigue, vagueness of items). Missing data is often problematic for the researcher, because it not only reduces the credibility of the data set but also raises questions about why certain items were not answered (e.g., some items may be perceived as too sensitive for some participants making them uncomfortable). These nonrandom missing values may be a threat to external validity or generalizability of a study's results (see Heppner et al., 1999). Thus, you should investigate if there are consistent patterns in the missing data (e.g., missing items from participants in a certain age range or only from women participants). For example, in a questionnaire with demographic and attitudinal questions, quite a few respondents refused to answer questions about their educational level. If the researcher had just deleted the data with missing values on educational level, it could have been problematic because of the potential distortion in the sample values on the attitudinal variable. In this case, we would recommend that researchers test to determine if there are significant differences in the mean scores on the attitudinal variable between two groups (i.e., cases with missing versus cases with nonmissing values on educational level). The researcher may use an independent sample t test by constructing a dummy variable (e.g., 1 = cases with missing values; 2 = cases with no missing values) to test the group differences. If there are no differences, the issue of missing values may not be crucial. On the contrary, if there is a significant difference based on the t statistic and associated p value, separate analyses should be conducted for the cases with missing values and without missing values on educational level. We strongly recommend that researchers also provide detailed discussion on the limitation of generalizing the findings to the specific population with a certain educational level.

If missing values are randomly scattered throughout cases and variables, we encourage students to use one of the following two strategies. First, if only a few missing data points are found in a large data set, delete the specific participants whose data contained the missing values. Note that, unfortunately, no firm guideline is yet established for determining how small missing values can be tolerated at a given sample size (Tabachnick & Fidell, 1996). The strategy to delete missing values has a limitation in that it reduces the sample size (i.e., the number of participants). Thus, we more typically recommend the second strategy, which is to replace the missing items with the group mean for those items. This strategy is more commonly used because the group mean for an item is expected to represent the central tendency (or average) of that item. This strategy also has the advantage of maintaining the sample size. Note that the statistical mean of a variable can be easily calculated by using common statistical programs (e.g., descriptive analysis commands in both SPSS and SAS). Regardless of the specific strategy employed for handling missing data, we recommend that researchers examine descriptive statistics (e.g., means, standard deviations, percentages, etc.) for both samples (i.e., the original data set including cases with missing values versus the revised data set).

Step 3 *Check outliers.* Sometimes a data set may be complete but other problems are present in the data. For example, perhaps one of the participants misread the directions for one of the inventories and, subsequently, that respondent's score is very different from the other respondents. In essence, if a participant's score is considerably different from others when the data set is examined in a scatterplot (which is an SAS- or SPSS-generated visual depiction of participant's scores on one or more variable), the person's score is considered to be an *outlier*. Outliers in a data set are often the result of mistakes, such as misunderstanding directions and/or items, but also can be related to random responding of a participant (e.g., responding without reading the items, such as marking 6 for all responses), purposeful faking of responses (e.g., faking bad, or faking good), as well as accurate but deviant responses. The problem is that extreme scores, or outliers, can have a disproportionate effect on the data analysis or, in essence, distort the results of a study.

To identify univariate outliers, researchers should convert each raw score in the data set into a standardized score (e.g., Z score or T score) and determine whether there is an outlier, referred to as a case that is deviant from the mean of all cases (e.g., ± 2 SD from the mean; note that the M is 0, SD is 1 in Z scores). In addition, to identify multivariate outliers (i.e., cases that reveal an unusual pattern of scores by their combination), Mahalanobis distance statistic is typically used. *Mahalanobis distance* refers to "the distance of a case from the centroid of the remaining cases where the centroid is the point created by the means of all the variables" (Tabachnick & Fidell, 1996, p. 67). Once Mahalanobis distance statistic is calculated for each case, a certain criterion to indicate multivariate outliers is set based on the degrees of freedom (*df*) and the critical value of chi-square statistics. The SPSS program provides an option under Regression Analysis to calculate Mahalanobis distance statistic.

Once either univariate or multivariate outliers are identified, several strategies can be utilized to reduce the influence of outliers, such as the deletion of the case, alteration of the case score by replacing it with the mean of all cases, or a transformation procedure of the variables (for more details, see Tabachnick & Fidell, 1996). However, note that these strategies may also distort the nature of the data. Thus, the researcher must address (a) the presence of outliers; (b) possible distortions when deletion, alteration, or transformation is employed; and (c) limitations in generalizing the study results to a different population.

Step 4   *Examine the normality of distributions.* Another potential problem within data sets pertains to the violation of the normality assumption regarding the distribution of the data set. The distribution of most data sets follows a normal distribution curve (see Figure 12.1). That is, most people's scores are located in the middle of the distribution, with only a few people at either end of the distribution. The critical point is that most statistical techniques are based on the assumption of normality, that is, that the data follow a normal distribution curve. The problem is that sometimes the distribution of scores for a particular variable may not be normally distributed. Figure 12.2 represents a distribution of scores for an inventory of suicidal ideation that is strongly

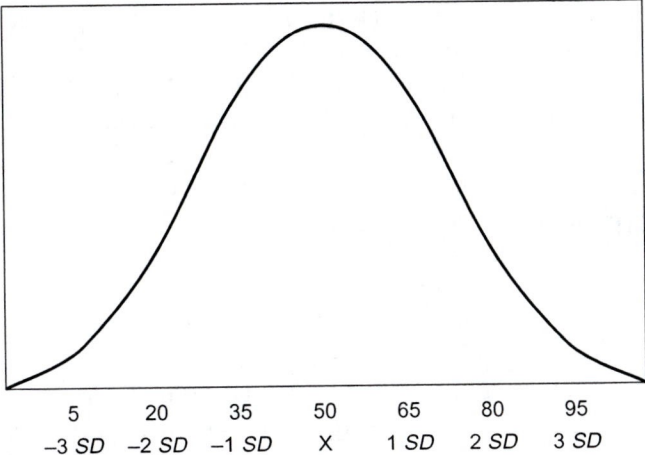

5	20	35	50	65	80	95
–3 SD	–2 SD	–1 SD	X	1 SD	2 SD	3 SD

FIGURE **12.1**

Normal distribution curve.

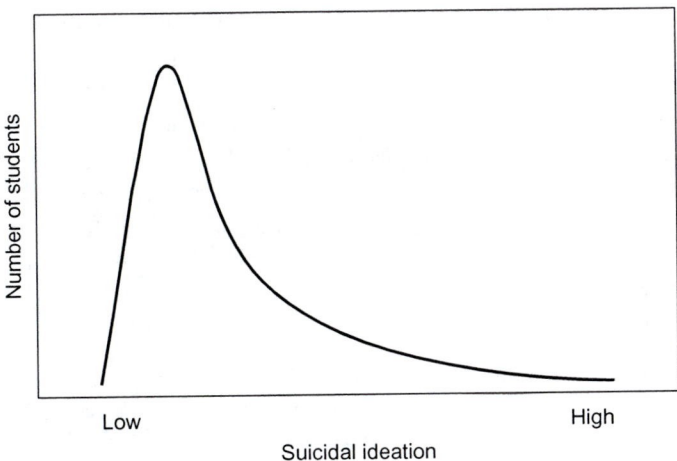

FIGURE **12.2**

Positively skewed distribution.

skewed to the left (i.e., positively skewed); that is, most college students typically report relatively low levels of suicidal ideation.

Skewness and kurtosis statistics are useful to check the deviation from normality of a distribution. *Skewness* involves the symmetry of the distribution; if a variable is skewed, its mean is not in the center but in the left (i.e., positively skewed) or in the right (i.e., negatively skewed) of the distribution. *Kurtosis* refers to the peakedness of the distribution and has three general types of curves—platykurtic (relatively flat), leptokurtic, and mesokurtic (relatively peaked). Values for skewness and kurtosis are available in several common statistical programs (e.g., under descriptive commend in SPSS). Although no firm guideline exists for determining acceptable values for skewness and kurtosis, the closer to 0 the better, and less than the absolute value of 2 is desirable. For advanced readers, the significance tests for both skewness and kurtosis against the null hypothesis of 0 are available (see Tabachnick & Fidell, 1996, pp. 72–73).

Step 5 *Determine the appropriateness of data transformations.* In Step 4, if the data failed to meet the assumption of normality (e.g., too skewed in the distribution), then data-transformation procedures would be recommended (e.g., a square root, a logarithm, the inverse transformations, or a ranked transformation, see Tabachnick & Fidell, 1996, pp. 82–84). Data transformations should be conducted with caution because interpreting the meaning of the transformed scores is sometimes difficult. For example, the logarithm transformation (i.e., transform the scores with a log function) of IQ scores may be harder to interpret. Nonetheless, transformation procedures are often used in research because they may have the advantage of reducing the impact of influential observations or what we call *outliers,* which could distort the central tendency of the distribution, as well as the relationships among the variables of interest. Note that the researcher needs to check whether the transformation resulted in a normal distribution (i.e., the values for skewness and kurtosis are close to zero). Readers are referred to statistics textbooks for how to perform the transformation (e.g., Tabachnick & Fidell, 1996).

Following is a short example from Wei (2000) about how to write the *transformation procedure:*

> The skewness and kurtosis of almost all the measured variables were less than 1, indicating the scores from this sample could be normally distributed. The only two measured variables that revealed kurtosis of greater than 2 were the BDI (skewness = 1.4, kurtosis = 2.5) and the HS (skewness = 1.7, kurtosis = 3.6). However, these findings are typical of previous studies with large samples (e.g., Kendall, Hollon, Beck, Hammen, & Ingram, 1987). Nonetheless, these suggested the two variables deviate from a normal distribution and thus the rank formation was conducted. Two variables after the transformation were called T-BDI and T-HS (note that T means "transformed"). The skewness and kurtosis for the T-BDI (.07 and − .28, respectively) and T-HS (.12 and − .31, respectively) indicated a normal distribution after the transformation. However, the correlations between T-BDI and BDI as well as T-HS and HS were very high ($r = .95, p < .001$, and $r = .93, p < .001$). In addition, there were very little differences between the original variables (the BDI and HS) and the transformed variables (the T-BDI and T-HS) in terms of correlations with other variables. For example, the correlations between T-BDI and other variables, as compared with the correlations between BDI and other variables, were very similar: 5 out of 21 pairs were identical, 13 out

of 21 had only .01–.02 differences, and 3 out of 21 had only .03–.04 differences. Thus, taking into account these results, the BDI and HS were remained in the subsequent analyses. (Modified from Wei, 2000, pp. 47–48)

Note that Wei had two variables—the Beck Depression Inventory (BDI) and the Hopelessness Scale (HS)—that revealed kurtosis values greater than 2 (i.e., 2.5 and 3.6, respectively), which were thus considered to lack a normal distribution. To remedy this problem, she conducted the rank transformation for the variables, which converted the original scores into the new scores ordered by their rank. Note that Wei provided the values for skewness and kurtosis for the transformed variables in order to ensure that the distribution of the variables changed closer to a normal distribution. However, also note that Wei finally chose not to use the transformed scores for her main analyses because the original scores and the rank-ordered scores after the transformation were highly correlated (r ranged from .93 to .95) and their correlations to other variables yielded a very similar fashion. In such a case, researchers are encouraged to retain their original data.

Following is an example of how to write results concerning *data screening:*

Prior to main analyses, all the variables of interests were examined through SPSS 10.0 program for accuracy of data entry, missing values, the normality of distributions, and multivariate outliers. Several miscoded scores of 8 on the Problem-Solving Inventory (PSI: Heppner, 1988; the item scores only range from 1–6) were corrected after examining the original responses from participants. The single missing value on the Social, Attitudinal, Familial, and Environmental Acculturation Stress Scale (SAFE: Mena, Padilla, & Maldonado, 1987) was replaced by the mean of all cases on the variable. The values for skewness and kurtosis fitted into an appropriate range (i.e., below the absolute value of 2), indicating the normal distribution of the scores across all variables of interest. No cases were found to have univariate outliers by examining whether there are extreme Z scores. Two cases were detected as multivariate outliers between the PSI and SAFE variables through Mahalanobis distance statistics (Tabachnick & Fidell, 1996) with $p < .001$, and thus deleted, leaving 98 cases for the main analyses. (Giovanna, 2002, pp. 40–42)

Note in this example that both univariate and multivariate outliers were examined. According to Tabachnick and Fidell (1996), *univariate outliers* are cases with extreme standardized scores (e.g., Z scores) on one or more variables, and *multivariate outliers* are defined as cases that have an unusual pattern or combinations of scores on two or more variables. Note that having multivariate outliers may be possible even in the case of having no univariate outliers. Although it may be an advanced topic for those who do not have an extensive statistical knowledge, we recommend using Mahalanobis distance to identify multivariate outliers (refer to Tabachnick & Fidell, 1996, for more details). The Mahalanobis statistic allows for determining a case that has an unusual combination of scores by providing information on how far the case is from the rest of the cases, as well as its significance based on its p value. In addition, as illustrated in the preceding example, the researcher should present the final sample size (i.e., the number of participants) after the deletion of any cases with outliers. This may help readers be informed of the total numbers of participants for the main analyses, which is often critical to determine statistical power or effect sizes of the subsequent analyses.

Preliminary Analyses

The purpose of descriptive analyses is to examine whether basic characteristics of the current data set (e.g., means, standard deviations, percentages, skewness, kurtosis, etc.) are comparable to those reported in previous research. Thus, in a broad sense, descriptive analyses can be considered a part of preliminary analyses. However, given the importance of the descriptive analyses in writing the results section, we fully describe it in a later section and concentrate only on the preliminary analyses here.

Preliminary analyses may include several analyses such as examining (a) if scores on the dependent variable are different across demographic variables, (b) reliability coefficients or factor structure for the measures, and (c) correlations among variables.

Step 1　*Check if scores on the dependent variable(s) are different across demographic variables.* The purpose of this step is to demonstrate that specific demographic groups (e.g., sex, race, age, education level, etc.) do not limit scores on the variable of interest (usually dependent variable). To achieve this goal, *t* tests, analyses of variance (ANOVAs), and chi-square analyses (particularly for frequency data) are typically utilized, especially when the demographic variables are discrete variables such as sex or race (these statistical techniques are described later in this chapter). For example, if researchers want to examine whether there are differences on the scores of the Beck Depression Inventory (BDI; Beck, Steer, & Garbin, 1988) due to sex of the participants (i.e., males versus females), they may conduct an independent samples *t* test and examine whether the *p* value of the *t* statistic is larger than the established alpha level (e.g., .05). If so, the researchers have some assurance that the BDI scores do not differ between male and female, and thus the BDI scores for men and women can be combined for the main analyses. If the *p* value is less than .05, or is statistically significant, it is recommended that the researchers conduct main analyses on the BDI separately by male and female groups.

If the demographic variables are continuous variables such as age, *t* tests, ANOVAs, or chi-square analyses are not appropriate to utilize. In this case, researchers may choose one of two strategies. The first strategy is to make the age variable into a discrete variable by dividing it into two (or more) subgroups (e.g., below the age of 25 versus 25 or above) and then conduct the *t* tests or ANOVAs. However, this strategy has a limitation in that the significance of the tests may depend on how the researcher chooses the subgroups. For example, there may be no significant difference on the scores of the dependent variable (let us say the BDI) between the two groups (below 25 versus 25 or above), whereas there may be a significant difference between another arbitrary age group (below 20 versus 20 or above). Thus, we recommend a second strategy, that is, conducting a regression analysis with age as the predictor and the BDI as the criterion variable and examining whether age significantly predicts the scores on the BDI. If the regression analysis with age as a predictor on the BDI is not found to be significant, the researcher can be less concerned about the influence of age on the dependent variable throughout the main analyses. If the result turns out to be significant, the researcher should (a) qualify the results pertaining to depression across age groups and (b) discuss in the discussion chapter how age may theoretically contribute to the dependent variable.

Following is an example of a *preliminary analysis* from Wang's (1994) thesis:

> To determine whether academic level influenced the results, a series of Student's *t* tests [one type of *t* test] were computed for each variable between undergraduates and graduates. The findings revealed that no statistically significant differences (positive *t* values indicate greater mean for undergraduate students) were found among observed variables except for problem-solving confidence (t (303) = 3.03, $p < .01$) and approach-avoidance style (t (300) = 4.27, $p < .01$). Thus, academic level did not seem to differently influence most of the variables; thus, for all analyses, the data from undergraduate and graduate students were combined. (Modified from Wang, 1994, p. 29)

Note that Wang (a) identified the specific statistical technique used to determine the influence of demographic variables (in this case, academic level; undergraduate versus graduates) on the variables of interest (e.g., problem-solving confidence) and (b) provided a brief summary of the findings across the variables of interest. Particularly, note that she added a comment in parentheses to aid the reader in understanding the meaning of the positive *t* values. However, note that, given the significance of the *t* tests for problem-solving confidence and approach-avoidance style subscales, the researcher should use caution in generalizing her main findings to all academic levels of students.

Step 2   *Assess the reliability coefficients and/or factor structure of the measures.* Typically the next step in the preliminary analyses is to assess the reliability coefficients of the measures (i.e., inventories) used. Note that several types of reliability can be considered. Most commonly, researchers are interested in whether the items for a particular inventory—and items for separate factors on a particular inventory—are internally consistent with each other. This type of reliability is called *internal consistency* and is calculated by obtaining an alpha coefficient.

The purpose of examining estimates of internal consistency from the sample is to determine if the measures used in this particular study have acceptable reliability levels and reliability estimates that are comparable to those found in previous studies. This is a very important preliminary analysis step because, without acceptable range of reliability coefficients (typically higher than .70 to .80 in social science research), the results could be adversely affected by the error variance associated with inadequate reliability and, thus, not equivalent to those reported in previous research. Establishing adequate and comparable reliability is very helpful particularly in cross-cultural or cross-national studies to evaluate the internal reliability of the inventories when used in a culture other than on those for which they were initially developed. For example, let us suppose that researchers want to measure South Africans' perceived problem-solving appraisal (i.e., individuals' belief in their problem-solving capabilities) by using the Problem-Solving Inventory (PSI; Heppner, 1988) developed in the United States. In this case, the assessment of internal consistency (typically coefficient alpha, see Cohen & Swerdlik, 1999) is crucial to evaluate the PSI in the South African sample, as well as to make a comparison between the findings from South Africans with their counterparts in the United States.

The following example from Heppner, Pretorius, Wei, Lee, and Wang (2002) illustrates *how to efficiently present estimates of internal consistency* for several measures in a cross-cultural study. Note that as a preliminary analysis, the authors first address the magnitude of reliability estimates across the three subscales and total of the PSI, and note the comparability with the findings of a previous researcher:

Reliability

Estimates of internal consistency were examined for the PSI total and each of the factors. The alpha coefficients were as follows: .89 for PSI total, .79 for PSC, .84 for AAS, and .71 for PC. These initial estimates of reliability suggest that the PSI and the three factors have acceptable levels of internal consistency in the South African sample. Similarly, Pretorius (1996) reported an alpha coefficient of .84 for the PSI total.

Factor Intercorrelations

Similarly to the research in the United States (Heppner, 1988), an intercorrelation matrix of the factor scores indicated moderate intercorrelations among the three factors: PSC/AAS = .50, PSC/PC = .47, and AAS/PC = .53. Thus, these moderate interrelations suggest that the three factors are somewhat interrelated but still represent distinct constructs. (p. 487)

Note that earlier in the paper the authors presented comparable internal consistency estimates for the PSI based on a demographically similar U.S. sample. In addition, the authors provide information about how the three factors are related to each other in the South African sample by providing information on the intercorrelations among the three factors, which provides more information about how the PSI performed in the South African sample (relative to U.S. samples). Note that the researchers presented reliability estimates for each subscale of the PSI as well as the total inventory, which provides reliability information at two levels. The total score is especially relevant for their study since this was the score utilized in their main analyses.

In addition to internal consistency estimates, inter-scorer or inter-rater reliability estimates (typically Kappa coefficients, see Cohen & Swerdlik, 1999) are needed when a researcher uses an open-ended questionnaire, then asks two or more judges or raters to sort participants' responses into the established categories, and wants to report the degree of agreement or consistency that exists between or among the raters. In this case, it is strongly recommended that the researcher report an inter-rater reliability coefficient in the preliminary analyses section so that readers can be confident that the main findings using the questionnaire are valid throughout the subsequent analyses.

Step 3 *Analyze and report intercorrelations among variables.* This last step of the preliminary analyses is important for several reasons. First, reviewing intercorrelations among variables can provide another opportunity to detect potential errors in the data set through the identification of unusual correlations among the variables. For example, if a strong negative correlation was found between measures for depression and anxiety, this would contradict the moderate to high positive correlations between the two variables from a myriad of previous research studies. Such a contradictory finding could be a warning signal that something may be wrong with the data set (e.g., there could be mistakes in calculating reversed score items). In such a situation, researchers should return to the data-screening step and carefully check the data to make sure the data and scoring of the inventories are correct.

Second, correlation analyses among variables may provide a researcher with helpful hints for further analyses. For example, if a researcher finds a very high correlation (typically over $r = .70$) between variable A (e.g., intelligence test scores) and variable B (e.g., creativity scores), this provides important information about these two variables in this data set. One immediate concern is that these two variables seem to share so much variance (49%) that in some forms of analyses, such as regression analyses, the results will be adversely affected by what is called *multicollinearity* (i.e., the potential adverse effects of correlated independent variables on the estimation of regression statistics, Pedhazur, 1997, p. 294). Thus, the researcher may want to either combine the two variables into a new variable C for the main analyses, or eliminate one of the two variables (A or B). (For more details, see Pedhazur, 1997.)

Finally, reporting intercorrelations among variables not only can provide readers with a general idea of the relationship among the variables of interest but also can provide answers for some specific research questions. In the latter case, the correlation analyses can be included as a part of the main analyses. For example, a research question of Heppner, Lee, Wei, Anderson, and Wang (2001) was "Does negative affectivity confound the problem-solving–psychological-adjustment link?" Even though they used structural equation modeling (refer to the statistical analyses section later in this chapter) to answer the research question, correlational analyses between NA and other variables such as the PSI and BDI were also used to provide basic answers to their research question. The following paragraphs and the correspondent intercorrelations table provide an example for how the researchers use findings from intercorrelations among variables to describe the general relationships among variables and also to answer their research question:

ZERO-ORDER CORRELATIONS
BETWEEN THE PSI AND OTHER VARIABLES

It was hypothesized that the PSI [Problem-Solving Inventory] would correlate significantly with the NA [Negative Affectivity] as well as the four indices of psychological adjustment. To guard against alpha inflation, a Bonferroni correction was used to establish the alpha level at .006 (.05/8), which is the original alpha level (.05) divided by the number of statistical tests. As shown in Table [12.1], the correlations between the PSI and almost all indices of psychological adjustment as well as the NA were statistically significant (all $ps < .0001$) except for the relations between the AAS [Approach-Avoidance Style] and the BAI variable [Beck Anxiety Inventory]. More specifically, the PSI was significantly correlated with the NA, BDI [Beck Depression Inventory], BHSR [Transformed Beck Hopeless Scale], and LS [Loneliness Scale]. In sum, the first hypothesis was supported by the findings of this study. (Adopted from Heppner, Lee, et al., 2001)

Note that a Bonferroni correction procedure in the preceding example refers to a statistical guideline on which researchers attempt to inhibit the inflation of alpha error due to multiple pairwise comparisons like a fishing

TABLE 12.1	MEANS, STANDARD DEVIATIONS, SKEWNESS, KURTOSIS, AND ZERO-ORDER CORRELATIONS AMONG PSI, PC, AAS, PSC, NA, AND PSYCHOLOGICAL DISTRESS VARIABLES

Variable	1	2	3	4	5	6	7	8	9	10
1. PSI	—									
2. PC	.73***	—								
3. AAS	.92***	.55***	—							
4. PSC	.81***	.51***	.56***	—						
5. BDI	.38***	.48***	.22***	.40***	—					
6. BAI	.18**	.29***	.08	.20**	.64***	—				
7. BHS	.38***	.33***	.27***	.40***	.64***	.39***	—			
8. T-BHS	.44***	.38***	.33***	.44***	.62***	.42***	.90***	—		
9. LS	.33***	.33***	.20***	.34***	.56***	.40***	.48***	.52***	—	
10. NA	.31***	.42***	.17***	.33***	.70***	.67**	.50***	.52***	.49***	—
N	274	274	274	274	275	273	274	274	275	272

Note. PSI = Problem Solving Inventory; PC = Personal Control; AAS = Approach-Avoidance Style; PSC = Problem-Solving Confidence; BDI = Beck Depression Inventory; BAI = Beck Anxiety Inventory; BHS = Beck Hopelessness Scale; T-BHS = Transformed BHS; LS = UCLA Loneliness Scale; NA = Negative Affectivity Scale; N = sample size; ** $p < .001$, *** $p < .0001$. Modified from Heppner, Lee, et al., 2001.

Source: From "Does Negative Affectivity Confound the Problem Solving-Psychological Adjustment Link?," by P. P. Heppner, D. G. Lee, M. F. Wei, C. anderson, and Y. W. Wang, 2001, Paper presented at the annual convention of the American Psychological Association, p. 25. Adapted with permission.

expedition. The alpha error is also called Type I error and refers to an error in decision to reject the null hypothesis (H_0) even if it is true. In the simplest form of the Bonferroni correction procedure, researchers can reduce the alpha error by dividing the original criteria (i.e., $\alpha = .05$) by the number of such comparisons. Suppose that a researcher decided on five comparisons in a study. If the researcher evaluated each comparison at a conventional alpha level ($\alpha = .05$), the estimated alpha level combined in the entire study could be as high as .25 (i.e., $.05 + .05 + .05 + .05 + .05 = .25$). To solve this problem, the researcher needs to establish a more stringent alpha level. In the Bonferroni, the new alpha level ($\alpha = .01$) for this study can be obtained by dividing the conventional alpha of .05 by the number of comparisons (in this case, 5) [$.05 / 5 = .01$]. Note that this new alpha level ($\alpha = .01$) is much less than the estimated alpha for five comparisons ($\alpha = 5 \times .05 = .25$). See Keppel (1991) or Myers and Well (1995) for more details.

Note in Table 12.1 that only those values below the diagonal were presented to represent correlation coefficients among the variables because the numbers above the diagonal are symmetric with those below the diagonal. Also note that the *Note* at the bottom of the table explains full names for the variables when acronyms are used in the table.

Descriptive Statistics

It is often useful for readers to understand how the participants responded as a group to the inventories in a study. For example, suppose that researchers are investigating variables that predict depression. It is important to know, as a group, how depressed participants were (e.g., extremely depressed? mildly depressed?) to understand the context of the study. Thus, one of the first tasks is to describe how the sample responded as a group on all of the central variables in the hypotheses as well as on the demographic variables. Statistics used to describe the main tendencies of a variable are called *descriptive statistics*. Mean *(M)* and standard deviation *(SD)* are the most frequently used statistics for this purpose. In addition, median, mode, frequency, and/or percentages may also be used in some situations. For example, researchers cannot calculate mean of the sex of the participants. Instead, researchers typically report frequencies with percentages [e.g., The participants were 56 women (69.1%) and 25 men (30.9%).] to describe this type of situation. The skewness and kurtosis of each variable may also be presented in this section; this information is useful for readers to ascertain to what extent the distribution of scores is normally distributed, which is often a basic assumption for many statistical analyses. In cases in which the data set contains many variables or categories, presenting a descriptive summary table in addition to a brief explanation of the descriptive nature of variables is typically recommended to succinctly communicate all of this information.

Following are examples of presenting *descriptive statistics:*

Means, standard deviations, skewness, and kurtosis for the 22 indicators are shown in Table [12.2]. The means for Depend, Close, and Anxious [the three variables assessing attachment styles used in the study] (M = 20.1, 22.6, and 14.1, respectively) are close to the means reported by Robert, Gotlib, and Kassel (1996) in a study with college students (M = 17.1, 21.3, and 15.9, SD = 5.5, 4.7, and 5.1, respectively). The means for the three Problem-Solving Inventory (PSI) subscales are comparable to the means reported in the PSI Manual (Heppner, 1988) for college students. Specifically, the range for the Problem-Solving Confidence (PSC) subscale is from 22.9 to 26.2, while 26.1 was found in this sample; the range for Approach-Avoidance Style (AAS) subscale is from 40.7 to 44.2, while 45.6 was found in this sample; and the range for Personal Control (PC) is from 16.6 to 17.5, while a mean of 17.2 was found in this sample. However, the means of Suppressive Style and Reactive Style (M = 23.2 and 17.7, respectively) in this sample are higher than the means (M = 12.7 and 13.7; SD = 4.2 and 4.0) reported by Heppner, Cook, Wright, and Johnson (1995) with a college sample. (Modified from Wei, 2000; p. 54)

Note in this example that Wei described the sample not only by reporting the means and standard deviations but also by comparing the means in her study with the findings from previous research.

Table 12.2 illustrates how Wei summarizes the paragraph in the preceding example by using a table format. This format can be helpful for readers to easily identify basic characteristics (e.g., M, SD) of variables of interest. Note that in addition to M and SD, she also presents skewness and kurtosis statistics (as was discussed earlier in the data-screening section), which enables her to efficiently provide readers with the fact that all of the variables are normally distributed (generally considered if the absolute numbers are less than 2). Also, note that Wei presents a typical way of identifying the acronym by explaining them in a *Note* at the bottom of the table. Acronyms are often used in tables to save space

TABLE 12.2 MEANS, STANDARD DEVIATIONS, SKEWNESS, AND KURTOSIS FOR THE INDICATORS

Variable	Mean	SD	Skewness	Kurtosis
AAS:				
Depend	20.7	5.0	−0.28	−0.12
Close	22.6	4.2	−0.34	−0.23
Anxious	14.1	5.0	0.53	−0.24
PSI:				
PSC: Problem-Solving Confidence	26.1	7.5	0.41	0.30
AAS: Approach-Avoidance Style	45.6	11.4	−0.14	−0.48
PC: Personal Control	17.2	4.5	−0.22	−0.14
PF-SOC:				
Suppression Style	23.2	4.3	−0.65	0.16
Reactive Style	17.7	4.1	−0.51	−0.14

Note. AAS = Adult Attachment Scale; PSI = Problem-Solving Inventory; PF-SOC = Problem-Focused Style of Coping. Modified from Wei, 2000, p. 59.

Source: From "Attachment, Coping, Conflicted Emotion, and Psychological Distress: Testing a Modeational Model," by M. Wei, 2000, Unpublished doctoral dissertation at the University of Missouri–Columbia, p. 59. Adapted with permission.

in creating the table; if it is not necessary to conserve space, use the full variable name, which makes it easier for the reader to understand the variables. However, if it is necessary to conserve space in creating a table by using acronyms, then it is necessary to provide a key explaining what the acronyms stand for in an explanatory note at the bottom of the table (see the fifth edition of the APA *Publication Manual*, 2001, for a discussion of stylistic features of tables).

Sometimes a researcher can use a table format to present a great deal of data—especially more complex arrangements of data—in efficient ways. Table 12.3 illustrates how Deffenbacher and Swaim (1999) arranged means by sex across groups. Again, note that all acronyms are explained at the bottom of the table so that a reader can decipher the variables in the table.

WRITING STATISTICAL ANALYSES TO DESCRIBE THE RESULTS

This section describes a variety of quantitative statistical techniques (e.g., chi-square, *t* test, ANOVA, Structural Equation Modeling, etc.) that students often use in analyzing the results of their studies. We very briefly describe various statistical techniques and, primarily, discuss key components in writing the results for the various statistical analyses. The descriptions and respective examples should serve as a helpful reference in writing your results sections after you have the output analyses in your hands. Again, note that the purpose of this section is not to provide statistical knowledge itself

TABLE 12.3 MEANS AND STANDARD DEVIATIONS OF AGGRESSIVE FORMS OF ANGER EXPRESSION ARRANGED BY GENDER, ETHNICITY, AND DEVELOPMENTAL LEVEL

| | White Non-Hispanic | | | | Mexican American | | | |
| | Males | | Females | | Males | | Females | |
Measure	M	SD	M	SD	M	SD	M	SD
PAQ								
MS	9.49	3.51	8.12	3.24	7.53	3.39	9.35	3.46
HS	7.82	3.14	8.36	3.32	7.24	3.15	7.93	3.21
PAP								
MS	7.01	3.38	5.72	2.59	6.57	3.31	6.47	3.06
HS	6.42	3.83	5.44	2.27	6.36	3.06	5.85	2.69
VA								
MS	9.32	3.77	9.05	3.61	7.97	3.54	8.81	3.71
HS	10.15	3.42	10.23	3.37	8.92	3.51	9.36	5.52

Note. PAQ = Physical Assault—Objects; PAP = Physical Assault—People; VA = Verbal Assault; MS = middle school; HS = high school. Reproduced from Deffenbacher and Swaim, 1999, p. 66.
Source: From "Anger Expression in Mexican American and White Non-Hispanic Adolescents," by J. L. Deffenbacher & R. C. Swaim, 1999, *Journal of Counseling Psychology, 46,* p. 66. Copyright 1999 by the American Psychological Association, Inc. Reprinted with permission.

in great detail but to help you to learn how to write the statistical analyses in an appropriate manner. Specifically, each of the statistical analyses consists of the following three subsections: (a) a very general introduction and purpose of when to use the specific statistical technique, (b) steps in writing the results of that statistical analysis, and (c) actual writing examples from published research and/or previous students' theses and dissertations. For convenience, we categorize the quantitative statistical techniques into two categories: (a) univariate analyses and (b) multivariate analyses. The first category involves any analyses that contain only one dependent variable, such as chi-square test, t test, several types of analysis of variance (ANOVA), analysis of covariance (ANCOVA), and multiple regressions. The second category can be used when multiple dependent variables are involved; for example, multivariate analysis of variance (MANOVA), cluster analysis, factor analysis, and structural equation modeling (SEM). If you are not comfortable in choosing appropriate statistical techniques to examine your research questions and hypotheses, refer to Tabachnick and Fidell's (1996) guideline (see pp. 30–32). Before proceeding to the specific statistical techniques, note that a common mistake that students occasionally make in writing their results is interpreting or even commenting on findings that approach statistical significance (e.g., $p = .052$ when the alpha level is established at $p < .05$). Do not report nonsignificant results however close the p value may approach the established alpha levels for science (i.e., conventionally $p < .05$ for social science or $p < .01$ for some medical research). If you freely increase the alpha level in determining the significance, readers cannot ascertain whether the findings are practically meaningful or just attributable to the chance probability (e.g., random errors). Alpha levels are set for an important reason; thus, discussing results that do not meet this basic a priori level is inappropriate.

Chi-Square

The chi-square statistic (χ^2) is used when the research question is aimed at examining the frequency of a certain categorical or discontinuous variable (e.g., sex, race) or, more technically, the extent in which an observed or actual frequency count differs from the expected frequency count. For example, Vera, Speight, Mildner, and Carlson (1999), using open-ended questions, asked clients to describe the ways in which they were similar to and different from their counselors. One of the main categories identified by clients was demographic variables such as gender and race. Chi-square tests were used because one of the research questions was to examine whether the actual frequencies of perceived similarity and difference in demographics (i.e., gender and race) were statistically different from the expected frequencies.

Writing the Results Using Chi-Square Once the chi-square analysis has been computed, the first task is to examine two numbers central to chi-square analyses: the χ^2 (pronounced chi-square) statistic and the associated p value. If the associated p value for the χ^2 statistic is less than the alpha level established in a study (e.g., .05), the result is statistically significant.

The results of the chi-square are typically reported in the following narrative format: "A chi-square analysis revealed that the frequency of [observed events] was significantly different from that of [expected events], χ^2 (a, N = b) = c, p < d." The following numbers are to be provided for each letter: (a) the degree of freedom (*df*), which is calculated by [(the numbers of levels in the row variable –1) × (the number of levels in the column variable –1)]; (b) the number of sample size (i.e., number of participants); (c) the value of the chi-square statistic; and (d) p value.

Vera et al. (1999) summarized the results of their chi-square analyses in the following example. Note that the authors first reported the frequency of numbers they observed from clients as well as the expected frequencies. Subsequently, they simply reported the two chi-square analyses, using a very similar format to that we have suggested.

> Eleven participants of 47 (23%) reported gender as a similarity and 2 of 47 (4%) reported race as a similarity. In actuality, 53% of the clients had a counselor of the same gender and 56% of the sample were racially matched. Ten of the 47 participants (21%) mentioned gender as a difference and 4 of 47 (9%) mentioned race as a difference. In actuality, 47% of the clients had a counselor of a different gender and racially 44% were unmatched. Chi-square analysis revealed that gender similarities, $\chi^2(1, N = 47) = 16.77$, $p < .05$, and racial similarities, $\chi^2(1, N = 47) = 47.32$, $p < .05$, were significantly underreported by the participants. The same was true for the reporting of gender differences, $\chi^2(1, N = 47) = 13.88$, $p < .05$, and racial differences, $\chi^2(1, N = 47) = 29.05$, $p < .05$." (p. 280)

Sometimes summarizing chi-square analyses in a table is efficient, most often if there are a number of analyses. For example, we constructed Table 12.4 to summarize the chi-square analyses conducted by Vera et al. (1999) to illustrate how this might appear.

For more statistical understanding of the chi-square analysis, please refer to Cohen (1996).

t Tests

t tests are typically used when a researcher wants to compare the mean differences on a dependent variable [which should be a continuous variable (e.g., reading scores)] between two groups [i.e., the independent variable, which should be a discrete (or categorical) variable (e.g., sex)]. The only exception is the case of a one-sample t test (see Green et al., 2000; pp. 139–140). Suppose that a researcher has a research question to determine if there is a significant difference on the Beck Depression Inventory (BDI) between men and

TABLE
12.4   CHI-SQUARE ANALYSIS SUMMARY

Variable	Observed Events (%)	Expected Events (%)	χ^2
Similarity			
Gender	23	53	16.77*
Race	4	56	47.32*
Difference			
Gender	21	47	13.88*
Race	9	44	29.05*

Note. *$p < .05$.

women. In this case, an independent-samples t test can be used; the sex of the participants (i.e., male and female) is regarded as the independent variable, and the BDI scores are the dependent variable.

Writing the Results Using t-Tests   The first step is to examine two numbers central to t tests, the t statistic and its associated p value. If the associated p value is less than the alpha level established in a study (e.g., .05), the results suggest that the mean difference between the two groups is statistically significant. The results of the t test are typically reported in the following format: "The [group 1] showed significantly higher mean scores on the [the name of the dependent variable] (M = a, SD = b) than [group 2] (M = c, SD = d), t (e) = f, $p < $ g." It is important to specify the means and standard deviations of the scores of the dependent variable between the two groups (a, b, c, and d), as well as the degree of freedom (e), the value of the t test statistic (f) and the p value (g). In the previous example, the means (M) tell the reader the extent to which the participants experienced depressive symptoms and the standard deviations (SD) tell the reader how far away participants' scores were in relation to the mean. The t statistic (f) gives the reader an indication of the size of difference between the two means; the higher the number, the larger the size of the difference. The number in parentheses after t (e) indicates the degree of freedom that is calculated by N_1 (the sample size for group 1) + N_2 (the sample size for group 2) − 2 (in the case of the independent-samples t test).

Rice and Mirzadeh (2000) were interested in examining the differences between adaptive perfectionists and maladaptive perfectionists (the independent variable) on the level of academic integration (the dependent variable). A t test was performed to examine the mean difference between the two groups on a measure of academic integration. The result of the t test was reported in the following manner:

> We conducted t tests to examine the mean differences between adaptive and maladaptive perfectionists on the measure of academic integration. . . . Adaptive

TABLE
12.5 *T* TEST ANALYSIS SUMMARY

Measure	Adaptive Perfectionists		Maladaptive Perfectionists		
	M	*SD*	*M*	*SD*	*t*
Academic integration	12.32	2.36	10.09	2.51	–5.69***

Note. ***$p < .001$.

perfectionists exhibited, on average, significantly higher scores on academic integration (M = 12.32, SD = 2.36) than maladaptive perfectionists (M = 10.09, SD = 2.51), $t(153)$ = –5.69, $p < .001$, d = 0.89. (p. 247)

Note in this example that the authors explicitly stated which group scored higher and then indicated the means, which illustrate, on average, how much higher. Thus, readers can easily see that one group was not only higher than the other but also how much higher. In addition, the authors included another statistic, d, which provides an index of the effect size. The effect size indicates how much variance in the dependent variable (academic integration) was accounted for by the independent variable (type of perfectionists). In this case, d was .89. Please note that regardless of sign (i.e., + or –), d values of .2, .5, and .8 traditionally represent small, medium, and large effect sizes, respectively (Green et al., 2000, p. 151). Thus, the effect size presented here would be considered large.

Sometimes results are summarized by a t test table. However, this may not always be necessary unless a researcher needs to summarize the results from several independent t tests. Again, for illustrative purposes, we created Table 12.5 from Rice and Mirzadeh (2000).

Note in the table that the means and standard deviations of each independent variable should be presented separately under the title for each group.

Interested readers can find detailed statistical explanations of using t tests, as well as different types of t tests (i.e., the independent-samples t test, and paired-samples t test), in most of the basic statistical textbooks such as Hays (1988) and Cohen (1996).

Analysis of Variance (ANOVA)

The analysis of variance (ANOVA) is used when a researcher wants to examine the mean differences of two or more levels of an independent variable on one dependent variable. In this section, we briefly discuss one-way and two-way ANOVAs.

One-Way ANOVA   A one-way ANOVA is used when a researcher wants to compare the mean differences across multiple levels of one independent variable on one dependent variable. For example, Ferrell-Swann (1999) was interested in examining whether participants' age (i.e., a dependent variable) would be different in three types of counselors (i.e., an independent variable that has three levels: novices, experienced nonexperts, and experts). Thus, she asked three levels of counselors to respond to a survey that included demographic variables such as age and sex. The *novices* were defined as master's students in counseling psychology; the *experienced nonexperts* referred to licensed psychologists who do not hold the American Board of Professional Psychology (ABPP) Diplomas or Fellow status in the American Psychological Association (APA); and *experts* referred to those who meet one of two criteria: individuals (a) who are licensed psychologists and who have achieved the ABPP Diplomas or (b) who are licensed psychologists who hold Fellow status in counseling related divisions in the APA.

Writing the Results Using a One-Way ANOVA   Once you have a computed ANOVA analysis in hand, then you should examine two numbers central to a one-way ANOVA analysis, the F statistic and its associated p value. If the associated p value is less than the alpha level established in a study (e.g., .05), the results suggest that the mean differences among the groups are statistically significant. The results of one-way ANOVA could be reported in the following format: "There was a significant effect of [the name of independent variable] on the [the name of dependent variable], F (df_1, df_2) = a, p < b." Note that specifying the value of the two degrees of freedom (df_1 and df_2) is necessary, along with the F test statistic (a) and the p value (b). The number for the first degree of freedom (df_1) is calculated by k (i.e., the number of levels of the independent variable) – 1, and the number for the second degree of freedom (df_2) is calculated by N (i.e., total sample size) – k.

Even if the overall result of the one-way ANOVA was statistically significant, the researchers do not know which of the three groups are statistically different from each other. Thus, the results from the ANOVA only indicate that there is a difference somewhere among the three groups. The next step is to conduct the follow-up tests (i.e., post hoc comparisons across more than two levels of the independent variable) in order to identify specifically which groups (i.e., conditions or levels) show significant mean differences out of all the groups in the independent variable. In this case, Tukey's and Scheffé's tests are two commonly used post hoc comparison methods. The difference between the two tests involves the fact that (a) the former usually requires equal sample size, whereas the latter does not; and (b) the Tukey's test deals with only pairwise (e.g., group 1 versus group 2) comparisons, whereas the Scheffé's test deals with every possible comparison (e.g., the average between group 1 and 2 versus group 3) resulting in a more conservative alpha level to guard against alpha inflation (for more details, refer to Keppel, 1991, and Myers & Well, 1995). Also, note that Tukey's or Scheffé's tests are not necessary if the independent variable has only two levels; in this case, the overall F statistic, along with means for each group themselves, reveals the size of difference as well as its significance by reviewing the p value. In essence, post hoc comparisons tests should be used only if there are three or more levels of the independent variable and the overall F statistic and its associated p value from the ANOVAs are significant.

Unlike post hoc tests, planned comparisons (or contrasts) can be used if researchers are interested in only comparing specific group means (e.g., control group versus treatment group; or treatment group A versus group B) depending on a priori theoretical hypotheses (e.g., treatment group will outperform control group; or treatment group A will outperform group B). As compared to post hoc tests, planned comparisons have advantages in (a) higher statistical power (i.e., higher probability to reject the null hypothesis when it is not true), and (b) less probability to commit Type 1 (or α) error (i.e., the mistake in decisions to reject the null hypothesis when it is true) by conducting only a few comparisons following theoretical hypotheses. See Keppel (1991) for more details.

For illustrative purposes, a *one-way ANOVA analysis and subsequent post hoc comparisons* from a dissertation by Ferrell-Swann (1999) follow:

> To determine if there was statistically significant difference among the three types of counselors on their age scores, one-way analysis of variance (ANOVA) procedures were conducted. The result revealed that there was a statistically significant difference in the mean scores of age among the three types of counselors, $F (2, 60) = 94.71$, $p < .001$. Post hoc comparisons with Tukey's statistic suggest that significant differences existed between the novice (M age = 26.22 years; ranged from 22 to 43 years) and experienced nonexpert groups (M age = 48.75 years; ranged from 32 to 64 years), novice and expert groups (M age = 57.63 years; ranged from 43 to 75 years), and experienced nonexpert and expert groups (all $ps < .001$). (Modified from Ferrell-Swann, 1999, pp. 88–89)

The research question was whether there is statistically significant mean difference in participants' age among the three types of counselors (i.e., novices, experienced nonexperts, and experts). Note in the example that the author utilized Tukey pairwise comparisons because the omnibus F test was significant and she wanted to identify which type of counselors were significantly different. Also note that, although the author provided the range of age variable in the example, it is more common to report standard deviations for the dependent variable across the levels of the independent variable(s).

Two-way ANOVA   A two-way ANOVA is used when researchers want to examine the effects of two independent variables (i.e., factors) and one dependent variable. In a two-way ANOVA, researchers examine three kinds of effects: (a) a main effect of the first factor (i.e., independent variable A), which examines the mean differences of a dependent variable across the levels of the first factor; (b) a main effect of the second factor (i.e., independent variable B), which examines the mean differences of dependent variable across the levels of the second factor; and (c) an interaction effect of the first and second factors (i.e., A × B), which examines whether the mean differences of dependent variables on the levels of the first factor vary as a function of the levels of the second factor (see Keppel, 1991, for better understanding of the interaction effect). The same principles could be applicable to studies with three or more independent variables.

For example, suppose that educators are interested in determining which instructional methods (e.g., lecture versus discussion) are more effective on students' final test scores in statistics considering students' previous knowledge levels (e.g., experience versus no experience in statistics). In such a case, a two-way ANOVA (i.e., 2 × 2 factorial design; note each independent variable has two levels) could be used because the study design included one continuous dependent variable (i.e., final test scores in statistics) and two categorical independent variables (i.e., instructional methods and students' previous knowledge levels).

Writing the Results Using a Two-Way ANOVA   As with the one-way ANOVA, in a two-way ANOVA, it is recommended that students examine the F statistic and the associated p value. However, note that in a two-way ANOVA students need to report three p values associated with three effects (i.e., two main effects from each independent variable and one interaction effect between the two variables). If each p value associated with two main effects and one interaction effect is less than the alpha level established in a study (e.g., .05), the results suggest that each effect, corresponding with each p value, is statistically significant. The results of a two-way ANOVA are often reported in the following format: "There was a main effect of [factor 1], F (df_1, df_2) = a, p < b; a main effect of [factor 2], F (df_3, df_4) = c, p < d; and an interaction effect of [factor 1 × factor 2], F (df_5, df_6) = e, p < f on [the dependent variable]." Note that the values of the F statistic (a, c, and e) with the degrees of freedom (df_1, df_2, df_3, df_4, df_5, and df_6) and p values (b, d, and f) should be reported by the two main effects and one interaction effect. If any effect of the three effects is statistically significant, the results of post hoc comparisons should follow.

The next example illustrates how Ambrose (1987) reported his results of a *two-way ANOVA*. Note that he used a two-way ANOVA procedure because he wanted to examine the main effects of the two independent variables [IV$_1$: Seriousness of offense (Serious Offenders versus Non Serious Offenders); and IV$_2$: Recidivism (Recidivists versus Non Recidivists)] and the interaction effect on the dependent variable (autism subscale of the Jesness Inventory: Jesness, 1971). For illustrative purposes, we selected only one dependent variable (autism) from 11 subscales of the Jesness Inventory. Readers can refer to Table 12.6 to examine the way to present results using a two-way ANOVA. Note as mentioned earlier that the two-way ANOVA results should have three components (i.e., two main effects of the independent variables and one interaction effect). Also note that, although we do not present Appendix A due to space considerations, we would recommend that researchers present the means and standard deviations across the independent variables. In addition, please be informed that no post hoc tests were used in this example because the Seriousness of Offense had only two levels although the main effect was significant. Keep in mind that post hoc tests should be utilized only when (a) the F statistic is significant at the desired alpha level *and* (b) the independent variable has more than two levels. Ambrose's results follow:

Hypothesis 1

There are no significant differences among Recidivists and Non Recidivists, Serious and Non Serious Offenders on the Autism scale of the Jesness Inventory.

The statistical test used to test this hypothesis was a two-way analysis of variance (ANOVA). The results (see Table [12.6]) indicate statistically significant difference between Serious Offenders and Non Serious Offenders on the Autism subscale in the Jesness Inventory, F $(1, 273)$ = 4.94, $p < .05$, suggesting that Serious Offenders demonstrated significantly higher scores on the Autism subscale of the Jesness Inventory when compared to Non Serious Offenders. However, the two-way ANOVA results fail to indicate that there is a main effect for the Recidivism variable as well as an interaction effect between Seriousness of Offense and Recidivism on the dependent variable. Group means and standard deviations are also presented in Appendix A.

Note in Table 12.6 that, although the author did not present the statistics for error variances (i.e., within group variance) and the total (note researchers need to report only Sums of Squares and associated *df* for the total), we highly recommend reporting the statistics for error variance and the total. The mean square for the error variance should be presented because it contributes to the denominator part of the F ratios (e.g., the F ratio for the main

TABLE 12.6 **TWO-WAY ANOVA SUMMARY TABLE FOR PERSONALITY VARIABLE DIFFERENCES**

Source	Sum of Squares	df	Mean Squares	F
Autism				
Seriousness of Offense	511.89	1	511.89	4.94*
Recidivism	94.29	1	94.29	.91
Interaction effect	128.24	1	128.24	1.24
Error				
Total				

Note. *$p < .05$. Modified from Ambrose, 1987; p. 64.

Source: From "A Comparison of Personality, Intelligence and Learning Disability Factors Among Juvenile Offenders," by P. A. ambrose, 1987, Unpublished doctoral dissertation at the University of Missouri–Columbia, p. 64. Adapted with permission.

effect of the first independent variable (A) can be calculated by the formula: $F_A = MS_A / MS_{error}$).

For more details about statistical issues related to ANOVA, see Hays (1988), Cohen (1996), and Keppel (1991).

Analysis of Covariance (ANCOVA)   Sometimes in the design of a study using an ANOVA, a researcher may want to control for the effects of a third variable that potentially is confounded with the effect of independent variable(s). This variable is called a covariate(s) or nuisance variable(s). According to Keppel (1991), a nuisance variable is a variable that if left uncontrolled could exert systematic influences on the main effects of the independent variable(s). Usually, covariates are assumed to be highly correlated with the dependent variable prior to the experiment. If there is a good possibility of the presence of covariates, a statistical procedure needs to be conducted called the analysis of covariance (ANCOVA). A typical example of a covariate examined in the ANCOVA is participants' pretest scores. The pretest scores should be considered as a covariate with the posttest scores because a person's performance at the pretest is often highly related to that of his or her posttest. If a researcher did not control for the influence of the pretest scores on the posttest scores, that researcher could misinterpret the size of the treatment effect of interest on the posttest. For another example, if a researcher is interested in examining the effects of two different math-teaching methods (i.e., treatment groups) on students' math scores (dependent variable), students' IQ scores or math abilities prior to the treatment should be considered as possible covariates.

There are two ways to control covariates in the ANCOVA depending on the nature of the specific covariate(s). First, if the covariate is a continuous variable (e.g., pretest scores), an ANCOVA procedure is recommended using a combination of a linear regression analysis and an ANOVA. Specifically, in an ANCOVA, the influence of the covariate (i.e., pretest scores) on the dependent measure (e.g., posttest scores) can be calculated by the regression coefficient. Next, the adjusted means for each treatment group are analyzed by the typical ANOVA analysis. Because the statistical calculations are beyond the scope of this chapter, for more interested readers, see Keppel (1991) or Myers and Well (1995). The second variation of the ANCOVA is to use a completely randomized block design in which the covariates is a categorical variable (e.g., sex). In this study design, the covariate can be treated as a blocking variable that means that the covariate blocks the treatment effect of interest. Specifically, in this design, the covariate (or blocking variable) can be controlled by considering it as another independent variable and then the main effect of the covariate, as well as the interaction effect between the covariate(s) and the main independent variable, can be tested. If there is no main effect of the covariate and the interaction effect between the two, the "pure" relationship between the main independent variable and the dependent variable is assured. If there is a significant main effect of the covariate and the interaction effect, the researcher needs to mathematically subtract the size of the covariate effects from the treatment group effects on the dependent variable. See Keppel (1991, pp. 313–314) for the statistical procedure.

Next we describe how to write the results for an ANCOVA. Given that it may be more frequent to have more than one independent variable, we explain the typical ways of writing a two-way ANCOVA.

Writing the Results Using a Two-Way ANCOVA   First of all, note that writing the results using a two-way ANCOVA is exactly the same as a two-way ANOVA after the adjustment of the means by eliminating the influence of a covariate from the scores in the dependent variable. If researchers have the computed output from a two-way ANCOVA in hand, it should contain not only the typical components in a two-way ANOVA but also new information on the covariate [i.e., the sums of squares *(SS)*, *df*, means of squares *(MS)*, and *F* statistic with associated *p* value for the covariate]. Thus, students should find that the *df* for the mean squares of within-group variance $(MS_{A \times B})$ in a two-way ANCOVA is 1 less than the typical within-group variance in a two-way ANOVA, because one additional *df* should be consumed to estimate the covariate. Given that writing the results for a two-way ANCOVA is exactly the same as for a two-way ANOVA except for the covariate part (note that the covariate part may not be often reported because the other components of the ANCOVA already reflect the adjustment by the covariate), we do not reiterate this discussion; instead, interested readers are referred to the earlier section for the two-way ANOVA.

Following is an example of a *two-way ANCOVA* from O'Rourke (1978). He was interested in examining the main effects of the two independent variables (i.e., IV_1: control versus treatment groups, and IV_2: male versus female) on the dependent variable (i.e., a measure of self-esteem). This would be the typical example for a two-way ANOVA, but in addition the author wanted to control for the pretest scores on the posttest scores (i.e., the dependent variable). In this case, the pretest scores would be considered a covariate, and thus the adjusted means of the two-way ANCOVA procedure should be used for the analysis of variance. Note in the example that O'Rourke presented two tables: (a) adjusted means after the ANCOVA procedure (Table 12.7), and (b) the two-way ANCOVA table (Table 12.8). Also note in Table 12.8 that although the researcher included the statistics for the covariate, it may be acceptable to delete the component for the covariate because the rest of the components (i.e., the main effects and interaction effect) already reflect the adjusted means. Readers should find that the ANCOVA table is the same as the ANOVA table except for the covariate and the *df* for the within-group variance as mentioned earlier.

The data were collected on the Self-Total (STOT) scale of the Barclay Classroom Climate Inventory (Barclay, 1974) and grouped according to treatment condition.

<table>
<tr><td>TABLE
12.7</td><td>POSTTEST MEANS ON THE SELF-TOTAL (STOT) SCALE, ADJUSTED FOR PRETEST PERFORMANCE, BY TREATMENT AND BY SEX</td></tr>
</table>

Group	N	Mean (Adjusted for Pretest Scores)
Total	39	14.56
Treatment		
Control	21	15.00
Experimental	18	14.04
Sex		
Female	17	15.50
Male	22	13.83

<table>
<tr><td>TABLE
12.8</td><td>ANALYSIS OF COVARIANCE OF SELF-TOTAL (STOT) SCALE BY TREATMENT METHOD AND SEX</td></tr>
</table>

Source of Variation	Sums of Squares	df	Mean Squares	F
Covariate (pretest)	82.95	1	82.95	4.96*
Treatment	8.28	1	8.28	.49
Sex	12.16	1	12.16	.73
Treatment × Sex	19.78	1	19.78	1.18
Error	569.04	34	16.74	
Total	699.59	38	18.41	

Note. *$p < .05$. Modified from O'Rourke, 1978, p. 70–71.

Source: From "The Effects of A Selected Guidance Program on the Self-development of Urban Fourth Grade Students," by B. W. O'Rourke, 1978, Unpublished doctoral dissertation at the University of Missouri–Columbia, p. 70. Adapted with permission.

The dependent variable (i.e., the STOT) was subjected to a two-way analysis of covariance to adjust for differences in pretest scores and to examine the effects of both treatment group (experimental or control) and sex of posttest performance. An analysis of covariance (ANCOVA) was employed to adjust the groups' posttest scores for pretest differences. The ANCOVA was carried out using the SPSS program. Significance tests on posttest means for each STOT were done by means of the F-ratios computed in the ANOVA after the adjustment of the group means.

Hypothesis 1

There is no difference between students who have received and the students who have not received a selected guidance program in self-competencies as measured by the STOT.

The results of the analyses for this measure are reported in Table [12.7] and [Table 12.8]. The overall group mean on the STOT was 14.56. The adjusted mean for the control group was 15.00, and 14.04 for the experimental group. The adjusted mean for females was 15.50 and 13.83 for males. The results of the ANCOVA on the STOT scale by treatment method and sex is presented in Table [12.8]. The F-ratio for the main effect of treatment did not reach significance, $F (1, 34) = .494$, $p > .05$. Therefore, Hypothesis 1 was not rejected for the criterion measure of self-esteem. Additionally, neither the main effect of sex nor the sex by treatment interaction was found to be significant.

Note in Table 12.8 that the F ratio for the covariate was significant at the $p < .05$ level, which means that the pretest scores were significantly associated with the posttest scores of the STOT. Note that after the adjustment procedure by the covariate, no main effects and interaction effect were significant.

Repeated-Measures ANOVA   Sometimes a researcher may want to examine the change on the dependent measure(s) over time. We call this a repeated-measure design because the dependent measure(s) need to be repeatedly measured with certain intervals (e.g., weekly). For example, suppose that researchers want to examine if the efficacy of a cognitive-behavioral therapy (CBT) group, is significantly different over time with a week interval on the depression scores as measured by the Beck Depression Inventory (BDI; Beck, Steer, & Garbin, 1988). In this case, the researcher can use repeated-measures ANOVA to examine the efficacy of the treatment with the primary independent variable as the time or sessions. The question of interest would be whether patients in the CBT group demonstrated a greater reduction in depressive symptoms over time. Note that we did not incorporate a control group in order to simplify the illustration, but usually researchers need a control group in order to interpret the treatment effect.

Note that a repeated-measures ANOVA with multiple measurements over time has advantages over a regular ANOVA in that (a) the former has more statistical power by separating the subject variable (i.e., individual difference in the performance on the dependent variable) from general random errors in a regular ANOVA and treating the subject variable as another independent variable, and (b) a repeated-measures ANOVA does not require the independence assumption (i.e., every score on the dependent variable should be independent of one another) as required by a general ANOVA. See Weinfurt (2000) and Keppel (1991) for more details.

In short, the repeated-measures analysis is used when a researcher is interested in the effects of the independent variables when dependent variables are repeatedly assessed from the same sample on the same measure. Note that in the example, the BDI scores are obtained from the same patients several times. Repeated measures could be applied to a variety of statistical analyses, such as an ANOVA and a MANOVA on the basis of the numbers of the dependent variables measured over time.

Writing the Results Using Repeated Measures   Once a researcher has a computed repeated-measures analysis in hand, then it is recommended that he or she examine two numbers central to analysis, the F statistic and its associated p value. If the associated p value is less than the alpha level established in a study (e.g., .05), the results suggest that the effect of time or sessions over time on the dependent measure are statistically significant

For example, Kivlighan and Shaughnessy (2000) investigated the development of the working alliance of different client groups obtained by cluster analysis through four times of counseling sessions. The Working Alliance Inventory (WAI; Horvath & Greenberg, 1986) was utilized as the dependent variable. In their study, the repeated-measures ANOVAs were used because the WAI scores were measured from the same clients four times. Kivlighan and Shaughnessy (2000) reported their results of *repeated-measures ANOVAs* as shown in the following example:

> To further examine these observed patterns of working alliance development, a series of repeated-measures analyses of variance (ANOVAs) were conducted to test the significance of these temporal changes in WAI ratings. Each repeated-measures ANOVA was followed up with a trend analysis testing for linear, quadric, and cubic trends. . . . For Cluster 1, the repeated-measures ANOVA was significant, Wilks's Λ = .35, $F(3, 12)$ = 8.42, $p < .05$. The linear trend was significant only for Cluster 1, $F(1, 14)$ = 27.33, $p < .017$. The quadratic trend, $F(1, 14)$ = 0.93, $p > .017$, and cubic trend, $F(1, 14)$ = 0.32, $p > .017$ were both non-significant. (Reproduced from Kivlighan & Shaughnessy, 2000; pp. 365–366)

Note that the Wilk's Lambda (Λ) statistic was used as an F value in their results. Also, the authors used a trend analysis that is usually used to depict the trend of participants' changes in scores over time. Technically, in trend analysis, the researchers want to determine if the trend of the change is linear, quadratic, or even cubic. For the statistical calculations for trend analysis, see Myers and Well (1995).

Three Types of Multiple Regression

Regression is the statistical technique used when a researcher is interested in predicting a dependent variable (i.e., criterion or outcome variable) from one or more *independent variables* [i.e., predictor(s)]. We prefer to use the term *predictor(s)* over *independent variable(s)* because in regression we cannot manipulate or control the predictors; likewise, we prefer the term *criterion* to the term *dependent variable,* because it is not dependent upon the manipulation of the independent variable. However, note that some researchers use these terms interchangeably. Also note that a researcher can have only one criterion variable in regression analysis and the predictor needs to be continuous with some exceptions (e.g., dummy coding). See Pedhazur (1997) for more details on this issue.

Suppose that researchers want to know how much variance on the outcome of counseling can be predicted by several factors such as counselors' perceived self-competence in their interventions, the client's motivation, and the degree of working alliance between counselor and client. In this example, the outcome of counseling is the criterion variable and the three predictor variables are the counselor's perceived competence, client's motivation, and the working alliance. Given the multiple predictors, this a *multiple regression*. If a researcher examines the effects of one predictor on one criterion, it is called a *simple linear regression*. In applied psychological research, multiple regressions are more often used because there is frequently more than one predictor for a criterion variable of interest. There are three types of multiple regression: simultaneous regression, stepwise regression, and hierarchical regressions. In this section, we briefly discuss how to report the results of these three types of multiple regression.

Note that a common mistake that students make in entering the predictors in the regression equation is entering the total scores of an instrument with its subscales. This is problematic, because the total score and the subscale scores are often highly correlated, which may cause *multicollinearity* problems—the potential adverse effects of correlated independent variables on the estimation of regression statistics (Pedhazur, 1997, p. 294).

Simultaneous Regression   Simultaneous regression is used when researchers are interested in examining the unique effects of each predictor on a criterion *at the same time*. The main purposes of simultaneous regression are to find how much unique variance each predictor contributes to the criterion and to determine whether each prediction by the predictors is significant. The advantage of simultaneous regression is that this method identifies the amount of unique variable contributed by each predictor after the shared variance of the predictors is removed.

Writing the Results Using Simultaneous Regression   Once researchers have a computed simultaneous regression analysis in hand, then we recommend that they examine three numbers central to simultaneous regression analysis, the R^2, the F statistic, and its associated p value. If the associated p value for the overall F is less than the alpha level established in a study (e.g., .05), the results suggest that the overall regression model is statistically significant. The results of simultaneous regression analysis could be reported in the following format: "It was found that the model was significant, adjusted R^2 = a, $F(df_1, df_2)$ = b, $p < c$. [Predictor 1] and [predictor 2] were found to be significant unique predictors in [the dependent variable]." Note that it is necessary to specify the value of the two degrees of freedom (df_1 and df_2) along with adjusted R^2 (a), F statistic (b), and p value (c). The R^2 refers to the percentage of the variance in the criterion explained by the predictors in total, which would be equivalent to the estimate of the effect sizes (omega squared; ω^2). The adjusted R^2 (which is also sometimes called "shrunken R^2; see Cohen & Cohen, 1983) is preferred to R^2 as an unbiased (i.e., which is less influenced by sample size) measure of strength between criterion and predictors in regression. For more details, refer to Keppel (1991, p. 66).

Following is an example of simultaneous regression from an article by Komiya, Good, and Sherrod (2000). They were interested in examining simultaneously the effects of several predictors such as emotional openness, gender, and other attitude variables (e.g., individual's perception of stigmatizing in receiving psychological help, levels of psychological and behavioral distress) on the attitudes toward seeking psychological help (i.e., the criterion). Specifically, the researchers asked university students to complete a set of inventories, which measured emotional openness (Test of Emotional Styles [TES], Allen & Hamsher, 1974), individual's perception of stigmatizing in receiving psychological help (Stigma Scale for Receiving Psychological Help [SSRPH], Komiya et al., 2000), the degree of psychological and behavioral distress (Hopkins Symptom Checklist—21-Item Version [HSC-21]; Derogatis, Lipman, Rickels, Uhlenhuth, & Covi, 1974), and attitudes toward seeking psychological help (Attitudes Toward Seeking Professional Psychological Help, Short Form [ATSPPH-S], Fischer & Turner, 1970). In this example, ATSPPH-S was utilized as the criterion variable; gender, TES, SSRPH, and HSC-21 were utilized as predictors. Note in the example that the authors described which variables were entered in the regression equation to predict the criterion variable and then reported such statistics as F and p value along with the percentage of variance in the criterion explained by the predictors as suggested earlier. Also note that gender was entered as a predictor by using a dummy coding although it is a categorical variable. *Dummy coding* is a method to convert a dichotomous (i.e., categorical variable with only two categories; in this case men and women) into a continuous variable by assigning 0 and 1 to each category (for more details, see Pedhazur, 1997). The example follows:

> The predictor variables (Gender, SSRPH, HSC-21, and TES) were entered into a simultaneous regression model predicting ATSPPH-S (help-seeking attitudes). The results, shown in Table [12.9], indicate that the model was significant, $F(4,$

	TABLE 12.9	SIMULTANEOUS REGRESSION ANALYSIS PREDICTING HELP-SEEKING ATTITUDES			

Variable	B	SE B	β	t
Gender	−2.70	0.66	−0.22	−4.10**
Stigma (SSRPH)	−0.60	0.10	−0.30	−5.83**
Emotional Openness (TES)	0.10	0.04	0.13	2.41*
Distress (HSC-21)	0.07	0.03	0.11	2.09*

Note. Gender = gender of participants (female = lower scores, male = higher scores); SSRPH = Stigma Scale for Receiving Psychological Help; TES = Test of Emotional Styles, Orientation subscale; HSC-21 = Hopkins Symptom Checklist—21-Item Version. *$p < .05$, **$p < .001$. Reproduced from Komiya, Good, & Sherrod, 2000, p. 141.

305) = 25.88, $p < .001$, and accounted for 25% of the variance in ATSPPH-S scores (adjusted $R^2 = .24$). Gender, SSRPH, TES, and HSC-21 were each found to be significant unique predictors of ATSPPH-S.

Note in Table 12.9 that the authors reported both the unstandardized beta (B) and its standard error estimates (SE B), and the standardized beta (β). Sometimes authors report either B and SE B, or β. Typically, researchers report the association between the predictor and criterion based on the β statistic. Note that the β statistics indicate the regression slope that provides readers with information about how many units in the criterion variable can increase or decrease (in case of the negative value on the β). In the table, for the stigma variable, the β statistic of $- .30$ indicates that every one unit of change in the stigma score brings a correcting $- .30$ unit change in help-seeking attitudes. Also note that the t statistic and associated p value indicates whether the β statistic is significantly different from 0. Only if the t statistic is significant should the researcher interpret the corresponding β statistic.

Stepwise Regression   Stepwise regression is one of the most popular types of multiple regression and is typically utilized to identify (a) how much total variance a set of predictors can account for in a criterion variable and (b) which predictors can explain more variance in the criterion. Thus, the advantage of a stepwise regression is that it can identify which predictors account for the most overall variance in the criterion, as well as identify how much of the total variance can be accounted for. A statistical program identifies and orders the predictor variables that account for the most variance, as well as the significance level for each predictor. The main disadvantage of stepwise regression is that the strongest predictor will take all of the variance it can, which will also include any shared variance that other predictors may have with the criterion; thus, the strongest predictor often may appear that it accounts for relatively more variance than it actually does relative to other predictions. Technically, stepwise regression is the combination of the forward selection and the backward selection. The predictors are entered into the regression equation one at a time if the predictor meets the desired alpha level; however, the predictor can be deleted later if it does not add a significant amount of the total variance to the regression equation. According to Tabachnick and Fidell (1996), stepwise regression is regarded as the path to the best prediction equation. Researchers often use stepwise multiple regressions particularly in cases where the researcher does not have a priori or theoretical hypotheses on the relationship between the criterion and the predictors of interest.

Writing the Results Using Stepwise Regression   Once researchers have a computed stepwise regression analysis at hand, then they should examine three numbers central to stepwise regression analysis, the adjusted R^2, the F statistic, and its associated p value. The writing format for the stepwise regression is almost identical to that of simultaneous multiple regression. If the associated p value is less than the alpha level established in a study (e.g., .05), the results suggest that the stepwise regression model is statistically significant. The results of stepwise regression analysis are often reported in the following format: "In the first step, [the first predictor] accounted for a significant amount of variance in the [dependent variable] (R^2 = a, F (df_1, df_2) = b, p < c). In the second step, [the second predictor] accounted for a significant amount of additional variance of [the dependent variable] after controlling the variance explained by [the first predictor] (R^2 = d, R^2 change = e, F (df_1, df_2) = f, p < g)."

Following is an example of a *stepwise regression* from Binen (1998). In the example, the author was interested in examining whether variables such as therapist level of training and the number of counseling sessions significantly predict client change scores (the criterion) on the Brief Symptom Inventory (BSI; Derogatis, 1993). Note that the author chose a stepwise regression given that she wanted to identify the relative associations between multiple predictors and the criterion without specific theoretical suggestions. Also note that the components of Table 12.10 are the same as Table 12.9 in the section of simultaneous regression.

> Hypothesis 4 posited that resources invested in treatment (i.e., therapist level of training and number of sessions) will have a significant effect on the BSI change scores. A stepwise multiple regression was run with the residual change score as the criterion variable, number of sessions as the predictor variable in step 1, and counselor level as the predictor variable in step 2 (Table [12.10]). Number of sessions ranged from 3 to 12 with a mean of 7.2 (*SD* = 2.19), a median of 7, and a mode of 8. Counselor level included 8 staff members, 6 interns, 9 doctoral level practicum students, and 8 master's level doctoral students. Step 1 of the regression indicated that number of sessions was not a significant predictor of change scores (t = –1.13, p = .27). The addition of counselor level in step 2 also did not add to the prediction of change score. Therefore, Hypothesis 4 was not supported.

Hierarchical Regression Hierarchical regression analysis, unlike simultaneous regression or stepwise regression, is used when researchers are interested in the effects of the specific *order* of the predictors as determined by a

TABLE 12.10	REGRESSION OF RESOURCES INVESTED IN TREATMENT ON RESIDUALIZED CHANGE SCORES OF THE GSI			
Variables	**B**	*SE* B	β	*t*
Number of Sessions	–.09	–.08	–.21	–1.12
COUNS LVL	–.16	.21	–.14	–.79

Note. GSI = Global Severity Index of the Brief Symptom Inventory. COUNS LVL = Counselor Level (1 = Staff, 2 = Intern, 3 = Doctoral Level Practicum, 4 = Master's Level Practicum). Modified from Binen, 1998, pp. 151.
Source: From "Treatment Outcome at a University Counseling Center," by L. M. Binen, 1998, Unpublished doctoral dissertation at the University of Missouri–Columbia, p. 151. Adapted with permission.

priori theory or hypotheses. For example, Chang and Rand (2000) were interested in examining the predictive utility of the dimensions of perfectionism (i.e., self-oriented perfectionism; other-oriented perfectionism; socially prescribed perfectionism) and stress on two criterion: psychological symptoms and hopelessness (note there are two criterion variables here, so the authors conducted two sets of hierarchical regression—one for each criterion). The authors asked college students to complete a set of inventories that included the Multidimensional Perfectionism Scale (MPS; Hewitt & Flett, 1991), the Perceived Stress Scale (PSS; Cohen, Kamarck, & Mermelstein, 1983), the Symptom Check List-90-Revised (SCL-90-R; Derogatis, 1983), and the Beck Hopelessness Scale (HS; Beck, Weissman, Lester, & Trexler, 1974). In this example, the three dimensions of the MPS (i.e., self-oriented perfectionism, other-oriented perfectionism, socially prescribed perfectionism) and PSS were utilized as the predictors, whereas the SCL-90-R and HS were each utilized as criterion variables. In the hierarchical regression equation, the authors set the specific order of predictors: perfectionism as the first step, perceived stress as the second step, and the interaction term (perfectionism × perceived stress) as the final step. Note that the authors put the perfectionism variable in the first step and the stress variable in the second step in the equation because they wanted to examine how much remaining variance on the criterion can be accounted by the stress variable over and beyond the perfectionism variable based on the personality vulnerability—stress model (e.g., Abramson, Metalsky, & Alloy, 1989).

Writing the Results Using Hierarchical Regression   Once a researcher has a computed hierarchical multiple regression analysis, then the researcher should examine four numbers central to hierarchical regression analysis, the values of R^2 and additional R^2 change, the F statistic, and its associated p value. Again, if the associated p value is less than the alpha level established in a study (e.g., .05), the results indicate that the hierarchical regression model is statistically significant. In addition, we recommend using a new statistic, R^2 change. This is an important statistic because this tells a researcher how much additional variance on the criterion is explained by the predictor in the second step in addition to the first predictor in the regression equation.

The results of a hierarchical regression analysis are often reported in the following format: "In the first step, [the first predictor] accounted for a significant variance in the variance of [the dependent variable] ($R^2 = a_1$, F (df_1, df_2) = b, $p < c_1$). In the second step, [the second predictor] accounted for a significant amount of additional variance in [the dependent variable] after controlling the variance explained by [the first predictor] ($R^2 = a_2$, R^2 change = d, F (df_3, df_4) = f, $p < c_2$)." Note that the values of R^2 (a_1 and a_2) along with the F statistic (b), the associated p values (c_1 and c_2) and degrees of freedom (df_1, df_2, df_3, and df_4), and finally R^2 change (d) should be reported in the sequence.

Following is an example of *hierarchical multiple regression* modified from Chang and Rand (2000). Note that for illustration purposes, we reconstructed the following paragraph as well as the subsequent Table 12.11. Note in the example that the R^2 for the socially prescribed perfectionism (the MPS-Social) in the first step was .21 [i.e., 21% of the variance on the psychological symptom (the criterion variable) was explained by perfectionism]. In addition, the R^2 for the stress (PSS) in the second equation was .41 and the R^2 change statistic was .20. This means that 20% of additional variance on the psychological symptoms can be explained by the second predictor, the PSS, over and beyond the variance by the first predictor, perfectionism. Note that the researcher can also calculate the amount of the R^2 change in the second equation (i.e., the percentage of the variance in the criterion explained by the PSS) easily by subtracting the R^2 at the first step from the R^2 at the second equation (.41 − .21 = .20). In Table 12.11, we summarized the results of hierarchical multiple regression. Again, note that we simplified the table from that of the authors just for the illustrative purposes. For those who are interested in the relationship among all of the variables in this study, we recommend the original reference (Chang & Rand, 2000, p. 132).

> In the first step, the socially prescribed perfectionism accounted for a significant amount of variance in psychological symptoms (R^2 = .21, F (1, 213) = 6.87, p < .07). In the second step, the perceived stress was found to explain a significant additional variance in the variance of psychological symptoms after controlling the variance accounted for by socially prescribed perfectionism (R^2 = .41, R^2 change = .20, F (1, 213) = 64.98, p < .001). In the final step, the interaction term (socially prescribed perfectionism × perceived stress) accounted for a significant additional amount of variance in the variance of psychological symptoms after controlling the variance explained by both socially prescribed perfectionism and perceived stress (R^2 = .43, R^2 change = .02, F (1, 213) = 7.04, p < .01).

Note that in the table the authors provided new symbols for reporting the results of hierarchical multiple regression, such as R and R^2 (i.e., how much the variance on the criterion variable can be explained by the predictor in a specific

TABLE 12.11 HIERARCHICAL REGRESSION ANALYSES SHOWING AMOUNT OF UNIQUE VARIANCE IN SUBSEQUENT ADJUSTMENT ACCOUNTED FOR BY PERFECTIONISM AND STRESS

	R	R^2	ΔR^2	$F(1, 213)$
	Psychological symptoms			
Step 1: MPS-Social	.46	.21		6.87**
Step 2: PSS	.64	.41	.20	64.98***
Step 3: MPS-Social × PSS	.66	.43	.02	7.04**

Note. N = 215. MPS-Social = Multidimensional Perfectionism Scale—Socially Prescribed Scale; PSS = Perceived Stress Scale. *p < .05. **p < .01. ***p < .001. Reproduced from Chang & Rand, 2000, p. 133.
Source: From "Perfectionism as a Predictor of Subsequent Adjustment: Evidence for a Specific Diathesis-stress Mechanism among College Students," by E. C. Chang and K. L. Rand, 2000, *Journal of Counseling Psychology, 47*, p. 133. Copyright 2000 by the American Psychological Association, Inc. Reprinted with permission.

step), and ΔR^2 [i.e., the R^2 change: How much additional or remaining variance in the criterion can be accounted for by the specific step over and above (or controlling for) the previous step(s)?] Note that the R^2 was reported in both the simultaneous and stepwise regressions in the previous sections but not in the tables. In a hierarchical multiple regression table, however, researchers typically report the ΔR^2 with the associated F statistic and p value. In the second step of the preceding example, note that the PSS variable accounted for 20% of the remaining variance on the psychological symptoms (i.e., the criterion) after controlling for the variance explained by the MPS-social.

Testing Moderating Effect in a Hierarchical Multiple Regression As a specific variation of the hierarchical multiple regressions, we next discuss how to write the results of a moderator with a regression equation. According to Baron and Kenny (1986), a *moderator* is defined as a variable that affects the direction and/or strength of the relationship between a predictor (or independent variable) and a criterion (or a dependent variable). Since a moderator interacts with the predictor to predict the criterion, it could be understood as similar to a second independent variable that interacts with the main independent variable. As suggested by the label *moderator,* in a regression a moderator *moderates* (or changes) the relationship between the predictor and the criterion. For example, individuals' social support can be depicted to buffer or moderate the relationship between negative life events and persons' psychological maladjustment (e.g., anxiety). Specifically, when social support is low, there may be a significant positive association between negative life events and anxiety; however, when social support is high, the relationship between the two variables may be significantly lower (or attenuated). In other words, even though a person experiences negative life events, it does not necessarily result in higher levels of anxiety if there is a high level of social support. [Note: sometimes moderators are confused with mediators; for more details on these concepts, interested readers could consult Baron and Kenny (1986), Holmbeck (1997), and Heppner et al. (1999)].

The steps to test the moderating effect in a regression are the same as the steps in a general hierarchical multiple regression. Specifically, in the first step, a predictor and a moderator are entered at the same time. In the second step, the interaction term between the predictor and the moderator (the predictor × the moderator) is entered to identify how much remaining variance in the criterion can be explained (or accounted for) by the interaction term (i.e., the size of moderating effect). Similar to the general hierarchical regression, the R^2 change (ΔR^2) is interpreted for this purpose.

Writing the Results of Testing a Moderator in a Hierarchical Multiple Regression Once a researcher has a computed moderating effect analysis in hand, we recommend reviewing the F of change value and associated p value for the interaction term to determine whether the moderating effect is significant. If the p value is less than the alpha level of the study (e.g., .05), the results indicate that the moderating effect is statistically significant. If the p value is bigger than .05, the researcher should stop and simply conclude that there is no significant moderating effect of [the moderator variable] in the relationship between [the predictor variable] and [the criterion variable]. Second, if a researcher obtains a significant moderating effect, we recommend that the researcher identify how much variance is accounted for by the moderator. In essence, the R^2 change indicates how much remaining variance in the criterion can be explained by the interaction effect between the predictor and the moderator, over and above the variance accounted for by the predictor and the moderator entered simultaneously in the first step. Third, we recommend that the researcher identify the nature of the moderating effect by plotting two regression lines using two values to represent the levels of moderator [i.e., high $(M + 1SD)$ versus low $(M - 1SD)$] (see Figure 12.3 for an example).

Following is an example from Lee et al. (2001) that depicts how to write the results of *testing a moderating effect.* In the study, the authors examined the moderating effect of the counselor-client working alliance (as measured by

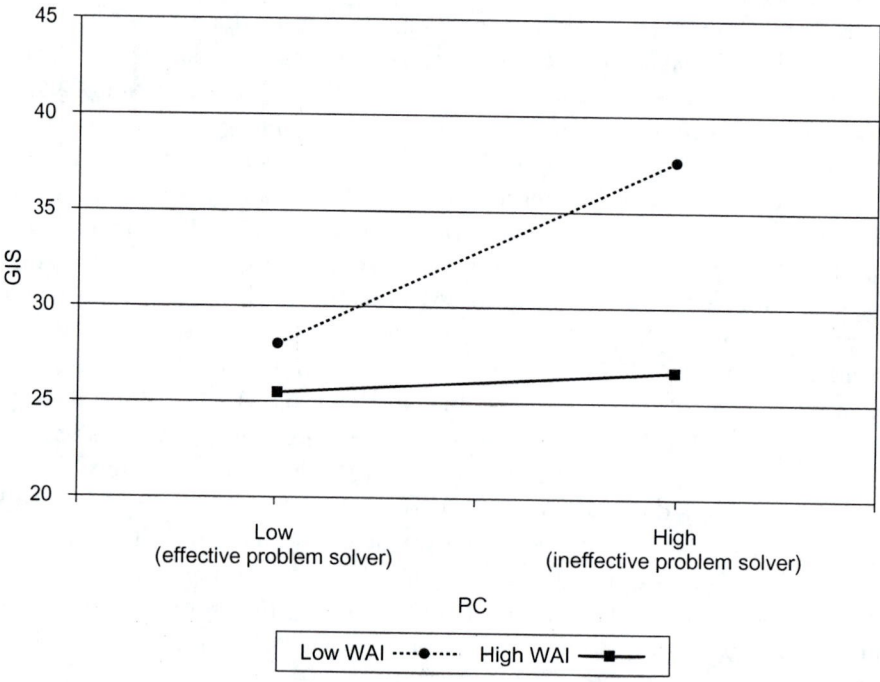

FIGURE 12.3

Interaction between personal control (PC) and the working alliance (WAI) predicting therapeutic outcomes (GIS). $N = 96$. Values for WAI and PC are plotted using low (one standard deviation below the mean) and high (one standard deviation above the mean) values of the WAI and PC. The slope for low and high WAI = 2.47, .31, respectively.

the Working Alliance Inventory: WAI, Horvath & Greenberg, 1986) between clients' problem-solving appraisal (the predictor as measured by the Problem-Solving Inventory: PSI, Heppner, 1988) and clients' counseling outcome (as measured by the Goal Instability Scale: GIS, Robbins & Patton, 1985). Note that the authors presented Table 12.12 to specify the steps in the hierarchical multiple regression as well as depict the interaction in Figure 12.3 to illustrate the nature of the moderating effect. Also note that the authors provide a brief statement to explain the nature of the moderating effect in the paragraph.

> Will clients' problem-solving appraisal interact with the working alliance in influencing therapeutic outcomes?
>
> Before examining the moderating effect in the regression equations, the predictor (i.e., the PSI and its three subscales), the moderator (i.e., the WAI), and their interaction terms (e.g., the PC × the WAI) were "centered" (i.e., scores were put into deviation score form) to eliminate multicollinearity problems (see discussion and more details by Holmbeck, 1997). Results depicted in Table [12.12] revealed that there was one significant moderating effect of the WAI with the PSI subscale, Personal Control (PC). This appeared in the relationship between the PC and the GIS, F_{change} (1, 92) = 5.52, $p < .05$, accounting for 4% of an additional variance in the GIS. Following recommendations by Holmbeck (1997) for the interpretation of the moderating effect, simple slopes and the regression lines for each level of the predictors (i.e., one standard deviation above or below the mean for high and low levels, respectively) were calculated. As depicted in Figure [12.3], subsequently higher levels of goal instability were reported by clients who perceived themselves as having less precounseling levels of Personal Control and experienced less working alliance with their counselors after the third session in counseling.

Multivariate Analysis of Variance (MANOVA)

A multivariate analysis of variance (MANOVA) is used when a researcher wants to compare the mean differences among two or more groups on *multiple dependent variables simultaneously.* Note that a MANOVA is different from an ANOVA in that it deals with multiple dependent variables. It is increasingly

TABLE 12.12	HIERARCHICAL MULTIPLE REGRESSION ANALYSES EXAMINING THE MODERATING EFFECT OF THE WAI BETWEEN THE PSI AND ITS SUBSCALES AND GIS

Criterion/Predictor Predictor Statistics

Step	R^2	Adjusted R^2	Change of R^2	F of Change
GIS				
Step 1. PC	.35	.33	.35	24.77***
WAI				
Step 2. PC × WAI	.39	.36	.04	5.52*

Note. PC = Personal Control; WAI = Working Alliance Inventory; GIS = Goal Instability Scale. *$p < .05$, ***$p < .001$.

common for researchers to use multiple dependent variables in order to examine the complexities of human behavior. In addition, MANOVA, as compared with a series of independent ANOVAs, has merit because it reduces the inflation of Type 1 error [i.e., the probability of rejecting the null hypothesis (H_0) when it is true] (for more details, see Tabachinick & Fidell, 1996). Similar to conducting ANOVAs, researchers can conduct both one-way and two-way MANOVAs. Specifically, in a one-way MANOVA, there is one independent variable but multiple dependent variables. In a two-way MANOVA, there are two independent variables and multiple dependent variables.

Writing the Results Using a MANOVA   Once a researcher has computed a MANOVA analysis, then we recommend that the researcher examine two statistics central to MANOVA, the F statistic and its associated p value. If the associated p value is less than the alpha level established in a study (e.g., .05), the results suggest that the mean differences between groups are statistically significant. Basically, the format of reporting MANOVA analyses (including one-way and two-way MANOVAs) is similar to that of the ANOVA analyses, respectively. But note that in MANOVA, the F statistic should be chosen among several indexes such as Wilks' Lambda, Pillai's Trace, Hotelling's Trace, and Roy's Largest Root. Wilks' Lambda (Λ) statistic is usually used for the F statistic in MANOVA.

Following is Vivona's (2000) summary of her results using a *MANOVA analysis:*

> The MANOVA of AS scores by attachment style and sex revealed effects for sex, $F(3, 100) = 6.23, p = 0$, but not attachment style, $F(6, 202) = 0.96$, *ns*, or interaction, $F(6, 202) = 0.59$, *ns*. As predicted, women received higher Sensitivity to Others scores than men, $F(1, 102) = 14.83, p = 0$. In addition, men received higher scores for Self-Awareness, $F(1, 102) = 5.00, p = .03$. (p. 325)

The author was interested in examining the effects of three attachment styles (i.e., avoidant, ambivalent, and secure) and sex as a variable on the three subscales of a person's perceived self-autonomy. A MANOVA analysis was conducted on the three subscales (the Self-Awareness scale, the Capacity to Manage New Situations scale, and the Sensitivity to Others scale) of the AS (Autonomy Scale; Bekker, 1993). Note that because there were two independent variables (i.e., attachment styles and sex) and three dependent variables (i.e., three subscales of the AS), a two-way MANOVA was performed. Thus, in the example, the author reported the results of the main effects of two independent variables as well as an interaction effect. Also note that because the overall F statistic for sex was significant, the author presented further explanation of effects for sex using a one-way ANOVA as a post hoc analysis. Note that the author added a brief statement about the contents and direction of the sex effect (e.g., women received higher scores than men) on the dependent variable. The notation of *ns* represents that there was no significance in the testing of F statistic across the different attachment styles.

Cluster Analysis

A cluster analysis (CA) is one of the popular multivariate classification techniques particularly in applied psychology where individual differences are one of the main foci of inquiry. CA is also typically thought of as a "typology," "classification analysis," or "numerical taxonomy" (Hair & Black, 2000), with the most common goal of classifying people into subgroups. For example, Larson et al. (1988) used CA with multiple measures (e.g., Problem-Solving Inventory: PSI, Heppner, 1988; Career Decision Scale: CDS, Osipow, Carney, Winer, Yanico, & Koschier, 1976; Vocational Preference Inventory: VPI, Holland, 1978) to identify different subtypes of individuals who are undecided about their careers. As a result, they found four different types of people: (a) planless avoiders in their career decision making (i.e., lack career-planning information and perceive themselves as relatively poor problem solvers), (b) informed indecisives (i.e., very well informed about career planning but still unable to make a decision perhaps because of a negative appraisal of themselves), (c) confident but uninformed (i.e., have a positive appraisal of their problem-solving abilities but lack information about the career-planning process), and (d) uninformed (i.e., lack some career-planning information).

Technically, CA is used when a researcher is interested in grouping members (e.g., people or objects) on the basis of their common characteristics. Each group with members that have similar characteristics is called a *cluster.* The members within a cluster are characterized by their homogeneity, whereas the members between clusters are considered as heterogeneous in their characteristics. In essence, it is desirable in CA to have the minimum within-cluster differences and the maximum between-cluster differences in members' characteristics.

CA is useful for providing a statistical tool for researchers who have a large number of respondents or objects in a data set that could be difficult to understand unless classified into meaningful subgroups. The other way CA is useful is when it is combined with other statistical techniques. For example, once clusters are identified, the researcher can utilize ANOVA to examine whether clusters are different from one another on the scores of some dependent variables. In the example of different types of people who are undecided about their careers, the researcher can conduct ANOVA to examine if the career decisiveness score (i.e., dependent measure) is different according to the membership of the cluster. On the contrary, it should be noted that the nature of CA is totally "exploratory" and it needs a researcher's judgment in choosing the best solutions in terms of the numbers of clusters that will be formed. A researcher needs to keep in mind that the addition or deletion of a new variable in the CA equation could impact the numbers of cluster as well as the membership of an individual observation across clusters. For more statistical procedure in CA, see Heppner et al. (1999), Hair and Black (2000), Wampold and White (1985), and Borgen and Weiss (1971).

Writing the Results Using Cluster Analysis   There are a variety of ways of writing results using CA; thus in this section we provide some examples of some basic writing strategies. Once students have computed the CA, a typical way of presenting the results is as follows: (a) the purpose of using CA (e.g., to identify patterns of people); (b) the specific statistical methods chosen for CA (e.g., Ward technique); (c) detailed description of multiple scales entered into the CA equation to identify the patterns of people; (d) description of the procedure to determine the number of clusters on the basis of theoretical relevance as well as statistical considerations (e.g., two-cluster solution as compared to three-cluster solution to maximize the differences between clusters, as well as minimize the differences within clusters, etc.); (e) providing a visual overview of difference among the clusters using a graph format (see Figure 12.4 from Jones's example, which follows); and (f) presenting results from additional analyses (e.g., MANOVA and subsequent post hoc tests) to interpret distinctive features of each cluster and naming each cluster (e.g., cluster 1 as compared to cluster 2 was characterized by significantly higher scores on [the A scale] and lower scores on [the B scale] based on the post hoc test [the name of specific post hoc test] with associated p value). We recommend students study Jones's example carefully to obtain a better understanding of how to write results using CA.

Jones (2000) was interested in classifying different subtypes of substance abuse clients in treatment programs. She used CA because one of her research questions was to identify patterns of personality styles and psychopathology syndromes. Note in the following example that she started with the description of the statistical procedure of CA and combined statistical strategies (i.e., MANOVAs and post hoc comparisons); this helps readers who may be interested in replicating the study. In addition, Jones provided a clear procedure and associated rationale in choosing the six-cluster solution. In order to graphically depict her results, she provided a figure of the six-cluster solution (see Figure 12.4), which is very helpful for readers to see the graphic representation of each cluster. In the next step, Jones conducted ANOVAs and associated post hoc analyses to examine whether demographics, as well as dependent measures (alcohol and drug dependence), are different across the six clusters, which enables readers to understand distinctive features of the six clusters. For example, Cluster 1 (criminal type/high substance use disorder), as compared with every other cluster was characterized by its higher scores on alcohol and drug dependence. Note that Jones used Table 12.13 to present effectively the demographic characteristics of the six-cluster solution, as well as the effects of the demographic variables on the clusters. Also note that we omit detailed information on Cluster 2 to Cluster 6 because of the space limitations for this chapter. However, understand that the study of writing the results for Cluster 2 through Cluster 6 should be identical to those Jones used for Cluster 1. Finally, only Figure 12.4 and Table 12.13 are presented here because of the restrictions of space.

CLUSTER ANALYSIS—PERSONALITY AND PSYCHOPATHOLOGY SUBTYPES

A cluster analysis was conducted to identify patterns of personality styles and psychopathology syndromes. The 14 personality subscales (antisocial, negativistic, depressive, avoidant, dependent, schizoid, narcissistic, masochistic, sadistic, histrionic, compulsive, borderline, paranoid, and schizotypal) and the 10 clinical subscales (anxiety disorder, dysthymic disorder, bipolar: manic disorder, major depression post-traumatic stress disorder, somatoform disorder, thought disorder, delusional disorder, alcohol dependence, and drug dependence) were used as grouping variables. The specific clustering technique used to generate the cluster solution was Squared-Euclidian distance and Ward's minimum variance clustering method (Ward, 1963).

A proximity matrix of the Squared-Euclidian distance between all pairs of participants was calculated and within-group variance was heuristically examined by analyzing the dendogram and the values of the fusion coefficients to discover a significant "jump" in the value of the coefficient, which implied that two relatively dissimilar clusters had merged. Upon examination of the dendogram and fusion coefficients, a range of four to nine clusters were examined and each solution was carefully analyzed as to conceptual and statistical distinction and interpretive value. Once each cluster solution was derived, the specific selection process included: (a) computing MANOVAs within each solution; (b) computing post hoc one-way comparisons using Tamhane post-hoc comparisons between all psychometric variables within each subgroup within each solution; (c) comparing all derived solutions for their cluster memberships and dissimilarity coefficients; and (d) examining each subgroup for theoretical congruity, conceptual distinction, and practical significance.

After carefully reviewing each cluster, the six-cluster solution was chosen for subsequent cross-validation (see Figure [12.4] for a line graph of the six-cluster solution). The seven-, eight-, and nine-cluster solutions were omitted because they lacked interpretative significance relative to the six-cluster solution. Specifically, cluster memberships were broken down into smaller group memberships that were virtually identical to those in the six-cluster solution. For the seven-cluster solution, the third-cluster membership of the six-cluster solution ($N = 71$) was broken into two distinct clusters ($N = 27$ and $N = 44$) with no significant differences between the two clusters. In the same pattern, the eight-cluster solution kept the split of the third cluster (as in the seven-cluster solution) and in addition, split the fourth cluster ($N = 61$) of the six-cluster solution in half ($N = 40$ and $N = 21$) with no significant differences between the two clusters. Finally, the nine-cluster solution was the same as the eight-cluster solution but further split the cluster of $N = 44$ into two more clusters ($N = 18$ and $N = 26$), again, with no significant statistical or interpretive value. The four- and five-cluster solutions were omitted because in both solutions, clusters were considered theoretically distinct. In addition, these two clusters remained stable within the six-, seven-, eight-, and nine-cluster solutions, which provided further evidence of their stability as distinct clusters.

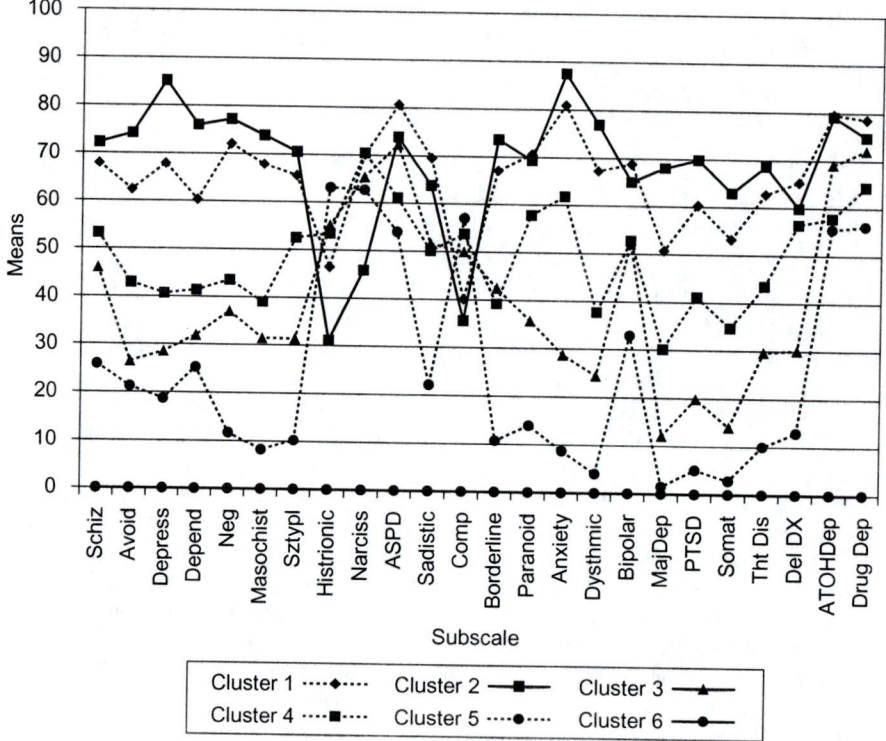

FIGURE **12.4**

Mean scores for personality and pathology subtypes. The scores for Cluster 6 were all 0 because this cluster contains the participants who were considered invalid by their random responses.

Personality and Psychopathology Syndrome—Six-Cluster Solution

The demographic characteristics of the six-cluster solution are presented in Table [12.13]. The effects of the demographic variables can be found in Tables 2 and 3 [note that we omitted these tables because of space restrictions]. Hypothesis 2 predicted there would be no significant differences among clusters on all demographic variables. Univariate analyses of variance conducted on the interval data found significant effects for age, F (5, 370) = 6.33, $p < .001$; highest grade completed, F (5, 356) = 2.68, $p < .01$; and number of times in treatment as a juvenile, F (5, 201) = 3.45, $p < .01$. Scheffé's post hoc comparisons revealed that for age, Clusters 2, 3, 4, and 5 were significantly older than Cluster 6 at the $p < .01$ level for Clusters 2, 3, and 5 and at the $p < .05$ level for Cluster 4. Regarding highest grade completed, post hoc comparisons revealed no significant between-groups effect. For number of times in treatment as a juvenile, follow-up comparisons found that Cluster 6 had been in treatment as a juvenile significantly more than Cluster 3 at $p < .05$ level. Chi-square analyses were conducted on the nominal and ordinal data and significant overall effects were found for level of education, χ^2 (10) = 31.42, $p < .001$ and for type of occupation, χ^2 (25) = 54.35, $p < .001$.

TABLE
12.13

DEMOGRAPHIC DATA—PERSONALITY AND PATHOLOGY SIX-CLUSTER SOLUTION

	Cluster 1	Cluster 2	Cluster 3	Cluster 4	Cluster 5	Cluster 6
Age [M, (SD)]	28.90 (9.18)	31.45 (8.84)	32.66 (8.70)	29.98 (8.32)	34.00 (7.07)	23.08 (5.50)
Last grade completed in school [M, (SD)]	10.48 (1.80)	10.51 (1.37)	10.86 (1.45)	10.93 (1.23)	11.00 (1.59)	9.83 (1.47)
# Arrests—Adult [M, (SD)]	7.15 (9.08)	7.00 (6.29)	6.58 (6.75)	6.60 (11.59)	7.33 (5.77)	6.53 (7.46)
# Arrests—Juvenile [M, (SD)]	2.61 (5.30)	1.59 (2.24)	2.24 (7.17)	3.14 (4.94)	.88 (1.63)	3.27 (3.24)
# times in SU treatment—Adult [M, (SD)]	2.23 (3.79)	2.80 (4.46)	1.84 (1.59)	1.95 (1.84)	1.67 (1.20)	1.53 (1.26)
# times in SU treatment—Juvenile [M, (SD)]	.27 (.58)	.24 (.74)	2.38 (.15)	.59 (1.32)	.23 (.44)	1.13 (2.56)
Treatment facility (%)						
Western Regional	69.2	72.5	70.4	82.0	84.0	83.3
Cremer Therapeutic Treatment Center	24.0	19.8	23.9	18.0	16.0	16.7
Mineral Area Treatment Center	5.8	7.7	5.6	0.0	0.0	0.0
Boonville Treatment Center	1.0	0.0	0.0	0.0	0.0	0.0
Marital status (%)						
Married	9.7	21.1	18.3	14.8	20.0	12.5
Never married	52.4	46.6	50.7	50.8	32.0	62.5
Divorced/ Widowed	19.4	20.0	14.0	19.7	36.0	4.8
Separated	2.9	8.9	2.8	4.9	8.0	4.2
Engaged	15.5	3.3	5.6	9.8	4.0	20.8
Race (%)						
Black	40.4	25.3	18.3	30.0	12.0	54.2
White	55.8	65.9	71.8	63.3	84.0	41.7
Other	3.9	8.8	5.8	6.7	4.0	0.0
Highest degree (%)						
GED	20.0	20.7	35.3	32.8	16.7	18.2
High-school diploma	31.0	24.1	35.3	37.9	58.3	13.6
Neither	49.0	55.2	29.4	29.3	25.0	68.2

(continued)

TABLE
12.13

DEMOGRAPHIC DATA—PERSONALITY AND PATHOLOGY SIX-CLUSTER SOLUTION (*CONTINUED*)

	Cluster 1	Cluster 2	Cluster 3	Cluster 4	Cluster 5	Cluster 6
Job prior to incarceration (%)						
Welfare/No regular	5.0	3.4	2.8	1.7	8.0	4.5
Working poor	27.0	36.0	15.5	20.3	24.0	36.4
Middle, blue-collar	51.0	42.7	67.6	44.1	56.0	36.4
Middle, white-collar	8.0	12.4	11.3	13.6	12.0	9.1
Upper, professional	4.0	1.1	0.0	18.6	0.0	4.5
Substantial income—inheritance/nonjob	5.0	4.5	2.8	1.7	0.0	9.1
County where adjudicated (%)						
Jackson	31.1	26.4	34.3	32.8	32.0	45.8
St. Louis City	20.4	13.2	2.8	8.2	12.0	8.4
Other	54.4	60.3	62.9	59.0	56.0	45.8
# days incarcerated before treatment (%)						
0 days	1.0	1.1	1.4	6.7	4.0	4.2
1 day–1 month	20.2	26.4	18.3	26.7	24.0	45.9
1 month–6 months	50.9	53.9	59.2	38.4	40.0	33.3
6 months–1 year	9.6	4.4	7.0	8.3	16.0	4.2
More than 1 year	18.3	14.3	14.1	20.0	16.0	12.5

Note. Number of subjects varies as participants did not respond to all demographic information questions. Modified from Jones, 2000, pp. 138–141.

Source: From "Comorbidity, Typologies and Treatment Outcome in a Correctional Substance Abuse Treatment Population," by N. T. Jones, 2000, Unpublished doctoral dissertation at the University of Missouri–Columbia, pp. 143–146. Adapted with permission.

The multivariate analyses of variance conducted on the six-cluster solution found that the overall effect was significant, λ (24, 347) = 1373.46, $p < .001$. Tamhane post hoc comparisons were conducted to analyze statistical differences across clusters. Mean differences scores from these follow-up analyses are presented in Table 4 [note we that omitted the table because of space restrictions].

Cluster 1: Criminal Type/High SUD (CT/High SUD; N = 104)
This subtype was characterized by the overall elevation of scores across subgroups. This cluster was significantly higher than Clusters 3, 4, 5, and 6 on all subscales (except for histrionic, narcissistic, and compulsive subscales). Average scores for persons in this subtype were over the BR of 75 for the following subscales: antisocial personality disorder, anxiety disorder, alcohol dependence, and drug dependence. This subtype was characterized by its scores on the antisocial PD ($M = 80.70$, $SD = 10.62$) and sadistic (aggressive) PD ($M = 69.63$, $SD = 11.62$) subscales, which were significantly higher in this cluster (including Cluster 2) than all other clusters at the $p < .01$ level.

The alcohol ($M = 79.67$; $SD = 13.18$) and drug dependence ($M = 78.63$, $SD = 12.82$) subscales were significantly higher than every other cluster ($p < .01$) except Cluster 2, in which the two mean scores were not significantly different from each other. (Modified from Jones, 2000, pp. 67–69)

Factor Analysis

Factor analysis is a statistical technique to examine the underlying relationships (i.e., latent structure) among variables of interest by discovering coherent subsets that are assumed relatively independent of one another. In research, factor analysis is usually utilized in constructing a scale or inventory that attempts to measure an abstract construct (e.g., attitudes toward sexual violence). For example, a researcher may be interested in developing a new scale to measure an individual's intelligence. Because intelligence is an abstract construct that cannot be observed directly, the researcher devises a variety of tests (e.g., comprehension, vocabulary, picture completion, object assembly, etc.) in which an individual's score can be obtained directly. Here, factor analysis can be utilized to discover an underlying structure of intelligence by obtaining a correlation matrix among the test scores. Suppose that comprehension scores are highly correlated with vocabulary (e.g., $r = .80$) but not with the rest of test scores; likewise, picture completion scores are highly correlated with object assembly but not with comprehension or vocabulary scores. These results indicate that comprehension and vocabulary scores are associated with each other whereas picture comprehension and object assembly scores are also associated with each other very well. Thus, the researcher can assume that intelligence may consist of two subsets; one is verbal ability to encompass comprehension and vocabulary, and the other is performance ability that includes picture completion and object assembly. Note that verbal and performance abilities are not observed directly from individual scores but assumed by the correlation structure among variables obtained from factor analysis.

Factor analysis usually consists of two variations, exploratory factor analysis (EFA) and confirmatory factor analysis (CFA). In EFA, a researcher is interested in summarizing data by grouping coherent (i.e., intercorrelated) subsets or subscales as was shown in the example of intelligence. Note that in EFA, the researcher does not know a priori how many subscales or factors can be extracted before conducting the factor analysis, and therefore the nature of the subscales is unknown, and therefore the analysis is considered totally "exploratory." Thus, researchers need to keep in mind that the addition or deletion of a new item could impact the number of factors.

On the contrary, the CFA is a more sophisticated technique that tests if the number of the factors (i.e., subsets) and their latent relations are valid as suggested by the EFA or a priori theory. In the example of intelligence, a researcher can conduct the CFA on the basis of knowing that intelligence consisted of two factors (verbal and performance abilities) and test if these two factors represent well the latent structure of intelligence. Note that the CFA can be also considered a part of structural equation modeling (SEM) because of its nature of testing the latent structural of a psychological construct.

Many technical statistical procedures are related to factor analysis that are beyond the scope of this chapter. For statistical procedures related to factor analysis, see MacCallum, Widaman, Zhang, and Hong (1999) as well as Fabrigar, Wegener, MacCallum, and Strahan (1999).

Exploratory Factor Analysis

Writing the Results Using an Exploratory Factor Analysis   Assuming that a researcher has the computer output of an EFA, we recommend describing the following components. Briefly, the results of an EFA typically contain the following components: (a) factorability indexes (e.g., the KMO and/or Batlett's test of sphericity), (b) initial factor extraction method (e.g., principle component analysis or principle axis factoring), (c) procedure and results extracting the number of factors (e.g., eigenvalues, results of the scree plot, information on the total variance explained by the factors), (d) rotation method [e.g., varimax (a type of oblique rotation) or promax (a type of orthogonal rotation)] and its rationale. In addition, a researcher typically needs to provide a summary table that includes information such as the name of each factor, the list of items for each factor, and the factor loading for each item. In addition, in the text it is necessary for the author to explain why the factor name was selected, then define the factor name and include the number of items for the factor, as well as sample items that loaded highest on this factor. Estimates of alpha coefficients indicating the amount of internal consistency of the items within each factor are also typically reported. Finally, information such as the inter-correlations among the factors, estimates of skewness and kurtosis, as well as communality estimates (i.e., shared variance among factors) are usually discussed. Refer to Tabachnick and Fidell (1996) for more details, as well as the theoretical and practical relevance. Note this process requires a number of judgment calls by the researcher.

We include two examples of exploratory factor analysis (EFA), one from Inman, Ladany, Constantine, and Morano (2001) and one from Heppner, Heppner, et al. (2002). We recommend that you review the two examples with care, particularly focusing on different ways of presenting EFA results.

In the first example, Inman et al. (2001) were interested in the development of an inventory to measure the cultural values conflict scales for South Asian women. They conducted an EFA because they wanted to discover the existence of any subscales in their cultural conflict scale. Note that they included components that were discussed earlier. For example, they provided a Kaiser-Guttman criterion along with the number of eigenvalues greater than 1.00, which is equivalent to the KMO statistic suggested earlier. Also they mentioned that they reviewed a scree plot in addition to the eigenvalue criterion. Moreover, they identified the criteria for retaining items in terms of factor loadings (i.e., the correlation coefficients that are associated with each factor), which helps readers to understand clearly the procedure that the authors followed in terms of deleting and retaining items.

EXAMPLE 1: THE EXPLORATORY FACTOR ANALYSIS

A common factor analysis with an orthogonal varimax rotation and a Kaiser-Guttman criterion of eigenvalue greater than 1.00 was used for the 28-item scale (Floyd & Widaman, 1995). Two-, three-, four-, and five-factor solutions were obtained. Although all the factor solutions except the five-factor solution met the eigenvalue criteria, the two-factor solution had the highest eigenvalues (Factor 1 = 6.00, Factor 2 = 3.87). The general rule of eigenvalue greater than 1.00 may at times misjudge the most suitable number of factors (Gorsuch, 1983). Thus, the second criterion looked at was the scree test. The scree test suggested two, three, and four factors; the majority of the variance was accounted for by the first two factors (i.e., 21.4, 13.8, 3.7, 3.6).

Because the purpose of the exploratory factor analysis was to identify the most plausible model with meaningful factors underlying the CVCS (the Cultural Values Conflict Scale; Inman et al., 2001), three criteria were used in retaining a preliminary factor structure: (a) retaining factor loadings that exceeded .40 (Floyd & Widaman, 1995); (b) retaining factors that had at least three items per factor (Comrey, 1988); and (c) items loading significantly (i.e., .40 and above) on more than one component after the rotation was eliminated. The intent was to maintain theoretical as well as conceptual meaningfulness. The two-factor solution provided the cleanest factor structure. Only four items loaded on more than one factor; these items were deleted. The two-factor solution not only was statistically sound but also maintained the theoretical integrity of the model. Thus, in examining the interpretability and conceptual resilience of the loadings (Gorsuch, 1983), the two-factor model made the most sense and hence was retained. Neither the four-factor nor the three-factor solutions provided a clear conceptual difference between factors. Furthermore, there was a significant overlap between factors; a majority of the items loaded on more than one component. This would have resulted in deleting even more items from the scale, thus compromising the theory as well as conceptual resilience.

The new model reduced the 28-item set to a 24-item set with two factors. Table [12.14] presents the two factors with their respective items, factor loadings, communality estimates (h^2), means, and standard deviations. Factor 1 consisted of 11 items, including all the previously hypothesized items from the Dating/Premarital Relations subscale, three items from the Marriage subscale, and one item from the Family Relations subscale. Thus, Factor 1 was renamed "Intimate Relations" because it deals with intimate/sexual relations. Factor 1 had an eigenvalue of 6.00, accounting for 21% of the total variance. Factor 2 consisted of 13 items, including 6 from the Sex Role Expectation subscale, four from the Family Relations subscale, and three from the Marriage subscale. Factor 2 was renamed "Sex Role Expectations" because it deals with themes related to familial and societal expectations of the South Asian female gender role. Factor 2 had an eigenvalue of 3.87, accounting for 14% of the total variance. The interscale correlation coefficient between the two-factor scales was .11.

Internal Consistency

The corrected item correlations were all positive and ranged from .11 to .56. The coefficient alphas for the entire normative sample of 319 women were .84 for the total scale score, .87 for the Intimate Relations subscale, and .85 for the Sex Role Expectations subscale.

Convergent Validity

To establish convergent validity of the CVCS and to test the hypothesis that CVCS scores were related to the CADC scores, a multivariate multiple regression analysis was performed. For this analysis, the predictor variables were the two subscales, IR [Intimate Relations] and SRE [Sex Role Expectations] of the CVCS and the criterion variables were the two subscales, AD [Acculturative Distress] and IC [Intercultural Competence] on the CADC [Cultural Adjustment Difficulties Checklist: Sodowsky & Lai, 1997]. The overall proportion of the variance in ratings of AD and IC accounted for by the combination of the CVCS subscales was significant, Pillai's trace = .31, $F(2, 105) = 9.98$, $p < .01$, $\eta^2 = .15$, in which η^2 is the multivariate effect size (Hasse & Ellis, 1987). Thus the CVCS scales in combination were related to cultural adjustment difficulties. . . . (Inman et al., 2001, p. 23)

Note in the preceding paragraphs that the authors reported an estimate of internal consistency of each factor and the total scale, which provides readers with the information concerning the homogeneity of the total scale and each subscale. Also note that they reported information on convergent validity with the Cultural Adjustment Difficulties Checklist (CADC: Sodowsky & Lai, 1997). The convergent validity estimates can reveal that a newly developed inventory is highly correlated with another inventory to measure a similar construct. Note that the high correlation between a new scale and another established scale to measure a similar construct enables readers to ascertain that the new scale has a good psychometric property. In relation to the ways to evaluate psychometric properties of a newly developed inventory, note that several types of validity estimates such as convergent validity, discriminant validity, and criterion-related validity are available (see Cohen & Swerdlik, 1999, for

TABLE 12.14   ITEMS, COMPONENT LOADING, COMMUNALITY ESTIMATES, MEANS, AND STANDARD DEVIATIONS FOR THE TWO-FACTOR CULTURAL VALUES CONFLICT SCALE

Item	Factor Loading	h^2	M	SD
Factor 1: Intimate Relations (11 items)				
I believe dating is acceptable only in a mutually exclusive relationship leading to marriage. (DPR)	.53	.40	2.35	1.24
I would experience anxiety if I decided to marry someone from another racial/cultural/ethnic group. (MAR)	.67	.61	3.24	1.30
I feel guilty when my personal actions and decisions go against my family's expectations. (FR)	.40	.33	3.76	.99
I would feel guilty if I were dating someone from another cultural/ethnic group. (DPR)	.79	.62	2.48	1.25
Despite cultural expectations, I would not experience anxiety if I engaged in premarital sex with someone I was in love with. (DPR)	.68	.57	2.95	1.45
I would not experience discomfort if I were to engage in premarital sexual relations with someone I was physically attracted to. (DPR)	.70	.57	3.32	1.36
I would experience guilt engaging in premarital sexual relations due to the social stigma attached to it within my culture. (DPR)	.64	.51	2.91	1.28
Marrying within my own ethnic group would be less stressful than marrying outside of my racial/ethnic group. (MAR)	.57	.41	3.93	1.18
The idea of living with a partner prior to marriage does not create anxiety for me. (DPR)	.56	.36	3.41	1.25
I believe that premarital sexual relations are acceptable only after being engaged to the person. (DPR)	.41	.26	2.19	1.05
An interracial marriage would be stressful to me. (MAR)	.65	.61	3.19	1.26
Factor 2: Sex-Role Expectations (13 items)				
I feel that I do not belong to either the South Asian culture nor the American culture when it relates to my role as a woman. (SRE)	.44	.29	2.88	1.32
I experience anxiety at the thought of having an arranged marriage. (MAR)	.53	.32	3.71	1.24
I feel like a pendulum in my role as a woman, wherein within my ethnic culture, I am expected to be dependent, submissive, and putting other's needs before mine, but in the American culture, I am encouraged to be independent, autonomous, and self-asserting of my needs. (SRE)	.64	.51	2.93	1.26

(continued)

TABLE
12.14

ITEMS, COMPONENT LOADING, COMMUNALITY ESTIMATES, MEANS, AND STANDARD DEVIATIONS FOR THE TWO-FACTOR CULTURAL VALUES CONFLICT SCALE (*CONTINUED*)

Item	Factor Loading	h^2	M	SD
I struggle with the value attached to needing to be married by age 25. (MAR)	.54	.42	3.17	1.32
I feel guilty for desiring privacy from my family. (FR)	.42	.35	2.52	1.17
I feel conflicted about my behaviors and options as a woman within the South Asian and in the American culture. (SRE)	.69	.51	2.98	1.14
I feel frustrated in going back and forth in my role as a woman within the South Asian community and within the American community. (SRE)	.71	.54	2.83	1.09
I often find it stressful balancing what I consider private and what my family considers to be public and vice versa. (FR)	.56	.43	3.01	1.09
I struggle with the double standard within my ethnic culture, wherein women more so than men are expected to be equally attentive to both their professional roles (e.g., maintaining career) as well as their home lives (e.g., household chores, parenting). (SRE)	.57	.36	3.60	1.10
I struggle with the pressure to be married and the lack of option to remain single within my culture. (MAR)	.49	.43	3.15	1.25
My family worries about me becoming too Americanized in my thoughts and behaviors. (FR)	.43	.24	2.98	1.29
I am bothered by the fact that in my ethnic culture marriage for a woman is considered to be more important than having a career. (SRE)	.40	.36	3.69	1.18
I struggle with my family's need to be involved in my day-to-day activities. (FR).	.51	.36	2.75	1.18

Note. DPR = dating/premarital sexual relations; MAR = marriage; FR = family relations; SRE = sex role expectations; h_2 = communality estimates. Reproduced from Inman, Ladany, Constantine, and Morano, 2001, p. 22.

more details). In essence, we recommend that researchers report reliability and validity estimates in addition to main results from factor analysis particularly in reporting the results from a test construction process in order to obtain information of the psychometric properties of a measure newly developed.

As illustrated in Table 12.14, we recommend that researchers include the following information in a summary table: the title of each factor and number of items contained [e.g., Factor 1: Intimate Relations (11 items)], each item and corresponding factor loading, communality estimate (h^2: the common variance shared by factors), means, and standardized deviations. Note that the means tend to be close to the scale midpoint, and the standard deviations are sizable; these numbers suggest that there is variability in people's responses to the items and that the distribution of scores are not strongly skewed (both are typically desirable qualities of a scale). In addition, we might suggest that researchers put "R" in front of each item if the item is reverse-scored and explain the meaning of "R" in the *Note* at the bottom of the table (e.g., "R" = reverse-scored item). Also note that the authors omitted the information on cross-loadings across factors. In general, low correlations between (or among) the factors and high correlation within a factor are desirable. Typically, researchers present the exact cross-loadings between (or among) the factors, as in Table 12.15 in Example 2.

In Example 2, Heppner, Heppner, et al. (2002) used an EFA because their research question aimed to investigate the factor structure of their scale, East Asian Coping and Resolution of Trauma (E-ACART) with a sample of 344 Taiwanese college students. Note that the authors provided the following information: (a) factor extraction method (e.g., principal component analysis), (b) factor rotation method (e.g., varimax and promax methods), (c) numbers of items as well as participants in total, (d) criteria to determine the number of factors (e.g., eigenvalue of greater than 1, retaining factor loadings that exceeded .50), (e) the total variance explained by the specific factors, (f) factor loadings, (g) the name of the factors, (h) internal consistency estimates (i.e., alpha coefficients) for each factor and the total scale, and (i) interfactor correlations.

EXAMPLE 2: THE EXPLORATORY FACTOR ANALYSIS

An iterated principal component analysis was conducted on the 70-item E-ACART scale ($N = 308$) to estimate the number of factors. Prior to the main analysis, the appropriateness of factor analysis was supported by Bartlett's test of sphericity, $\chi^2 (2415, N = 308) = 10917.72, p < .0001$, and the Kaiser-Meyer-Olkin measure of sampling adequacy of .86 (see discussion by Tabachnick & Fidell, 1996). Seventeen components (or factors) with a Kaiser-Guttman criterion of eigenvalue greater than 1.00 were extracted. The total variance explained by the 17 factors was 65.7%. However, the general criterion of eigenvalue greater than 1.00 may misjudge the most appropriate number of factors (Gorsuch, 1983), thus the scree plot was carefully examined. The scree plot indicated three to eight factors.

Thus, three-, four-, five-, six-, seven-, and eight-factor solutions were examined initially both on orthogonal and oblique rotation on the 70-item scale. The following criteria were applied in retaining a preliminary factor structure: (a) only retaining items with factor loadings over .50; (b) only retaining factors with at least five items; and (c) deleting items with cross-loadings over .30 after the rotation. Based on these criteria, and given the moderate to high intercorrelations among factors (i.e., half of the interfactor correlations exceeded .37), a five-factor solution with an oblique rotation (i.e., promax) seemed the most conceptually and statistically appropriate.

The five-factor oblique model reduced the 70-item set to a 35-item set with five factors. The total variance accounted for by the five factors was 52.8%. Table [12.15] presents the five factors with their respective items, factor loadings, communality estimates (h^2), means, standard deviations, and percentage using the specific coping strategy. Factor 1 was named "Accommodation with Reflection and Volition" because the items reflected the individual's combined efforts to reflect, accept, or accommodate to existing realities, redefine the meaning of the trauma, as well as their volition in responding to the trauma (13 items, accounting for 21% of the variance). Nine of the items were secondary control items reflecting Interpretive, Illusory, and Predictive control as well as Distancing while four items reflected primary control. Items contained a mix of reframing, fatalism, efficacy, and active problem solving. Highest loading items were "Believed that I would grow from surviving the traumatic event" and "As a starting point, tried to accept the trauma for what it offered me."

Factor 2 was named "Family/Elders Support and Guidance" because the majority of the items related to seeking support from family and respected elders (six items, accounting for 11% of the variance). This factor was an equal blend of three primary and three secondary control items pertaining to a mix of family support, respect for elders/ancestors, and efficacy. Highest loading items were "Shared my feelings with my family" and "Knowing that I could ask assistance from my family increased my confidence."

Factor 3 was named "Religion/Spirituality" in that all of the items reflected coping with the trauma through the use of religion or spirituality and all items reflected vicarious (secondary) control (five items, accounting for 10% of the variance). Items contained a mix of reframing, fatalism, efficacy, and active problem solving. Highest loading items were "Found comfort from my religion or spirituality" and "Found guidance from my religion."

Factor 4 was named "Saving Face and Detachment" in that all of the items dealt with the individual's desire to "save face" as well as efforts to avoid thinking about the trauma for either short or long periods of time (six items, accounting for 6% of the variance). All six items reflected secondary control and pertained to detachment, saving face, and protecting family members. Highest loading items were "Saved face by not telling anyone" and "Pretended to be OK."

Factor 5 was named "Professional and Personal Resources" because the majority of the items related to the individual's efforts to use professional resources (e.g., counselors) or personal resources (e.g., people on the Internet, food) to cope with the trauma (five items, accounting for 5% of the variance). These items were an equal blend of primary and secondary control reflecting distancing, respect for authority figures, peer support, and saving face. Highest loading items were "Saved face by seeking advice from a professional I did not know personally" and "Actively sought advice from professionals." The items were also a blend of seeking assistance from professionals and peers as well as using strategies to distance oneself from the trauma, such as eating in excess or traveling; nonetheless, all items loaded positively on this factor.

| TABLE |
| 12.15 |

EXAMPLE ITEMS, COMPONENT LOADING, COMMUNALITY ESTIMATES, MEANS, STANDARD DEVIATIONS, AND PERCENTAGE USING THE COPING STRATEGY FOR THE FIVE-FACTOR EAST ASIAN COPING AND RESOLUTION OF TRAUMA SCALE

| Example Items | Factor Loadings | | | | | h^2 | M | SD | Percentage Using This Strategy |
	F1[a]	F2	F3	F4	F5				
Factor 1: Accommodation With Reflection and Volition							3.12[b]	1.24[b]	87.5
Believed that I would grow from surviving the traumatic event.	**.74**	.00	-.02	-.21	-.05	.54	3.56	1.20	94.4
As a starting point, tried to accept the trauma for what it offered me.	**.68**	-.12	.03	.01	.04	.45	3.10	1.20	90.8
Factor 2: Family/Elders Support and Guidance							2.57[b]	1.15[b]	60.5
Shared my feelings with my family.	.03	**.82**	.00	-.17	.01	.70	2.74	1.25	61.5
Knowing that I could ask assistance from my family increased my confidence.	.07	**.80**	.00	-.07	-.02	.66	2.81	1.26	65.5
Factor 3: Religion/Spirituality							2.43[b]	1.18[b]	40.1
Found comfort from my religion or spirituality.	.00	-.03	**.92**	.01	-.05	.80	2.46	1.16	43.8
Found guidance from my religion.	-.03	.01	**.89**	.00	.00	.79	2.42	1.20	41.4
Factor 4: Saving Face and Detachment							2.45[b]	1.27[b]	66.7
Saved face by not telling anyone.	-.20	.02	.02	**.75**	.15	.62	2.34	1.31	43.6
Pretended to be OK.	-.03	.00	-.01	**.73**	.03	.54	2.12	1.28	74.6
Factor 5: Professional and Personal Resources							2.60[b]	1.23[b]	39.1
Saved face by seeking advice from a professional (e.g., counselor, social worker, psychiatrist) I did not know personally.	-.01	.09	.02	.02	**.80**	.68	2.76	1.27	37.2
Actively sought advice from professionals (e.g., counselors, social workers, psychiatrists).	.07	.02	.08	-.08	**.79**	.66	2.74	1.35	35.9

Note. h^2 = communality estimates;[a] Factor labels: F1 = Accommodation With Reflection and Volition, F2 = Family/Elders Support and Guidance, F3 = Religion/Spirituality, F4 = Saving Face and Detachment, and F5 = Professional and Personal Resources.[b] = M and SD were calculated based on the responses of those who reported using the specific coping strategy.

Intercorrelations Among Factors

The interfactor correlation coefficients among the five factors ranged from .03 (between Factor 2 and 4) to .34 (between Factor 2 and 3). These results indicate that each factor has distinctiveness. (Heppner, Heppner, et al., 2002)

Note that the 10 items in Table 12.15 are just listing two items from each factor of the original E-ACART with 35 items. Please refer to Heppner, Heppner, et al. (2002) for the whole listing of items. Note also in the table that the authors provided similar information as in the first example, an EFA by Inman et al. (2001), such as the name of a factor (i.e., subscales of the E-ACART), all lists of items, internal consistency estimates of each factor, communality estimates (h^2), means, and standard deviations. However, note that, unlike the example by Inman et al., Heppner, Heppner, et al. provided other important information, factor loadings of each item across all of the factors. This information enables readers to know how each item loaded on all of the factors, providing the information of the distinctive nature of each item. For example, one item of Factor 1 (i.e., "Believed that I would grow from surviving the traumatic event") is more likely to be associated with Factor 4 (i.e., saving face and detachment; $r = -.21$) than Factor 2 (i.e., family/elders support and guidance; $r = .00$). More important, a review of these numbers indicates the degree to which items are strongly associated with other factors or whether they load primarily on one factor. Also note that the authors used the bold font as well as underlining to indicate which items belong to the specific factor, which helps readers easily identify the items that loaded on each factor.

Confirmatory Factor Analysis

Writing the Results Using a Confirmatory Factor Analysis   Although there are some variations in writing the results from the CFA, we recommend that a researcher include the following typical components: (a) the method of estimation (e.g., typically the maximum likelihood estimation), (b) statistical software used for the CFA [e.g., the LISREL 8 (Jöreskog & Sörbom, 1996), the AMOS 3.6 (Arbuckle, 1997), or the EQS 5.0 (Bentler, 1995)], (c) the description of the hypothesized factor structure on the basis of the EFA or a priori theory [e.g., a three-factor solution for the Working Alliance Inventory (Horvath & Greenberg, 1986)], (d) the goodness-of-fit indicators used (e.g., chi-square statistic, the ratio of chi-square to the degree of freedom, the GFI, CFI, NFI, AGFI, AIC, RMSEA, etc.; see Quintana & Maxwell, 1999, for more details), and (e) a brief statement indicating whether or not the hypothesized factor structure was confirmed by the CFA. In addition, it is usually recommended to present information on the reliability and validity estimates of the factors.

The next example is the description of a CFA from Neville, Lilly, Duran, Lee, and Browne (2000). They were interested in confirming the three-factor structure of the Color-Blind Racial Attitudes Scale (CoBRAS) that was obtained from their previous research using EFA. Note in the example that Neville et al.

not only included the suggested components in writing the results of the CFA but also presented a table that summarized the goodness-of-fit indicators used in their research in order to help readers compare a variety of fit indexes. Also note that the authors compared the three-factor solution and two competing factor solutions (i.e., three-factor versus two-factor solutions as well as a two-factor versus a one-factor solution) in order to find the relative strength of the three-factor structure as suggested by their first study. For this comparison, note that the authors used two chi-square difference tests with their associated p values (for more details, see Hatcher, 1994) and provided a rationale for why they chose a three-factor solution over a two- and a one-factor solution. Finally, note that the authors also presented information on reliability and validity estimates in their results section, which provides readers with information on how the three factors confirmed from the CFA were well represented by homogeneous indicators (i.e., items), as well as how the three factors had construct validity, particularly as compared with another scale measuring a similar construct.

CONFIRMATORY FACTOR ANALYSIS

A confirmatory factor analysis (CFA) with robust maximum likelihood estimation was conducted on the 20 items of the CoBRAS, using the LISREL 8.2 (Jöreskog & Sörbom, 1998). Comparisons between the three-factor oblique model identified in Study 1, a global factor model, and a two-factor conceptual model were made using a variety of statistics including a chi-square statistic, root mean square error of approximation (RMSEA), Akaike information criterion-of-fit index (AGFI). Differences between chi-square statistics were also computed to test for an improvement in fit from the two-factor model over the global factor model and from the three-factor model over the two-factor model using the likelihood ratio or chi-square difference test (Bollen, 1989). Across several indexes, it appears the three-factor oblique model was the best fit compared with the competing models, primarily because it had the following lowest statistics: [χ^2, χ^2/df], AIC, and RMSEA (see Table [12.16]). Results also suggest that the three-factor model was a good fit of the data as indicated by the GFI (.90) and the AGFI (.87), which were above .85 (as suggested by Jöreskog & Sörbom, 1993). In addition, results of the differences

TABLE 12.16 **GOODNESS-OF-FIT INDICATORS FOR NULL MODEL AND COMPETING HYPOTHESIZED MODELS FOR CoBRAS IN STUDY 2**

Model[a]	df	χ^2	χ^2/df	RMSEA	AIC	Hoelter N	GFI	AGFI
Factor 1	170	1,053	6.20	.10	1,089	121	.82	.77
Factor 2	169	1,048	6.20	.10	1,081	121	.82	.77
Factor 3	167	526	3.10	.06	653	210	.90	.88

Note. RMSEA = root mean square error of approximation; AIC = Akaike information criterion; GFI = goodness-of-fit index; AGFI = adjusted goodness-of-fit index; CoBRAS = Color-Blind Racial Attitudes Scale.
[a]For the independent model, χ^2 (190) = 2,639. Reproduced from Neville, Lilly, Duran, Lee, & Browne, 2000, pp. 65.
Source: From " construction and Initial Validation of hte Color-Blind Racial Attitudes Scale (CoBRAS)," by H. A. Neville, R. L. Lilly, G. Duran, R. M. Lee, and L. Browne, 2000, *Journal of Counseling Psychology, 47*, p. 65. Copyright 2000 by the American Psychological Association, Inc. Reprinted with permission.

in the chi-square statistic test indicated that the model was the best fit of the data, $p < .001$. Using the likelihood ratio difference test, the χ^2 difference statistics for 2 versus 1 factor and 3 versus 2 factors were significant ($p < .05$).

Reliability

To further examine reliability of the CoBRAS, the test was divided into two equal lengths, yielding an acceptable Guttman split-half reliability estimate of .72. Cronbach's alpha for each of the factors and the total score were acceptable and ranged from .70 (Blatant Racial Issues) to .86 (CoBRAS total).

Concurrent Validity

The correlations among the CoBRAS factors and the two Belief in a Just World Scales were examined to investigate the concurrent validity of the CoBRAS. Results indicate significant correlations among the Global Belief in a Just World (GBJW) Scale (Lipkus, 1991), Multidimensional Belief in a Just World Scale—sociopolitical subscales (SS) (Furnham & Procter, 1988), the three CoBRAS factors, and the CoBRAS total score. Correlations ranged from .39 (between Institutional Discrimination and GBJW) to .61 (among MBJWS and Racial Privilege as well as the CoBRAS total).

Structural Equation Modeling

Structural equation modeling (SEM) is a statistical technique used when a researcher wants to test the plausibility of a theory or a model about the predictive relationships among variables (e.g., variable A$\rightarrow$ B $\rightarrow$ C; note arrows represent hypothesized predictive effects). The nature of the variables analyzed in SEM can be either latent (i.e., scores or values on a scale that cannot be observed directly) or manifest (i.e., scores or values that can be observed directly). In general, SEM can be considered as a combination of factor analysis and path analysis for the following two reasons. First, SEM is used for analyzing unmeasured or latent variables (i.e., factors), and thus it is viewed as having a factor analytic feature. In this regard, the confirmatory factor analysis (CFA) can be a part of SEM because it deals with both latent variables and a test of a hypothesized model or factor structure. In addition, SEM includes path analytic features in the sense that it deals with the predictive relationships among variables. The only difference between path analysis and SEM is that the former can analyze the predictive orderings of only "measured or manifest" variables; the latter is able to analyze both manifest and latent variables. For more details in SEM, see recent resources such as Loehlin (1998), Quintana and Maxwell (1999), Kline (1998), and Klem (2000).

In short, the two facets of SEM (i.e., factor analysis and path analysis) consist of the following two parts. First is the *measurement part* of the model, which corresponds to the CFA and concerns how well the latent variable(s) can be represented by the manifest variables (i.e., indicators or observed variables) as hypothesized by the theory or results from the EFA. Second is the *structural part* of the model that corresponds to path analytic properties and depicts the direct or indirect effects of the relationships among latent variables

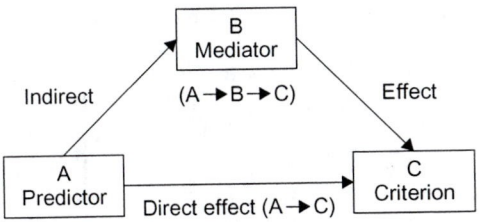

12.5

Direct and indirect effects among variables.

---

or factors. Specifically, the direct effect from variable A to C can be illustrated by variable A → C, whereas the indirect effect from A to C is depicted by A → B → C where B is a mediator variable. Figure 12.5 depicts the direct and indirect effects among the predictor, mediator, and criterion variables (see also Baron & Kenny, 1986, for more on these effects).

Writing the Results Using Structural Equation Modeling (SEM)   First of all, note that there are many variations in writing the results using SEM (for more details, see Hatcher, 1994). Nonetheless, common features of SEM pertain to the two main parts: (a) the measurement model and (b) the structural model. Note however that the measurement model and the structural model are quite similar in the type of analyses. Whereas the measurement model is quite similar to that of CFA, the following components are common for the structural model: (a) the method of estimation (e.g., typically the maximum likelihood estimation); (b) statistical software used for the SEM [e.g., the LISREL 8.2 (Jöreskog & Sörbom, 1998), the AMOS 3.6 (Arbuckle, 1997), or the EQS 5.0 (Bentler, 1995)]; (c) the description of the hypothesized latent variables structure as well as their causal relationships on the basis of a priori theory; (d) the goodness-of-fit indicators used (e.g., chi-square statistic, the ratio of chi-square to the degree of freedom, the GFI, CFI, NFI, AGFI, AIC, RMSEA, etc.; see Quintana & Maxwell, 1999, for more details); (e) results of comparing several equivalent models (e.g., partially mediated model and fully mediated model, etc.); and (f) a brief statement of indicating whether or not the hypothesized latent variables structure, as well as predictive relationships among variables, is accepted by the SEM.

Following is an example of SEM from Heppner, Pretorius, et al. (2002):

Measurement Model

A two-step procedure recommended by J. C. Anderson and Gerbing (1988) was used in the present study to test the mediational model. In the first step, a CFA was used to develop an acceptable measurement model, then the structural model was tested in the second step. Similarly to Study 1, we created 4 item-bundles to operationalize the AAS latent variable and 3 item-bundles for the PSC latent variable. The bundles consisted of the same items in Study 2 as in Study 1. In addition, we determined the adequacy of the model fit on the basis of the CFI, BL89, NNFI, Mc, and RMSEA. As noted in Study 1, the CFI, BL89, and NNFI (close to .95 or greater), the Mc (close to .90 or greater), and the RMSEA (close to .05 or less) are considered to be desirable. We also used chi-square difference tests to compare nested structural models.

In the measurement model the latent variables are allowed to covary with each other. The maximum-likelihood analysis using CALIS in SAS (SAS Institute, 1991) was used to estimate the measurement model (see Figure [12.6]). An initial test of the measurement model yielded a very good fit for the model, χ^2 (59, N = 213) = 93.39, p < .01, CFI = .95, BL89 = .95, NNFI = .93, Mc = .92, RMSEA = .05. In addition, all of the factor loadings were significant (p < .001), suggesting that the four latent variables (AAS, PSC, intrapersonal distress, and interpersonal distress) were well represented by all of the indicators. Moreover, the correlations among the four variables were significant at the .01 level, except for the correlation between AAS and interpersonal distress (r = .03, p > .05). Given this lack of significance in the measurement model, there was no effect to mediate. Thus, interpersonal distress was removed from the subsequent structural models.

Structural Model for Tests of Mediation

The structural model (see Figure [12.7]) was tested with a maximum-likelihood analysis using CALIS in SAS (SAS Institute, 1991). According to Holmbeck (1997), three models must be estimated in structural equation modeling to test for a mediational effect. First, a direct-effect model tests the effect of AAS on intrapersonal distress in the absence of the mediator, PSC. For the mediation to exist, the path coefficient (from the AAS to intrapersonal distress) in the direct-effect model must be significant to continue to test the mediational effect of PSC. If the path coefficient from AAS to intrapersonal distress were not significant, no mediational effect would exist. The direct path coefficient from AAS to intrapersonal distress was significant (r = .26, p < .01), which met Holmbeck's (1997) first step criterion for examining a mediational model.

The second step in Holmbeck's (1997) procedure is to test the partially mediated structural model that estimates the direct effect from AAS to intrapersonal distress and adds the paths from AAS to PSC as well as from PSC to intrapersonal distress. The results of the partially mediated structural model were very good: χ^2 (41, N = 216) = 51.36, p > .05, CFI = .98, BL89 = .98, NNFI = .98, Mc = .98, RMSEA = .03 (90% lower confidence limit = 0; 90% upper-confidence limit = .06). The direct effect of AAS on intrapersonal distress was reduced in the first direct-effect model (r = .26, p < .01) and nonsignificantly associated in the partially mediated model (r = − .20, p > .05). Note that although the correlation was not significant, the size of the correlation was almost as large as the former correlation but in the opposite direction, suggesting the possibility of a suppressor.

The final step in Holmbeck's (1997) procedure is to compare the partially mediated model with the fully mediated model, in which the direct path from AAS to intrapersonal distress is constrained to zero. The fully mediated model revealed very good fit indexes as well: χ^2 (42, N = 216) = 52.97, p > .05, CFI = .98, BL89 = .98, NNFI = .97, Mc = .98, RMSEA = .03 (90% lower confidence limit = 0; 90% upper confidence limit = .06; see Figure [12.7]). A chi-square difference test showed no significant difference between the two models, $\Delta\chi^2$ (1, N = 216) = 1.62. For parsimonious purposes, the fully mediated model is considered a better fit for the data (as suggested by J. C. Anderson & Gerbing, 1988). In Figure [12.7], the magnitude of the mediational effect (i.e., the standardized estimate of the indirect effect size; see Kline, 1998) from AAS via PSC to intrapersonal distress is given by multiplying the path coefficients, .69 × .48 = .33. In other words, nearly 11% of

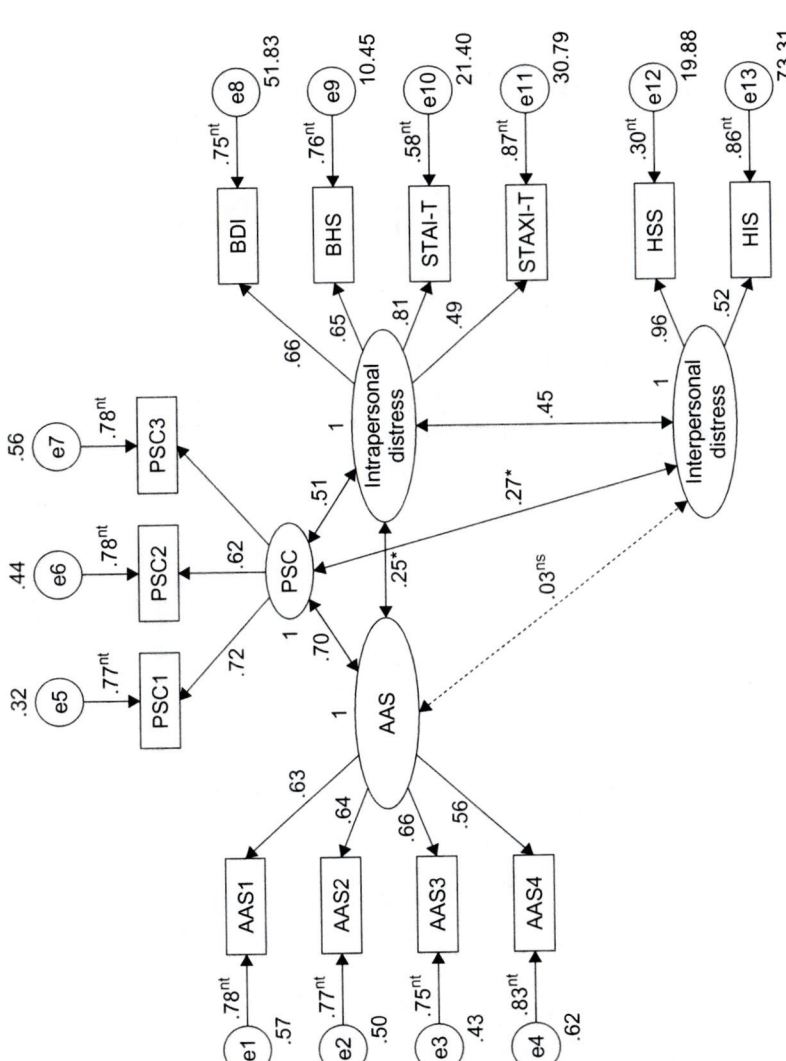

FIGURE 12.6

The measurement model. The rectangles are measured variables, the large ovals are latent constructs, and the small circles are residual variances. Factor loadings are standardized and all are significant (*p* < .001), except for these designated paths: *p* < .001); ns = not significant, nt = fixed at 1. AAS = Approach-Avoidance Style; PSC = Problem-Solving Confidence. Intrapersonal distress latent variables: BDI = Beck Depression Inventory; BHS = Beck Hopelessness Scale; STAI-T = State-Trait Anxiety Inventory-Trait; STAXI-T = State-Trait Anger Inventory-Trait. Interpersonal distress latent variables: HSS = Hard to Be Sociable Scale; HIS = Hard to Be Intimate Scale.

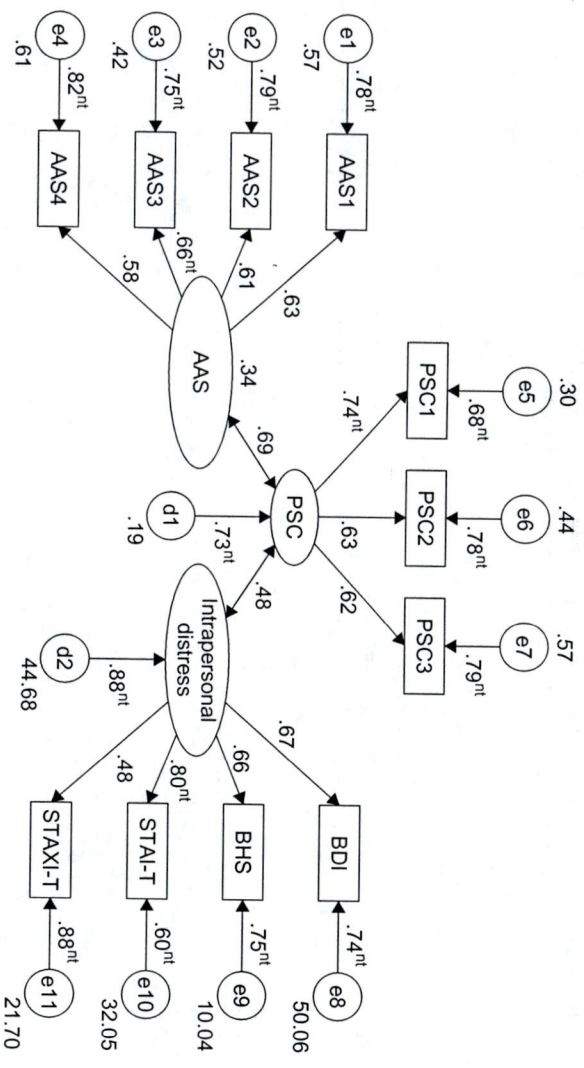

FIGURE 12.7

The fully mediated model. The rectangles are measured variables, the large ovals are latent constructs, and the small circles are residual or disturbance variances. Factor loadings are standardized and all are significant ($p < .001$), except for the paths designated "nt," which were fixed at 1. AAS = Approach-Avoidance Style; PSC = Problem-Solving Confidence. Intrapersonal distress latent variables: BDI = Beck Depression Inventory; BHS = Beck Hopelessness Scale; STAI-T = State-Trait Anxiety Inventory-Trait; STAXI-T = State-Trait Anger Inventory-Trait.

variance in intrapersonal distress was accounted for by the mediation effect of PSC between AAS and intrapersonal distress. In addition, all factor loadings were significant ($p < .001$), indicating that the AAS, PSC, and intrapersonal distress variables were well represented by the indicators. In sum, the result suggests that PSC fully mediated the relationship between AAS and intrapersonal distress but not the relationship between AAS and interpersonal distress. Thus, the second hypothesis was partially supported. Parenthetically, an alternative model was explored that examined whether AAS could serve as a mediator between PSC and psychological distress. The result indicates that AAS failed to mediate the relationship PSC and intrapersonal distress because the path from AAS to intrapersonal distress was not significant ($r = -.20, p < .05$) in this model. (Reproduced from Heppner, Pretorius, Wei, Lee, & Wang, 2002, p. 494)

They were interested in testing a problem-solving mediational model, which postulates that the Problem-Solving Confidence (PSC) mediates the relationship between Approach-Avoidance Style (AAS) and multiple indexes of psychological distress (see Figure 12.7). They utilized SEM because the main purpose of the study was testing their hypothesized model to describe the relationship among a variety of latent variables. Note in the path diagram in Figure 12.6 that latent variables have an oval shape while manifest variables (or indicators) are represented by a rectangular shape. Also note that the small circles represent residual (i.e., error) or disturbance variances (see Kline, 1998, for more details on the symbols). In addition, the one-way arrows represent a prediction from variable A to B (A $\rightarrow$ B), whereas the two-way arrows signify a bidirectional prediction between variables A and B (A $\leftrightarrow$ B). The numbers on arrows represent path coefficients that depict the strength of prediction or association between the variables.

First, note that they presented two models [i.e., the measurement (see Figure 12.6) and the structural model (see Figure 12.7)], as we discussed earlier. Second, the authors introduced a variety of goodness-of-fit indexes and their desired levels (see Quintana & Maxwell, 1999, for more details), which helps readers determine the degree to which the hypothesized model fits the actual data. Third, they presented the fit indexes for the measurement model as well as a brief summary of the overall meaning for readers. Finally, note that all the latent variables in their measurement model were represented well by their indicators, which thus allowed the researchers to proceed in testing their structural model. Note that if the measurement model was not represented by all the indicators, it would have been inappropriate for them to test the structural model. Also note that Heppner, Pretorius, et al. (2002) used 7 item-bundles (or parcels) for the PSC (3 bundles) and AAS (4 bundles) instead of using the 27 individual items of the PSC (11 items) and AAS (16 items). Heppner, Pretorius, et al. used item-bundles in order to (a) guard against estimating an unnecessary large number of parameters (i.e., factor loadings and error terms), and (b) reduce the possibility of distortion from idiosyncratic characteristics of individual items in fitting the model to the data. For more details about item-bundles, refer to the discussion by Russell, Kahn, Spoth, and Altmaier (1998).

In the structural model (see Figure 12.7), Heppner, Pretorius, et al. (2002) tested the direct effect (i.e., A → C) and indirect effect (i.e., A → B → C) among the latent variables. For example, one of the latent variables, the PSC (i.e., variable B), was assumed as a mediating variable between the AAS (i.e., variable A) and the intrapersonal distress (i.e., variable C). Note that the size of mediating effect of variable B can be obtained by multiplying the path coefficient between variable A and B with the path coefficient between variable B and C. Specifically, note that, in their study, the size of mediating effect was $.69 \times .48 = .33$, indicating that 11% (i.e., $.33 \times .33 = .11$) of variance in Intrapersonal Distress is accounted for by the mediation effect of the PSC between AAS and Intrapersonal Distress. Heppner, Pretorius, et al. provided a detailed description on meeting the criteria for mediating effects (as suggested by Holmbeck, 1997), as well as on how to calculate the size of mediation effect. We recommend that readers carefully study their structural model in the example along with Figure 12.7 that depicts the model with path diagrams.

CONCLUSIONS

This chapter discussed common components used to write a quantitative results chapter while writing a thesis, dissertation, or manuscript for publication. In general, this chapter provided guidelines with examples on how to present a clear road map for each major section and how to conduct and write preliminary analyses, as well as main analyses, across a variety of statistical techniques. Additionally, the chapter provides resources such as checklists for writing the results of various statistical techniques, as well as references regarding other advanced statistical techniques not fully covered in this chapter.

The importance of appropriately employing various statistical techniques and subsequently writing the results of those analyses cannot be overemphasized. The goal of this chapter was to present a step-by-step guide to writing results for quantitative studies, as well as present a number of examples, all in efforts to clarify the writing of quantitative results. However, when authors are in doubt about applying the correct statistical analyses for their study, we strongly suggest that authors consult a statistician. If the wrong statistical analyses are conducted, the study will be greatly weakened regardless of how well the results are written.

CHECKLIST FOR CHAPTER 4 OF THE THESIS OR DISSERTATION

Readers can find a step-by-step checklist in writing results using specific statistical techniques as well as preliminary analyses. We recommend that students follow the steps carefully in the checklist and make a mark in the box located before the statement for each step after they complete the specific step.

The Chapter Road Map

Did you . . .

❑ Provide the reader with a guide to each of the major sections in the paper?

Data Screening

Did you . . .

❑ Check the accuracy of the data entry either by reviewing the data file or by using frequency tables and graphic methods (e.g., histograms)?

❑ Confirm the accuracy of the data entry by using frequency tables?

❑ Check if missing values reveal any consistent patterns?

❑ Check missing data with random patterns either by deleting the participants whose data contained the missing values or by replacing the missing items with the group mean for that item?

❑ Check both univariate and multivariate outliers by reviewing relevant statistics such as standardized scores and Mahalanobis distance?

❑ Check the normality of distributions of your data by calculating and reviewing the values for skewness and kurtosis?

❑ Conduct the appropriate data transformation for the variables that failed to meet the assumption of normality?

❑ Report the data-transformation procedure as well as the values for skewness and kurtosis for the transformed variables?

❑ Report the final sample size after completing all the relevant data screening procedures?

Preliminary Analyses

Did you . . .

❑ Check whether scores on dependent variable(s) are different across demographic variables either by using t tests and/or analysis of variance (in case of discrete variables) or by using regression analysis (in case of continuous variables)?

❑ Provide the reliability coefficients of the measures used and check whether the internal consistency estimates of the measures reach appropriate levels (e.g., greater than .70)?

❑ Conduct intercorrelation analyses among the primary variables of interest in your study and report the result?

Descriptive Statistics

Did you . . .

❑ Report means and standard deviations as well as other relevant descriptive statistics (e.g., median, mode, frequency, percentage, skewness, and kurtosis) of your sample?

❑ Italicize *M* (for the means) and *SD* (for the standard deviations)?

❑ Provide a descriptive statistics summary table of your variables of interest?

❑ Provide a *"Note"* at the bottom of the table and identify the acronyms?

Chi-Square Analysis

Did you . . .

❑ Report the degree(s) of freedom (*df*), the number of participants, the χ^2 statistic, and its associated *p* value?

❑ Report the observed frequencies and the expected frequencies as well as their percentages?

❑ Italicize *N* (for the number of participants) and *p* (for the *p* value), but not italicize χ^2?

❑ Provide a chi-square analysis summary table along with the percentages of the variables and the χ^2 statistic, if necessary?

❑ Provide a *"Note"* at the bottom of the table and identify the acronyms?

t test Analysis

Did you . . .

❑ Report the degree(s) of freedom (*df*), the *t* test statistic, and its associated *p* value?

❑ Report the means and standard deviations of the scores on the dependent variable between the two groups?

❑ Italicize *M* (for the means), *SD* (for the standard deviations), *t* (for the *t* test statistic) and *p* (for the *p* value)?

❑ Provide a t test summary table along with the means and standard deviations of the variables and the t test statistic, if necessary?

❑ Provide a *"Note"* at the bottom of the table and identify the acronyms?

One-Way Analysis of Variance (ANOVA)

Did you . . .

❑ Report two degrees of freedom (dfs), the F test statistic, and its associated p value?

❑ Conduct the follow-up tests (i.e., post hoc comparisons; Tukey's test or Scheffé test) only when the F statistic is significant at the desired alpha level and the independent variable has more than two levels or conditions?

❑ Report the results of the follow-up tests along with the means and standard deviations for the dependent variable?

❑ Italicize M (for the means), SD (for the standard deviations), F (for the F test statistic) and p (for the p value)?

❑ Provide a one-way ANOVA summary table along with sum of squares, the degree of freedom (df), mean squares and the F test statistic for the variable as well as the error variance and the total variance, if necessary?

❑ Provide a *"Note"* at the bottom of the table and identify the acronyms?

Two-Way Analysis of Variance (ANOVA)

Did you . . .

❑ Report two degrees of freedom (dfs), the F test statistic, and its associated p value for two main effects and one interaction effect?

❑ Conduct the follow-up tests (i.e., post hoc comparisons; Tukey's test or Scheffé test) only when the F statistic is significant at the desired alpha level and the independent variable has more than two levels or conditions?

❑ Report the results of the follow-up tests along with the means and standard deviations for the dependent variable?

❑ Underline M (for the means), SD (for the standard deviations), F (for the F test statistic) and p (for the p value)?

❑ Provide a two-way ANOVA summary table along with sum of squares, the degrees of freedom (df), mean squares and the F test statistics for two main effects, one interaction effect, the error variance, and the total variance, if necessary?

❑ Provide a *"Note"* at the bottom of the table and identify the acronyms?

Two-Way Analysis of Covariance (ANCOVA)

Did you . . .

❑ Define the covariate and describe the procedure of adjusting the group means in the ANCOVA?

❑ Adjust the means by eliminating the influence of a covariate from the scores on the dependent variable using either regression analysis (when the covariate is a continuous variable) or a completely randomized block design (when the covariate is a categorical variable)?

❑ Report the adjusted means and standard deviations for the dependent variable?

❑ Report two degrees of freedom (*df*s), the *F* test statistic, and its associated *p* value for two main effects and one interaction effect just like the case of general two-way ANOVA after controlling for the covariate?

❑ Conduct the follow-up tests (i.e., post hoc comparisons; Tukey's test or Scheffé test) only when the *F* statistic is significant at the desired alpha level and the independent variable has more than two levels?

❑ Report the results of the follow-up tests if significant?

❑ Italicize *M* (for the means), *SD* (for the standard deviations), *F* (for the *F* test statistic) and *p* (for the *p* value)?

❑ Provide a table of adjusted means after the ANCOVA procedure?

❑ Provide a two-way ANCOVA summary table along with sum of squares, the degrees of freedom (*df*), mean squares and the *F* test statistics for two main effects, one interaction effect, the error variance, and the total variance, if necessary?

❑ Provide a *"Note"* at the bottom of the table and identify the acronyms?

Repeated-Measures ANOVA

Did you . . .

❑ Report two degrees of freedom (*df*s), the *F* test statistic, and its associated *p* value?

❑ Report the statistic that you used as the *F* value (e.g., Wilks's lambda)?

❑ Conduct the relevant follow-up test (e.g., trend analysis) when the main effect was significant and report the results of the follow-up test?

❑ Italicize F (for the F test statistic) and p (for the p value)?
❑ Provide a repeated-measures ANOVA summary table along with sum of squares, the degrees of freedom (df), mean squares and the F test statistics for the variable as well as the error variance and the total variance, if necessary?
❑ Provide a *"Note"* at the bottom of the table and identify the acronyms?

Simultaneous Regression Analysis

Did you . . .

❑ Define the predictor variables and the criterion variable?
❑ Report two degrees of freedom (dfs), both R^2 and the adjusted R^2, the F test statistic, and its associated p value?
❑ Report how much variance the predictor variables accounted for in the total variance of the criterion variable?
❑ Italicize R^2 and the adjusted R^2, F (for the F test statistic), and p (for the p value)?
❑ Provide a simultaneous regression summary table along with the unstandardized beta (B), its standard error estimates (SE B), the standardized beta (β), and the t test statistic of each predictor, if necessary?
❑ Provide a *"Note"* at the bottom of the table and identify the acronyms?

Stepwise Regression Analysis

Did you . . .

❑ Define the predictor variables entered into the regression equation in each step as well as the criterion variable?
❑ Report two degrees of freedom (dfs), both the R^2 and adjusted R^2, the F test statistic, and its associated p value?
❑ Report how much variance the predictor variable by each step accounted for in the total variance of the criterion variable?
❑ Italicize R^2 and the adjusted R^2), F (for the F test statistic), and p (for the p value)?
❑ Provide a stepwise regression summary table along with the unstandardized beta (B), its standard error estimates (SE B), the standardized beta (β), and the t test statistic of each predictor, if necessary?

❑ Provide a *"Note"* at the bottom of the table and identify the acronyms?

Hierarchical Regression Analysis

Did you . . .

❑ Define the predictor variables entered into the regression equation in each step as well as the criterion variable?

❑ Provide the rationale for entering the predictors in a specific order in the steps?

❑ Report two degrees of freedom (*dfs*), both the R^2 and the additional R^2 change, the *F* and the *F* of change statistics, and their associated *p* value by each step?

❑ Report how much variance the predictor variable by each step accounted for in the total variance of the criterion variable over and above the variance explained by its previous step?

❑ Italicize R^2 (for both the adjusted R^2 and the R^2 change), *F* (for the *F* test statistic), and *p* (for the *p* value)?

❑ Provide a hierarchical multiple regression summary table along with the value of R^2 and the R^2 change (ΔR^2), and the *F* test statistic with two degrees of freedom in each step, if necessary?

❑ Provide a *"Note"* at the bottom of the table and identify the acronyms?

Multivariate Analysis of Variance

Did you . . .

❑ Check if the numbers of dependent variables are more than two?

❑ Report two degrees of freedom (*dfs*), the *F* test statistic (i.e., Wilks's Lambda), and its associated *p* value?

❑ Conduct the follow-up tests (i.e., post hoc comparisons; Tukey's test or Scheffé test) only when the omnibus *F* statistic is significant at the desired alpha level and the independent variable has more than two levels or conditions?

❑ Report the results of the follow-up tests along with the means and standard deviations for the dependent variable?

❑ Italicize *M* (for the means), *SD* (for the standard deviations), *F* (for the *F* test statistic) and *p* (for the *p* value)?

❑ Provide the follow-up ANOVA's summary table along with sum of squares, the degree of freedom (*df*), mean squares, and the *F* test statistic for the variable as well as the error variance and the total variance, if necessary?

❑ Provide a *"Note"* at the bottom of the table and identify the acronyms?

Cluster Analysis

Did you . . .

❑ Describe the purpose of using CA (e.g., to categorize types of people)?

❑ Describe the specific method you chose for CA (e.g., Ward method)?

❑ Provide the rationale to determine the numbers of clusters both theoretically and statistically?

❑ Provide a visual overview of difference among the clusters using a graph format?

❑ Provide a table that includes means and standard deviations of the multiple measures that contributed to determining the clusters, if necessary?

❑ Provide the title of each cluster as well as detailed description of its distinctive features?

Factor Analysis I: Exploratory Factor Analysis (EFA)

Did you . . .

❑ Check the statistics to determine whether the sample is factorable (e.g., the KMO and/or Bartlett's test of sphericity)?

❑ Describe the initial factor extraction method (e.g., principle component versus principle axis factoring) as well as the rotation methods (e.g., oblique versus orthogonal)?

❑ Provide the rationale to choose specific numbers of factors both theoretically and statistically (eigenvalue greater than 1.0 along with scree plot)?

❑ Report the following information in both paragraphs and a table (if necessary), once you determine the numbers of factors: title, each item, eigenvalues, factor loadings, communality (h^2), means and standard deviations for each factor, and the total variance explained by each factor?

❑ Provide reliability estimates (e.g., internal consistency) for both subscales and the total score as well as validity estimates (e.g., convergent and discriminant validity)?

Factor Analysis II: Confirmatory Factor Analysis (CFA)

Did you . . .

❑ Describe the method of estimation (e.g., the maximum likelihood estimation) as well as the software program used (e.g., LISREL, EQS, or AMOS)?
❑ Present the rationale for constructing and testing the model?
❑ Report necessary fit-indexes such as GFI, CFI, NFI, RMSEA, etc.?
❑ Provide a brief statement indicating whether or not the hypothesized factor structure is supported by the actual data?
❑ Provide figures that include the path diagram for the measurement model (CFA)?

Structural Equation Modeling (SEM) Analysis: Mediational Model Testing

Did you . . .

❑ Review all required steps aforementioned in the section of the CFA to determine whether or not the measurement model fits well with data?
❑ Describe the method of estimation (e.g., the maximum likelihood estimation) as well as the software program used (e.g., LISREL, EQS, or AMOS) for the structural model?
❑ Present the hypothesized structural models to be tested such as the partially mediated model or fully mediated model?
❑ Check the conditions to test a mediational model as suggested by Holmbeck (1997)?
❑ Report necessary fit-indexes such as GFI, CFI, NFI, RMSEA, etc.?
❑ Provide a brief statement indicating whether or not the hypothesized factor structure is supported by the actual data?
❑ Provide figures that include the path diagram for the measurement model as well as relevant structural model(s)?

USEFUL REFERENCES FOR OTHER STATISTICAL TECHNIQUES

You are encouraged to refer to the following references to find statistical knowledge on the three other statistical techniques that are less frequently used and were not included in this chapter due to space limitations: Hierarchical Linear Modeling, Discriminant Functional Analysis, and Canonical Correlation Analysis.

Hierarchical Linear Modeling (HLM)

HLM is "an approach to longitudinal repeated measures data that begins by modeling individual growth curves (level I model). Then, variations in people's growth curve parameters are modeled using other predictors (level II model)" (Weinfurt, p. 356). For example, HLM can be utilized when a researcher wants to know how much each student in a study changed by comparing students' characteristics of the "fast learners" and "slow learners" based on their rates of change over 6 months.

Useful References

Bryk, A. S., & Raudenbush, S. W. (1987). Application of hierarchical linear models to assessing change. *Psychological Bulletin, 101*, 147–158.

Bryk, A. S., & Raudenbush, S. W. (1992). *Hierarchical linear models: Applications and data analysis methods.* Newbury Park, CA: Sage.

Pedhazur, E. J. (1997). *Multiple regression in behavioral research: Explanation and prediction* (3rd ed.). Fort Worth, TX: Harcourt Brace College Publishers.

Rogosa, D. (1988). Myths about longitudinal research. In K. W. Schaie, R. T. Campbell, W. Meredith, & S. C. Rawlings (Eds.), *Methodological issues in aging research* (pp. 171–209). New York: Springer.

Rogosa, D., Brandt, D., & Zimowski, M. (1982). A growth curve approach to the measurement of change. *Psychological Bulletin, 92*, 726–748.

Weinfurt, K. P. (2000). Repeated measures analysis: ANOVA, MANOVA, and HLM. In L. G. Grimm & P. R. Yarnold (Eds.), *Reading and understanding more multivariate statistics* (pp. 317–361). Washington, DC: American Psychological Association.

Discriminant Function Analysis

Discriminant function analysis is a multivariate statistical technique "to predict group membership from a set of predictors. For example, can a differential prediction of diagnosis between a group of normal children, a group of children with learning disability, and a group with emotional disorder be made readily from a set of psychological test scores?" (Tabachnick & Fidell, 1996, p. 507).

Useful References

Betz, N. E. (1987). Use of discriminant analysis in counseling psychology research. *Journal of Counseling Psychology, 34*, 393–403.

Brown, M. T., & Wicker, L. R. (2000). Discriminant analysis. In H. E. A. Tinsley & S. D. Brown (Eds.), *Applied multivariate statistics and mathematical modeling* (pp. 209–235). San Diego, CA: Academic Press.

Tabachnick, B., & Fidell, L. C. (1996). *Using multivariate statistics.* New York: Harper Collins College Publishers.

Canonical Correlation Analysis (CCA)

The canonical correlation analysis is a multivariate statistical technique "that can be used to investigate relationships among two or more variable sets.

Each variable set usually consists of at least two variables" (Thompson, 2000; p. 285). For those who are familiar with multiple regression (i.e., predictions by several predictors on one criterion), canonical analysis can be understood as an extension of multiple regression with multiple criteria variables (i.e., dependent variables). For example, the canonical correlation analysis can be used when a researcher is interested in predicting the composite of two dependent variables to measure an individual's credit usage (i.e., number of credit cards held by the family, and average monthly dollar expenditures on all credit cards) by two independent variables (i.e., family size, and family income) (see the example by Hair, Anderson, & Tatham, 1987, p. 189).

Useful References

Campbell, K. T., & Taylor, D. L. (1996). Canonical correlation analysis as a general linear model: A heuristic lesson for teachers and students. *Journal of Experimental Education, 64,* 157–171.

Tabachnick, B., & Fidell, L. C. (1996). *Using multivariate statistics.* New York: Harper Collins College Publishers.

Thompson, B. (2000). Canonical correlation analysis. In L. G. Grimm & P. R. Yarnold (Eds.), *Reading and understanding more multivariate statistics* (pp. 285–316). Washington, DC: American Psychological Association.

QUALITATIVE RESULTS

*The Meaning-Making Process**

Say not, "I have found the truth," but rather, "I have found a truth." Say not, "I have found the path of the soul." Say rather, "I have met the soul walking upon my path." For the soul walks upon all paths. The soul walks not upon a line, neither does it grow like a reed. The soul unfolds itself, like a lotus of countless petals. (Gibran, 1923/1972, p. 55)

The great philosopher and poet Kahlil Gibran talked about self-knowledge in *The Prophet*. His words and wisdom may help authors understand the process of writing qualitative results. As we depicted in the chapter on qualitative research methods, doing qualitative research is a process of discovery. The interactive results between your own and participants' knowledge become the "treasure" you discover in the journey. The depths of the knowledge gained in this process may be "measureless" as it unfolds itself. Yet, what you need to do is not find out the ultimate "truth" of the phenomenon you investigate but, rather, present one of the "truths" you discover on the path of the journey.

The process of writing about the findings is both "artful" and "political" (Denzin & Lincoln, 1998). Writing can be viewed "as a method of inquiry that moves through successive stages of self-reflection. As a series of writings, the field-worker's texts flow from the field experience, through intermediate works, or later work, and finally to the research text that is the public presentation of the ethnographic and narrative experience" (p. 21). In accordance with the ontology of the qualitative research (there are multiple realities), there are numerous ways to interpret the materials obtained in the field. In this chapter, strategies to write the results are illustrated with various examples that utilize grounded theory, consensual qualitative research, or phenomenology/hermeneutics as strategies of inquiry. Finally, a conclusion and some tips for writing the results chapter are provided.

*This chapter co-authored with Yu-Wei Wang.

GROUNDED THEORY

As indicated in Chapter 8, the data of grounded theory can be analyzed by using Glaser's comparative approach (1992); the dimensionalizing, axial coding, and conditional matrix strategies suggested by Strauss and Corbin (1990); or dimensional analysis formulated by Schatzman (1991). You need to identify the approach you choose for your thesis or dissertation and write the results section in accordance with the particular approach selected. Following are two examples that used the frameworks developed by (a) Strauss and Corbin (1990) and Schatzman (1991) and (b) Glaser and Strauss (1992), respectively.

In the first example, the author identified the analytic approach that he utilized in the beginning. Then, he presented the dimensional analysis model for his grounded theory and outlined each category that emerged from his data in the beginning of the results chapter. Subsequently, he described each category with excerpts from the interviews to explain the meaning of the categories.

RESULTS SECTION OF A GROUNDED THEORY STUDY
THAT FOLLOWED STRAUSS AND CORBIN'S MODEL

The dimensional analysis model for experiences of gay and lesbian supervisees in counseling supervision, evolving from Strauss and Corbin's (1990) framework for grounded theory analysis and developed from the present investigation, is presented in Figure [13.1].

The model in Figure [13.1] is explained in this section with quotations from the data to illustrate each part of the model. Quotations used throughout the text will end with a catalogue of the code of the interview from which the statement was taken as well as the line numbers of the actual statement quoted in the text of this document. Brackets in the quotations either sanitize the quotes from revealing information that could be used to identify those participants or clarify instances when participants were referencing something they had talked about previously in the interview.

Emergent Core Categories: Central Issues
Distinctive to Gay and Lesbian Supervisees

The experiences of gay or lesbian individuals in counseling supervision (conditions dictated by the research question of this investigation) suggest two central issues as reported by participants: (a) questioning safety, and (b) reacting to GLB (gay, lesbian, and bisexual) clients. More specifically, the first category refers to supervisees feeling some degree of uncertainty about how their supervisors would react to their GLB orientations or to GLB-relevant materials raised during their supervision session. Ultimately, these experiences were raised with regard to the level of safety supervisees felt when being honest about themselves and discussing sexual orientation with their supervisors. The second category involves the experiences these supervisees had while working with GLB clients. When working with clients with this critical characteristic, these supervisees discussed having reactions to them unique to those they experienced with clients generally;

Context
- Timing of clinical experience
- Location of clinical experience
- Degree of outness and view of self as gay or lesbian

Core Categories/ Conditions
- Questioning safety
- Reacting to GLB clients

Intervening Condition
- Sexual orientation of the supervisor (heterosexual)

Strategies (Actions/Processes)
- Gauging the environment
- Gauging the supervisor
  - Determining supervisor's comfort level with GLB people and issues
  - Determining supervisor's knowledge of GLB people and issues

Consequences
- Ability to make assumptions regarding supervisor's response to sexual orientation prior to supervision
- Determination of "safety" in supervision
- Degree to which supervisee will discuss GLB-related concerns in supervision
- Perceived need to "educate my supervisor"

FIGURE **13.1**

Dimensional analysis model of gay and lesbian supervisees' strategies for supervision.

---

also, they expressed a desire for guidance and discussion regarding these reactions with their supervisors.

Questioning Safety

This research indicates feelings of uncertainty or reluctance regarding how a supervisor will react to minority sexual orientations as these supervisees entered into supervisory relationships. Most, but not all, of these supervisees experienced cautiousness about how their supervisors would respond to them because of their GLB status or GLB issues; all participants experienced a degree of uncertainty about their supervisors' response to their sexual orientations. Michael (all names used are pseudonyms) intimated the existence of this phenomenon in his interview statement about coming out to his supervisor:

Coming out is a part of being gay and it's something that you do for your entire life. It takes on special significance in the supervisory relationship because, you know, it's a power relationship. So, it's meaning that I need to, you know, basically, be vulnerable to a person that I don't know that well and who has power over me. (2-02-01: 16–23)

His thoughts are echoed throughout the data, although others more specifically labeled the feelings behind questioning how their supervisor would react to their being gay or lesbian. Kristin, who had not been out in a professional setting previous to supervision, stated:

So, I guess that the piece of that was not having been out in a professional situation. I was reluctant to be out in this new professional situation. I was just kind of, figuring out how that was going to work . . . figuring out where it was safe. (1-26-01: 416–423)

Rebecca talked about being out to her supervisor and the type of response she hoped to receive:

Knowing that it was a safe environment—it puts me, I want to use the phrase "on equal playing field" but I don't know if I really want to use that phrase. That it's— I didn't want to be an issue. I didn't want it to be anything special. I wanted to, you know, be just like the other people in the program who had heterosexual relationships or were single. Whatever their orientation was. I didn't want to be, "Oh that's a lesbian in the program." I didn't want to be singled out as having that as my sole identity. (1-20-01: 182–193)

Discussing her experience as a lesbian in supervision, Bridget commented:

I think going in initially I was a little uncertain about—you kind of have to feel your way out through every supervisor and, kind of, see where they're at with those kind of issues. (1-18-01: 6–10)

Each of these statements is exemplary of the questioning and uncertainty that these gay and lesbian supervisees experienced regarding how their supervisors would react to their sexual minority status. This uncertainty led to a strategy of gauging supervisors' responses to their own sexual orientations or to GLB-relevant materials; this strategy will be discussed in more detail later. (Rooney, 2000, pp. 95–98)

In this example, the author utilized the dimensional analysis model to illustrate his grounded theory and thus presented the categories along the following dimensions: Context, Core Categories/Conditions, Intervening Condition, Strategies, and Consequences. This provided a clear understanding of the various dimensions related to the phenomenon under investigation and depicted the relationships among those dimensions and categories. Before describing the various categories, the author also informed the readers how he was going to explain each part of the model. The information about the quotations helps the readers to learn how to use the quotations to understand the results.

Also, note how the author explained the core categories/conditions. He clearly defined each core category to lead the readers to understand the central dimension related to the phenomenon. Then, in explaining a specific category, the author provided a more detailed definition of the category in the beginning and then stated how common this experience was among the supervisees who were interviewed in the study. He also gave examples from several interviews to support the credibility of the category and finally explained how this core category (condition) is related to the strategy used by the supervisees. In short, this example illustrates the strategies used to write the results section of a grounded theory study.

Following is another example, which followed the model proposed by Glaser and Strauss (1967). The author studied how and what mothers of children of color learned about their White racial identity.

This section of the results chapter will focus upon highlighting the important themes derived from the interviews. The analysis and more lengthy descriptions are a part of the next chapter. The themes will be organized around the research questions(s): What is the learning for White women who have children of color as they become aware of their racial identity? Or what is the process of the learning about their racial identity and what is the content of that learning?

PROCESS—HOW THE LEARNING OCCURRED

The way that the women interviewed learned about their racial identity took many forms. A lot of them involved noticing the differences between their child's experience and their own. Their learning process includes concentrating participation in multicultural environments; becoming involved with more people of color; and, for some, learning how to handle discrimination. The security of the home environment in contrast to the differences and sometimes discrimination that get highlighted from contact in the external environment was also a factor in the learning processes. . . .

The Experience of Discrimination

The women in this study talked about discrimination on two levels. One involved looks, stares, comments or questions from people at large. This kind of prejudice I called interpersonal discrimination. Eleven of the 13 participants described incidents of this kind. The other 2 interviews, both mothers of Asian children, didn't discuss any incidents.

Some common examples of this kind of discrimination follow. One example is that four of the woman told stories that had the same refrain. It involved the experience of people not believing that they were the mothers of their child because of the difference in skin color. Carol typifies this phenomenon as she talks about her experiences with her first child, a Latino.

> CM: *I remember when C was really little, when he was a baby, the first time I went back to Tennessee, and I was carrying him on my lap in the airplane, that was the first time someone asked me, he goes, "What a beautiful child! Is that your child! Is that your child?" So, it always shocks me, but it happens all the time that people don't believe that I'm the mother. People don't expect that I'm the mother, because I look so different from them. That happened in Chile as well as here.*
>
> KS: *So, it's sort of like when you go outside—in the family, you don't even think about it.*
>
> CM: *Right.*
>
> KS: *But when you go in the outside world—*
>
> CM: *Right. Well, again, it probably happens less in Berkeley and Oakland than anywhere. I mean, people here are so accustomed to biracial families and children that it's not surprising. In—in Chile, it was surprising to people. And definitely, in Tennessee, people really—people would comment just, "Where are they from?" or "They have really beautiful color. Where are they from?" Because they don't look Black, and they don't look White. And in Tennessee, there aren't a lot of Latinos. Although there are more now. There are migrant workers in Tennessee and they're all over the East. It's not common.* (Stoddart, 1999, pp. 63–67)

In this example, the author first provided the readers with a road map for presenting her analytic results (i.e., The themes derived from the data would be organized according to the research questions, and the detailed analyses would be included in the discussion chapter). In addressing each research question, she summarized the themes related to the question and presented each theme separately with quotes from the interviews. In describing each theme, she also provided information on the number of participants who mentioned that particular type of experience so that the readers would know how many participants share the same experience. In addition to the sample of the results cited here, the author used another 12 pages to illustrate each theme. Then, she presented the grounded theory developed from this study in the next chapter. Following is a sample of the grounded-theory section:

> The basic, underlying premise to theory, derived from the women's stories themselves, is that a dialectic develops between the mother and partner or child of color around racial identity. As the White mothers become aware of the racial identity of their partner or child, it impacts the view of their own racial identity—and vice versa. This dialectic undergirds how the White mothers learn about their racial identity and what they eventually learn. A stronger dialectic leads to an increased differentiation around racial identity and the development of a more multifaceted awareness. How this process unfolds is the basis of this dissertation and will be covered in the following pages.
>
> With birth mothers the dialectical process begins with their relationship with their partner of color but intensifies once their child is born. For the White women with adopted children, the dialectic begins during the adoption proceedings and builds once the child is placed with them.
>
> This dialectical relationship can be visualized as follows.

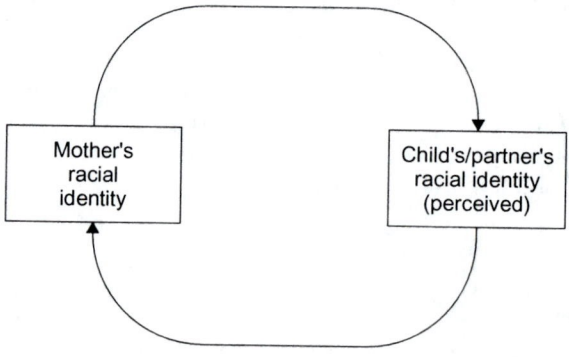

. . . As will be developed later in this theory, the incongruencies between the White woman's racial socialization and that which is experienced by her child of color are learning elements for this grounded theory. However, whatever the women's starting position in regard to racial identity, they are influenced on some level by their relationship to their partner/child of color. The development of her White racial identity is inextricably tied to the kind of exposure to and learning about the racial identity of her partner/child of color and the experiences they have together as a family . . .

Differentiation

This next aspect encompasses delineating the White women's own learning process about their racial identity in more details and outlining its characteristics. Let's get right to the diagram.

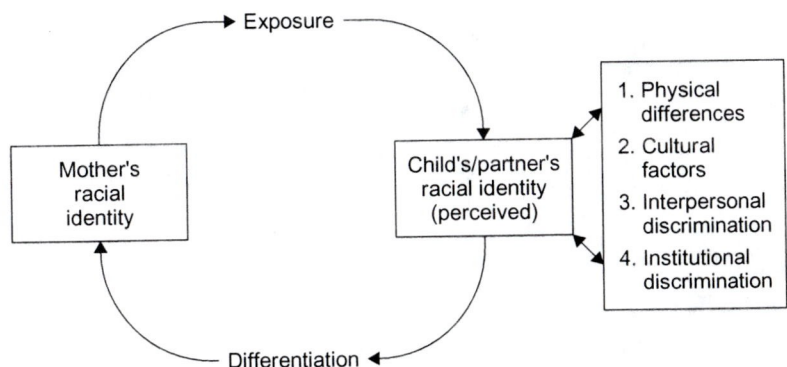

The element that we add now to the figure is differentiation. This is how the White women make sense of their experience of the child's/partner's racial identity. It involves the participants perceiving the differences in or between their socialization and their child's or partner's. It also implies a change or alteration in the White women's racial identity because of their exposure to and experience with their child's racial identity.

. . . The amount of differentiation about racial identity varied among the participants and will be detailed into three "stages" below. The first group had a limited exposure to the world of color. This group will be called Nondiscriminators. The second segment, called Active Differentiators, took more action and change about their exposure and experience and were more heavily involved in making comparisons and distinctions about their White racial identity. They seemed to be in more of an active stage of learning. Integrators were the final group of participants in terms of differentiation and had a more multifaceted view of the racial identity of themselves, their family, and others at large. The three stages on our ever-evolving chart would look like the following:

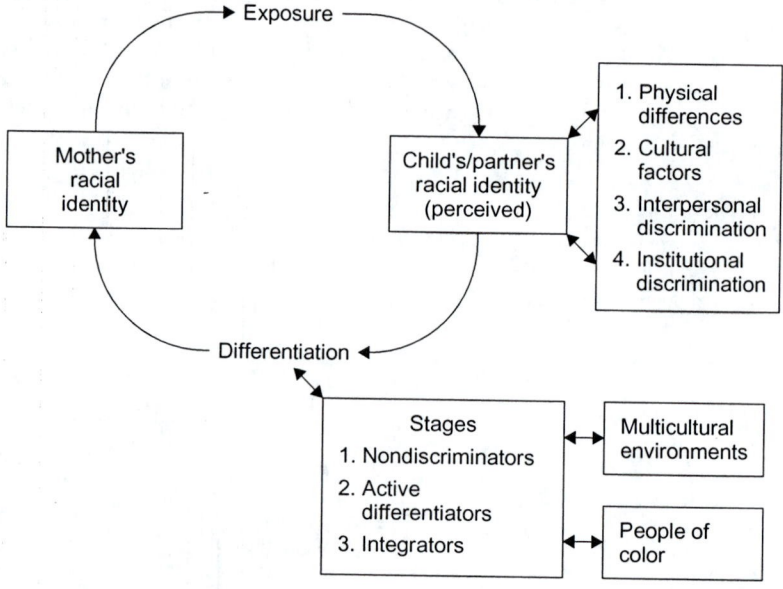

(Stoddart, 1999, pp. 80–91)

The author went on to describe her grounded theory in another 70 pages of text. We encourage you to refer to the dissertation for more details. As indicated in the example, the theory is grounded in the data. The author utilized figures to depict the dynamic relationships between mother's racial identity and child's/partner's racial identity. Readers could easily see how the theory evolved over time.

CONSENSUAL QUALITATIVE RESEARCH

The results from the consensual qualitative research (CQR) strategy are most often presented following the guidelines listed in Hill, Thompson, and Williams (1997). The categories that emerged from the cross-analysis are often separated into three types (general, typical, and variant) and summarized in a table. Following is an example from a CQR study that investigated the meaning of career and relevant concepts for adult American Indians:

DESCRIPTION OF THE GENERAL FINDINGS IN A CQR STUDY

Analysis of the participants' interviews generated a variety of categories, with some variation occurring between the participants who had attended or completed college and those who had attended or completed high school. Within two domains—meaning of career and success is a collective experience—the cate-

TABLE 13.1	CATEGORIES WITHIN THE DOMAINS OF MEANING OF CAREER AND SUCCESS IS A COLLECTIVE EXPERIENCE	

Domain	Category	Frequency
Meaning of career	Lifelong endeavor	Typical
	Pursuit of a chosen goal	Typical
	Promoting American Indian traditions	Variant
Success is a collective experience	Contribute to well-being of others	Typical
	(a) American Indian community or tribe	Typical
	(b) Family members	Typical
	(c) The next generation	Typical
	Personal satisfaction	Variant
	Material gain	Variant
	Explicit rejection of material gain as an indicator of success	Variant

gories were consistent across the entire sample, with educational level appearing to not make a difference in the participants' beliefs and experiences. For the remaining three domains—supportive factors, obstacles, and living in two worlds—unique categories emerged between the two groups. The results presented below [sic] are organized around the domains. Categories that arose in fewer than three cases were dropped from further consideration, as they were not considered sufficiently stable. (Juntunen et al., 2001, pp. 277–279)

In the preceding example, the tables help the readers to understand the results and inform the readers about how many different categories emerged within each domain and how common these experiences were among the American Indians who participated in the study. In particular, the authors found that the participants with different educational levels had similar as well as different experiences in their career journey. Thus she grouped the categories according to the commonness of the experiences in Table 13.1 and then also separated the two groups in Table 13.2 to reflect the different experiences between the participants with postsecondary education and those with secondary education. Finally, the authors stated under what situations the categories were excluded from the findings and the rationale for setting the criteria. As Hill et al. (1997) suggested eliminating the categories that only applied to one or two cases, the authors informed the reader that they complied with Hill et al.'s suggestion and decided to eliminate the categories that applied to less than three cases.

In the following example, the authors further explained one of the domains that emerged from the findings. Due to space limitations in this chapter, only a sample of the results is included here. Notice that the authors first explained the typical categories (more common experiences); they told the readers how many participants shared the same experience and provided more detailed information on the meaning of the experience for the participants. As

TABLE
13.2

TABLE 13.2 CATEGORIES WITHIN THE DOMAINS OF SUPPORTIVE FACTORS, OBSTACLES, AND LIVING IN TWO WORLDS, BY EDUCATIONAL LEVEL

Domain	Secondary Education Participants		Postsecondary Education Participants	
	Category	Frequency	Category	Frequency

Supportive factors	High value on education	General	Family influences
			  (a) Family support
			  (b) Being a provider
			Sobriety
				Typical
				Typical
				Variant
				Typical

Obstacles	Lack of family support	Typical	Discrimination Alienation from tribal community Restrictions of reservation	Typical Variant Variant
Living in two worlds	Two distinct and distant worlds	Typical	Moving between two worlds Creating holistic third world	Typical Variant

mentioned earlier, the categories that only applied to one or two cases were dropped from the categories. However, the authors still noted their uniqueness and provided some explanation of those particular barriers. Although these barriers were not found in more than two cases, they may reveal some important individual differences. Finally, the authors included quotations from the interviews to illustrate each category. These quotations helped the readers to understand the meaning of and variations within each category for the participants.

EXAMPLE: DESCRIPTION OF THE DOMAINS AND CATEGORIES IN A CQR STUDY

Obstacles

A typical category for obstacles among the participants who had attended or completed high school was a lack of support from significant others, relevant for 4 of the 7 participants in this group. This lack of support sometimes occurred passively, as neither family members nor school personnel discussed career opportunities or exposed the participants to the ideas of work when they were growing up. Two female participants reported that their male partners actively discouraged them from working or pursuing an education. Although they were not mentioned in sufficient number to be included as a category, several other specific barriers were noted: being a single parent and a lack of resources for child care (2 participants), domestic violence, alcohol use, and oppression (1 participant each). These respondents generally described the ways in which they had overcome these barriers. However, the individual who identified oppression as a barrier was less hopeful. In his words, "We never had opportunities to have careers, I always felt. They (White people) always hold you down" (Participant 7).

Among participants with postsecondary education, discrimination was a typical category for obstacles, connected to the career experience by 9 of the 11 participants. Six participants had experienced discrimination toward American Indians from the majority culture, occurring in work, educational, and other settings. One woman with a long career history, referring to a powerful board position she had held previously, said, "I was really the token Indian that they had. I was being used as a token Indian" (Participant 10).

Work-related discrimination was also identified in attitudes colleagues held about affirmative action and related programs. One woman, who worked in a predominantly male career, reported, "They more or less hired me because I was an Indian and I was a woman" (Participant 9). However, she felt that the discrimination she experienced was due more to being a woman in a male-dominated field than it was to being American Indian.

. . . A variant category of alienation also emerged for people who left the tribal community and returned. For 3 participants, their decision to leave the reservation to pursue education created a barrier to their desire to return home to work and live. Some participants felt ridiculed for their achievements by family and neighbors.

[Referring to friends at home on the reservation] *You see them at home . . . [they] sit around at home, and that's kind of bad, and then they criticize the people who do try to reach their goals . . . [call them] "wannabes" and stuff like that.* (Participant 14)

Others felt like they did not, or would not, fit in again when they returned home . . .

In some instances, participants who saw the reservation as placing limits on the ability of individuals to leave, which may in turn lead to resentment toward people who do ultimately leave, also expressed this sense of alienation. One person, who had lived both on and off the reservation, expressed his concerns as follows:

I noticed it is harder to go to school there [on the reservation] and be productive. They [young people on the reservation] don't look forward to the future as being something to look forward to. On the reservations, I think that there's definitely a set of circumstances where people are not encouraged to go out. (Participant 17)

. . . For a small number of participants, the feeling of alienation and discrimination from the dominant culture was a significant factor in their overall life satisfaction. Others recognized discrimination and indicated their belief that it was more harmful to the source of the racism than to the target.

I'm not going to say the whole society's racist, because that's not the case. I've seen individuals that are and actually, I feel sad for them, because they narrow their experiences so greatly by that. (Participant 11) (Juntunen et al., 2001, pp. 280–281)

PHENOMENOLOGY/HERMENEUTICS

As discussed in Chapter 8, researchers who conduct a phenomenological or hermeneutic study typically present the essence of the participants' lived experiences through exhaustive descriptions. The exhaustive descriptions provide the readers an understanding of "what happened" and "how the phenomenon was experienced by the participants." Within these descriptions, various themes that emerge from the data are presented with quotations from the data. In this section, two examples are provided to illustrate various ways to present the findings in a phenomenological or a hermeneutic study.

In a phenomenological or hermeneutic study, the authors usually provide a very detailed profile for each participant in the results chapter, which includes general background information, observations of the researcher, and raw data. These profiles help the readers to obtain a sense of the "whole" experience of the participants. Also, after the readers review the findings, they can always refer back to individual profiles to evaluate the credibility of the findings.

After providing the descriptions of the participants, a general overview of the results should be depicted. In the next paragraphs, examples from a phenomenological study will be introduced followed by examples from a hermeneutic study. Consider the first example from a phenomenological study on the resilience of the elderly:

Collectively, these are the results of 880 years of life and living. The participants' phenomenological perceptions and meanings of resilience have been explored. These results are the researcher's best understanding of their views, which integrate all of the data collected and the methods of analysis utilized.

The participants' responses to the broad questions from Chapter I, which guided this study, are summarized in this chapter. There was a great amount of overlap across those questions and the participants' responses, which became apparent through both manual and software analysis. Therefore, participants' responses were categorized into the topical areas of resilience that are presented here.

Themes of the participants' major life transitions and the coping skills that aided them in overcoming them are summarized. Participants' holistic perceptions of resilience are presented, including social, spiritual, emotional, and physical aspects. The emerging patterns of internal characteristics of resilience and the participants' values, which may influence resilience, are summarized. Themes of the participants' responses concerning innate and developmental aspects of resilience are presented. The participants' resilience definition themes have been synthesized into a resulting definition. A brief summary concludes this chapter. (Adams, 1997, pp. 181–182)

In this example, the author summarized the approach he utilized to organize the findings. Note that he also outlined all of the themes that emerged from the data. The accounts of the themes collectively provided the readers an exhaustive description of the phenomenon of interest. Thoroughly describing the similar and different themes across the participants constitutes an important part of the results chapter. To demonstrate how to provide this type of exhaustive description, examples for illustrating thematic similarity and differences that emerged in Adam's (1997) study are presented next:

COPING SKILLS THAT AIDED PARTICIPANTS IN OVERCOMING

The participants identified numerous coping skills that aided them in overcoming major life transitions. Childhood memories of others who modeled coping behaviors was a major theme that surfaced. These role models were described as offering expectations and discipline, nurturance, and encouragement toward the participants' independence. Such findings are consistent with the research literature on childhood resilience (Werner, 1989; Werner & Smith, 1982).

Participants thematically described that the maintenance of oneself with care, respect, and discipline helped them to cope. A sense of identify, self-esteem, and personal power were important characteristics. This is consistent with the professional literature. The literature implied that preserving one's self-identify and psychological well-being is primary (Lieberman & Tobin, 1983).

Prayer, meditation, and spiritual guidance were considered a strength-evoking theme for the participants. There was a strong emphasis by the participants on keeping worry to a minimum and accepting life as it is. Participants' advice for coping was to remain responsible for what is within one's power and let go of what one is powerless over. This is certainly an example of the strengths model suggested in the literature (Jordaan, Meyers, Layton, & Morgan, 1968; Super, 1955; Wister, 1990).

All of the participants strongly credited involvement in their work, purpose, desires, goals, and concerns as a primary coping mechanism. Keeping one's mind active and making independent choices were thematically reported by the participants as crucial in maintaining self-determinism. The power of one's will and commitment were suggested as important tools for overcoming.

> Care and love from significant relationships (e.g., family, friends, partners, teachers) were thematically described as crucial in overcoming difficult transitions. A sense of the interdependence with one's community was an important theme. Feeling valued, wanted, and purposeful were crucial to the participants' desires to overcome life transitions and focus their hope on the future. A strong theme of generativity, concern for future generation, surfaced as important to participants' sense of self-fulfillment. The theme that social roles are important to coping is consistent with the professional literature. (Adams, 1997, pp. 184–186)

In this description of the theme *coping,* the author summarized his observations of the data and presented the common experiences of those participants. Any consistency between the findings and the existing literature was also reported. In the following paragraphs, the author further compared the differences across the participants:

> Although individual differences are always an important consideration, the thematic differences between the participants' responses are presented here. Participants acknowledged that they had not previously contemplated about specific aspects of themselves that became apparent through the interviews, while other participants had acutely developed those same aspects. Marriage was experienced by some participants as positive and supportive, enhancing resilience, while others described marriage as an experience that tore them down, inhibiting resilience.
>
> The participants described various relationships with the deceased as a means to cope with the loss. Some participants continued expressive communication with their dead loved ones. Some appeared to find resolve about significant deaths while others carried great emotional burdens. Relative to dead parents, the difference in grief resolve between the participants who were orphaned as children and those who were orphaned as adults was substantial. Participants who lost parents during childhood presented with difficulty adjusting to that change and had long histories of unresolved grief. Those who lost parents as adults were much more accepting of those losses and appeared to have the coping skills necessary to adjust.
>
> Negative and positive childhood experiences were strongly emphasized by participants and continued to affect their meanings and perceptions throughout their lives. This was most apparent in the various emotional undercurrents throughout the interviews. Some participants described long histories of remorse and resentment concerning childhood shame, abuse, and neglect. Participants reported still feeling anger, sadness, depression, joy, and contentment relative to their childhood experiences. Some participants had experienced depression and desperation, while other participants reported never having felt depressed or desperate.
>
> Some participants clarified a vast difference between what they considered as spiritual and what they considered as religious. Others described the religious and spiritual as synonymous.
>
> The female participants identified more strongly with their roles in the workforce than did the males. The male participants identified more with their roles in personal and social relationships than their roles in the workforce. (Adams, 1997, pp. 196–197)

In this example, the author contrasted the different themes that emerged from the experiences of the participants (e.g., relationship with their partners, childhood experiences, and gender differences) and emphasized their relationships to the phenomenon of interest (i.e., resilience). This helps the reader to obtain more in-depth understanding of the phenomenon. You are also encouraged to present quotations from the interviews to illustrate the differences. Although not presented here, a summary of the results is typically provided at the end of the description of themes (see Adams, 1997, for an example).

Next is an example of the results section from a hermeneutic study. The author presented an outline of the results chapter in the beginning of the chapter:

> The results chapter of this paper contains seven sections. Section A contains a description of the sample including basic demographic data. Section A also contains four general categories into which the sample was grouped; it was felt that these categories, more than any other factors about the participants, accounted for the greater part of the variance among the interviews and so seemed to provide natural organizational divisions. These categories are Age, Gender, In Treatment or Not In Treatment, and "Psychological Mindedness." This last category related to the general depth of self-reflective thinking exhibited by the participants as well as their willingness to discuss sensitive and potentially painful issues in an open and cogent fashion. These categories were discussed further in the thematic analysis sections and were considered in presenting the significant contextual data in *Section F.*
>
> To investigate the impact of adoption on the adolescent participants, and to provide greater clarity in the interview process and in its interpretation, a number of research questions were developed (pp. 71–72) out of four general areas of inquiry (p. 25). After the completion of the interviews and the organization of the data, these research questions were further distilled into four Thematic Research Propositions that specifically addressed the objectives of this study and encapsulated a number of the salient themes that emerged from the interviews. From this point forward I have referred to the Thematic Research Propositions as TRPs (i.e., TRP #1, TRP #2, TRP #3, and TRP #4).
>
> Thematic Research Propositions 1, 2, 3, and 4 were explicated in Sections B, C, D, and E, respectively. Each of these sections contains 5 subsections (numbered 1–5); subsection 1 presented a concise summary of the TRP, subsection 2 contains a statement of the number of the participants who made comments relevant to the TRP, subsection 3 presented the thematic analysis of the interview data that illustrated the specific TRP, subsection 4 presented an analysis of any sharply divergent or contradictory responses, and subsection 5 presented or restated exemplars, which were particularly strong or representative examples of that section's theme. Due to its length, Section D also included, in list form, the major distinguishing elements of TRP #3.
>
> In subsection 3, the participants' narratives were examined for references, stories, and statements that were interpreted as either consistent or not consistent with the themes expressed by the specific TRP. These interpretations were presented and illustrated using quotes from the interviews; furthermore, these quotes were conceptualized by reference to where they occurred in the interviews, i.e., whether or not they were offered by the participant in response to a specific question on the Interview Schedule (Appendix A). If they occurred in response to a specific question, I summarized or restated the actual interview

questions in order to provide a more complete context for the participant's response. Further information was also given where helpful, such as the emotional tone of the participant's response, or whether the comment was tangential, suggested by the researcher, or spontaneously offered. (Abbott, 1999, pp. 75–76)

In the preceding example, the author very clearly described how he analyzed the data and organized his results sections. This type of presentation helps the readers to understand how the findings addressed each of the initial research questions and the research objectives. Following are examples from each of the five subsections for one of the TRPs. For this TRP, the author used 18 pages to explain all of the subsections. Due to limited space in this chapter, sometimes only parts of each subsection were cited to illustrate how to present this type of results. You are encouraged to read the original dissertation for more details.

DESCRIPTION OF THE THEMATIC RESEARCH PROPOSITION (SUBSECTION #1)

TRP #1 proposed that adopted persons, and adolescents in particular, have a sense of not "being-at-home," "rootlessness," or in general of "not-belonging" that was disturbing to them and related to some aspect of their adoption. Illustrations of this proposition included statements the participants expressed about the "meaninglessness of life," a sense of emptiness, or a general sense for the instability of relationships, their own sense of self, and human being in general, depending on the context in which the statement was made. Expressions of feeling lost or alone in the world evinced this theme, as did the contrary expression of being "found" (e.g., through a search for biological parents).

The background for this proposition is the use of the hyphenated term "not-at-homeness" proposed by Martin Heidegger in describing the authentic condition of Dasein (see Theoretical Framework, pp. 56–59). For the purpose of clarity in the presentation of the data, participants' statements were contextualized and related to Heidegger's hermeneutic insights through a brief description. A more complete explication of the relationship of the participants' statements and Heidegger's use of this term was reserved for the discussion chapter. (Abbott, 1999, pp. 85–86)

In the first subsection of the TRP, the author briefly described the proposition and the origin of this proposition. He also informed the reader how he would present data related to this proposition and referred the reader to a later chapter for the discussion on the relationships between the findings and existing literature, which was used to generate the proposition.

NUMERICAL RESULTS (SUBSECTION #2)

Of the group of participants who were currently in treatment (64%), or who had had significant psychological treatment in the recent past, seven of seven (100%) made statements or discussed situations that were interpreted as strong or moderately strong evidence of the existence and importance of TRP#1. In the non-treatment group, which comprised 36% of the participants, two of four (50%) made similar statements. Three participants also made comments or gave answers that indicated that this theme was not salient; of these, two were from the non-treatment group and one was in treatment. Obviously, one participant made contradictory statements at different points in the interview. Since contradictions such as these did occasionally occur, these statements or excerpts of a participant's narrative were included in Section #4 below [sic]. (Abbott, 1999, p. 86)

In essence, in this example, the author provided some numerical information to help the reader understand the pervasiveness of the theme across the participants.

EXPLICATION OF THE THEMATIC
RESEARCH PROPOSITION (SUBSECTION #3)

This TRP was richly expressed by a wide variety of comments and stories. A sense of various participants' feelings of "not fitting in," "not belonging," "being a stranger," feeling "unconnected" or "unnatural," or "not having a real home," or having "missing parts" or a "hole inside," and even of "not existing" were frequently repeated. Although some of these feelings might be thought of as characteristic of adolescence in general, or as in the case below [sic], of children of divorce, when placed in the context of the interviews, their relevance to the experience of adoption became obvious. As an introduction to this section, one participant described her childhood home in a way that lent a particular poignancy to the experience of this theme:

I felt like in the basement that my mom and I lived in, like a real cold, like eerie feeling kind of. Because, like it was . . . I mean, just even like the set up of it, like there was like a staircase that led to nowhere. You know what I mean? Like in the middle of our apartment there was a staircase and it went up to the top floor, but they kind of put like a thing like right there. It was just weird. I don't know. And I was home a lot by myself at that point. And just real cold. And like . . . I don't know. I know my mom loved me, but I just remember my room like smelling and like . . . cold, like, bare. I don't know. And like my mom got me kittens and stuff to play with, but still was . . . I don't like it. It was cold and eerie. My mom tried to make it nice, but it wasn't. So. The next house that we rented—same thing; kind of cold and empty and . . . that's a better word, just empty. Like, not much life to the place at all. And my dad's . . . well, my dad's apartment was always like, kind of like creepy and eerie and gross. I mean, it's, like, physically dirty. His apartment. I mean, he doesn't live there now, but it was like gross. It was dirty.
(CE, f, 18, Tx, L, E, p. 13)

This comment was a response to questions about how adoption affected her as a child or her sense of childhood in general. For CE it mattered very little where she and her mother physically resided; each new place felt as empty and "un-homelike" as the last. CE linked this directly to adoption later in the interview by using some of the same words to describe her early feeling for herself, calling herself an "outcast" and explicitly discussing the sense that something was "missing" from her or her life (p. 14):

There's part of me that doesn't understand why she gave me up. Umm, I think . . . I just fight a lot in my head, like, she was 15, you know, she had to give me up. She couldn't have a kid. But there's a part of me that's just like, well, why did you do that. Like, why did you go and like, get pregnant and do all that shit. And, like, just give me away. Like I'm some, life gift or some, lie, some object, like . . . umm . . . I don't know. I just have . . . I get angry a lot of times, like . . . I mean, I think a bigger part of me is just sad that, like, I don't know her, like there is a part of me that's missing . . . I feel that there is a part that's like, a hole in my heart that, umm, is gone. (CE, f, 18, Tx, L, E, pp. 16–17)

She was struggling to understand and accept that her biological mother had few choices in regard to "giving her up"; however, the anguish in her voice was unmistakable, as was the clear indication that there was a sense of "something lacking" or of the existence of an emptiness that felt internal and that she carried from place to place. There was, in fact, a "hole" or emptiness in what appeared to be the most central and "essential" part of her; the very heart of things was plagued by this lack or emptiness.

Earlier in this study it was proposed that adoption seems to "rip the veil" off the fiction that one's experience of life, the meaning of being, and the nature of one's relation to other persons (even family) is given and unproblematic (p. 22). This quote from CE was, I believe, a fair indication of this process and established a linkage with Heidegger's discussion of the existential consequences for human beings when we are jarred or fall out of the ordinary and come face to face with profound challenges to our essentialist notions about reality or Being.

. . . Similar expressions of feeling "outcast" or like a "stranger" in the world came up for 8 of 11 (73%) participants. Another example of the theme of "nonbelonging" occurred during the interview with SM, whose responses implied that he had felt like a stranger in his home, that he felt different from everyone else, and like an outcast in general. . . .

In the feeling of being an outcast and in the sense that something was missing from his self/life, SM's concerns were interpreted as similar to CE's, though he downplayed them to some degree. However, it also seems clear that part of the solution to his alienation or estrangement from others was, in fact, meeting his biological mother. In having had this opportunity, he differed significantly from CE at least in terms of the emotional context of his (verbally similar) comments.

The difference in the meaning of these ideas for these two participants showed up more clearly in the different levels of psychological distress displayed by CE and SM. Therefore, this was more a matter of understanding the consequences of these issues and the conclusions various participants had drawn from them, i.e., [sic] the effect these adoption-related themes had on their functioning and self-esteem. This is an issue that pertained to TRP #4 and as such was more thoroughly addressed in Section E and in the discussion of the results. (Abbott, 1999, pp. 86–90)

The author continued, using another six pages to explain the similar theme revealed in the interviews with some other participants. In addition, he also noted the differences across the participants. The author did a very good job of presenting representative quotes that are followed by his interpretative process and outcomes. This writing strategy provides the reader with a very clear picture of how interpretations are made based on the data. Note that he used the first two quotes to demonstrate that the same theme was observed at different parts of the interview with the same participant. Furthermore, the author paid special attention to not only the verbal content of the interviews but also the emotional context of the participants' comments. He stressed the importance of understanding the various meanings of the same theme (e.g., "not-belongingness") assumed by the participants.

Following the explication of the themes, the author discussed the contradictions that appeared in the data, as indicated in the following example:

Contradictions (Subsection #4)

There were certain notable responses throughout several of the interviews that appeared to contradict the importance of various aspects of TRP #1 in participants' lives. One salient contradiction came from JA who, though he appeared to be affected by adoption, particularly in terms of abandonment anxieties and loyalty issues, also said that he understood why he was placed and that he really felt quite happy about both the decision and the outcomes. In fact, despite JA's many anxieties about the search and reunion process he was contemplating, telling his biological parents that things were better was identified by him as a primary goal of the search. Again being sensitive to the feelings of the other, he also wanted to express his gratitude.

> I just want to go there just to kind of tell them that thank you, that you let me be adopted and just I'm not mad at you guys because you had to do what you had to do. Because it doesn't bother me. Because I'm glad she let me get adopted at her young age. Because it set a better life for me and maybe a better life for her. And then she let me be adopted and not have to, like, drag me though like all the drug thing and alcohol thing, and, and having a bad life. Because I think about that. . . It worked out great. (JA, m, 14, NonTx, L, E, p. 18)

JA went on to express a number of reasons why he believed he was able to accept being adopted fairly easily, and to turn his anxieties into more positively framed emotions. The contextual and intrafamilial factors he listed were important to look at and were examined in Section F and the discussion section. For the purpose of this section it was enough to note that JA had struggled with some difficult issues similar to those of other more troubled adoptees, and had either avoided or transformed some of the worst possibilities into a more positive outlook. (Abbott, 1999, pp. 96–97)

The author went on to use another three pages to explain the other contradictions that were revealed in the interviews with two other participants. Note in the example cited that the author described the contradiction that he observed in the interview with JA and then he presented his understanding of the contradiction. From a hermeneutic perspective, any contradiction needs to be understood from a broader perspective. As the author stated, other factors, such as the context, may have led to the verbal contradiction. Thus, authors should present their interpretation of any such contradictions and use data (e.g., quotes from the interviews) to support their reasoning.

After providing descriptions of the themes, numerical results, explication of the themes, and any contradictions in the data, authors often present exemplars of the theme:

Exemplar(s) of the Thematic Research Proposition

TR made a comment that could serve as an exemplar for both the "emptiness" theme and the notion of "not-belonging" in their most extreme manifestations. TR was discussing how "not-at-home" she felt with her adoptive parents, now divorced, and she remarked, "I just have ongoing dreams about it. Every time I think about my dad and my mom at home and wanting to go home it always ties in to my real family. And kind of that I'd like to know who I really am" (TR, f, 16, Tx, L, G, p. 8). I asked her about the connection between going home and knowing "who she is" and where this self-understanding would develop if it were to occur; TR is not sure, but replied, "Yeah. Well, it's not in (her current home residence), I know that. I have no idea where she is; I have no idea who she is. Nothing. I guess it's just kind of a fear . . . of . . . being" (p. 8).

The pronoun "she" in the above [sic] passage could refer to either her conception of her true self or to her biological mother. It was not clear which TR intended. What does seem clear, however, is that there was a very strong connection for TR between knowing her biological mother, knowing where home would be, and in knowing who she "really" was as a person. Without having the first two questions answered, she was unable to generate an adequate or satisfying answer to the third.

Her use of the word "nothing" was also very striking, as was the look on her face when she said it; she appeared to be very distant or removed from the room and looked intensely self-absorbed at this moment. The word itself was chilling; it had the quality of a decision or of a carefully considered and irrevocable judgment. She seemed to be pronouncing judgment on her experience, herself, and on existence in general at the same time.

I initially believed that she was going to explain this "fear" or problem as a fear of something specific. However, she said "fear of being" and then seemed to weigh this and then consciously decided to leave it at that. This passage reflected her experience of "non-being" and her sense for Being in itself on a generalized, or background level, rather than expressing a specific and more psychological fear or concern. This notion was to some degree confirmed a few moments later when she responded to a murmur of sympathy on my part with:

Yeah. It's a big hole. It's like . . . I'm not even really existing. I mean, I've had several thoughts of killing myself. I don't express all of them because here if you say well, I'm going to kill myself they take away your shoelaces, your belt, everything. (TR, f, 16, Tx, L, G, p. 8)

This was the logical next step: if she was nothing, if there was "nothing," then death or, in this case self-eradication, would bring congruence to her inner experience and her judgment about the existential state of affairs she found in the world around her. This was a very clear rendition of what TRP #1 was designed to illustrate, albeit in an extreme form; that is, the idea that there are connections at a very primal level between the experience of some adopted persons and what Heidegger meant by Dasein's "not-at-homeness."

TR expressed the equation in the following fashion: (1) I do not know who or what I am in any clear, certain, or unproblematic (essentialist) manner, i.e., I do not know who I am or where I belong, and am therefore "homeless" in the sense of being adrift/not belonging or not being "at-home-in-the-world"; (2) this "not-knowing" is linked to her historical dislocation from her biological family (mother); (3) since TR doesn't feel that she has a place in the world, this had led to a profound alienation and despair. To the degree that TR can understand that this experience is, as Heidegger had argued, an authentic encounter with Dasein's primordial ontological state or reality, to that same degree she may be able to face and overcome this despair. However, everything in the context around TR contests this along positivistic lines (our heritage of Cartesian modernism); and, therefore, (4) this state feels intolerable/unbearable and hopelessly pathological to her; death is the only option she can think of that would establish as a visible, undeniable, and concrete fact of her "true" experience, i.e., of her own "essential/essentialist" non-existence.

Also, it seemed likely that this inherently difficult experience was made more difficult in part because of her age and because of the lack of understanding and support offered by her parents and/or significant mentors in her life. There were important clinical and parenting implications to be gleaned from TR's struggle with this sense of alienation and despair. Given this, and that this was only the briefest sketch of an interpretation of TR's experience, this exemplar in particular is further explicated in the discussion section of this study, pp. 194–196. (Abbott, 1999, pp. 100–102)

The exemplar often provides readers a holistic understanding of a representative case for a particular theme. Note that the author integrated both the verbal and nonverbal contents into his interpretation of the theme (i.e., "emptiness") in one participant's experience. The author also presented his initial impression of the data and how that was changed throughout the interview. This helps the readers to understand how his interpretations evolved in the interview process. Next, the author presented his reasoning process and conclusion for the "fear of being" experienced by the participant. This demonstrates how to engage in a hermeneutic dialogue with the data, the interviewees, and the researcher him/herself. Finally, the author stated that the contribution of his findings to developing clinical and parenting interventions would be presented in the discussion chapter. (Readers who want to apply the findings of this exemplar in their practice could refer to that section for more details.)

CONCLUSIONS

Because most of the qualitative research findings are written in a narrative fashion, which is often different from your previous research training, we suggest you seek additional writing skills to enhance your ability to develop and elaborate your narratives in a clear, interesting, logical, and even artful way in order to most accurately depict the findings. In general, authors conducting qualitative research rely primarily on language, not numbers, to depict the phenomenon of interest or the lived experiences of the participants. Good writing can make the data come "alive." You may find it helpful to study creative writing techniques or read literature. Likewise, it may be helpful to form a reading and writing group where group members can exchange readings (e.g., qualitative research or literature) and provide feedback to each other's writing. Finally, the reading and writing group can serve as a source of emotional support for you because writing sometimes can be a lonely process and some of the research topics may be very emotionally laden (i.e., child abuse). Having social support from others who are writing a qualitative study or who are interested in the same topic may help you to overcome fears and obstacles related to writing (e.g., writing blocks).

THE DISCUSSION

Making the Data Sing

Arriving at the point of your thesis or dissertation when you have analyzed all your data and are now ready to write can be a very exciting time. The discussion chapter is where you can reflect on your findings and help the reader understand the significance and implications of your project. This chapter first discusses the affective reactions you may have when you arrive at this point in your research. We discuss the three most common reactions that can create barriers for students: (a) running out of steam, (b) doubting the significance of the research, and (c) fear of making their work public. Next, we describe the seven elements that a discussion chapter should contain. Throughout this section are examples from other students' discussion chapters that can serve as models. Finally, a Checklist for Chapter 5 of the Thesis or Dissertation is included to assess the completeness of your discussion chapter.

AFFECTIVE REACTIONS

Throughout the various tasks of a thesis or dissertation, students typically experience a range of feelings. These have been explored throughout this book. Similarly, at the point of writing their discussion chapter, students typically experience various affective reactions that may hinder progress on writing this chapter or limit its quality. While having emotional reactions is a normal part of the process, you should be aware of these reactions and develop strategies to keep them from derailing the writing process. Three of the most common feelings are described in the following section.

Running Out of Steam

Probably the most common reaction students have at this point is running out of steam. Students have typically expended a great amount of time and energy on conducting their research up to this point. The process may have taken longer and been fraught with more obstacles than expected. Perhaps they have had difficulty analyzing their data and writing their results chapter. By the time they arrive at the point of writing their discussion chapter, they may feel that they just want the project to be completed. Thus, in our experience, students often shortchange this final chapter. Although this practice may be understandable, this chapter is critical to a reader's perception of the importance and quality of the whole research project. Thus, you must find ways to keep your focus for this last but critical chapter of your thesis or dissertation.

Doubting the Significance of the Research

Another very common reaction from students at this stage of their research is doubting its significance. Sometimes students have been disappointed with their findings; perhaps the findings have fallen short of their expectations. They may have hypothesized certain findings and become personally invested in proving certain things; nonsignificant findings or findings that are contrary to what was expected may seem disappointing. At times like these, you should remember Carl Rogers' simple but powerful statement: The data are always friendly. Thus, no matter what you find in your research and whether or not it is expected or contrary to predictions, the data are important to the knowledge base. Thus, rather than feeling disappointed about the findings and thus perhaps avoiding writing the discussion chapter, you should view all data as friendly and try to understand and discuss the results.

Fear of Making Your Work Public

The discussion chapter signals the end of the project. It also indicates that you will soon need to "defend" your research to the larger scholarly community. This can bring about anxiety. Will your research be considered important? Will your committee think that your project meets the requirements for a thesis or dissertation? Will people quarrel with your results or criticize various decisions you have made in the design or analysis of the research? These questions are very common ones for researchers to experience. Even seasoned scholars may have these concerns. Just remember that research is, by nature, a public activity. Although research may be designed and conducted in a private fashion, the purpose of research is to build a public knowledge base and, thus, the results of research are ultimately for public consumption. As such, they are subject to criticism and skepticism, as well as praise and adulation. Remember also that all research is flawed in some ways. The perfect study is nonexistent. All research is a trade-off; building strength in one methodological area may bring weakness to another. Thus, make the best decisions you can throughout the research process and realize there will be limitations to your research that you will delineate in the discussion chapter.

Most Important Elements of a Discussion Chapter

Although the elements that constitute a discussion chapter vary, some key elements are consistent. In this section, we describe global elements that need to be integrated throughout the discussion chapter: (a) the "so what?" factor, and (b) staying close to the data. Next, seven elements are presented that should be present in all discussion sections: (a) a road map, (b) a discussion of the results of the hypotheses, (c) the relationships of the results to previous theory or research, (d) methodological implications, (e) a discussion of the implications of this research for practice or future research, (f) a limitations section, and (g) a summary and conclusion section. We also present examples from students' theses and dissertations to help clarify these seven elements.

The "So What?" Factor

As you will clearly discern from the examples presented in this chapter, woven throughout the entire discussion chapter is an emphasis on the very basic question of "so what?" In the overview chapter, we emphasized how vital it is to build a case for the importance of conducting this particular research. We talked about leaving readers with the thought that "this is exactly the study that should be conducted on this area." Now, in the discussion chapter, it is important to discuss the relevance and importance of the study and its findings. In our experience, we find that students sometimes get so immersed in the details of their study that they cannot "see the forest for the trees." To help them focus on the forest we often ask them to imagine themselves describing the importance of their study to an average lay person who has little or no background in the field. What stands out? Why is it important? This is the kind of information that needs to be included so that the reader can appreciate the significance of the research and appreciate its take-home uses.

Staying Close to the Data

When discussing the importance of findings, the researcher must stay very close to the data. When making statements about what the data mean or why they are important the researcher must be able to point to the specific data that allow those claims. Sometimes students take "leaps of faith" with their data and make claims that are unwarranted by their actual data. Thus, as you read through drafts of your thesis or dissertation, you must ask yourself the question, Where, specifically, do I have data that allow me to make that statement?

A Road Map

As we have stressed in other parts of this book, providing the reader with a "road map" to structure the chapter can serve as an important advanced organizer in helping the reader understand what will comprise the chapter. In the following example, Ferrell-Swann (1999) provides an effective road map for her discussion chapter:

> This chapter will discuss the implications of the results presented in Chapter 4. First, the findings of the main and supplemental analyses will be discussed in reference to possible explanations of the findings and their convergence or divergence with previous literature. Next theoretical and research implications of the study will be discussed. Finally limitations of the study will be reviewed and suggestions for future directions within psychological expertise research will be made. (Ferrell-Swann, 1999, p. 101)

A Discussion of the Results of the Hypotheses

Probably the most important element of a discussion chapter is a thorough and engaging description and analysis of the results of each hypothesis of the study. As you may recall, in Chapter 4, the results chapter, you simply present your results—just the facts of what you found. In the discussion chapter, you have the opportunity to discuss, analyze, and explain the findings of each hypothesis, as well as any additional post hoc analyses.

This discussion of the results can be presented in a number of ways. Some advisors recommend "leading with your strongest suit" or, in other words, presenting your most important or scientifically meaningful results first. This strategy allows you to reflect on the "big picture" of your results and to present those findings prominently in the first part of the chapter. These can then be followed by findings that may have less scientific importance.

For example, Ji's (2001) discussion on the role of attachment status in predicting longitudinal relationships between counseling session impact events and the working alliance in an adolescent population led with his strongest and most scientifically important findings:

> The main findings of this study include the significant cross-correlations between (a) the dimensions of the working alliance and session impact events over time, and (b) adolescents' self-reports of having generally positive therapy experience with their therapists. Adolescent clients reported having strong working alliances with their therapists. Furthermore, adolescents who reported their sessions as having strong relationship and task impacts led to increases in the three dimensions of the working alliance, bonds, tasks, and goals, over time. Consequently, increases in working alliance dimensions led to stronger ratings of the sessions' relationship and task impacts over time. The SIS hindering impacts demonstrated adverse effects on the three dimensions of the working alliance over time. The results are consistent with the hypothesis that over time, session impact events will lead to the formation of the working

alliance, which increases the likelihood that adolescents will perceive their sessions as having positive impacts. The qualitative and quantitative findings demonstrate that the adolescents in this study reported gaining benefits from therapy. (p. 93)

Another strategy that is often recommended, especially if you have a number of complex findings, is to present them in the order they were presented in the results section of the thesis or dissertation. This symmetry of discussing the results of each hypothesis may assist the reader in understanding the results of each hypothesis in turn.

For example, Zook (2000), in her discussion of the predictive influence of academic achievement, career exploration, self-esteem, and feminist identity to the career self-efficacy and outcome expectations of college women, proposed six hypotheses and chose to discuss each hypothesis in turn, just as she had presented them in Chapter 1 and Chapter 4. For space considerations, we present three of her hypotheses in the following example. As you can see, this approach provides the reader with a very clear understanding of the results of her hypotheses and the level of support she found for each:

Hypothesis 1 stated that ratings of efficacy and outcome would be significantly different for male-dominated, female-dominated, and sex-balanced careers. This hypothesis was soundly supported by the results. Significant differences in efficacy and outcome expectations between male-dominated, female-dominated, and sex-balanced occupations were found. The women in this study expressed the highest efficacy and outcome expectations for sex-balanced occupations and the lowest efficacy and outcome expectations for male-dominated occupations.

The importance of self-efficacy expectations to such critical variables as choices, effort, performance, persistence (Bonet, 1994; Brown, Lent, & Larkin, 1989; Hackett, Betz, Casas, & Rocha-Singh, 1992), career exploration intentions and career indecision (Betz & Voyten, 1997), has been soundly established in prior studies. Self-efficacy has been found to be an important variable to the career development of both men and women for a range of occupations and has been shown to be especially important for women, particularly those considering careers in nontraditional or male-dominated fields (Betz, 1992; Nevill & Shlecker, 1988.)

The relatively low ratings of self-efficacy and outcome expectations for male-dominated occupations found in this study are consistent with the findings of past research (Betz & Hackett, 1981; Campbell & Hackett, 1986; Matsui, 1994; Matsui, Ikedo, & Ohnishi, 1989; Sinner, 1995). This consistency across time suggests that poor perceptions of efficacy and outcome for male-dominated occupations continue to be an issue for traditionally aged college women, and that, to a degree, differences in efficacy and outcome expectations appear to remain split along gender lines. In spite of this, it does appear that some progress has been made over the past two decades. While ratings for male-dominated occupations were low, ratings of efficacy and outcome for sex-balanced occupations were high, surpassing even those for female-dominated occupations. This finding is encouraging, indicating that efficacy and outcome expectations for sex-balanced careers have increased significantly since the time of Betz and Hackett's original work in

1981. The past 20 years have evidenced an influx of women into careers traditionally dominated by men, resulting in a more balanced sex ration for these occupations. The results of this study indicate that perceptions of efficacy and outcome expectations for these careers have shifted as well.

Hypothesis 2 stated that sorority membership status would be significantly predictive of career self-efficacy and outcome beliefs for female-dominated, male-dominated, and sex-balanced occupations. This hypothesis was not supported by the results of this study. Sorority membership status was not found to account for any significant variance in efficacy or outcome ratings for any occupational grouping. Likewise, the interactive efforts of sorority membership status with academic achievement, career exploration behaviors, and ratings of feminist identity development were not found to account for a significant portion of variance in efficacy or outcome scores for male-dominated, female-dominated, or sex-balanced occupations. The interaction effect between sorority membership status and self-esteem did not account for a significant portion of variance in efficacy or outcome ratings for sex-balanced or female-dominated occupations, nor did it account for a significant portion of variance in ratings of outcome expectations for male-dominated occupations.

Taken together, these findings indicate that differences in career self-efficacy and outcome expectations between sorority-affiliated and non-sorority-affiliated college women are negligible for female-dominated and sex-balanced careers but may have significant implications for efficacy and outcome expectations for male-dominated careers. These findings are inconsistent with previous research that has indicated that Greek affiliation may significantly influence such constructs as attitude, development, self-esteem, and group-oriented behavior (Jacobsen, 1986; Smith & Tyler, 1996).

Hypothesis 3 stated that academic achievement would add significant explanation in addition to the efforts of sorority membership status. Results of this study soundly supported this hypothesis. As anticipated, academic achievement accounted for a significant portion of the variance in efficacy and outcome expectations for all occupational groupings. Achievement was found to account for more variance in female-dominated occupations. Achievement accounted for slightly more variance in efficacy and outcome expectations for sex-balanced occupations than for female-dominated occupations. These findings mirror those of Kelly (1993), and are consistent with those of Hackett (1985), and Lapan et al. (1989).

It appears that academic achievement may be more critical to the development of efficacy and outcome beliefs for male-dominated occupations than for female-dominated or sex-balanced careers. One possible explanation for this finding is that the consideration of careers in male-dominated [occupations] may require a confidence factor that is not necessary for female-dominated or sex-balanced options. It stands to reason that women with higher levels of prior academic achievement would be more likely to develop such a confidence level.

An alternate explanation for the inflated importance of academic achievement to the development of efficacy and outcome expectations for male-dominated careers relates to the relative lack of visible female role models for male-dominated careers. The visibility of female role models for any given occupation has been speculated to increase the likelihood that young women will develop personal efficacy expectations for the occupation in which the role models were observed (Kelly, 1993). In the absence of such role models other factors, such as achievement, might take on increased significance in the development of efficacy and outcome expectations.

Academic achievement was by far the most influential of the variables examined in this study. Across all occupational groupings, academic achievement accounted for between 5.1% and 13% of the total variance in ratings. This finding is encouraging as it supports Kelly's (1993) conclusion that ability is generally more influential to the development of career self-efficacy and outcome expectation for college-aged women than are oppressive gender attitudes or sociocultural pressures. (Zook, 2000, pp. 46–50)

A combination of these first two strategies consists of clustering the hypotheses and then discussing the results within that cluster. For example, perhaps a student's first three hypotheses all related to one central construct while the last four related to another construct. The student may discuss the first three as a group, perhaps leading with the most important finding in the cluster. In the following example, Ferrell-Swann (1999) groups her hypotheses and discusses the major findings of these hypotheses:

The results of the main analysis suggested that there was a multivariate dimension that distinguished among novices, experienced nonexperts, and experts. The hypotheses were that there would be two dimensions, one comprised of performance variables related to the hypothesis formation task and the other comprised of dispositional variables such as problem-solving self-appraisal or self-esteem. Additionally, it was hypothesized that performance and dispositional variables would accurately classify members of each of the groups. The results did not completely support the hypotheses in that the multivariate dimension that was found consisted of a combination of the performance variables quality of hypothesis formation and self-rated self-confidence, and the dispositional variable of counselor self-efficacy. However, the theoretical and empirical literature examining expertise in psychology has suggested that both performance and dispositional variables may be crucial to the development and expertise. For example, Goodyear (1997), and Jennings and Skovholt (1999), both suggest that personality characteristics are an essential part of the counselors' ability to work effectively with clients, therefore possibly contributing to the development of expertise. Additionally, Lichtenberg (1997) argues that performance on a counseling-related task should be an integral part of defining expertise in psychologists. He further suggests that "the quality of performance of the counselor on domain-relevant tasks should be the defining characteristics of expert performance in counseling psychology" (Lichtenberg, 1997, p. 229). It appears that performance on a counseling-related task and dispositional traits of the counselor may both be related to expertise; therefore expertise in counseling may be comprised of both performance and dispositional variables.

Interpretation of the Discriminant Function
Although the multivariate dimension correctly classified many members of the groups, it appeared to most effectively distinguish the novice group from both the experienced nonexpert and expert groups. The dimension was less accurate in distinguishing experienced nonexperts from experts. Low self-efficacy and quality of hypothesis formation were negatively related to the discriminant function and self-rated self-confidence was positively related. Further exploration of these variables indicated that lower self-efficacy was associated with novices, whereas a lower quality of hypothesis formation and higher self-rated

self-confidence were associated with experienced nonexperts and experts. To understand why these findings developed, exploration of the factors comprising the dimension is merited.

Self-Efficacy

The fact that low self-efficacy was associated with novices makes intuitive sense in that novices have had much less counseling experience than the other two groups and may feel less capable in their performance as counselors. This finding is consistent with literature examining self-efficacy in counselors. That is, it has been generally found that beginning counselors gain self-efficacy in their counseling ability over the course of training (Johnson et al., 1989; Larson et al., 1992; Melchert et al., 1996; Leach, Stoltenberg, McNeill, & Eichenfield, 1997), and that counselors with higher degrees and more experience have higher perceptions of self-efficacy than beginning counselors (Larson et al., 1992; Sipps, Sugden, & Faiver, 1998). The current finding appears to support the previous literature regarding neophyte counselors and to provide additional information about the previous literature regarding neophyte counselors and to provide additional information about the self-efficacy of experienced nonexperts. In this study, experienced nonexperts reported their self-efficacy as being similar to that of individuals classified as experts in this study. It is possible that the self-efficacy of these two groups was not discernibly different because each group had experience past the doctorate. The literature discussed above [sic] seems to suggest that self-efficacy is related to the amount of training and experience attained by the individual. The findings from this study appear to support these suggestions.

An alternative explanation that must be considered for the loading of this variable is the effect of sex and age. The novice group was primarily composed of young female participants. Some research in the domain of self-efficacy has suggested that females are more likely to have lower self-confidence when compared to males. This research has also suggested that younger individuals are more likely to have lower self-efficacy than older individuals. Therefore, it is possible that the loading of this variable on the discriminant function is related to sex and age differences among the groups. (pp. 104–106)

Ferrell-Swann (1999) then went on to the dispositional variable of self-care confidence and additional results.

You should think about what order is most effective in discussing your particular results. You should also consult with your advisor about the appropriate strategy. Regardless of the order, you must thoroughly discuss your findings for each hypothesis and research question. Omitting results because they were nonsignificant or uninteresting is not appropriate. Much can be learned from all data, so it is important that all data be thoroughly discussed.

Remember that the results and discussion chapters serve two very different purposes. The results chapter is only for presenting the facts and not discussing them; the discussion chapter is for discussing results and not (re)presenting them. Thus, numbers should be very rare in a discussion chapter. All numbers from the various analyses should already have been presented; now the task is to "make the results sing"—bring them to life and engage the reader in their importance and implications.

The Relationship of the Results to Previous Theory or Research

An important task in the discussion chapter is to position your results within the larger literature of the area and discuss how it supports, contradicts, or extends that scholarship. Being able to position research generally requires a great deal of reading and reflection. It requires that you go back to the literature you reviewed in Chapter 2 and carefully analyze your current findings in relationship to previous findings in the literature. If you find that your research supports previous research or theory, highlight points of similarity. At other times, your results may extend previous findings. For example, your findings may replicate earlier findings but with a more diverse sample or with a more sophisticated or rigorous methodology. Other times, your results may be contrary to what has been found in previous research or has been predicted by theory in the area. Discuss this contradiction and hypothesize about the reason for this difference.

A scientific base for any given area is strengthened when different researchers examine aspects of the area using different samples and different conditions. Thus, a contribution is made when researchers can highlight how their particular study relates to the larger knowledge base. Therefore, whenever possible, discuss how the current study relates to theory in the area. If the study was guided by theory, discuss the findings in the context of that theory and highlight similarities and differences with the theoretical framework. For example, the following excerpt from Ferrell-Swann's (1999) discussion highlights important theoretical implications:

Theoretical Implications
The results of the study have theoretical implications for understanding expertise in psychology. The following area will be discussed in reference to possible ways the current study clarifies or extends our theoretical understanding of expertise: The relevance of dispositional characteristics to understanding expertise and defining expertise.

Dispositional Characteristics
One of the theoretical aims of this study was to explore the relevance of dispositional variables in the understanding of expertise. Previous research has suggested that personality characteristics might be important components of expertise that have been ignored in the past (Goodyear, 1997; Jennings, 1996; Jennings & Skovholt, 1999). Although all the dispositional variables studied were not predictors of the experimental groups, this study provides some evidence that dispositional variables such as self-efficacy are critical to the development of expertise.

An important contribution of this study that extends the previous literature and theoretical understanding of expertise is that it explored dispositional characteristics and provided a performance measure for counselors to complete. The majority of literature that has incorporated performance tasks has neglected to include dispositional variables (Brammer, 1997; Hillerbrand & Claiborn, 1990; O'Byrne & Goodyear, 1997). Previous studies have explored dispositional or personality characteristics of "master therapists" (Harrington, 1998; Jennings, 1996;

Jennings & Skovholt, 1999) without attempting to link these traits to the participant's performance on a counseling-related talk. If an important defining characteristic of expertise is expert performance (Orlinsky, 1999; Lichtenberg, 1997), then these studies have provided us with limited information. This study extends the current literature and theoretical conceptualization of expertise by incorporating and comparing performance and dispositional variables.

Furthermore, the findings of this study suggest that dispositional and performance variables may both be important characteristics of expertise. Currently, the theoretical and empirical literature has failed to consider the interactive role of these two variables. It may be that [the] counselor's characteristics affect the way that he or she performs counseling tasks. From this perspective, it may not be possible to separate expert performance from the dispositional traits of the individual; the traits that make the individual a unique person may be the same traits that have helped him or her become an expert psychologist. Future research should continue to explore this possibility by examining additional dispositional variables within the context of different types of counseling-related tasks. (pp. 119–120)

Implications for Practice and Future Research

As an expert in the specialized area that your thesis or dissertation covers, you are in a unique position to provide an in-depth section on the implications of your investigation. Most topics in applied psychology have implications for both practice and future research. Implication for practice should include ways your findings may guide the work of practitioners. How could a teacher, counselor, or parent make use of the findings from this investigation as they work with others? Some practitioners criticize research in psychology for having no relevance for them (Heppner et al., 1999), while others contend that scientists have just been ineffective at synthesizing their findings in ways that would be useful to practitioners. Although drawing those implications for practitioners is sometimes challenging, applied psychologists must be able to make those connections. Similarly, in the area of research, the student who has conducted a thesis or dissertation in an area is in a unique position to guide future researchers in the area. When our students, for example, are searching for good researchable topics, we often advise them to go to the literature and examine the discussion chapters of theses and dissertations or the discussion sections of journal articles to get ideas of what those experts perceive as the next important studies that need to be conducted on a given topic. Although graduate students sometimes have difficulty perceiving themselves as experts capable of guiding the field, the fact is that, after thoroughly reviewing the literature and conducting an ambitious study in the field, they know more perhaps than anyone about their particular topics. Thus, presenting an in-depth discussion of the investigation's implications is a highly important contribution to the literature.

Thus, for example, Zook (2000) presented a discussion of the implications her study has for providing career counseling to women:

The findings of this study in context with past research have significant implications to the provision of career counseling to women. Taken as a whole, the results of this study indicate that the career development of women is still interwoven with societal concepts of gender and that the development of a positive feminist identity may facilitate career efficacy and outcome expectations. This appears to be especially true for the career self-efficacy perceptions and outcome expectations for male-dominated occupations.

As noted by Juntunen (1996), career counselors are in a unique position to help their female clients focus on sex-role socialization and to encourage women to actively assume responsibility for their career development in spite of societal restrictions. Career counselors should take care to become aware of their own gender attitudes as well as those of the society in which we live. Likewise, care should be taken to assess the gender attitudes and socialized learning experiences of the women with whom they work. Counselors should encourage women to examine and explore their beliefs as they apply to career choice and development, and to explore a range of career choices and options. Efforts should be made to assist women in making informed career decisions based on interests, ability, and lifestyle choices unencumbered by restrictive societal gender roles.

The unexpectedly high rating of efficacy and outcome expectations for sex-balanced careers indicates that significant societal shifts have occurred over the past two decades. One potential explanation for this shift in perceptions is the fact that more visible female role models are available for sex-balanced occupations. The availability of female role models for sex-balanced occupations is significant, as it increases the likelihood that girls and women will be exposed to more vicarious learning experiences relevant to the development of career self-efficacy and outcome perceptions. Career counselors are now in a position to capitalize on the availability of observational role models for sex-balanced and female-dominated occupations. As in the past, efforts should be made on the part of the career counselor to provide the client with opportunities to observe female role models in male-dominated occupations when possible.

Few universities or colleges employ a sufficient number of career counselors to meet the needs of the student body in its entirety. Fortunately, the implications of this study are not restricted to the counseling dyad. Counselors and other professionals dedicated to fostering student growth and development should consider resources available to them through which they might impact the gender attitudes and stereotypes of undergraduate students. Outreach presentations and workshops sponsored by women's centers, residence life offices, counseling or career centers for example, may effectively and economically reach a large number of students.

The results of this study clearly demonstrated that career exploration activities were related to the development of positive career self-efficacy and outcome expectations. The obvious implication here is that undergraduate women can benefit from opportunities to participate in activities designed to foster career exploration behaviors. In addition to career counseling, programs designed to facilitate career exploration early in the college experience could allow for substantial planning and growth. For instance, career exploration workshops or even a guided tour of the campus career center during freshman orientation would encourage young women to consider career exploration activities [that] might in turn lead to career exploration behaviors. Beyond this, a career exploration course during the first year of study would provide a structured environment for career exploration behaviors to flourish. Whatever the vehicle, the introduction of career exploration early in the college experience might lead to a broader range of career opportunities for college women. (pp. 53–55)

Similarly, Flores (1999) suggested specific ideas for future research that may help other scholars build on her work on the factors contributing to the career orientation of Mexican American adolescent women:

> According to the results, the data fit the model adequately. However, because there were several paths that were not significant, it is suggested that future research explore alternative models to investigate whether a modified model better explains the career orientation among Mexican American adolescent women. Based on the Wald and Lagrange Multiplier tests, it seems that eliminating the path between acculturation and self-efficacy and adding paths from mother role modeling to career interest, acculturation to career orientation, and feminist attitudes to career orientation would improve the model fit. Additional model testing with several samples of Mexican American girls is necessary.
>
> A longitudinal study that assesses these participants' career orientation at different times following high-school graduation is recommended. It would be interesting to investigate the characteristics of the students who achieved the educational and career goals they had during their senior year of high school and those whose plans changed. Such a study would provide information regarding the factors that affect the career orientation of Mexican American women at different times of their life. Given that this population is rarely studied, this program of research would forward the knowledge in vocational psychology.
>
> Additionally, since this study only included Mexican American girls, additional studies that examine the validity of the Lent et al. (1994) model with Mexican American boys are needed. It would be interesting to investigate the career orientation among Mexican American boys and to test whether the Lent et al. (1994) model adequately explains their career orientation. Also, the differences and similarities between Mexican American boys and girls should be researched.
>
> Finally, conducting separate path analyses using the traditional, nontraditional, and gender-neutral occupations may be beneficial and could possibly lead to stronger path coefficients and a better model fit. Such analyses would provide information as to how interests and self-efficacy for these occupations contribute to career orientation. (pp. 74–75)

Methodological Implications

In addition to recommendations about global research directions that may be fruitful, many studies highlight important methodological implications that can help future researchers develop more rigorous and effective designs. For example, Berry (1996) provides the following discussion in his master's thesis on predicting depression using problem-solving appraisal and reflective judgment:

> This study has methodological implications for counseling research in general. The improvement in prediction afforded by the use of multiple indicators of the constructs reiterates the need for multiple measures to control for measurement error. To make use of the multiple measures in this way would require the use of structural equation modeling, employing the estimation of latent variables. More

frequent use of latent variables would likely result in operationalizations that are much better representations of the constructs of interest and parameter values that are more accurate estimates of the true functional relations among these constructs. In addition, the inclusion of a variable not previously considered in this area of research allowed for the expansion of the conceptualization of the relation between problem solving and depression. Linear models, such as regression and SEM, are all vulnerable to model specification errors, which can distort the depiction of the functional relations revealed among the variables (Pedhazur, 1982; Wood, 1994b). Only by trying new variables, especially from other, related areas of research, will this threat to the validity of the models be adequately addressed. (p. 51)

Ferrell-Swann (1999) also provided a number of methodological advances in her study of counselor expertise that could increase the rigor and methodological sophistication of future studies:

Research Implications

This study has several methodological implications that can strengthen future research in the area of expertise for counseling. The methodological purpose of this study was threefold: (1) to provide solid definitions of the experimental groups that could be replicated in future expertise studies; (2) to use external criteria to define expertise rather than experience; and (3) to explore expertise as a developmental variable by the inclusion of an experienced nonexpert group. The results of this study extend our understanding of the expertise literature in each of these areas. Further discussion of these areas and their implications for future research is warranted.

Definition of Groups

As discussed earlier in this paper, previous research has neglected to clearly and consistently define the experimental groups used in expert-novice studies. The result of this methodological flaw has been a body of research that is ill-defined and that is difficult to compare in that none of the studies are using the same criteria to define experts and novices. Most of this research clearly identifies difficulties in demarcating experts and often calls for future studies to address this issue. However, few studies consider the inconsistency in the definition of novice to be of relevance. This issue seems critical in that both groups with expertise cannot be clearly delineated without a comparison group of neophytes.

A common weakness among the expert-novice studies is that novices are often individuals who are not practicing within the domain of psychology. For example, some studies use undergraduates as novices and compare their performance to doctoral level psychologists (Brammer, 1997; Thompson, 1986; Worthington, 1984). These studies find significant results, but what meaning do they have? As the theoretical literature argues that expertise is domain-specific, it seems frivolous to compare experts within psychology to individuals who are not trained in the field. Instead, novice groups need to be comprised of individuals who have some experience and training within the domain of applied psychology. Using these criteria would allow researchers to determine if there are truly differences in expert performances when they are compared with novices who have training in the domain rather than individuals with no experience or training in applied psychology.

The novice group in this study was comprised of individuals with one to three completed practicum experiences. This criterion was selected because it assured that novices would have completed basic training that would allow them to make reasonable judgments about a fictional client. As there has been a call in the literature to link expertise with performance measures (Lichtenberg, 1997), it seems essential that the comparison group be one that has the basic skills to complete the experimental task. From the findings of the current study, it appears that using these criteria to define novices provides an appropriately trained comparison group within the domain of applied psychology. (pp. 120–122)

Limitations

All studies have limitations, and these need to be acknowledged in the discussion chapter. For example, limitations always exist about the extent to which you can generalize your findings; no matter how diverse a sample, it will by nature never be inclusive of everyone. A study may have many other limitations as well. A list follows of some of the most common limitations prevalent in applied psychological research. We encourage you to reflect on your research and determine which are the primary limitations of your investigation:

SAMPLING LIMITATIONS
- Generalizability of sample
- Insufficient numbers of participants
- High levels of attrition

INSTRUMENT LIMITATIONS
- Self-report nature of most studies
- Insufficient validity of instruments

PROCEDURE LIMITATIONS
- Generalizability of intervention (e.g., analogue research)
- Fidelity of intervention (e. g., noncompliance with protocol)

METHODOLOGICAL LIMITATIONS
- Cross-sectional data

In constructing the limitations section, you should highlight significant limitations yet not be overly critical of every small aspect of the study that could be improved. Limitations sections should generally be a paragraph or two, not pages.

As we mentioned in the chapter on methodology, at that point, a researcher should be thinking ahead to the limitations sections and making every attempt to eliminate as many potential limitations as possible. For example, if a researcher indicates that a major limitation was the instruments selected, the committee or reader may rightfully ask why that particular instrument was selected. Likewise, if insufficient participants to adequately test the hypotheses were used in the study, a question may be, Why were more participants not obtained? Thus, you must be designing the most rigorous methodology—one that limits as many threats to internal and external validity as possible. At the same time, you should acknowledge the limitations that do exist and discuss these in as clear and concise a manner as possible.

For example, Mayfield (1999) presented limitations related to the labeling of his participants, their generalizability to the population of gay men as a whole, the self-report nature of the instruments, the cross-sectional nature of the study and the inattention to potentially important factors that may also influence psychological adjustment:

> As with all studies, this study has several limitations. Although the participants were recruited from all areas around the [United States], the sample cannot be described as a random and representative sample of gay men. Research with sexual minorities is plagued by this problem because in order to be identified as a sexual minority, participants must be willing to label themselves as such. It is no accident that much of the research on identity development has had a problem finding sufficient number of participants in the earlier stages of identity development. Many gay men in such stages either do not label themselves "gay," or, if they do, they may not be willing to do so with researchers whom they do not know. Thus, it is reasonable to assume that the sample used in this study is more representative of gay men in the later stages of identity development.
>
> Another limitation was the methods used to recruit participants. Given that there are no definitive data about who is "gay," there are surely no data about what portion of the gay community uses the Internet. However, Koch and Schockman (1998) conducted a large-scale survey of gay men who use the Internet ($N = 7,210$) and found that, although most were White, college educated, and under the age of 46, gay men who were members of minority groups, were less educated, and older than 46 were also Internet users. The fact that other recruitment methods were used both helps and hinders the problem of representativeness. On the one hand, it is good to have multiple sources of participants; on the other, to what extent do these other methods additionally bias the sample? There are no definitive answers to this question. By posting announcements on listserves aimed at Latino and African American gay men, I hoped to recruit a more racially diverse sample. My efforts were rewarded; nearly 29% of the sample identified as something other than European American.
>
> The self-report nature of all the instruments is another limitation. Because of common method variance and the possibility of response set, the use of self-report measures tends to inflate the correlations found among variables. In addition, when using self-report measures, researchers cannot know how truthfully respondents answer. Social desirability might affect the way participants answer the items. Another limitation related to the instruments is the assumption that self-report instruments measure what they purport to measure. Although the instruments used exhibit appropriate levels of reliability and validity, various researchers have encountered problems with the Superiority scale (Robbins & Patton, 1985), which serves as an example for researchers to be cautious about drawing conclusions about a construct from a single scale.
>
> Yet another limitation is the cross-sectional nature of the study. Although age was used as a covariate, it is likely that there are important cohort differences in gay men that have arisen due to changes in general societal attitudes toward homosexuality. This last point brings me to another limitation. This study was correlational in nature. Even though SEM techniques were employed, hopefully

guided by sound theory, the causal relationship inferred from such correlational data do not constitute strict causality in the experimental sense. No independent variables were manipulated to determine what the effects of such manipulations were on dependent variables. Thus, causal inferences and conclusions drawn from the results of this study are tempered by the fact that they were derived from correlational data.

A final limitation of this study is the inattention given to other important factors that influence identity as well as psychological adjustment. The roles of race, ethnicity, social class, and other important identity variables were not examined in this study, although they surely play an important part in the ways in which self-psychology constructs, gay identity, and psychological well-being are related. (pp. 140–142)

Mackert (2001) presented a number of limitations inherent to studying an organization undergoing change. This type of field research often makes control of variables considerably more of a challenge than laboratory research. As Mackert highlights, this unique sample increases the generalizability and validity of his results while also increasing the number of factors that were out of his control:

Although great measures were taken to ensure a strong study, there were still a number of limitations due to its nature. Prior to listing the limitations, however, it is important to note one unique and vital strength to this research: the use of employees from an organization undergoing change as participants. As opposed to the majority of research in this area that used the traditional sample of convenience (i.e., college students), this research was able to receive the support of an organization able to realize the importance of the study and agree to allow the recruitment of their employees as participants. This greatly enhanced the validity of the study and the generalizability of the results. However, as with any study, there were still limitations that occurred. These limitations will be listed and briefly discussed in this section.

1. The overall sample was not representative of the population. It was overwhelmingly female (80%) and Caucasian (92.5%). In addition, as this research was only conducted with an organization in the Midwest, the cultural values of the individuals and the organization likely reflected Midwestern values. Due to the unequal representation in this study, the results may not be generalizable to other organizations, ethnicities, or across genders.

2. The organization in this study was just entering their change initiative. While they had involved employees in one round of meetings, many of the employees were unsure of what the change entailed. In fact, the employees had not been provided a detailed description of the change, just that a change was coming and that it was still to be determined. The meetings were an attempt at getting the employees to see themselves as the change agents, similar to the "buy in" discussed throughout this chapter. This could have extreme implications for the ability to replicate the results across different time points in a change program. This is discussed further in the point below [sic].

3. As conductivity has been posited as being state dependent to a certain extent, it could show differences across time. However, this study only investigated one change initiative at only one point in time. Therefore, the

results might be dependent upon the time of the change in this case, and may not remain the same if the scale were administered at a different point in a change process. This again limits the generalizability of the results to the starting phase of change initiatives.

4. Due to the nature of this research, in a real organization actually engaged in business, there was an inability to control for any independent variables. This directly limits statements about causation of differences in scores, as any number of factors could be responsible for the differences found to exist.

5. While this study included marker variables for purposes of validity, it did not include a true measure of personality. With the relationship found between PA and NA, thought to be trait characteristics, this appeared to be an important limitation. The inclusion of a personality inventory would have allowed for further detection of relationships between personality styles and conductivity, as well as for the statistical control of at least some potentially mediating variables.

6. Similar to any exploratory technique, this study only serves as an initial snapshot of the phenomenon of conductivity. There is a definite need for further replication of the results through confirmatory factor analysis with other samples.

7. The first step in a larger scale construction project, this study could only provide limited reliability and validity evidence. As a result, further use of this scale should be limited to continued scale development projects.

8. The last few factors on the Conductivity Inventory were small in size. Only consisting of four items each, the Organizational Fig and Knowledge and Investment factors could not possibly measure the full extent of the concepts they represent. With only four items, the spread of information within the concept is simply not large enough. (pp. 103–105)

Summary and Conclusions of the Discussion Chapter

The summary and conclusion section of the discussion chapter is especially important because it is the summary and conclusion for the whole study. Thus, the reader must be able to obtain a clear and concise statement of what the researcher concludes from the study and what summary comments are possible. Sometimes students do not provide this section, and readers feel as though they have been dropped without appropriate closure. Thus, completing the thesis or dissertation with a strong summary and conclusion can serve the purpose of emphasizing the "take-home message" or what the researcher hopes the reader will take away from reading the study.

As Sherrod (2002) demonstrated, a summary and conclusion section can be concise and still provide the reader with the essential message her work contributed:

Results of this study support the prediction stated in Chapter 1, that is, that college men at extremes of a continuum could be distinguished by a wide variety of masculinity and personality-related constructs. This study provides empirical support for the theorized notion that men at high risk for perpetrating sexual assault are characterized by personality disturbances. The study also provides empirical support for the theorized notion that men at high risk for perpetrating sexual assault are characterized by acceptance of traditionally held beliefs about gender roles. Further, this study provides empirical support for the idea that men at low risk to perpetrate rape are psychologically healthy. The suggestion that personality disorder features are implicated in high-risk individuals provides fuel for future researchers and innovators in rape prevention. The findings about masculinity-related constructs lend empirical support to those working to change traditional conceptions of gender roles in order to combat rape. (p. 142)

Similarly, Mackert (2001) proposed four key conclusions he hopes the reader takes away from his study of resistance to organizational change:

Based on the preceding discussion of the results, several conclusions were drawn from this study. First, it appeared that this study achieved one of its primary goals in serving as a sound initial step in the construction of an inventory designed to measure individuals' reactions to organizational change. More specifically, the Conductivity Inventory provided a promising index of the degree to which an individual is engaged in an organizational change initiative. While this conclusion is tentative due to the exploratory nature of an initial study, the sound theory based text construction steps used, in addition to the reliability and validity evidenced in the study, provided enough support to allow such an assertion.

It was also concluded that the second main goal of this study, creating a neutral and transtheoretical model explaining the internal processes engaged within individuals involved in organizational change, was also met. Through the review of the literature, the concept of conductivity for schematic conversion was created. This model integrated thoughts from both the organizational development and psychological fields. Further, examination of the factors on the Conductivity Inventory and their relationships to the marker variables provided support for the neutrality of the concept and its emphasis on the unconscious forces of growth motivation and homeostatic motivation schemas.

This study also asserted that the single most important factor influencing an individual's level of conductivity toward organizational change was Alliance. Defined as a sense of connectedness the individual has with the change agent and change process, this concept revolved around the individual's agreement with the tasks and goals of the change process and a bond with the change agent. As Alliance accounted for the majority of the variance explained by the Conductivity Inventory, it clearly displayed the most importance. Given this, one can only conclude that organizations contemplating change should pay special attention to creating interventions that create higher agreement on the tasks and goals of the change and a strong relationship with the person(s) in charge of the change.

Lastly, building from the previous point, it was concluded that this study provided crucial theoretical and research-based knowledge to the field of organizational development. Prior to this study, organizational development theorists had discussed resistance to change from unitary theoretical standpoints. In addition, the term resistance appeared to have been misappropriated from Lewin's (1947) original conception. This study served as a catalyst for returning the understanding of individual reactions to organizational change to a more useful and integrative one that has great potential for future theoretical, research, and applied uses. (pp. 102–103)

CONCLUSIONS

In essence, the discussion chapter is one that gives you an opportunity to discuss the importance and implication of your research. When readers pick up a thesis or dissertation, they often turn right to the discussion chapter to find out how the research turned out. You must do a lot of thinking about your findings and how best to organize these findings into a meaningful discussion chapter. As the expert on the topic, you are in the best position to interpret and discuss the results within the context of the broader professional literature. By writing an effective discussion chapter, you can help the reader understand the important contribution your research is making to the professional literature. Following is a checklist for you to assess your discussion chapter before giving it to your advisor or others for critique.

CHECKLIST FOR CHAPTER 5 OF THE THESIS OR DISSERTATION

Did You . . .

1. . . . . Discuss the results of each of the hypotheses, research questions, and post hoc analyses?
2. . . . . Avoid numbers and a listing of results and, rather, discuss the findings?
3. . . . . Organize your discussion of the results by leading with your strongest results, by presenting them using the order they were presented in the results chapter, or some conceptually meaningful combination?
4. . . . . Integrate your results with previous theory?
5. . . . . Discuss methodological implications?
6. . . . . Integrate results with previous research?
7. . . . . Provide your thinking about reasons for theoretically or empirically inconsistent results?
8. . . . . Provide a clear answer to the "so what" question?
9. . . . . Stay close to your data and not make statements that were unsupported?
10. . . . . Provide clear implications for practice?
11. . . . . Provide clear implications for future research?
12. . . . . Discuss the limitations of your study in appropriate depth?
13. . . . . Provide a thoughtful and engaging summary and conclusion?

CHAPTER 15

CITATIONS AND REFERENCE LISTS

The Devil Is in the Details

Researchers have a responsibility to acknowledge the original contributions of other writers and to distinguish their own observations from the scholarly insights of others (see American Psychological Association, 2001). A failure to acknowledge the contributions of other authors is more than an oversight. Appropriately acknowledging and giving credit to previous authors is an important ethical obligation and, in essence, is a matter of fairness and integrity. Moreover, the accuracy of citing others' work is essential to create reliable and valid knowledge bases in a profession. Conversely, multiple citation inaccuracies, such as the year of publication or author order, not only do a disservice to the cited author's work but also lower the desired level of professional standards in the literature. Thus, whenever you are referring to an idea, empirical finding, methodological procedure, or scholarly contribution of another professional, you should not only reference that professional's work but also do so accurately. Thus, an important aspect of the thesis and dissertation is to appropriately and accurately reference relevant citations (see Heppner et al., 1999, for a more thorough discussion of ethical issues and obligations related to this topic).

In addition, all those citations must be listed in a certain order (primarily alphabetically) in what is called the Reference List. This enables readers to find the complete reference for each citation in the text. This can often result in a hundred or more references in a comprehensive literature review in a relatively narrow topic. Committee members not only will often scan the reference list but also will sometimes examine the reference list first to assess the type and range of literature that is cited on a particular topic. Note that the reference list includes only those articles, chapters, and books that you used and cited in the text, as opposed to a bibliography, which is generally a more extensive list of relevant sources on a particular topic.

The most widely used style for citing references, as well as for developing the reference list, is what is commonly referred to as *APA style*, which is thoroughly described in the fifth edition of the *Publication Manual of the American Psychological Association* (APA, 2001). This book contains a myriad of stylistic guidelines for expressing ideas and reducing bias in language, punctuation, abbreviations, headings, numbers, tables, figures, appendixes, and reference lists, as well as suggestions for manuscript preparation, the publication process, and ethical issues. The APA *Publication Manual* is a "must" for students in many programs; we strongly encourage students to purchase this book and regularly consult it as they write their thesis or dissertation.

The purpose of this chapter is to discuss some of the most common stylistic errors in referencing sources both in the text and in the reference list. Specifically, we briefly discuss stylistic errors in citations within the text and then the many obstacles that are encountered in compiling the references. In the last section of the chapter, we discuss common errors in the reference list. In essence, we hope to reduce your hassles with what can be a very time-consuming and frustrating task. Moreover, appropriately acknowledging the contributions of previous authors is not only 'good science' but also the right thing to do. Accurately citing and referencing previous contributions create reliable knowledge bases in the literature and can make the work of future readers and researchers much easier.

STYLE OF CITING REFERENCES IN THE TEXT

Several stylistic features for citing references in the text are delineated in the fifth edition of the APA *Publication Manual*. Based on our experiences in working with students, three areas where mistakes are commonly made in citing references in the text follow:

1. *Order of citations.* References are arranged alphabetically by the first author's last names (and then, if necessary, first name, the second author's name, and then year). Semicolons are used to separate citations to different references (e.g., Johnston, 1995; Williams, 2002) except for multiple citations to the same single author where commas can be used (e.g., Baker, 1994, 1999, 2001).
2. *Use of ampersands and "and."* When a reference is made to two or more authors within parentheses, an ampersand is used (e.g., Baker & Williams, 1997). When a reference is made to authors in a typical sentence outside of parentheses, the word "and" joins the authors' names, such as Baker and Williams (1997); in this case the date of the publication is placed in parentheses.
3. *Et al.* When a publication has only two authors, each time a citation is made to this source, list both authors and the publication year (e.g., Baker & Williams, 1997). However, with three or more authors, the first

citation should list all authors (e.g., Baker, Williams, & Lopez, 2002) but thereafter cite the reference as (Baker et al., 2002). When a reference has seven or more authors, the first citation should use an "et al." (e.g., Baker et al., 2002).

COMMON PROBLEMS IN COMPILING REFERENCES

Each author has his or her own style of writing and compiling references. Some authors establish a habit of recording a complete reference each time they cite a new reference. Other authors compile their reference list after their proposal is completed. Other authors may vacillate between these two ends of the continuum. Sometimes authors are so involved in their writing that stopping to record their references seems like a disruption to their concentration. In this section, we briefly discuss common problems in compiling references and some possible solutions.

Few authors record each and every reference citation as they are writing. Perhaps the most common and significant problem is that when authors do attempt to compile the references, they are unable to do so. Sometimes authors cannot find the original reference source because it was mislaid or borrowed or because the source has now been borrowed from the library. Or, if the author is referencing an author that was cited in another article or book (i.e., using secondary sources), the author cannot recall what source the citation was taken from. In these situations, the author may spend a considerable amount of time relocating the appropriate source. Beware; relocating missing references is not only time-consuming but also frustrating.

Another common problem in compiling references is efficiently organizing the references. Sometimes authors record their references at the end of a writing period in a computer file; or, if they are writing away from a computer, such as in a library, they may write their references on a single sheet of paper. Other times they may record references in their notes they are taking about an article; or the author copies most of the references, and so, instead of recording and compiling references, they store the primary sources from which they will later compile the references. Sometimes an author uses all of these methods in writing the thesis or dissertation. In short, problems often occur in compiling the references; when references are misplaced or cannot be located, the author must use additional time to relocate the references.

Another problem that occurs is that the author did record the reference but it was not fully recorded according to the *Publication Manual* (APA, 2001). For example, the reference was missing the volume number for a journal article, or the initials of an author's first or middle name, or the publisher of a book. Another common omission happens when an author quotes verbatim a portion of an article or book chapter but does not record the page numbers on which the quote appeared in the original source (the page numbers are needed in citing the source of the direct quote). Yet another problem occurs when an author has two publications in the same year and then later the author cannot remember which reference matches which citation. These types of problems happen with authors who are less familiar with the *Publication Manual* and are not aware of all of the details that are needed for the reference list. Again, the author needs to spend additional time to relocate and record the references. Let the author beware.

Yet another problem occurs when using an older secondary source and the author records a citation for a chapter from an edited book that does not contain the page numbers of the chapter. (Note: Page numbers of book chapters were not required in earlier years and, subsequently, rarely were included in reference lists before the fourth edition of the *Publication Manual* in 1994.) Consequently, the author has an incomplete citation, which again necessitates additional time to search for the complete citation.

In short, a number of different kinds of obstacles prevent authors from easily and quickly compiling their list of references. A thesis or dissertation is very time-consuming; the various obstacles in compiling the reference list can add additional time to an already time-consuming process, not to mention the emotional frustration of finding the missing details.

Our experience has been that there is not one right way to create an efficient system to compile the reference list, but we do strongly recommend that you establish some kind of system for compiling the references. One system is to record all the new references cited on a computer file after each writing session; a variation of this method is to record the references on 4 × 6 file cards or even write them on a sheet of paper. Then, store the recorded references in a safe place and combine them over time. An advantage of 4 × 6 cards is that the references can be easily arranged, even as new references are added, to create an alphabetical ordering of the references (which is how they will appear eventually in the reference list). Some students create a running reference list on the computer at regular intervals (e.g., every week or month). A variety of software referencing programs are designed specifically for helping organize reference information.

UTILIZING BIBLIOGRAPHIC COMPUTER PROGRAMS FOR YOUR REFERENCES

Bibliographic computer programs are useful tools that help you to create your references more easily and accurately. *EndNote, Reference Manager,* and *ProCite* are three popular bibliographic computer programs. With these programs, you can create your own reference database by entering the bibliographic information of the articles and books that you want to cite in your thesis/dissertations. The reference data can be entered into the database either by directly typing the reference information or by importing the reference information from public databases (e.g., PsycInfo, ERIC, Medline). Based on your own reference database, the bibliographic programs automatically create citations and references in your manuscript according to the designated reference style (e.g., APA). The benefits of using bibliographic programs for your references are that you do not have to type all the references by hand and that the programs automatically match the reference style you want.

Whether the method of compiling references is a highly sophisticated computerized system is less important than whether some systematic method is used to compile and organize the references. Our experience has been that when students do not compile their references on a regular basis, more problems and emotional frustration occur.

COMMON REFERENCE LIST ERRORS

A number of errors commonly occur in compiling the references for the reference list. We have prepared a list of some of the most common errors that we have seen in theses and dissertations. Many other stylistic features are part of the widely utilized *Publication Manual* (APA, 2001) that are relevant for correctly preparing the reference list; we again encourage you to routinely consult the *Publication Manual* in developing your reference list.

Errors in compiling the reference list can occur just because you are unfamiliar with the style established in the *Publication Manual*. Errors may also be present if you copy other authors' references; if these references contain errors, those errors are then transferred. Although copying references from other authors' work is common, be aware that this practice makes you vulnerable to errors in the original authors' work.

Following is our list of errors that can occur in developing reference lists. In some cases, we immediately provide examples of references to illustrate the correct form. We also present a Sample Reference List at the end of the chapter that we encourage you to examine as you study the various errors in our list.

1. *Missing references.* A reference is cited in the text but is not included in the reference list.
2. *Incongruity between the text citation and reference list.* The most common error occurs when the dates in the text citation (Wampold, 1994) and in the reference list (Wampold, 1995) differ. Other times, the order of the author names or spelling of the author names differs.

3. *Spacing.* The reference should begin flush left, with all subsequent lines for this reference indented five spaces (see sample).

4. *Spelling.* Sometimes errors appear in the spelling of authors' names or journal or book titles.

5. *Alphabetical order.* References are to be arranged alphabetically by the first author's last (and, if necessary, first and middle) name (and date of publication, if necessary). In rare cases, an author might have published two or more articles in the same year; in such cases, the year of citation for the articles includes letters, such as 2002a, 2002b, and so on (see sample).

6. *Chronological order.* References for the same author are to be arranged chronologically, with the earliest reference first. If co-authors are involved in any citations to the same first author, the multiple-authored studies are placed after all single-authored publications; multiple-authored publications with the same first author are arranged alphabetically by several author names (and subsequent authors if necessary) and date of publication (if necessary). See sample.

7. *Author names.* Only the complete last name of each author is listed, along with initials of their first or first and middle names. References are then arranged with authors' last names appearing first, followed by the initials of their first and middle names.

> Fassinger, R. E. (1991). The hidden minority: Issues and challenges in working with lesbian women and gay men. *The Counseling Psychologist, 19,* 157–176.

There is one exception to watch for with the order of author first and last names. When a book chapter is referenced that is part of an edited book, it is customary to cite the book in which the chapter appeared and the editors of the book. In citing the editors of the book, the initials of the first and second names *precede* the authors' last names:

> Gilbert, L. A. (1992). Gender and counseling psychology: Current knowledge and directions for research and social action. In S. D. Brown & R. W. Lent (Eds.), *Handbook of counseling psychology* (2nd ed., pp. 383–418). New York: Wiley.

A very common error in the reference list occurs when the author names in multiple-authored publications are connected with the word "and"; the appropriate style is to use an ampersand (&) to connect author names in multiple-authored references. A comma separates each name (see example in Item 9 and sample).

8. *Year of publication.* The current style is to place the year of the publication after the list of authors' names within parentheses, followed by a period. (For convention presentations, in addition to the year, include the month of the presentation.) See example in Item 7 and sample.

9. *Titles of journal articles and book chapters.* The titles of journal articles and book chapters should *not* be placed within quotation marks, nor should they be italicized. Only the first word of the title should be

capitalized; all other words should not be capitalized, except when there is a colon in the title (in this case the first letter of the first word after a colon is capitalized) or a proper name appears in the title. Thus, a journal reference would typically be as follows:

Enns, C. Z., McNeilly, C. L., Corkery, J. M., & Gilbert, M. S. (1995). The debate about delayed memories of child sexual abuse: A feminist perspective. *The Counseling Psychologist, 23,* 181–279.

10. *Journal names.* All important words of the journal name should be capitalized. In addition, the journal name should be italicized (see preceding example).

11. *Titles of books.* Only the first letter of the first word of a book should be capitalized, except when there is a colon in the book title or when a proper name appears in the title. In the case of a colon, the first letter of the first word after the colon should be capitalized. The book title should be italicized. See example in Item 7 and sample.

12. *Journal volume and page numbers.* After the name of the journal (which is followed by a comma), the volume number (which is italicized) appears, followed by a comma, and then page numbers of the article (followed by a period). A common error is to omit either the volume number or the page numbers. There is one exception to note. In cases where journals begin each issue with page 1 (i.e., the issues are not continuously paginated across journal issues in a particular volume) and, thus, each issue is numbered (e.g., issue number 1, 2, etc.), then it is necessary to include the issue number after the volume number in parentheses but not italicized.

13. *Book edition.* If there are multiple editions of a book, the edition for the particular reference appears in parentheses after the book title and is abbreviated (e.g., 2nd ed.). Note the word *second* does not appear in the example, nor is the abbreviation of *edition* capitalized. The edition within the parentheses directly follows the title without a comma, and a period is placed after the parentheses. Thus, the book edition is a secondary part of the title but is not italicized, as is the book title (see example in Item 7).

14. *Book editors.* With an edited book, use Ed. (or Eds.) in parentheses to identify the editor(s).

15. *Book chapter page numbers.* In citing a chapter from an edited book, those numbers are placed after the book title within parentheses, followed by a period. See example in Item 7 and sample.

16. *Book publisher.* After the book title or page numbers of a chapter in an edited book, list the city and state (use postal state abbreviations) where the book was published, followed by a colon, and then the book publisher name (capitalizing the first letter of each word of the publisher). Thus, a book reference would typically appear as follows:

Helms, J. E. (1990). *Black and white racial identity: Theory, research, and practice.* Westport, CT: Greenwood Press.

A chapter in a book would typically appear as follows:

Fuhriman, A., & Burlingame, G. M. (1994). Group psychotherapy: Research and practice. In A. Fuhriman & G. M. Burlingame (Eds.), *Handbook of group psychotherapy* (pp. 3–40). New York: Wiley.

In short, a wide range of errors can occur in the reference list. Providing accurate citations for references used in research is important so that readers can easily locate references of interest. Moreover, multiple errors in the reference list can cause readers to question the care and attention to detail in conducting the research as well.

CONCLUSIONS

Accurately citing previous research and compiling the citations in a reference list are very important ethical obligations in writing a thesis or dissertation. Although there are many steps and details to consider in conducting a thesis or dissertation, there is a myriad of details to attend to in compiling the reference list. We maintain that you cannot be too attentive in compiling and organizing your reference list. Without careful attention to the details of each reference, you could have a devil of a time completing this part of the thesis or dissertation.

Sample Reference List

Aldwin, C., Folkman, S., Schaefer, C., & Lazarus, R. S. (1980, September). *Ways of coping: A pressure measure.* Paper presented at the annual meeting of the American Psychological Association, Montreal, Canada.

Bandura, A. (1980). Self-efficacy mechanism in human agency. *American Psychologist, 37,* 122–147.

Bandura, A. (1986). *Social foundations of the thought and action: A social cognitive theory.* Englewood Cliffs, NJ: Prentice-Hall.

Baumgardner, A. H., Heppner, P. P., & Arkin, R. M. (1986). Role of causal attribution in personal problem solving. *Journal of Personality and Social Psychology, 50,* 636–643.

Ben-Yishay, Y., & Prigatano, G. P. (1990). Cognitive remediation. In M. Rosenthal, E. R. Griffith, M. R. Bond, & J. D. Miller (Eds.), *Rehabilitation of the adult and child with traumatic brain injury* (2nd ed., pp. 393–409). Philadelphia: Davis.

Brown, S. D., & Lent, R. W. (Eds.) (2000). *Handbook of counseling psychology* (3rd ed.). New York: Wiley.

Butler, L., & Meichenbaum, D. (1981). The assessment of interpersonal problem-solving skills. In P. C. Kendall & S. D. Hollen (Eds.), *Assessment strategies for cognitive behavioral interventions* (pp. 197–225). New York: Academic Press.

Cheng, S. K., & Lam, D. J. (1997). Relationships among life stress, problem solving, self-esteem, and dysphoria in Hong Kong adolescents: Test of a model. *Journal of Social and Clinical Psychology, 16,* 343–355.

Chynoweth, G. H. (1987). *Problem solving: A rational process with an emotional matrix.* Unpublished manuscript.

Elliott, T. R. (1992). Problem-solving appraisal, oral contraceptive use, and menstrual pain. *Journal of Applied Social Psychology, 22,* 286–297.

Folkman, S. (1984). Personal control and stress and coping processes: A theoretical analysis. *Journal of Personality and Social Psychology, 46,* 839–852.

Neville, H. A., Heppner, P. P., & Wang, L. (1997). Relations among racial identity attitudes, perceived stressors, and coping styles in African American college students. *Journal of Counseling and Development, 75,* 303–311.

Nezu, A. M. (1986a). Efficacy of a social problem solving therapy approach for unipolar depression. *Journal of Consulting and Clinical Psychology, 54,* 196–202.

Nezu, A. M. (1986b). Negative life stress and anxiety: Problem solving as a moderating variable. *Psychological Reports, 58,* 279–283.

Sternberg, R. J. (1982). Reasoning, problem solving, and intelligence. In R. J. Sternberg (Ed.), *Handbook of human intelligence* (pp. 225–307). New York: Cambridge University Press.

Tobin, D. L., Holroyd, K. A., Reynolds, R. V., & Wigal, J. K. (1989). The hierarchical factor structure of the coping strategies inventory. *Cognitive Therapy and Research, 13,* 343–361.

Zeidner, M., & Endler, N. S. (Eds.). (1996). *Handbook of coping: Theory, research, and applications.* New York: Wiley.

PUBLISHING THE THESIS OR DISSERTATION

We have both been actively involved in writing for publication for over 25 years. We have chaired dozens of thesis and dissertation committees, as well as served on hundreds of committees for other students. We have also served on 10 or more editorial boards of major journals and reviewed hundreds of manuscripts over the years. Puncky has served as the editor for *The Counseling Psychologist* for 6 years where he has reviewed a hundred manuscripts each year. In short, we have worked in various capacities with many talented researchers and have seen a broad array of skills. At the same time, we have also seen many problems with manuscripts submitted for publication. Many of these problems are ones that can be avoided and that have been addressed throughout this text.

We strongly believe that more theses and dissertations should be published as journal articles. Sometimes very creative and innovative ideas can be found in dissertations and theses, but few people will ever read these studies if they are not published. The profession is losing important knowledge when these investigations are not published in mainstream journals and, thus, are not made easily available to researchers and practitioners. Although there may be a number of reasons that students' research does not get published, a primary one is that often times students are not familiar with the publishing process and subsequently do not adequately develop an article for publication review.

The goal of this chapter is to discuss the publication process. We first discuss some typical affective reactions to publishing, with the goal of acknowledging reactions such as anxiety and self-doubt as parts of a normal, developmental process of becoming an author in the professional literature. The second section discusses 10 myths related to the process of writing manuscripts for publication. The writing process itself is a very important topic but is often overlooked. Third, we provide an overview of the publication process, from identifying the most relevant publication outlets to submitting a manuscript. Our goal in this section is to provide information to which beginning authors may have had less exposure. The subsequent section discusses a number of common problems that reviewers often identify with manuscripts, as well as our suggestions for preventing such problems.

AFFECTIVE REACTIONS

Students and professionals alike commonly have a range of negative affective reactions at even the thought of pursuing a publication in a professional journal. Disbelief, trepidation, anxiety, and even terror not only are common reactions but also are appropriate responses to the process. We would like to normalize these kinds of reactions. Such reactions do not mean that authors will not be successful publishing papers; in fact, these feelings are often most acute when authors are initially pursuing professional publications.

For example, when Puncky was a beginning graduate student, he had some vague sense that conducting "research" was for people other than himself, perhaps for "trained scientists" who knew what they were doing. He did not think "they" would let people like him do this kind of work. When a faculty member suggested one day that they do a study together, Puncky had a number of feelings—from surprise, to shock, to feeling unprepared and incompetent to be involved in research. It was only after being on a research team with two faculty and one other student for several months that Puncky became aware that he was rather enjoying the process of working on the research team and that he began feeling satisfied with his contributions to the research project. Months later, when this same faculty member suggested that they now present their research findings at a national conference, Puncky was excited about the possibility but his overwhelming response was fear. Privately, he even hoped that the convention proposal would be rejected. To his dismay and terror, the proposal was accepted! He had never attended a professional conference before, and the thought of presenting a paper to a professional audience was very anxiety producing. To his surprise, the presentation was not a nightmare but actually went quite well. When his advisor later suggested they submit another convention proposal for the following year, he was surprised that he now thought this was a good idea; and this time he hoped the proposal would be accepted! In retrospect, Puncky never dreamed he would feel excited about the possibility of presenting a paper at a national conference.

A number of important issues are illustrated in this example. First it highlights that students often learn important skills by actually engaging in research activities; that is, they learn by doing. Conversely, if students do not become involved in research projects, it will be very difficult for them to acquire much procedural knowledge about how to actually conduct research. And, most important, as students acquire the necessary knowledge and skills, their affective reactions and subsequent sense of confidence also change. This is a good example of what Bandura (1986) calls the development of beliefs of self-efficacy, and his theory of self-efficacy has much importance for developing confidence in successfully writing for publication.

Bandura (1986) theorized that individuals can increase their self-efficacy beliefs in four different ways: First is performance attainment in which the person takes small steps and has success experiences. In this case, Puncky could assist with tasks on the research team and feel some success and reinforcement for his efforts. A second mechanism is verbal reinforcement, where a person whom the individual respects gives feedback indicating that person's belief in the individual's abilities to accomplish the tasks successfully. In this case, Puncky's advisor saying to him "Let's do a study together" implicitly communicated that "I believe in you and I want to work with you on a project we could publish." A third mechanism is modeling, or seeing other individuals similar to oneself who are attempting and being successful with the skill. In this case, it was seeing another graduate student who was also participating on the team being successful with various tasks. Finally, awareness of one's physiological state provides feedback, which affects one's level of self-efficacy. In this case, when Puncky's advisor proposed the second research project, Puncky noticed that he felt more relaxed and confident and his heart no longer raced.

Another important issue raised by Puncky's scenario pertains to gender differences. Traditionally, graduate programs have consisted of primarily male faculty; and, even though this is changing, the majority of full professors and even associate professors in many professions tend to be male. This can influence the amount of mentoring one receives to become a researcher. For example, in the scenario Puncky described, both of the faculty and the other graduate students were all white males. Women often have had fewer opportunities to see women scientists as role models or to be invited to become involved in the research training process. In the developmental process of becoming an author, working with mentors and learning the skills of research via the apprenticeship model are important. Women may at times need to work harder to find appropriate mentors, male or female, who can help them develop their skills at writing for publication.

A similar developmental issue happened as Puncky later became involved in submitting manuscripts for publication review. After being involved in several research projects, he apprehensively submitted a manuscript for editorial review. The paper was rejected. He felt embarrassed, his confidence was shaken, and he felt that his scholarship was simply "not good enough." He submitted a second manuscript with the same result; the manuscript was rejected. Faculty, however, were very instrumental in supporting and encouraging him. For example, when Puncky sheepishly disclosed that one of the manuscripts was rejected, the faculty member attributed this outcome to the reviewers, referring to them as "sticks in the mud"! As Puncky licked his wounds and persevered, he acquired more knowledge about writing professional papers, as well as about the review process (e.g., "It all depends on who will review the paper," he was told). To his surprise and delight, when he resubmitted those manuscripts after extensive revision and help from faculty, the manuscripts were reviewed more favorably and eventually accepted for publication.

This example again emphasizes that mentors can be extremely important in the learning process, not only about the process of publishing but also about the developmental process of learning to become an author in the professional literature. In short, sometimes authors feel as though they have to learn everything on their own. Remember that new authors do not need to reinvent ways of publishing in the professional literature; rather, many possible mentors in the applied professions can assist authors in learning how to publish professional articles.

Also introduced by Puncky's scenario is the range of emotions that are a normal part of the publication process. We have discussed the many affective reactions students have at each stage of the dissertation process in other chapters of this book, but there are also emotions unique to the process of preparing a journal article from a thesis or dissertation. These emotions may start as students start considering whether they want to publish their results. For example, many students who have worked very hard to get their thesis or dissertation project completed report feeling "burned out" and like they "never want to look at their thesis or dissertation again." Students often feel that they were able to get their thesis or dissertation passed by their committee but question whether it is worthy of publication; they tend to see all the flaws and question its value to the scientific community, as well as their ability to publish in a professional journal. Some students feel that they do not want their work to be provided in such a public forum as a journal for they fear that others will criticize their work. All of these feelings are very normal parts of the publication process.

After an author submits an article to a journal, a number of other affective reactions are common. Probably one of the times when the strongest affective reactions occur is when the editor's letter (often called an "action letter") arrives in the author's mailbox. Generally speaking, no matter how well conducted and written the manuscript is, reviewers are likely to identify a number of weaknesses, as well as suggestions for change. Even very experienced researchers receive action letters with pages of suggestions for change. This process is hard even for these seasoned authors, but the first time one receives such a letter can be very difficult! Many first-time authors, in talking about this experience, report reactions very similar to Greg's:

> I received the letter from the journal in the mail and I felt my heart pounding as I opened it. It was a very thick letter with several pages of single spaced comments. I scanned it quickly and saw the lines that "Unfortunately, they would be unable to offer publication at this time". . . but they were telling me I could choose to revise and resubmit if I felt I "could attend to the 'substantial revisions' that were being suggested." Then I started scanning the letters from the reviewers and my heart sank with despair. I felt embarrassed, confused, overwhelmed, and angry. They were saying things like I didn't have a clear rationale for the importance of the study, it was poorly written and rambled, that another analysis

would be more appropriate, and that it read more like a dissertation than a journal article. I couldn't keep reading, it felt so painful to work so hard on this for so
long and to be told, in effect, that it was no good. I threw the letter into a drawer
so I wouldn't have to look at it. I will never be a researcher. . . . I was afraid I
didn't have what it takes to do this and I was right.

We cannot emphasize enough how important it is to be aware of these
kinds of emotional reactions during the publication process and, most important, to take action to cope with these emotions. First of all, you need to know
that getting a "revise and resubmit" is typically as good as it gets; only very
rarely are manuscripts accepted on a first submission. Indeed, getting a revise
and resubmit on a first submission is really quite an accomplishment. In addition, even the most seasoned researchers get a great deal of feedback and suggestions for change; in fact, the task of the editorial review board is to carefully
evaluate the manuscript to identify weaknesses and ways of improving the
manuscript. Although Greg's emotional reactions were normal, he needed to
not perceive the editorial feedback as indicative that he was not able to be a
successful researcher.

Experienced researchers cope with these reactions in a variety of ways.
We briefly discuss 10 strategies we have found helpful in coping with editorial feedback:

1. After receiving and reading the action letter, let yourself have a few days
   to emotionally process the feedback, then re-read and carefully evaluate
   the feedback.
2. Do not allow yourself to avoid the action letter for many weeks. From
   our experience, the quicker we can approach the task of revision, the
   better we generally feel about revising the manuscript.
3. Analyze the action letter and carefully assess what is being asked; what
   suggestions will be easy to change and which will be more difficult?
4. Become aware of and modify (if at all possible) self-statements such as "I
   am a terrible researcher and they are making this abundantly clear in
   their critique" to "This is a normal part of the publication process and
   even very good researchers get this kind of review."
5. Most manuscripts are significantly improved from editorial feedback.
   Rather than focusing on your inadequacies, continually remind yourself
   how much the manuscript is being improved. The editorial feedback will
   really help the eventual contribution that this manuscript will make to
   the professional literature.
6. Take small and easy steps when starting to revise a manuscript. That is,
   start by revising all of the easy suggestions and then tackle the bigger,
   more daunting issues.
7. Identify any suggestions that are inappropriate or even impossible to
   make, and write a clear rationale for not responding as requested.

8. Realize that some reviewers' comments may not be well taken, and they may even review manuscripts in areas where they lack expertise. Take feedback as advisement and carefully consider whether it is valid or not.
9. Remember that authors do not have to make all the revisions alone and without consultation. Rather, consult with trusted faculty members, advisors, or other colleagues about ways to respond to certain issues.
10. Sometimes a particular comment or suggestion is particularly concerning and causes a student to avoid the revision process (e.g., a request for extensive data reanalysis). It is important to not let one suggestion derail the revision process; rather, approach the tasks one by one, and consult when necessary.

Thus, as throughout the thesis and dissertation process, you will typically have many affective reactions throughout the publishing process. Be aware of these common reactions and develop ways of coping with them as you enter into the world of professional publishing.

MYTHS ABOUT THE WRITING PROCESS

A very critical component of successfully publishing in the professional literature pertains to the process of writing itself. The process of writing is often taken for granted and, subsequently, overlooked and ignored. Our experience in working with students, as well as in examining our own writing process, suggests that the process of writing is a very important component to discuss with students and faculty alike. In this section, we organize our discussion of the writing process around 10 myths about professional writing.

Myth #1. Good writing happens when you are in the right state and mood and feel inspired and brilliant. Yes, an author is occasionally able to conceptualize some complex material and articulate it eloquently or forcefully on paper. Perhaps it was all the right conditions, a fresh mind, a healthy and fully functioning body, knowledge of the material, and, for some, the right amount of caffeine; and voila—the words flow and it sounds great! When you find such a scenario, by all means seize the moment! However, we also want to encourage you not to wait for the "stars to align in such a fashion" to allow such writing to occur. In fact, sometimes authors "excuse themselves" from writing because they do not feel they are in the "right mood." Rather we want to encourage you to create optimal conditions to successfully write.

It is impossible to specify optimal writing conditions that will fit everyone; authors have different schedules, different times of optimal performance (e.g., "morning" versus "night" people), and different writing styles. Our main point is that from our writing experience and working with other authors, we encourage you to establish regular, predetermined writing times in order to have consistent opportunities to prepare the manuscript for submission. In addition, we encourage you, if at all possible, to establish significant blocks of time in order to have enough time to accomplish substantial amounts of writing. For example, many authors have found it helpful while preparing manuscripts to reserve two or three half-days or one full day each week. Others find it hard to reserve so much time and so, instead, reserve 2 hours a day. We personally prefer significant writing blocks of 6 to 8 hours one or two times a week (but more if we have the time). We find that we are able to process the material at a deeper level with sustained time to write, and we are able to write more effectively to articulate our thinking.

In sum, although sometimes authors are able to capitalize on the "right mood," we encourage you to proactively plan and set aside regular predetermined blocks of writing time. Having regular and significant amounts of time greatly increases not only the level of writing productivity but also the quality of the writing.

Myth #2. You cannot force good writing. Sometimes students report that they find themselves unmotivated to write during their predetermined writing times and that they feel they have a "writer's block." In essence, they find it difficult to write during the time they have set aside to write. Sometimes the writing times that students have established are indeed not optimal times for them to productively write. In such cases, reexamining the suitability of the writing times may be useful and, perhaps, changing the times to better suit the individual. If, however, the writing times are suitable, other things may be blocking the writing process—perhaps psychological barriers. As a general rule, if you find it hard to write, we encourage you not to stop writing but, rather, to set your goal to just write a first draft. The level of writing does not have to be stellar; rather, focus on making some small level of progress during each writing time.

Some accomplished authors have learned over time the number of pages they can write (on average) in a particular period of time. For example, an author may consider eight typed pages as a good level of productivity for a full day of writing (8 to 9 hours). In order to increase the chances of having "successful writing days," the author then establishes a minimal goal of writing six typed pages in a full day of writing. Such goal setting often results in the author feeling successful at the end of the writing period and actually looking forward to the next writing period. Moreover, when the author has written six pages and still has 2 hours of writing time left, he or she may feel as though the day's work is already accomplished so can coast for the remainder of the writing day (but still work hard).

In short, we encourage you to not only establish a regular writing time but also establish obtainable writing goals that will help you feel you are making progress and thus becoming a successful writer. We have come to believe that making progress toward your goals is very important in the coping process (see Heppner, Cooper, et al., 2001), and writing manuscripts is no exception.

Myth #3. It is best to write a manuscript in a linear process from title page to the references.   Carefully planning the writing tasks, including the order of the manuscript sections, is very important. For many people, it is better not to write the manuscript from beginning to end. Some sections are more difficult to write than others; for example, for most authors, the methods section is the easiest section to write, while the introduction and discussion are often most difficult. Likewise, sometimes the title and abstract are easier to write after the first drafts of the other sections are written because the author now has the benefit of a significant amount of thinking about the manuscript.

However, a common assumption is that authors should start from the beginning, write the title and abstract pages, and continue sequentially through the manuscript. Our experience is that sometimes it is useful to carefully consider the order of the various writing tasks and plan strategically. Although we are advocating strategic planning, note that we also encourage authors not to plan rigidly but, rather, to allow the plans to be altered as the manuscript evolves and tasks change over time. For example, if the methods section is the easiest to write, an author may start there. Upon completion, many authors feel a sense of accomplishment. This feeling of success can be important for many writers, leaving them with a feeling that they are making progress and are more ready to focus on the next, slightly more difficult task. In essence, one suggestion is to start with the easiest task and progress toward the more difficult tasks. Sometimes there is a logical progression of the writing tasks. For example, the introduction should flow logically into the discussion, so some authors like to write the results second, followed by the introduction and discussion sections in order to have continuity between the introduction and discussion.

Many authors have indicated that it is often difficult to resume writing from where they stopped at the end of their last writing period, especially if a significant amount of time has elapsed (like a week or more). Thus, we suggest that the writing task for a particular writing period be planned relative to the amount of time available. For example, if the author has a 4-hour block of time available, this may be sufficient to write a good first draft of the introduction. However, one hour will not be sufficient to write the introduction and, perhaps, some smaller task would better fit this time.

Sometimes authors also report having lost their train of thought from the last writing session and have difficulty remembering exactly what they were about to write, or a particular strategy, or even key words to introduce into the manuscript. We suggest that authors record or even sketch such notes at the end of each writing session to help them remember such details until their next writing session.

In short, we encourage you to consider the various tasks and sections of the manuscript and carefully plan the order of the writing tasks based on factors such as the amount of time available for particular writing sessions, the level of difficulty or complexity of the writing task, and your energy level for any particular day. In addition, although you may sketch a plan, we encourage you to be open to altering your plan as the manuscript evolves.

Myth #4. The writing needs to be perfect.   Sometimes authors have the expectation that their writing needs to be perfect, even when they first write it. If the writing is not quite perfect, they delete it all from their screen and start all over. Students commonly report spending hours in such scenarios and leaving after a long and frustrating day with little or even nothing written. Such scenarios are obviously not desirable and result in making the writing process much more difficult—and even more painful—than is necessary.

We strongly suggest that you set your initial expectations to obtain a first draft, not a perfect section of writing. That is, the initial goal is to obtain a draft of a particular section; the goal is to just write, however rough or preliminary the draft. In addition, from our experience, it is helpful to let the draft "cool" a bit for a day or more, that is, to allow yourself to get some distance from the draft. We find it is then much easier to return to the first draft and revise it, rather than to start from the beginning if all previous writing was destroyed. In fact, we encourage authors to write, review, and rewrite various sections of manuscripts three to four times to prepare (and polish) the final manuscripts before submission.

In sum, it is a very rare person who has the ability to write excellent first drafts, and it is nearly impossible for a novice writer to do so. It is misleading to expect that one can write an outstanding manuscript in one draft. Thus, we encourage you to develop successive drafts of the various sections of your manuscript and allow yourself to start with a very rough draft.

Myth #5. Other tasks are more important than writing; my writing can wait.   For a variety of reasons, sometimes authors find it easier to avoid writing. Perhaps the author has a general tendency to procrastinate, or perhaps there is something in particular about a specific writing task that is causing the author to have some fears, either well-founded fears or not-so-well-founded fears. Sometimes authors report procrastinating by focusing on other tasks like cleaning their hall closet (as they have been wanting to do this for months!) or totally cleaning their office space (to help them really get organized for the big writing project), or reading more and more books before they start writing (in order to be more completely and fully informed). Or authors consciously or unconsciously create crises in their lives and, of course, no one could blame them for putting their writing temporarily aside. In essence, there are many ways that authors can consciously or unconsciously procrastinate and, in so doing, often convince themselves on some level that it is a good decision.

We encourage you to examine the psychological dynamics underlying your own tendencies to avoid writing. Sometimes friends can help increase your awareness; other times advisors or counselors can help. We strongly encourage you not to try to break an avoidance cycle alone if the avoidance persists. We further encourage you to keep your writing times strictly for writing. Resist the temptation to do other things during the writing periods. Students in our classes sometimes develop buddy systems, in which the goal is to check in with each other on a routine basis about how they are using their writing times and to discuss any writing barriers they are encountering.

In sum, although very good reasons arise to cancel a writing session, we want to encourage you to be aware of self-defeating avoidant patterns related to writing. If this is a persistent issue, find ways of getting help so you can move forward with your writing.

Myth #6. Writing ability is related to the author's level of knowledge about the content area.   Sometimes authors conceptualize writing as being only a function of their knowledge of a particular content area. That is, the more an author knows about a particular content area, the better he or she will be able to write on that particular topic. Content knowledge is obviously a very important factor in writing but most likely not the only factor. For example, psychological processes often can either interfere or enhance the writing process. Thus, affective processes (e.g., depression, anxiety) or cognitions (i.e., irrational beliefs) can disrupt, and even derail the writing process.

Identifying all of the possible reasons for the various cognitions and affective reactions that may disrupt the writing process is impossible. Suffice it to say that, if the writing process is significantly affected or consistently disrupted, then some interventions are needed, such as self-monitoring (e.g., thought listing), reflection, journaling, talking to friends, or counseling. Basically, you need to understand that various psychological processes (e.g., irrational beliefs specifically about oneself as a writer) play an important role in the writing process. Thus, we encourage you to monitor your cognitive and affective processes during the process of writing, as these activities may influence your ability to write.

If psychological processes can disrupt or derail the writing process, then psychological processes can also facilitate the writing process. For example, sometimes positive self-talk can be very helpful to promote persistence and perseverance in the long process of developing a manuscript. Likewise, in starting with the easy writing tasks first, a natural process of self-reinforcement and satisfaction typically occurs in making progress toward a goal. Thus, one strategy is to arrange the writing tasks (as discussed in Myth #4) so as to also increase your self-reinforcement. A variant of the self-reinforcement strategy is to arrange some kind of satisfying event upon reaching a writing goal (e.g., developing a complete draft of a manuscript). Thus, for example, upon reaching a particular goal, you may not only feel satisfaction but also buy a special treat (e.g., a favorite cheese or other food item, a new book, a special trip).

In short, conceptualizing the writing process as only consisting of content knowledge omits an important aspect of the process. Other activities such as psychological processes can play an important role in sustaining a high level of writing over time.

Myth #7. Once you have a good first draft, the manuscript is finished.

Once the author has a good draft of a manuscript, there is often a tendency to assume that the manuscript is finished and ready to submit for publication review. Another version of this myth is that writing for professional publication is not much different than writing a term paper; that is, if an author was successful in the past at writing term papers, their thinking is that they will be successful at writing professional manuscripts. Unfortunately, these assumptions are not necessarily true.

Professional writing typically requires a great deal of thought and reflection about a topic and a considerable amount of time to articulate precise meanings in a succinct and accurate style. Professional writing is typically not a quick process that happens in a single draft. Rather, experienced authors indicate that they often write and revise a manuscript three to four times. Sometimes, after they have left a manuscript to "cool" for a few days, they read and reread some part of the manuscript several times (such as the introduction and the discussion in succession) and, subsequently, add, delete, and polish subtle meanings.

Another writing strategy is to ask several colleagues to read the manuscript and provide editorial feedback after a manuscript is about ready to submit for publication review. We suggest that you specifically encourage your colleagues to provide critical feedback, from major conceptual issues to minor grammatical issues. In fact, you should be thinking of the areas of expertise of different colleagues and select colleagues for their specific skills. Such a strategy is often very helpful to identify very specific problems or confusing or unclear wording, as well as more general stylistic issues. In short, preparing a manuscript for editorial review typically requires a great deal of work and far more preparation and depth of thought than writing a term paper or even a first draft.

Myth #8. Writing is easier to do with others in a group.

Some people like to brainstorm and problem-solve in groups, while others prefer to problem-solve alone. Problem-solving and brainstorming are activities that lend themselves to group activities. Conversely, writing tends to be a more solitary activity and much less efficient to do within a group. Moreover, the level of concentration necessary for writing often prohibits group writing.

In fact, successful authors often arrange their writing environments to reduce social interruptions of all kinds (e.g., people stopping by, phone calls, emails) to increase their ability to focus on their writing; that is, they try to arrange a quiet and secluded environment in which to write. Sometimes such a location is in a professional office or in a private office at home. Writing alone is different from having co-authors and collaborating on a manuscript, as many students do with their advisors on their thesis or dissertation article. The most common strategy in group collaborative projects is for each individual to assume responsibility for writing a specific section, such as the introduction. The co-authors can then provide feedback and even help to revise the next draft of a section of a paper. Such collaborative effort can be very productive, but note that this is quite different from writing a manuscript in a group setting.

In sum, to fully concentrate on your writing, you probably need to be in a quiet, secluded environment that is relatively free of interruptions. Although it may appear easier and more fun to jointly write a manuscript with a group of co-authors, such a method usually is not very efficient in preparing a manuscript.

Myth # 9. The best writing happens under pressure.   Sometimes students report that they write best under pressure. In some ways, that is similar to writing a term paper under pressure or preparing for an exam under pressure. Indeed, the pressure of a deadline often does increase the motivation to write and sometimes even the level of writing performance. However, note that professional writing is more than the number of pages written. Moreover, professional writing requires a deeper level of thinking than is typically required in term papers; this deeper level of thinking is often not possible when working under pressure and a tight deadline. In essence, successful professional writing requires the time to reflect, time to read, time to talk to colleagues, time to write and to evaluate the writing, and time to repeatedly revise the manuscript.

In short, successful professional writing requires a deep level of thought, careful writing, and sustained reflection over time. External pressures may increase the motivation to write and, at best, facilitate the development of writing first drafts of manuscripts. From our experience in working with students, we do not believe the best writing happens under pressure. Rather, we encourage you to increase the quality and depth of your professional writing through reflection, reading, and a sustained course of writing and rewriting.

Myth #10. Writing just happens.   A final myth about writing is that it cannot be described, that it is too complex, and that the process of writing cannot be planned or altered—it just happens. Although the writing process is complex, involves many different processes, and defies description, we do not believe that "it just happens." Rather, we believe that each author has many choice points involved during the process of writing, and we urge authors to be more planful in their professional writing in ways we have suggested.

In sum, we have discussed 10 myths associated with professional writing. We do not believe that writing "just happens" magically but, rather, that authors can and do exercise control in the process. Belief in the 10 myths we discussed about writing all reduce authors' level of effort or control in the writing process. One of our central messages about successful writing for professional publication is that sustained effort over time is required to produce a high-quality product; thus, we encourage you to work toward exercising various types of control to allow yourself to reach your professional writing goals.

STEPS ON THE ROAD TO PROFESSIONAL PUBLICATIONS

Identifying Where to Send Your Manuscript

The first step in publishing a thesis or dissertation is to identify the best professional outlet for publishing a particular manuscript. Determining which journal outlet is "best" consists of two important issues: (a) finding appropriate journals and a relevant audience or readers for the type of manuscript you want to publish, and (b) identifying the highest quality journal that is appropriate for your work.

The first task is finding a journal that publishes the types of articles that are consistent with your thesis or dissertation. Although a particular discipline may have, let us say, 10 primary journals, they typically will have a specific focus in terms of the type of articles they publish, such as empirically based articles; theoretical articles; articles aimed at practitioners; short, in-the-field articles, and so on. For example, within counseling psychology, the *Journal of Vocational Behavior* publishes primarily empirical research on industrial/organizational psychology as well as career development and vocational behavior related articles. Rarely does this journal publish strictly theoretical articles, although there have been exceptions. *The Counseling Psychologist* publishes primarily major conceptual and empirical treatises (up to 120 pages) on topics related to counseling psychology. This journal also has several smaller sections or forums, such as Professional Issues or International Forum. These forums focus on professional issues such as training or development issues, or address international topics in counseling psychology. The *Journal of Counseling and Development* publishes primarily applied articles on counseling topics, as well as empirical articles with clear implications for practice. Thus, the first step is to identify the most appropriate outlet for your work. You should first read the mission statement to identify the focus of the journal; this is usually printed in the first few pages of each journal or in the first issue of each volume under a title like "Instructions for Authors" or "Guidelines for Manuscript Submissions." In addition, we suggest that you consult with advisors or other faculty who are knowledgeable about the journals in their field. Another strategy is to examine the last few years of various journals to determine if the type of manuscript you are thinking of preparing is similar to those already published in the journal. You should examine not only the content of the topics covered but also the style of manuscript. Most new editors when they assume their editorial responsibilities publish an editorial that describes what type of articles they will strive to publish during their editorial term. Reading these editorial statements can be very helpful in determining whether your manuscript would be appropriate for that particular journal. At times, you may even email a journal editor, briefly explain the type of article you will be writing, and inquire if such a manuscript would be appropriate for submission to that journal. Identifying the most appropriate journal is a very critical step in the publication process. If a manuscript is submitted to a journal that does not publish the type of papers submitted, the manuscript may not have much chance of being accepted for publication in that source and could be in the review process for many months. Thus, you need to make the best possible assessment for the most appropriate outlet.

A closely related issue pertains to the type of audience most relevant for your work. For example, some journals are read by a much larger audience, (e.g., the primary journals of associations). Other journals are read predominantly by practitioners; thus, the findings of a study may be adopted and used more readily than it would if it were published in journals read largely by researchers.

The placement of your work may also depend to some extent on your career goals. For example, if you are interested in becoming an academic psychologist and working in a setting that values empirical research, then publishing in top-tier, empirical journals is probably important. Your articles will be read and perhaps cited by other scholars. This can also be helpful as you network with professionals at conventions or even apply for employment. Conversely, if you are interested in developing a practice-oriented career, then publishing in a more practitioner-oriented outlet may be more relevant.

Another major activity is to determine the highest-quality journal that is appropriate for the manuscript. Many journals are available in any given field, and not all journals are of the same level of quality or scientific rigor. For example, some journals allow people to publish their work if they pay a fee to do so; other journals may not be "peer reviewed" (meaning they do not have an editorial board of peers that anonymously reviews articles) and may have very high acceptance rates; other journals have a peer-review process and have a very low acceptance rate. Some journals have high citation rates, while other journals are cited much less frequently, which reduces the potential impact of articles published in those journals. To determine which are the highest-quality, most scientifically rigorous journals in a given field, you again should talk with your advisor or other people who are knowledgeable about various journals. You can also access information from the journal regarding whether it is a peer-reviewed journal and what the acceptance rate is for manuscripts. Generally speaking, many journals in applied psychology have acceptance rates of 20–30%, meaning that 70–80% of manuscripts that are submitted to them are rejected. Generally speaking, the higher the rejection rate, the more likely a journal will be considered of high quality and only accept the very best manuscripts. In addition, some individuals and institutions place importance on what is called the *impact rating* of journals, which is a calculation of how often, on average, other researchers in the professional literature cite an article from a specific journal. The higher the impact rating, the more often the articles in that journal are cited in the literature and, thus, the more influential the journal is perceived to be. The impact ratings for most journals can be found in the Social Science Citation Index, which most libraries carry in their reference sections either in hard copy or CD-ROM.

After determining the level of quality of various journals, you then should evaluate the level of rigor and sophistication inherent in the manuscript. For example, perhaps your study examines the correlations between two variables. This type of article will probably not be accepted into a top empirical journal but may be accepted in a second- or third-tier journal. On the other hand, perhaps your research is an important test of a theory, using a traditionally under-represented sample and employing advanced-level statistical procedures. This type of article may have a possibility of being published in a top journal. Basically the process is one of identifying the best match between your manuscript and the type of manuscript and the level of manuscript quality journals typically publish. A common strategy is to submit a manuscript to a journal of similar or slightly higher level of quality and rigor; if the manuscript is not accepted by that journal, the author will often receive a helpful critique of the work that can strengthen the manuscript for submission to another journal.

The Structure of the Editorial Team

Although great variability exists across journals, some general organizational structures are quite common. Generally, an *editor* is selected for each journal. The editor's term may be for any amount of time, but perhaps most common is an editorial term of 4 to 6 years. The editor can generally set a mission for the journal under his or her leadership; thus, reading the editorial typically presented in the first issue of the editor's term can provide very helpful information about the type of articles desired. Most journals have *associate editors* to assist the editor in evaluating manuscript submissions. Thus, even though you may submit a manuscript to the editor, you may receive correspondence from one of the associate editors who has been assigned the responsibility of managing the review process for your particular manuscript.

The *editorial review board* is a group of scholars who regularly reviews manuscripts for a particular journal; they are selected by the editor and serve at that editor's discretion. The term of the editorial board members typically varies from 1 to 3 years and, sometimes, much longer. The editor typically asks these individuals to indicate their areas of expertise and assigns manuscripts accordingly. Note, however, that assigning manuscripts can sometimes be a difficult task for the editor. For example, sometimes the most qualified reviewers for a newly submitted manuscript have recently been assigned manuscripts to review. Thus, the editor may choose to send the manuscript to reviewers who do not have the exact expertise desired or, perhaps, will send it to an ad hoc reviewer with the desired expertise. Ad hoc reviewers are not permanent members of the review board but, rather, are individuals who occasionally review manuscripts for a journal. The editor generally assigns the manuscript to three editorial reviewers and asks them to provide a quantitative assessment of the article on such issues as the quality of the conceptualization, writing, analyses, the importance of the topic to the field, and so on. In addition, the reviews are supposed to write a thorough narrative review, highlighting both strengths and weaknesses of the manuscript. There are vast differences in the quality of reviews that are conducted for various journals. Some journals are known for very high quality, educational reviews. These can be very helpful to all authors, but especially to novice authors. Other journals provide very cursory reviews that provide little information on which to revise the manuscript. When these reviews come back from the editorial review board members, the editor or associate editor of the journal typically reads the manuscript and the reviewers' assessments, then, together with his or her own opinion, makes a decision about whether to accept, reject, or offer a revise and resubmit to the author.

Preparing the Manuscript for Publication

After identifying an appropriate journal, the next step is to prepare the manuscript for publication review. Most journal articles have the following sections: title page, abstract, introduction, methods, results, and discussion. These sections typically parallel the sections in thesis and dissertation manuscripts but must be much shorter and more focused. Most journals have a section called something like "Guidelines for Authors," which is very important to study to learn such things as the required length of the abstract, page limits, and so on. Not attending to such information can seriously damage an author's credibility with the editor and editorial review board members even before they start reviewing the manuscript.

The goal and focus of the various sections of a published article are typically very similar to those of the thesis or dissertation; for example, the methods section in both formats is to describe the participants, instruments, and procedures of the study. Thus, one task is to significantly reduce the length of the thesis or dissertation to anywhere from 15 to 30 typed manuscript pages, depending on the specific journal requirements. To prepare a manuscript for publication review, you should examine the APA *Publication Manual*, which briefly discusses the function and content of each section of the article. You will also find that many of the suggestions made in this book for the various sections of the thesis or dissertation apply to published articles as well, such as building a strong rationale in the introduction and "making the data sing" in the discussion section. Preparing a manuscript for publication review typically takes a great deal of time (e.g., several months) even for experienced writers. We strongly recommend—at a minimum—writing, revising, polishing, obtaining feedback from experienced writers, and revising again before submitting the paper for publication review. To also aid in preparing the manuscript, see the subsequent section in this chapter that discusses common problems identified in manuscript reviews.

Assuming that you have developed a manuscript that is now ready for editorial review, again closely examine the specifications of the journal outlet. We suggest that you double-check small details regarding any specific stylistic issues required by a particular journal, as well as instructions regarding the number of manuscript copies requested, where to send the manuscript for review, and so on—all details that are important to attend to in order to facilitate the review process. Submitting a manuscript to the wrong editor is less than impressive. For example, when the current editor of a journal receives a manuscript forwarded by a person who was editor of the journal 12 years earlier, there tends to be a certain loss of credibility for the author who is submitting the manuscript! [Yes, indeed, this has actually happened!] After submitting a manuscript for editorial review, you should receive a letter acknowledging that the manuscript has been safely received and that it has been sent to external reviewers for their assessment. If you do not receive such an acknowledgement letter within 4 weeks of submission, you should contact the editor (preferably by email, phone, or letter) to ascertain if the manuscript has been received.

The Editorial Review Process

After a manuscript is submitted for editorial review, the editor typically assigns the manuscript to three or more reviewers to assess the professional merits of the paper. These reviewers typically (a) rate the manuscript on various criteria established by the editor (e.g., importance of the paper), (b) make recommendations about the suitability of the manuscript for publication (i.e., from accept as is to reject, with varying levels in between), and (c) write a narrative evaluation of the specific strengths and weaknesses of the manuscript. The editor then evaluates all of the feedback, including his or her own reading of the manuscript, and makes an editorial decision on the manuscript. The editor then writes a letter to the author (often called an action letter), indicating his or her decision to accept or reject the paper or suggesting that the author revise and resubmit the paper. In addition, the editor typically includes the written narrative reviews provided by the reviewers to help the author understand how the reviewers assessed the strengths and weaknesses of the manuscript. The length of the editorial review process varies. Some journal editors typically return an editorial decision within 6 to 8 weeks after a manuscript is received for review; other editors may have a longer review process, up to 6 to 9 months.

The most common editorial decision for most journals is either to reject the manuscript or to recommend that the author revise and resubmit the manuscript. For most journals, it is less common for a manuscript to be accepted, even with revisions, on the first submission. Although sometimes authors with less publishing experience are disappointed at receiving an action letter recommending "revise and resubmit," we have come to realize that such letters are actually encouraging and often represent "good news." A "revise and resubmit" recommendation allows you to address various concerns raised by the reviewers and editor. Conversely, when an editor decides to reject a paper, that typically means the editor does not want to see that particular paper again, even if revised; in these situations, if you still believe in the paper, you should submit it to another journal. Only in extremely rare circumstances in which authors believe the manuscript was unfairly evaluated or misunderstood should authors contact the editor concerning a rejected manuscript.

If you receive a letter recommending that the paper should be revised and resubmitted, you must attend very closely to the editorial feedback and subsequently write a detailed cover letter indicating how the manuscript has been revised to incorporate the editorial feedback (see example of a cover letter in Appendix A). In our view, the best cover letter provides a point-by-point description of how the author revised the paper, starting with each point provided by the editor, then proceeding though the comments made by Reviewer 1, Reviewer 2, and so on. In any instance in which you choose not to follow the editor's suggestion, you must provide a rationale for your decision. It is not enough to say that you have "responded to the issues raised by the reviewers"; rather, the description in the cover letter should indicate exactly how the changes were made.

Many journal editors send the revised and resubmitted manuscript back to at least two of the original three reviewers. Thus, the same reviewer who raised suggestions about the original manuscript will again be reviewing the manuscript, along with the cover letter sent to the editor, and attending very closely to how you have responded to his or her critiques. Thus, you should be respectful and thorough (and not patronizing) in the cover letter regarding what has been done to respond to the original suggestions. It can be highly frustrating for an editorial review board member to spend a great deal of time studying and making suggestions for a manuscript, only to have the author ignore the feedback. Having a frustrated reviewer is not highly advantageous for an author resubmitting an article for publication.

Many editors prefer to make a disposition (accept or reject) about a manuscript upon the second submission of a manuscript (in the case of a revised and resubmitted manuscript). Even at this point, however, the editor may accept a manuscript providing that additional (and usually minor) revisions are made. Thus, it is fairly common even after a manuscript has been accepted to be asked to make minor changes to the manuscript. Thus, novice authors should be aware that this process takes a long time to reach closure.

Once the manuscript has been accepted, the author is usually asked to submit both a hard copy and a disk containing the manuscript. Authors are also generally asked to complete copyright permissions, which transfer the legal rights to the manuscript over to the journal. The manuscript then goes through a process of being prepared for publication by the journal publisher. Many journals hire a production staff to carefully edit the manuscript for grammatical and stylistic issues. In such cases, the author receives the carefully edited manuscript and is asked to evaluate the suitability of the stylistic changes. In addition, the author is usually asked to respond to a number of author queries, such as providing missing references, clarifying the correct spelling of author names in cases where two spellings occur in the manuscript, or adding missing information for articles cited in the reference list. Several months before the article will appear in the journal, the author receives *galley proofs*, which are the typeset pages that will appear in the journal. This is not the time for making any major changes to the article; rather, this is a time to check whether the article has been typeset correctly. Major changes, such as adding sentences, can be costly, as authors are often charged the cost of having that particular change re-typeset.

When the galley proofs arrive in the mail, the author is then asked to carefully review the galleys and make sure that everything is as it should be and that no typographical errors, missed sentences, or the like are still remaining in the manuscript. Although this can be a tedious process, authors must examine their manuscript galleys very carefully. We recommend that one person reads from the original paper that was submitted, while another person checks the galley proofs on a line-by-line basis. When the galley proofs are sent back as approved by the author, they are as they will appear in the journal. Any problems in the manuscript that are not caught at this stage will reflect on the author. Thus, use time and care to review the galley proofs. Journals often have very short time lines for authors to return the galley proofs, oftentimes within 48 hours. If authors do not return them in the allotted time, publication of the manuscript can be delayed. The lag between a journal article being accepted and actually appearing in a journal is often quite long, probably most typically between 12 to 18 months, but in some cases even longer than that.

Eventually, the publication appears in the journal. This is an exciting time and one that should be celebrated. As is evident from the process we have just described, getting to this stage takes time, skill, and perseverance. We encourage authors to savor the moment of publication and reflect on the journey to get to this point.

COMMON PROBLEMS IN MANUSCRIPTS SUBMITTED FOR PUBLICATION

As longtime editorial board members and journal editors, we have witnessed a number of problems with manuscripts submitted for publication. Throughout this book, we have made many recommendations and suggestions that were designed to reduce many of the most common problems related to writing manuscripts. Although it is impossible to discuss all of the many problems that can occur in submitting papers, we briefly discuss some of the most common problems: (a) manuscript length, (b) rationale and conceptualization of constructs, (c) measurement of constructs, (d) sampling procedures, (e) data collection, (f) data analyses, and (g) discussion of the results. We suggest that you review this section before submitting your manuscript for publication.

Manuscript Length

Perhaps first and foremost, manuscripts submitted for publication based on a dissertation/thesis are sometimes too long, rambling, and not tightly focused. Subsequently, reviewers' evaluations indicate that the paper "reads more like a dissertation" where page length is not an issue. Previously we indicated that submitted manuscripts should generally be no more than 30 pages, and often considerably shorter. A 30-page limit means roughly that the introduction should be 5 to 6 pages; methods, 5 pages; results, 5 to 6 pages; discussion, 5 to 6 pages; references, 5 pages; and title page, abstract page, tables, and figures, a total of 5 pages. Partly related to the length of the manuscript is the focus of the manuscript, which should provide a clear and strong rationale (or purpose) that is closely aligned to the methods, results, and discussion (more on this topic follows). In essence, preparing a manuscript from a thesis or dissertation takes a great deal of time for a succinct presentation.

Rationale and Conceptualization of the Constructs

The conceptualization of the constructs and variables and the accompanying rationale for the study often provide difficulties for authors. A critically important component of preparing a manuscript is developing a compelling rationale for conducting the study, which is the focus of the manuscript. The rationale should be integrated with the existing literature on the topic. Another common means of establishing a compelling rationale is to articulate the societal need for further examination of this topic, such as identifying the number of people affected by a certain topic (e.g., depression, eating disorders) and, especially, indicating the lack of information about some aspect of this topic. It is often insufficient as a rationale to maintain that this study has not been done previously; although it is obviously important that the study provides new information, it is usually more compelling if a researcher is developing or testing a model or theory (see Tracey & Glidden-Tracey, 1999) as one way of establishing the need for conducting a study.

A critical aspect of developing the rationale for a manuscript is clearly specifying the constructs that will be examined in the paper. Problems arise when a paper contains too many constructs (i.e., psychological entities that are assumed to exist)—like more than five constructs; and it becomes confusing for the reader to understand the constructs and their interrelationships. Problems also arise when there are too few constructs—like two constructs. Most professions have developed over the years so that a study that examines, let's say, two constructs and subsequent variables (that operationalize or measure the constructs) is typically too simple and does not contribute enough to warrant journal space over other more complex studies.

An issue related to the constructs in a quantitative study pertains to the hypotheses of the study. Problems sometimes occur when there are too few hypotheses (e.g., 1 or 2) but most often because there are too many hypotheses (e.g., more than 7 or 8). Typically too many hypotheses result in confusing the reader and expanding the focus of the study, which prevents the necessary depth to fully describe the constructs and their interrelationships. In short, the rationale and focus of the study need to be succinctly written and should make a compelling case for how the manuscript will add to the existing literature. Reviewers typically read the introduction first; thus, their first impression of the manuscript is based on the introduction. Thus, the rationale within the introduction merits not only careful writing but also several rounds of revision to publish it.

Measurement of Constructs

Perhaps the most common problems are using measures with inadequate psychometric properties and not providing psychometric estimates related to the measure of each construct. In essence, measures with inadequate or unknown psychometric properties will raise concerns by reviewers, resulting in unfavorable reviews. We recommend that you consult research design texts to obtain additional information about psychometric issues for measures (e.g., Heppner et al., 1999), as well as Chapter 7 in this book for examples of describing measures.

Sampling Procedures

Several issues often arise pertaining to the sample utilized in the study. How a sample was obtained affects the limitations related to the conclusions that can be drawn from the study, so sampling is a significant issue for reviewers who are assessing a manuscript. Perhaps the biggest problem is when researchers fail to describe their sample at all or describe it only minimally. Such situations raise concerns for reviewers about the adequacy of the sampling, which often weaken their evaluations of the study.

Another sampling issue pertains to using a *convenience sample,* a sample that is readily accessible but often is not appropriate for the research questions. In essence, the sample utilized in the study should generalize to the population for which the researcher has developed the research questions (see Chapter 9 of this book and Heppner et al., 1999). The more distant the sample is from the intended population, the more concerns reviewers tend to have about the sampling of participants. Thus, be aware of and articulate the strengths and limitations of the sample procedure.

A closely related issue pertains to the size of the sample, also know as *statistical power* (see Chapter 7 of this book and Heppner et al., 1999). In essence, you must have adequate statistical power to test the hypotheses under question. Thus, it is often useful to specify the level of statistical power to provide some justification for the size of the sample utilized in the study. Without such an analysis reported in the manuscript, reviewers may be concerned about the adequacy of the study, especially if the sample size appears low.

Data Collection

A number of problems can occur with data collection that can greatly weaken the results of a study. When a researcher administers a number of instruments, respondents may become fatigued and not respond as accurately or carefully over time. Respondent fatigue can introduce unnecessary bias or error into the data, thereby reducing the accuracy of the consultations of the study. Likewise, sometimes researchers operationalize a key construct with a single data source, which not only puts a great deal of weight on that data source but also increases the probability of measurement error. Reviewers examine whether bias or error could have significantly affected the accuracy of the data and, thus, the conclusions of the study (see Heppner et al., 1999, for more details).

Within applied professions, the effectiveness of various training interventions is often tested; but, many confounding variables (see Heppner et al., 1999, for more details) may introduce systematic bias and greatly affect the results of the study (not to mention the independent variables under examination). Therefore, reviewers are often keen to examine the details surrounding the training intervention; and authors should provide careful documentation of the intervention and describe what steps were taken to document the fidelity of the treatment intervention (see Heppner et al., 1999, for more details). Authors also should describe any procedures used to prevent experimenter or participant bias, such as keeping experimenters blind to the specific purpose of the study.

In short, a number of problems can significantly weaken the results of a study. Unfortunately, almost all of these kinds of problems are very difficult if not impossible to correct after the data are collected (i.e., short of collecting the data again). Subsequently, problems in data collection can be very difficult to rectify and, thus, merit careful attention before the study is conducted.

Data Analyses

A very common problem in manuscripts submitted for editorial review pertains to data analyses. Reviewers often question the appropriateness of a particular statistical analysis and suggest an alternative analysis—typically, a more advanced statistical analysis. These types of problems are not fatal flaws; the author can re-do the statistical analysis and revise the manuscript accordingly.

A more serious issue pertaining to data analysis occurs when the author has a very limited understanding of the statistical procedures and, thus, writes a confusing and ambiguous description of the analyses used. Another problem arises when authors do not organize the results section of the manuscript according to the aim of the study or hypotheses identified in the introduction; the lack of congruence between the introduction and the results section typically makes it very difficult for reviewers to understand the outcome of a study and often results in confusion. Because the results represent the core of a study, this problem is very serious and reduces the probability of publication. Be sure to consult Chapter 12 and Chapter 13 of this text; these chapters present examples of writing a results section and suggest consulting relevant statistical books and consultants.

Discussion of the Results

The discussion section is a critical section of a journal submission because it is here that the author must explain not only what was found in the study but also how these results intersect with the existing literature, as well as why these results are important. In essence, it is incumbent upon the author to make the data come alive, that is, to "make the data sing" (see Chapter 14 for more details on this topic). Authors sometimes fail to synthesize the results of the study within the existing literature or fail to describe the importance of the study in ways that others can easily understand. We sometimes find that students' discussion sections are one or even two more drafts away from being strong discussions, even though they have written and revised the discussion three times. Writing a very good discussion section typically requires a great deal of writing skill (see Chapter 14 for some writing strategies and examples). We encourage you to seek feedback and consultation from experienced writers to fine-tune your writing in the discussion section.

CONCLUSIONS

As researchers who passionately believe that more students' theses and dissertations should be published in the professional journals, we hope this chapter has helped to promote and demystify the publication process. Adding to the professional literature by conducting a thesis or dissertation is a big contribution in itself; the extra effort of publishing your research in a professional journal adds even more as it makes the work accessible to a much larger audience who will read and use the findings to improve future research or practice in the area.

Appendix A: Example Cover Letter

Editor Good Hope
Department of Accepted Manuscripts
Keep the Faith, MD

Dear Dr. Hope,

We are resubmitting our manuscript entitled "Increasing Students' Professional Identification and Confidence in Scholarly Contributions" for editorial review in the *Journal of Brilliant Thoughts*. We found the feedback very helpful and believe we have greatly strengthened and streamlined the manuscript. More specifically, we have attended closely to your feedback as well as that of the three reviewers and have done our best to incorporate almost all of the suggestions. We will delineate the changes, point by point, beginning with your letter, and then address each reviewer's comments.

1. We clarified and narrowed the focus of the manuscript, with the total number of pages now being 18 (including abstract, references, and table).
2. The purpose and design of the study is now clearly identified in the introduction, specifically indicating that the qualitative data is used to facilitate understanding of the quantitative data.
3. The participants are now more clearly identified as all of the members of the first-year doctoral class (and enrolled in Psychology 464, known as the "first-year class").
4. More information is provided about the coding system, and we clearly indicate that its function was to summarize the qualitative data into meaningful categories. The items were written as face-valid items to measure the hypotheses of the study.
5. With regard to ethical issues, we now also clarify the participants informed consent to allow their data to be used in this research. In

addition, we also specify that participants were given the opportunity to join a research team to develop a manuscript describing this study.

6. We explicitly chose two poster presentations, and of increasing difficulty, to allow for an adequate test of the effects of behavioral performance. This reason is now in the manuscript. We assessed participant responses after each performance because the two performances had two different audiences (the second included faculty and upper classmen, who are more likely to be perceived as a higher risk group), and thus might yield different responses. Because these were different experiences, we did not expect the successive presentations to necessarily be additive.

7. The tables have been combined into one table and reorganized to more closely match the primary and secondary purposes of the study. Likewise, the results are now explicitly organized along these lines, as well as the discussion.

With regard to reviewers, we will address issues not previously mentioned.

8. With regard to reviewer 005, we reduced the manuscript's length, including the section describing the instrument and procedures. We shortened the description of the instrument and refer to the table as suggested. We also now note that two items did not apply for the second administration and were thus dropped. The results section was also reorganized and streamlined to more concisely present the results. We combined the two tables into one, but did not include the t-tests because of space restrictions. We also shortened the narrative description of the qualitative data.

9. With regard to review 017, we chose not to revise the title because professional identification was the secondary purpose of the study (but now labeled more clearly as such). The first sentence in the abstract, and most of the abstract, was revised in line with the narrower and more specific focus of the manuscript. We did not include all names for the first citation of Heppner, et al. 1994 and 1995; rather, we followed the guidelines in the APA Manual of not listing all author names with six or more authors. We did, however, include all author names in the first citation for articles with less than six authors.

Older references were removed from the manuscript as suggested. We retained the "self-identified gay man" as this seemed necessary to describe the diversity within the group or participants. We now clearly identify which questions were similar of different to Heppner et al. (1995) in the methods. The items for the questionnaire are now in abbreviated form in the table and also available from the first author.

10. With regard to reviewer 014, we have now greatly revised the introduction and are much clearer in the stated purpose of the study. In addition, we now explicitly state in the introduction that the study is

both a quantitative and qualitative study. We also have clarified the use of the term "class," which indeed was the members of the introductory counseling class. The original manuscript was a bit confusing with regard to the class members; although all of the students were then new doctoral in counseling psychology, many of the students previously obtained masters degrees in fields other than counseling, which was confusing. We have now eliminated the reference to the students' previous training as masters students. We now provide much more specific information about informed consent of the participants. The study was approved by the University's Human Subjects Approval Committee. We have now also clarified that five of the authors of the study developed a coding system to categorize the data. Since the instrument was developed specifically for the purpose of this study, we do not have any estimates of validity for the inventory, and thus we did not elaborate on this issue. We are also much clearer now in terms for the items for the instrument pertained to each of the hyptheses of the study. The results and the discussion sections have been greatly reduced and are more clearly organized now around the purpose of the study. In addition, we have tried to articulate the significance of the study in the discussion much more clearly.

In sum, we have tried to respond to all of the issues identified by you and the reviewers. As a result, we believe that the manuscript has been greatly strengthened, and thus we are now resubmitting the manuscript for your review. We look forward to your response and any suggestions you may have for improving the manuscript.

Sincerely,

Destined T.B. Published, Ph.D
Assistant Professor

References

Abbott, S. (1999). *Where there is no place like home: Heidegger, hermeneutics, and the narratives of adopted adolescents.* Unpublished doctoral dissertation, The California School of Professional Psychology, Alameda.

Abramson, L. Y., Metalsky, G. I., & Alloy, L. B. (1989). Hopelessness depression: A theory-based subtype of depression. *Psychological Review, 96,* 358–372.

Adams, J. H. (1997). *Perspectives of the oldest-old concerning resilience across the life span.* Unpublished doctoral dissertation, New Mexico University, Las Cruces.

Aiken, L. S., & West, S. G. (1991). *Multiple regression: Testing and interpreting interactions.* Newbury Park, CA: Sage.

Al-Darmaki, F. R. (1998). *Attitudes toward women's roles and psychological adjustment: A study on the United Arab emigrants female college students.* Unpublished doctoral dissertation, University of Missouri, Columbia.

Allen, J. G., & Hamsher, J. H. (1974). The development and validation of a test of emotional styles. *Journal of Consulting and Clinical Psychology, 42,* 663–668.

Ambrose, P. A. (1987). *A comparison of personality, intelligence, and learning disability factors among juvenile offenders.* Unpublished doctoral dissertation, University of Missouri, Columbia.

American Psychological Association. (1994). *Publication manual of the American Psychological Association* (4th ed.). Washington, DC: Author.

American Psychological Association. (2001). *Publication manual of the American Psychological Association* (5th ed.). Washington, DC: Author.

Anderson, J. C., & Gerbing, D. W. (1998). Structural equation modeling in practice: A review and recommended two-step approach. *Psychological Bulletin, 103,* 411–423.

Arbuckle, J. L. (1997). *Amos user's guide.* Chicago: SmallWaters.

Baker, C. E. (1998). *Examining the role of problem-solving appraisal and narcissism in leader behavior: A test of Fiedler's prediction in an unfavorable situation.* Unpublished doctoral dissertation, University of Missouri, Columbia.

Bandura, A. (1986). *Social foundations of thought and action: A social cognitive theory.* Upper Saddle River, NJ: Prentice-Hall.

Bandura, A. (1997). *Self-efficacy: The exercise of control.* New York: W. H. Freeman & Company.

Barclay, J. R. (1974). *A user's manual: The Barclay Classroom Climate Inventory* (3rd ed.). Lexington, KY: Educational Skills Development.

Baron, R. M., & Kenny, D. A. (1986). The moderator-mediator distinction in social psychological research: Conceptual, strategic, and statistical considerations. *Journal of Personality and Social Psychology, 51*, 1173–1182.

Beck, A. T., Steer, R. A., & Garbin, M. G. (1988). Psychometric properties of the Beck Depression Inventory: Twenty-five years of evaluation. *Clinical Psychology Review, 8*, 77–100.

Beck, A. T., Weissman, A., Lester, D., & Trexler, L. (1974). The measure of pessimism: The Hopelessness Scale. *Journal of Consulting and Clinical Psychology, 42*, 861–865.

Bekker, M. H. J. (1993). The development of an autonomy scale based on recent insights into gender identity. *European Journal of Personality, 7*, 177–194.

Bem, D. J. (1995). Writing a review article for *Psychological Bulletin*. *Psychological Bulletin, 47*, 71–75.

Bentler, P. M. (1995). *EQS structural equations program manual*. Encino, CA: Multivariate Software.

Bergin, A. E., & Garfield, S. L. (Eds.). (1994). *Handbook of psychotherapy and behavior change*. New York: Wiley.

Berry, T. R. (1996). *Using problem-solving appraisal and reflective judgment to develop predictive models of depression*. Unpublished Master's thesis, University of Missouri, Columbia.

Binen, L. M. (1998). *Treatment outcome at a university counseling center*. Unpublished doctoral dissertation, University of Missouri, Columbia.

Bingham, R. P. (2000). 1999 Presidential address: Lessons learned at the half-century mark. *The Counseling Psychologist, 28*(1), 143–149.

Birnbaum, M. H. (2000). *Psychological experiments on the Internet*. San Diego: Academic Press.

Birnbaum, M. H. (2001). *Introduction to behavioral research on the Internet*. Upper Saddle River, NJ: Prentice-Hall.

Black, J. & Enns, G. (1998). *Better Boundaries: Owning and Treasuring Your Life*. Oakland, CA: New Harbinger Publishers.

Bollen, K. A. (1989). *Structural equations with latent variables*. New York: Wiley.

Borgen, F. H., & Weiss, D. J. (1971). Cluster analysis and counseling research. *Journal of Counseling Psychology, 18*, 583–591.

Brown, S. D., & Lent, R. W. (Eds.). (1984). *Handbook of counseling psychology*. New York: Wiley.

Brown, S. D., & Lent, R. W. (Eds.). (1992). *Handbook of counseling psychology*. (2nd ed.). New York: Wiley.

Brown, S. D., & Lent, R. W. (Eds.). (2000). *Handbook of counseling psychology*. (3rd ed.). New York: Wiley.

Browne, L. (1997). *The role of collective self-esteem and personal self-esteem in predicting the psychological well-being of African Americans*. Unpublished master's thesis proposal, University of Missouri, Columbia.

Browne, L. (1998). *The role of collective self-esteem and personal self-esteem in predicting the psychological well-being of African Americans*. Unpublished master's thesis, University of Missouri, Columbia.

Buboltz, W. C., Miller, M., & Williams, D. J. (1999). Content analysis of research in the *Journal of Counseling Psychology*. *Journal of Counseling Psychology, 46*(4), 496–503.

Bureau, U. S. C. (2001). *Population change and distribution: Census 2000 brief*. Washington, DC: U.S. Government Printing Office.

Cacioppo, J. T., & Petty, R. E. (1981). Social psychological procedures for cognitive response assessment: The thought-listing technique. In T. V. Merluzzi, C. R. Glass, & M. Genest (Eds.), *Cognitive assessment* (pp. 309–342). New York: Guilford Press.

Chang, E. C., & Rand, K. L. (2000). Perfectionism as a predictor of subsequent adjustment: Evidence for a specific diathesis-stress mechanism among college students. *Journal of Counseling Psychology, 47,* 129–137.

Charmaz, K. (2000). Grounded theory: Objectivist and constructivist methods. In N. K. Denzin and Y. S. Lincoln (Eds.), *Handbook of qualitative research* (2nd ed., pp. 509–536). Thousand Oaks, CA: Sage.

Chen, H. J. (2001). *The development of the Spiritual Attachment Inventory.* Unpublished doctoral dissertation proposal, University of Missouri, Columbia.

Cohen, B. B. (1995). *Evaluation of workshops to counter sexual harassment.* Unpublished doctoral dissertation, University of Missouri, Columbia.

Cohen, B. H. (1996). *Explaining psychological statistics.* Pacific Grove: Brooks/Cole.

Cohen, J. (1988). *Statistical power analysis for the behavioral sciences* (2nd ed.). Hillsdale, NJ: Erlbaum.

Cohen, J., & Cohen, P. (1983). *Applied multiple regression/correlation analysis for the behavioral sciences* (2nd ed.). Hillsdale, NJ: Erlbaum.

Cohen, R. J., & Swerdlik, M. E. (1999). *Psychological testing and assessment: An introduction to tests and measurement.* Mountain View, CA: Mayfield.

Cohen, S., Kamarck, T., & Mermelstein, R. (1983). A global measure of perceived stress. *Journal of Health and Social Behavior, 24,* 386–396.

Comrey, A. L. (1988). Factor-analytic methods of scale development in personality and clinical psychology. *Journal of Consulting and Clinical Psychology, 56,* 754–761.

Corrigan, J. D., Dell, D. M., Lewis, K. N., & Schmidt, L. D. (1980). Counseling as a social influence process: A review [Monograph]. *Journal of Counseling Psychology, 27,* 395–441.

Covey, S. R., Merrill, A. R., & Merrill, R. R. (1994). *First things first : to live, to love, to learn, to leave a legacy.* New York: Simon & Schuster.

Creswell, J. W. (1998). *Qualitative inquiry and research design: Choosing among five traditions.* Thousand Oaks, CA: Sage.

Croteau, J. M., Anderson, M. Z., Distefano, T. M., & Kampa-Kokesch, S. (2000). Lesbian, gay, and bisexual vocational psychology: Reviewing foundations and planning construction. In R. M. Perez, K. A. DeBord & K. J. Bieschke (Eds.), *Handbook of counseling and psychotherapy with lesbian, gay, and bisexual clients* (pp. 383–408). Washington, DC: American Psychological Association.

Davis, J. J. (1996). *The working alliance and internalization of the relationship in psychotherapy.* Unpublished doctoral dissertation, University of Missouri, Columbia.

Dawis, R. V. (1987). Scale construction. *Journal of Counseling Psychology, 34,* 481–489.

Deffenbacher, J. L., & Swaim, R. C. (1999). Anger expression in Mexican American and White non-Hispanic adolescents. *Journal of Counseling Psychology, 46,* 61–69.

Denzin, N. K., & Lincoln, Y. S. (Eds.) (1998). *The landscape of qualitative research: Theories and issues.* Thousands Oak, CA: Sage.

Denzin, N. K., & Lincoln, Y. S. (Eds.). (2000). *Handbook of qualitative research* (2nd ed.). Thousands Oak, CA: Sage.

Derogatis, L. R. (1983). *The SCL-90-R: Administration, scoring, and procedures manual II.* Baltimore: Clinical Psychometric Research.

Derogatis, L. R. (1993). *The Brief Symptom Inventory (BSI): Administration, scoring, and procedures manual III.* Minneapolis, MN: National Computer Systems.

Derogatis, L. R., Lipman, R. S., Rickels, K., Uhlenhuth, E. H., & Covi, L. (1974). The Hopkins Symptom Checklist (HSCL): A self-report symptom inventory. *Behavioral Science, 19,* 1–15.

Diener, E., & Crandall, R. (1978). *Ethics in social and behavioral research.* Chicago: University of Chicago Press.

Dixon, D. N., & Glover, J. A. (1984). *Counseling: A problem-solving approach.* New York: Wiley & Sons.

Dixon, D. N., Heppner, P. P., Peterson, C. H., & Ronning, R. R. (1979). Problem-solving workshop training. *Journal of Counseling Psychology, 26,* 133–139.

Dixon, W. A., Heppner, P., & Rudd, M. (1994). Problem-solving appraisal, hopelessness, and suicide ideation: Evidence for a mediational model. *Journal of Counseling Psychology, 41,* 91–98.

Dixon, W. A., Heppner, P., Burnett, J. W., Anderson, W. P., & Wood, P. K. (1993). Distinguishing among antecedents, concomitants, and consequences of problem-solving appraisal and depressive symptoms. *Journal of Counseling Psychology, 40,* 357–364.

Drew, C. F. (1980). *Introduction to designing and conducting research* (2nd ed.). St. Louis: C. V. Mosby.

Elliot, R. (1989). Comprehensive process analysis: Understanding the change process in significant therapy events. In M. J. Packer & R. B. Addison (Eds.), *Entering the circle: Hermeneutic investigation in psychology.* (pp. 165–184). Albany: State University of New York Press.

Elliott, R. (1993). *Comprehensive process analysis: Mapping the change process in psychotherapy.* Unpublished research manual. (Available from the author, Department of Psychology, University of Toledo, Toledo, OH 43606).

Ellis, A. (1962). *Reason and emotion in psychotherapy.* New York: Lyle Stuart.

Evans, R., & Donnerstein, E. (1974). Some implications for psychological research of early versus later term participation by college students. *Journal of Research in Personality, 8,* 289–374.

Fabrigar, L. R., Wegener, D. T., MacCallum, R. C., & Strahan, E. J. (1999). Evaluating the use of exploratory factor analysis in psychological research. *Psychological Methods, 4,* 272–299.

Ferrell-Swann, K. (1999). *An exploration of the components of counselor expertise.* Unpublished doctoral dissertation, University of Missouri, Columbia.

Fine, M. (1992). *Disruptive voices: The possibilities of feminist research.* Ann Arbor: University of Michigan Press.

Fischer, E. H., & Turner, J. L. (1970). Orientations to seeking professional help. *Journal of Consulting and Clinical Psychology, 35,* 79–90.

Fitzgerald, L. F., & Betz, N. E. (1994). Career development in cultural context: The role of gender, race, class, and sexual orientation. In R. W. Lent (Ed.), *Convergence in career development theories: Implications for science and practice* (pp. 103–117). Palo Alto, CA: CPP Books.

Flick, U. (1992). Triangulation revisited: Strategy of validation or alternative? *Journal for the Theory of Social Behavior, 22,* 175–197.

Flores, L. Y. (1999). *Factors contributing to the career orientation of Mexican American adolescent women.* Unpublished doctoral dissertation, University of Missouri, Columbia.

Floyd, F. J., & Widaman, K. F. (1995). Factor analysis in the development and refinement of clinical assessment instruments. *Psychological Assessment, 7,* 286–299.

Fonow, M. M., & Cook, J. A. (Eds). (1991). *Beyond methodology: Feminist scholarship as lived research.* Bloomington: Indiana University Press.

Furnham, A., & Procter, E. (1988). *The multi-dimensional just world belief scale* [Monograph]. London: London University.

Gershuny, B. S. (2000). *Structural models of psychologist trauma, dissociative phenomena, and distress in a mixed-trauma sample of females: Relations to fears about death and control.* Unpublished doctoral dissertation, University of Missouri, Columbia.

Gibran, K. (1972). *The prophet.* New York: Alfred A. Knopf. (Original work published 1923).

Giorgi, A. (1970). *Psychology as a human science: A phenomenologically based approach.* New York: Harper & Row.

Giorgi, A. (1985). Sketch of a psychological phenomenological method. In A. Giorgi (Ed.), *Phenomenology and psychological research* (pp. 8–22). Pittsburgh, PA: Duquesne University Press.

Giovanna, S.-R. (2002). *Examining the relationships of acculturation, acculturative stress, problem solving appraisal, and psychological symptoms among Mexican immigrants in the Midwest.* Unpublished doctoral dissertation, University of Missouri, Columbia.

Glaser, B. G. (1992). *Basics of grounded theory analysis: Emergence vs. forcing.* Mill Valley, CA: Sociology Press.

Glaser, B. G., & Strauss, A. L. (1967). *The discovery of grounded theory.* Chicago: Aldine.

Goetz, J. P., & LeCompte, M. D. (1984). *Ethnography and qualitative design in educational research.* New York: Academy Press.

Gorsuch, R. L. (1983). *Factor analysis.* Hillsdale, NJ: Erlbaum.

Green, S. B., Salkind, N. J., Akey, T. M. (2000). *Using SPSS for Windows: Analyzing and understanding data* (2nd ed.). New Jersey: Prentice-Hall.

Guba, E. G., & Lincoln, Y. S. (1998). Competing paradigms in qualitative research. In N. K. Denzin & Y. S. Lincoln (Eds.), *The landscape of qualitative research: Theories and issues* (pp. 156–184). Thousands Oak, CA: Sage.

Hair, J. F., Anderson, R. E., & Tatham, R. L. (1987). *Multivariate data analysis with readings.* New York: Macmillan.

Hair, J. F., & Black, W. C. (2000). Cluster analysis. In L. G. Grimm & P. R. Yarnold (Eds.), *Reading and understanding more multivariate statistics* (pp. 147–205). Washington, DC: American Psychological Association.

Hammond, M. S. (1999). *Impact of client personality on presenting problems and symptoms.* Unpublished doctoral dissertation, University of Missouri, Columbia.

Hardings, S. (1991). *Whose science? Whose knowledge? Thinking from women's lives.* Ithaca, NY: Cornell University Press.

Hasse, R. F., & Ellis, M. V. (1987). Multivariate analysis of variance. *Journal of Counseling Psychology, 34,* 404–413.

Hatcher, L. (1994). *A step-by-step approach to using the SAS system for factor analysis and structural equation modeling.* Cary, NC: SAS Institute.

Hatcher, L., & Stepanski, E. J. (1994). *A step-by-step approach to using the SAS system for univariate and multivariate statistics.* Cary, NC: SAS Institute.

Hays, W. L. (1998). *Statistics.* New York: Holt, Rinehart, & Winston.

Heppner, P. P. (1979). *The effects of client perceived need and counselor role on clients' behaviors.* Unpublished doctoral dissertation, University of Nebraska, Lincoln.

Heppner, P. P. (1988). *The Problem Solving Inventory: Manual.* Palo Alto, CA: Consulting Psychologists Press.

Heppner, P. P., Baumgardner, A., & Jackson, J. (1985). Problem-solving self-appraisal, depression, and attributional style: Are they related? *Cognitive Therapy & Research, 9,* 105–113.

Heppner, P., Baumgardner, A. H., Larson, L. M., & Petty, R. E. (1986). Different coping activities of perceived effective and ineffective problem solvers over time. Unpublished data.

Heppner, P. P., Baumgardner, A. H., Larson, L. M., & Petty, R. E. (1988). The utility of problem-solving training that emphasizes self-management principles. *Counseling Psychology Quarterly, 1*(2–3), 129–143.

Heppner, P. P., Casas, J., Carter, J., & Stone, G. L. (2000). The maturation of counseling psychology: Multifaceted perspectives, 1978–1998. In S. D. Brown & R. W. Lent

(Eds.), *Handbook of counseling psychology* (3rd ed., pp. 3–49). New York: John Wiley & Sons.

Heppner, P. P., & Claiborn, C. D. (1989). Social influence research in counseling: A review and critique. *Journal of Counseling Psychology, 36,* 365–387.

Heppner, P. P., Cook, S. W., Wright, D. M., & Johnson, C. (1995). Progress in resolving problems: A problem-focused style of coping. *Journal of Counseling Psychology, 42,* 279–293.

Heppner, P. P., Cooper, C., Mulholland, A., & Wei, M. (2001). A brief, multidimensional, problem-solving psychotherapy outcome measure. *Journal of Counseling Psychology, 48,* 330–343.

Heppner, P. P., & Dixon, D. N. (1981). A review of the interpersonal influence process in counseling. *Personnel & Guidance Journal, 59,* 542–550.

Heppner, P. P., Glauser, C., Wang, Y.-W., Armer, J. N., Whitlow, N. M., & Reynolds, A. (2002). *Breast cancer survivors with lymphedema: Stressors and the role of coping and social support.* Paper presented at the annual meeting of the American Psychological Association, Chicago, IL.

Heppner, P. P., Heppner, M. J., Lee, D.-G., Wang, Y. W., Park, H.-J., & Wang, L. (2002, August). *Development and validation of the East Asian Coping and Resolution of Trauma (E-ACART) Scale.* Paper presented at the annual convention of the American Psychological Association, Chicago, IL.

Heppner, P. P., Hibel, J., Neal, G. W., Weinstein, C. L., & Rabinowitz, F. E. (1982). Personal problem solving: A descriptive study of individual differences. *Journal of Counseling Psychology, 29,* 580–590.

Heppner, P. P., Kivlighan, D. M. Jr., & Wampold, B. E. (1999). *Research design in counseling* (2nd ed.). Belmont, CA: Wadsworth.

Heppner, P. P., & Krauskopf, C. J. (1987). An information processing approach to personal problem solving. *The Counseling Psychologist, 15,* 371–447.

Heppner, P. P., Lee, D.-G., Wei, M.-F., Anderson, C., & Wang, Y. W. (2001, August). *Does negative affectivity confound the problem-solving–psychological-adjustment link?* Paper presented at the annual convention of the American Psychological Association, San Francisco, CA.

Heppner, P. P., & Petersen, C. H. (1982). The development and implications of a personal problem solving inventory. *Journal of Counseling Psychology, 29,* 66–75.

Heppner, P. P., & Pew, S. (1977). The effects of diplomas, awards, and counselor sex on perceived expertness. *Journal of Counseling Psychology, 24,* 147–149.

Heppner, P. P., Pretorius, T., Wei, M.-F., Wang, Y. W., & Lee, D.-G. (2002). Examining the generalizability of problem-solving appraisal in Black South Africans. *Journal of Counseling Psychology, 49,* 484–498.

Hewitt, P. L., & Flett, G. L. (1991). Perfectionism in the self and social contexts: Conceptualization assessment and association with psychopathology. *Journal of Personality and Social Psychology, 60,* 456–470.

Hill, C. E., Thompson, B. J., & Williams, E. N. (1997). A guide to conducting consensual qualitative research. *The Counseling Psychologist, 25,* 517–572.

Hillenbrand-Gunn, T. L. (1995). *A qualitative examination of the differential impact of two psychological rape prevention interventions on college men.* Unpublished master's thesis, University of Missouri, Columbia.

Holland, J. L. (1978). *Manual for the vocational preference inventory* (3rd ed.). Palo Alto, CA: Consulting Psychologists Press.

Holmbeck, G. N. (1997). Toward terminological, conceptual, and statistical clarity in the study of mediator and moderators: Examples from the child-clinical and pediatric psychology literatures. *Journal of Consulting and Clinical Psychology, 65,* 599–610.

Holmes, P. F. (1999). *Counselor self-reflection.* Unpublished doctoral dissertation, University of Missouri, Columbia.

Horvarth, A. O., & Greenberg, L. (1986). The development of the Working Alliance Inventory. In L. S. Greenberg & W. M. Pinsoff (Eds.), *The psychotherapeutic process: A research handbook* (pp. 529–556). New York: Guilford Press.

Hoshmand, L. T. (1997). The normative context of research practice. *The Counseling Psychologist, 25,* 599–605.

Howard, J. K. J. (1998). *The development and validation of the Black experience inventory (BEI).* Unpublished doctoral dissertation, University of Missouri, Columbia.

Inman, A. G., Ladany, N., Constantine, M. G., & Morano, C. K. (2001). Development and preliminary validation of the Cultural Values Conflict Scale for South Asian women. *Journal of Counseling Psychology, 48,* 17–27.

Institute, S. (1991). *The CALIS procedure: Analysis of covariance structures.* Cary, NC: Author.

Jesness, C. F. (1971). *The Jesness Behavior Checklist.* Palo Alto, CA: Consulting Psychologists Press.

Ji, P. Y. (1998). *The role of attachment status in predicting longitudinal relationships between session-impact events and the working alliance within an adolescent client population.* Unpublished doctoral dissertation proposal, University of Missouri, Columbia.

Ji, P. Y. (2001). *The role of attachment status in predicting longitudinal relationships between session-impact events and the working alliance within an adolescent client population.* Unpublished doctoral dissertation, University of Missouri, Columbia.

Jones, N. T. (2000). *Comorbidity, typologies and treatment outcome in a correctional substance abuse treatment population.* Unpublished doctoral dissertation, University of Missouri, Columbia.

Jöreskog, K. G., & Sörbom, D. (1996). *LISREL 8: User's reference guide.* Chicago: Scientific Software International.

Juntunen, C. L., Barraclough, D. J., Broneck, C. L., Seibel, G. A., Winrow, S. A., & Morin, P. M. (2001). American Indian perspectives on the career journey. *Journal of Counseling Psychology, 48,* 274–285.

Kasai, M. (1997). *Self-construal, narcissistic vulnerability, and symptoms of psychological distress among Japanese college students.* Unpublished doctoral dissertation, University of Missouri, Columbia.

Kendall, P. C., Hollen, S. D., Beck, A. T., Hammen, C. L., & Ingram, R. E. (1987). Issues and recommendations regarding use of the Beck Depression Inventory. *Cognitive Therapy and Research, 11,* 289–299.

Keppel, G. (1991). *Design and analysis: A researcher's handbook.* Englewood Cliffs, NJ: Prentice-Hall.

Kerlinger, F. N. (1986). *Foundations of behavioral research* (3rd ed.). New York: Holt, Rinehart, & Winston.

Kivlighan, D. M., & Shaughnessy, P. (2000). Patterns of working alliance development: A typology of client's working alliance ratings. *Journal of Counseling Psychology, 47,* 362–371.

Klem, L. (2000). Structural equation modeling. In L. G. Grimm & P. R. Yarnold (Eds.), *Reading and understanding more multivariate statistics* (pp. 227–259). Washington, DC: American Psychological Association.

Kline, R. B. (1998). *Principles and practice of structural equation modeling.* New York: Guilford Press.

Knox, S., Hess, S. A., Petersen, D. A., & Hill, C. E. (1997). A qualitative analysis of client perceptions of the effects of helpful therapist self-disclosure in long-term therapy. *Journal of Counseling Psychology, 44,* 274–283.

Komiya, N., Good, G. E., & Sherrod, N. B. (2000). Emotional openness as a predictor of college students' attitudes toward seeking psychological help. *Journal of Counseling Psychology, 47*, 138–143.

Koss, M. P., Gidycz, C. A., & Wisniewski, N. (1987). The scope of rape: Incidence and prevalence of sexual aggression and victimization in a national sample of higher education students. *Journal of Consulting and Clinical Psychology, 55*, 162–170.

Ladany, N., O'Brien, K. M., Hill, C. E., Melincoff, D. S., Knox, S., & Petersen, D. A. (1997). Sexual attraction toward clients, use of supervision, and prior training: A qualitative study of predoctoral psychology interns. *Journal of Counseling Psychology, 44*, 413–424.

Larson, L. M., Heppner, P., Ham, T., & Dugan, K. (1988). Investigating multiple subtypes of career indecision through cluster analysis. *Journal of Counseling Psychology, 35*, 439–446.

Lee, D.-G., Heppner, M. J., McKinnon, L., Heppner, P. P., Multon, K. D., & Gysbers, N. C. (2001). *Examining the role of problem-solving appraisal in the process and outcome of career counseling.* Paper presented at the meeting of the American Psychological Association, San Francisco, CA.

Lincoln, Y. S., & Guba, E. G. (1985). *Naturalistic inquiry.* Beverly Hill, CA: Sage.

Lincoln, Y. S., & Guba, E. G. (2000). Paradigmatic controversies, contradictions, and emerging confluences. In N. K. Denzin and Y. S. Lincoln (Eds.), *Handbook of qualitative research* (2nd ed., pp. 163–188). Thousands Oak, CA: Sage.

Lipkus, I. (1991). The construction and preliminary validation of a Global Belief in a Just World Scale and the exploratory analysis of the Multidimensional Belief in a Just World Scale. *Personality and Individual Difference, 12*, 1171–1178.

Lloren, M. B. (1998). *GRIM for girls: Development and validation of a measure of psychological loss in adolescence.* Unpublished doctoral dissertation, University of Missouri, Columbia.

Loehlin, J. C. (1998). *Latent variable models: An introduction to factor, path, and statistical analysis* (3rd ed.). Mahwah, NJ: Lawrence Erlbaum.

MacCallum, R. C., Widaman, K. F., Zhang, S., & Hong, S. (1999). Sample size in factor analysis. *Psychological Methods, 4*, 84–99.

Mackert, M. J. (2001). *Conductivity for schematic conversion: A new conceptualization for resistance to organizational change.* Unpublished doctoral dissertation, University of Missouri, Columbia.

Mahathera, H. G. (1990). *Mindfulness in plain English.* Somerville, MA: Wisdom Publications.

Mahrer, A. R. (1988). Discovery-oriented psychotherapy research: Rationale, aims, and methods. *American Psychologist, 43*, 694–702.

Mayfield, W. A. (1999). *The relationships among narcissistic vulnerability, gay identity, masculinity ideology, and psychological adjustment in gay men.* Unpublished doctoral dissertation, University of Missouri, Columbia.

Mena, F. J., Padilla, A. M., & Maldonado, M. (1987). Acculturative stress and specific coping strategies among immigrants and later generation college students. *Hispanic Journal of Behavioral Sciences, 9*, 207–225.

Mohr, J. J., & Rochlen, A. R. (1999). Measuring attitudes regarding bisexuality in lesbian, gay male and heterosexual populations. *Journal of Counseling Psychology, 46*, 353–369.

Morrow, S. L., Rakhasha, G., & Castañeda, C. L. (2001). Qualitative research methods for multicultural counseling. In J. G. Ponterotto, J. M. Casas, L. A. Suzuki, & C. M. Alexander (Eds.), *Handbook of multicultural counseling* (2nd ed., pp. 575–603). Thousand Oaks, CA: Sage.

Morrow, S. L., & Smith, M. L. (1995). Constructions of survivals and coping by women who have survived childhood sexual abuse. *Journal of Counseling Psychology, 42,* 24–33.

Morrow, S. L., & Smith, M. L. (2000). Qualitative research for counseling psychology. In S. D. Brown & R. W. Lent (Eds.), *Handbook of counseling psychology* (3rd ed., 199–230). New York: John Wiley & Sons.

Moustakas, C. E. (1994). *Phenomenological research methods.* Thousand Oaks, CA: Sage.

Mulholland, A. M. (2000). *Validation of an eating disorders assessment on African American college women.* Unpublished doctoral dissertation, University of Missouri, Columbia.

Munley, P. H. (1974). A content analysis of the *Journal of Counseling Psychology. Journal of Counseling Psychology, 21,* 305–310.

Murray, S. E. (1997). *Working alliance and session impact in career counseling for Vietnam era veterans with and without post-traumatic stress disorder.* Unpublished doctoral dissertation, University of Missouri, Columbia.

Myers, J. L., & Well, A. D. (1995). *Research design and statistical analysis.* Hillsdale, NJ: Lawrence Erlbaum.

Neal, G. W. (1983). *Personal problem solving: Awareness and utilization of campus helping resources.* Unpublished doctoral dissertation, University of Missouri, Columbia.

Nelson, C., Treichler, P. A., & Grossberg, L. (1992). Cultural studies: An introduction. In L. Grossberg, C. Nelson, & P. A. Treichler (Eds.), *Cultural studies* (pp. 1–16). New York: Routledge.

Neville, H. A., Heppner, P., & Wang, L.-F. (1997). Relations among racial identity attitudes, perceived stressors, and coping styles in African American college students. *Journal of Counseling & Development, 75,* 303–311.

Neville, H. A., & Heppner, M. J. (1999). Contextualizing rape: Reviewing sequelae and proposing a culturally inclusive ecological model of sexual assault recovery. *Applied and Preventive Psychology, 8,* 41–62.

Neville, H. A., Lilly, R. L., Duran, G., Lee, R. M., & Browne, L. (2000). Construction and initial validation of the Color-Blind Racial Attitudes Scale (CoBRAS). *Journal of Counseling Psychology, 47,* 59–70.

Newcomb, M. D. (1994). Drug use and intimate relationships among women and men: Separating specific from general effects in perspective data using structural equation models. *Journal of Consulting and Clinical Psychology, 62,* 463–476.

O'Neil, J. M., Helms, B., Gable, R., David, L., & Wrightsman, L. (1986). Gender Role Conflict Scale: College men's fear of femininity. *Sex Roles, 14,* 335–350.

O'Rourke, B. W. (1978). *The effects of a selected guidance program on the self-development of urban fourth grade students.* Unpublished doctoral dissertation, University of Missouri, Columbia.

Osipow, S. H., Carney, C. G., Winer, J., Yanico, B., & Koschier, M. (1976). *The Career Decision scale.* Columbus, OH: Marathon Consulting and Press.

Patterson, W. L. (1994). *Police personality and stress: An aspect of role conflict.* Unpublished doctoral dissertation, University of Missouri, Columbia.

Patton, M. J. (1992). Counseling psychology and the organized health industry: The hazards of uniformity. *The Counseling Psychologist, 20,* 194–206.

Patton, M. Q. (1990). *Qualitative evaluation and research methods* (2nd ed.). Newbury Park, CA: Sage.

Pedhazur, E. J. (1997). *Multiple regression in behavioral research: Explanation and prediction* (3rd ed.). Fort Worth, TX: Harcourt Brace College Publishers.

Perez, R. M. (1993). *Problem solving appraisal of delinquent adolescents.* Unpublished doctoral dissertation, University of Missouri, Columbia.

Petty, R. E. & Cacioppa, J. T. (1986). *Communication and persuasion: Central and peripheral routes to attitude change.* New York: Springer-Verlag.

Pidgeon, N. (1996). Grounded theory: Theoretical background. In John T. E. Richardson (Ed.), *Handbook of qualitative research methods for psychology and the social sciences* (pp. 75–85). Leicester, UK: British Psychological Society Books.

Pidgeon, N., & Henwood, K. (1996). Grounded theory: Practical implementation. In J. T. E. Richardson (Ed.), *Handbook of qualitative research methods for psychology and the social sciences* (pp. 86–101). Leicester, UK: British Psychological Society Books.

Polkinghorne, D. E. (1989). Phenomenological research methods. In R. S. Valle & S. Halling (Eds.), *Existential-phenomenological perspectives in psychology* (pp. 41–60). New York: Plenum.

Ponterotto, J. G., & Casas, J. M. (1991). *Handbook of racial/ethnic minority counseling research.* Springfield, IL: Charles C. Thomas.

Pretorius, T. B. (1996). The family environment of students self-appraised as effective and ineffective problem solvers. *Psychological Reports, 79,* 915–921.

Pusateri, M. R. (1995). *The meaning of low-flat Holland code profiles.* Unpublished doctoral dissertation, University of Missouri, Columbia.

Quintana, S. M., & Maxwell, S. E. (1999). Implications of recent developments in structural equation modeling for counseling psychology. *The Counseling Psychologist, 27,* 485–527.

Rabinowitz, F. E. (1984). *An investigation of the supervision process over time.* Unpublished doctoral dissertation, University of Missouri, Columbia.

Reeder, B. L., & Heppner, P. (1985). Personal problem-solving activities of Black university students. *Journal of Multicultural Counseling & Development, 13,* 154–163.

Reis, S. D. & Heppner, P. (1993). Examination of coping resources and family adaptation in mothers and daughters of incestuous versus nonclinical families. *Journal of Counseling Psychology, 40,* 100–108.

Rice, K. G., & Mirzadeh, S. A. (2000). Perfectionism, attachment, and adjustment. *Journal of Counseling Psychology, 47,* 238–250.

Richardson, J. T. E. (Ed.). (1996). *Handbook of qualitative research methods for psychology and the social sciences.* Leicester, UK: British Psychological Society Books.

Robbins, S. B., & Patton, M. J. (1985). Self-psychology in career development: Construction of the Superiority and Goal Instability Scales. *Journal of Counseling Psychology, 32,* 221–231.

Robert, J. E., Gotlib, I. H., & Kassel, J. D. (1996). Adult attachment security and symptoms of depression: The mediating roles of dysfunctional attitudes and low self-esteem. *Journal of Personality and Social Psychology, 70,* 310–320.

Rooney, S. C. (2000). *A dimensional analysis of the experiences of gay and lesbian counseling supervisees.* Unpublished doctoral dissertation, University of Missouri, Columbia.

Ruelas, S. R., Atkinson, D. R., & Ramos-Sanchez, L. (1998). Counselor helping model, participant ethnicity and acculturation level, and perceived counselor credibility. *Journal of Counseling Psychology, 45,* 98–103.

Russell, D. W., Kahn, J. H., Spoth, R., & Altmaier, E. M. (1998). Analyzing data from experimental studies: A latent variable structural equation modeling approach. *Journal of Counseling Psychology, 45,* 18–29.

Schaefer, C. C. (1997). *The mother daughter relationship of female leaders: A qualitative study with implications for counseling psychology.* Unpublished doctoral dissertation, Seton Hall University, South Orange, NJ.

Schatzman, L. (1991). Dimensional analysis: Notes on an alternative approach to the grounding of theory in qualitative research. In D. R. Maines (Ed.), *Social organization and social processes: Essay in honor of Anselm Strauss* (pp. 303–314). New York: Aldine de Gruyter.

Schmidt, W. C. (1997). World-Wide Web survey research: Benefits, potential problems, and solutions. *Behavioral Research Methods: Instruments and Computers, 29,* 274–279.

Schwandt, T. A. (2000). Three epistemological stances for qualitative inquiry: Interpretivism, hermeneutics, and social constructionism. In N. K. Denzin & Y. S. Lincoln (Eds.), *The handbook of qualitative research* (pp. 189–213). Thousand Oaks, CA: Sage.

Sherrod, N. B. (2002). *A few good men II: Distinguishing between men with high and low endorsement of rape-supportive attitudes.* Unpublished doctoral dissertation, University of Missouri, Columbia.

Shoyer, B. G. (1998). *Psychotherapist self-care: Beliefs, practices, and outcomes.* Unpublished doctoral dissertation, University of Missouri, Columbia.

Sodowsky, G. R., & Lai, E. W. M. (1997). Asian immigrant variables and structural models of cross-cultural distress. In A. C. C. A. Booth & N. Landale (Eds.), *Immigration and the family: Research and policy on U.S. immigrants* (pp. 211–234). Hillsdale, NJ: Erlbaum.

Sörbom, D. (1993). *LISREL 8: Structural equation modeling with SIMPLIS command language.* Hillsdale, NJ: Erlbaum.

Sternberg, R. J. (1991). Editorial. *Psychological Bulletin, 109,* 3–4.

Stoddart, K. (1999). *Learning about White racial identity: Lessons from mothers of children of color.* Unpublished doctoral dissertation, The Fielding Institute, Santa Barbara, CA.

Strauss, A. L., & Corbin, J. (1990). *Basics of qualitative research: Grounded theory procedure and techniques.* Newbury Park, CA: Sage.

Strong, S. R. (1968). Counseling: An interpersonal influence process. *Journal of Counseling Psychology, 15,* 215–224.

Strong, S. R. (1971). Experimental laboratory research in counseling. *Journal of Counseling Psychology, 18,* 106–110.

Suarez-Renaud, G. (2002). *Examining the relationships of acculturation, acculturative stress, problem solving appraisal and psychological symptoms among Mexican immigrants in the Midwest.* Unpublished doctoral dissertation, University of Missouri, Columbia.

Tabachnick, B. G., & Fidell, L. S. (1989). *Using multivariate statistics.* New York: Harper & Row.

Tabachinick, B. G., & Fidell, L. S. (1996). *Using multivariate statistics.* New York: HarperCollins College Publishers.

Thompson, B. (2000). Canonical correlation analysis. In L. G. Grimm & P. R. Yarnold (Eds.), *Reading and understanding more multivariate statistics* (pp. 285–316). Washington, DC: American Psychological Association.

Towle, D. C. (1992). *Personality, alcohol consumption, alcohol expectancies, drinking situations, and alcohol consequences among college students.* Unpublished doctoral dissertation, University of Missouri, Columbia.

Tracey, J. G. T., & Glidden-Tracey, C. E. (1999). Integration of theory, research design, measurement, and analysis: Toward a reasoned argument. *The Counseling Psychologist, 27,* 299–324.

Travis, J. & Ryan, R. S. (1988). *Wellness Workbook.* Berkeley, CA: Ten Speed Press.

U.S. Census Bureau. (2001, January). *Resident Population Estimates of the United States by Sex, Race, and Hispanic Origin: April 1, 1990 to July 1, 1999, with Short-Term Projection to November 1, 2000.* Retrieved September 1, 2001, from Population Estimates Program, Population Division via http://www.census.gov/population/estimates/nation/intfile3-1.txt

Vera, E. M., Speight, S. L., Mildner, C., & Carlson, H. (1999). Clients' perceptions and evaluations of similarities to and differences from their counselors. *Journal of Counseling Psychology, 46,* 277–283.

Vivona, J. M. (2000). Parental attachment styles of late adolescents: Qualities of attachment relationships and consequences for adjustment. *Journal of Counseling Psychology, 47,* 316–329.

Vu, P. H. (2000). *Relations between acculturation and gender role conflict, shame-proneness, and psychological well-being among Vietnamese American men.* Unpublished doctoral dissertation, University of Missouri, Columbia.

Wampold, B. E., & White, T. B. (1985). Research themes in counseling psychology: A cluster analysis of citation in the process and outcomes section of the *Journal of Counseling Psychology. Journal of Counseling Psychology, 32,* 123–126.

Wang, L. (1994). *Gender-related personality traits, problem-solving appraisal, and perceived social support in predicting a model of psychological adjustment.* Unpublished doctoral dissertation, University of Missouri, Columbia.

Wang, L. (1995). *Development and validation of a scale to measure the discrepancy of parental expectation.* Unpublished doctoral dissertation, University of Missouri, Columbia.

Wang, Y.-W. (2003). *A feminist qualitative study of child sexual abuse victims in Taiwan: Coping, social support and sociocultural context.* Unpublished doctoral dissertation, University of Missouri, Columbia.

Ward, J. H. (1963). Hierarchical grouping to optimize an objective function. *Journal of the American Statistical Association, 58,* 236–244.

Warner, P. (1996). *The role of gender-related personality traits in predicting process and outcome variables in supervision.* Unpublished master's thesis, University of Missouri, Columbia.

Webb, C. D. (1996). *A phenomenological investigation of doctoral students' experiences with their dissertation committees.* Unpublished doctoral dissertation, University of Tennessee, Knoxville.

Wei, M. (1998). *Counselor problem: Solving appraisal, trustworthiness, attractiveness, expertness, client expectations on therapeutic working alliance.* Unpublished master's thesis, University of Missouri, Columbia.

Wei, M. (2000). *Attachment, coping, conflicted emotion, and psychological distress: Testing a mediational model.* Unpublished doctoral dissertation, University of Missouri, Columbia.

Weinfurt, K. P. (2000). Repeated measures analysis: ANOVA, MANOVA, and HLM. In L. G. G. P. R. Yarnold (Ed.), *Reading and understanding more multivariate statistics* (pp. 317–361). Washington, DC: American Psychological Association.

Weis, L., & Fine, M. (2000). *Construction sites: Excavating race, class, and gender among urban youth.* New York: Teachers College Press.

Whyte, W. F. (1943/1981). *Street corner society: The social structure of an Italian slum.* Chicago, IL: The University of Chicago Press.

Williams, E. N. (1997). *Perceptions of serendipity: Career paths of prominent women in counseling psychology.* Unpublished doctoral dissertation, University of Maryland, College Park.

Williams, E. N., Judge, A. B., Hill, C. E., & Hoffman, M. A. (1997). Experiences of novice therapists in prepracticum: Trainees', clients', and supervisors' perceptions of therapists' personal reactions and management strategies. *Journal of Counseling Psychology, 44*, 390–399.

Worthington, R. L., & Juntunen, C. L. (1997). The vocational development of non-college-bound youth: Counseling psychology and the school-to-work transition movement. *The Counseling Psychologist, 25*, 323–363.

Wright, D. M. (1989). *The relationship between coping variables and problem solving outcomes in adult children of alcoholics.* Unpublished master's thesis, University of Missouri, Columbia.

Wright, D. M., & Heppner, P. P. (1991). Coping among nonclinical college-age children of alcoholics. *Journal of Counseling Psychology, 38*, 565–572.

Wright, D. M., & Heppner, P. P. (1993). Examining the well-being of nonclinical college students: Is knowledge of the presence of parental alcoholism useful? *Journal of Counseling Psychology, 40*, 324–334.

Zook, C. E. (2000). *The predictive influence of academic achievement, career exploration, self-esteem, and feminist identity to the career self-efficacy and outcome expectations of college women.* Unpublished doctoral dissertation, University of Missouri, Columbia.

Credits

This page constitutes an extension of the copyright page. We have made every effort to trace the ownership of all copyrighted material and to secure permission from copyright holders. In the event of any question arising as to the use of any material, we will be pleased to make the necessary corrections in future printings. Thanks are due to the following authors, publishers and agents for permission to use the material indicated.

Index

TO THE OWNER OF THIS BOOK:

I hope that you have found *Writing and Publishing Your Thesis, Dissertation, and Research: A Guide for Students in the Helping Professions,* First Edition useful. So that this book can be improved in a future edition, would you take the time to complete this sheet and return it? Thank you.

School and address: _____

Department: _____

Instructor's name: _____

1. What I like most about this book is: _____

_____

_____

2. What I like least about this book is: _____

_____

_____

3. My general reaction to this book is: _____

_____

_____

4. The name of the course in which I used this book is:

_____

5. Were all of the chapters of the book assigned for you to read? _____

If not, which ones weren't? _____

6. In the space below, or on a separate sheet of paper, please write specific suggestions for improving this book and anything else you'd care to share about your experience in using this book.

_____

_____

_____

_____

BROOKS/COLE
CENGAGE Learning·

BUSINESS REPLY MAIL
FIRST-CLASS MAIL   PERMIT NO. 34   BELMONT CA

POSTAGE WILL BE PAID BY ADDRESSEE

Attn: Counseling Editor

Brooks/Cole
20 Davis Drive
Belmont, CA   94002-9801

FOLD HERE

OPTIONAL:

Your name: _____ Date: _____

May we quote you, either in promotion for *Writing and Publishing Your Thesis, Dissertation, and Research: A Guide for Students in the Helping Professions,* First Edition or in future publishing ventures?

Yes: _____ No: _____

Sincerely yours,

P. Paul Heppner and Mary J. Heppner